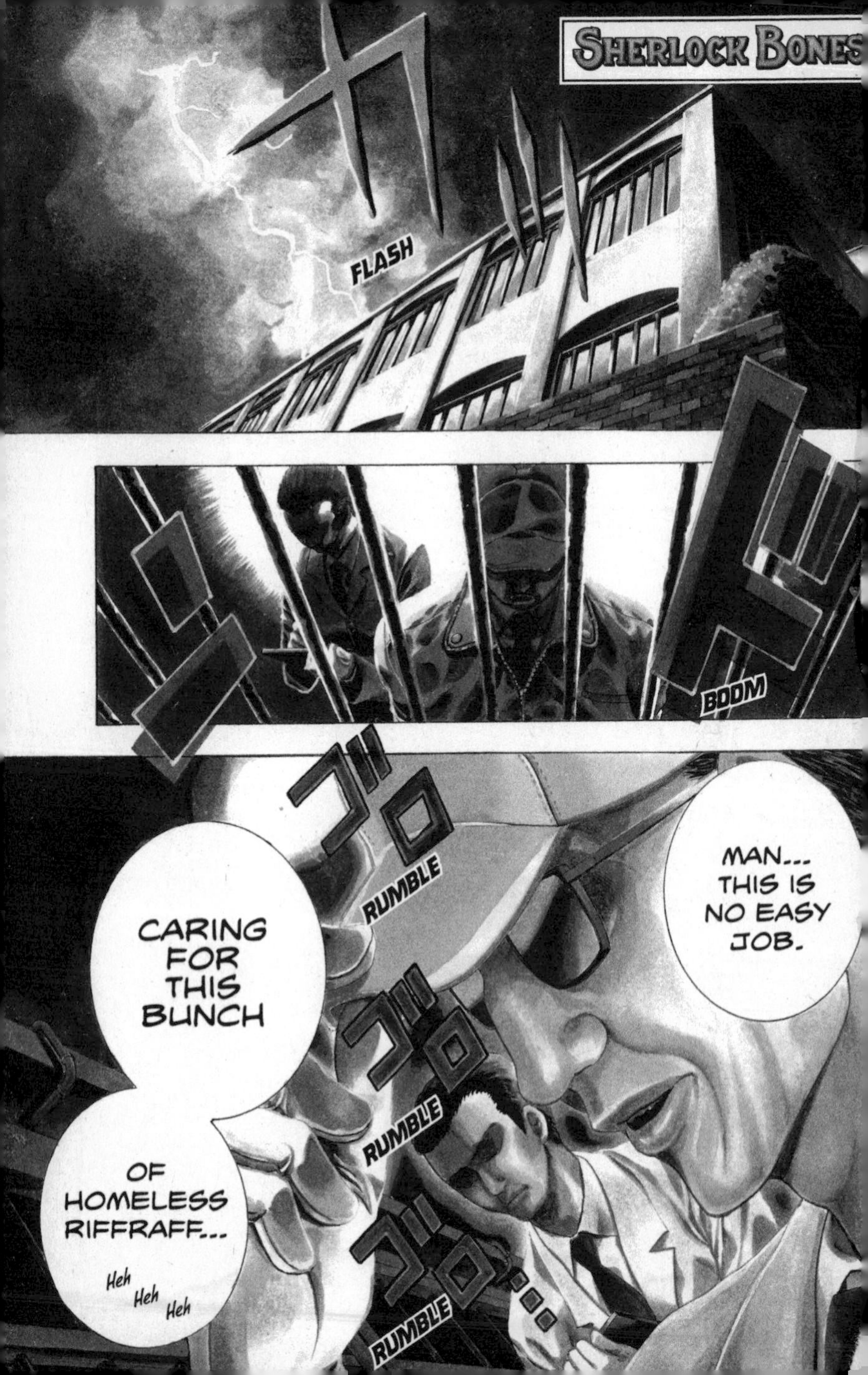
FLASH
BOOM
MAN... THIS IS NO EASY JOB.
RUMBLE
CARING FOR THIS BUNCH
OF HOMELESS RIFFRAFF...
Heh Heh Heh
RUMBLE
RUMBLE

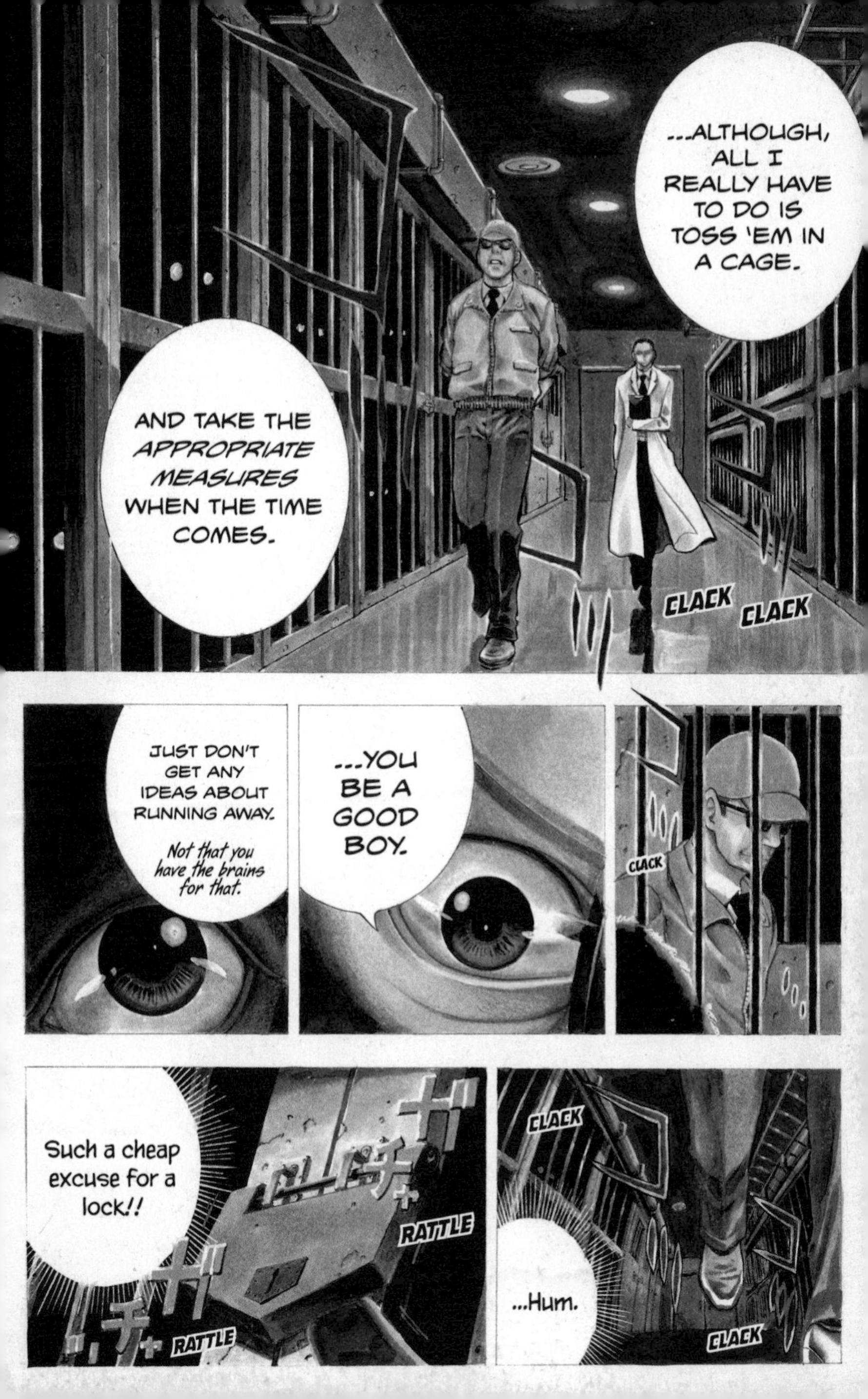
...ALTHOUGH, ALL I REALLY HAVE TO DO IS TOSS 'EM IN A CAGE.
AND TAKE THE *APPROPRIATE MEASURES* WHEN THE TIME COMES.
CLACK
CLACK
CLACK
...YOU BE A GOOD BOY.
JUST DON'T GET ANY IDEAS ABOUT RUNNING AWAY.
Not that you have the brains for that.
CLACK
...Hum.
CLACK
Such a cheap excuse for a lock!!
RATTLE
RATTLE

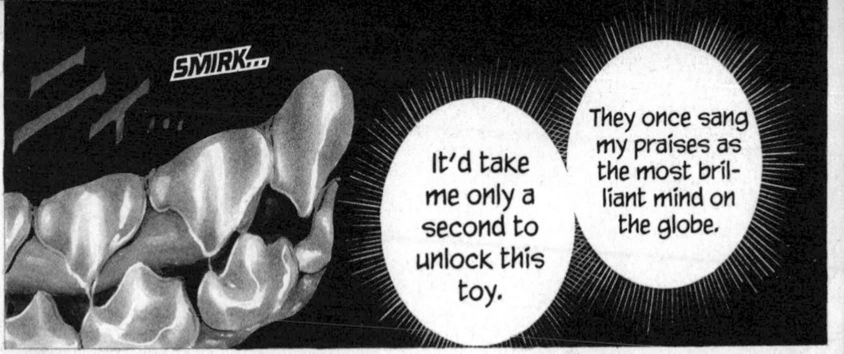
They once sang my praises as the most bril-liant mind on the globe.
It'd take me only a second to unlock this toy.
SMIRK...

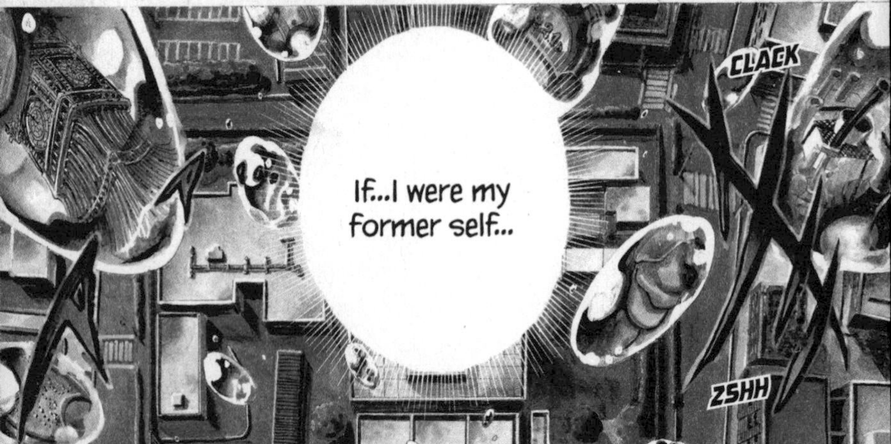
CLACK
If...I were my former self...
ZSHH

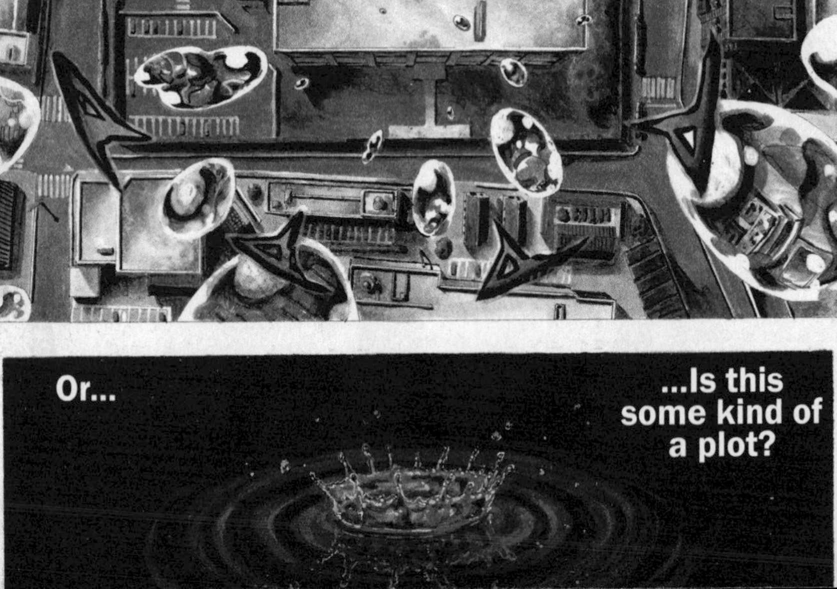
...Is this some kind of a plot?
Or...

Case 0 ⚜ Encounter of the100th Year

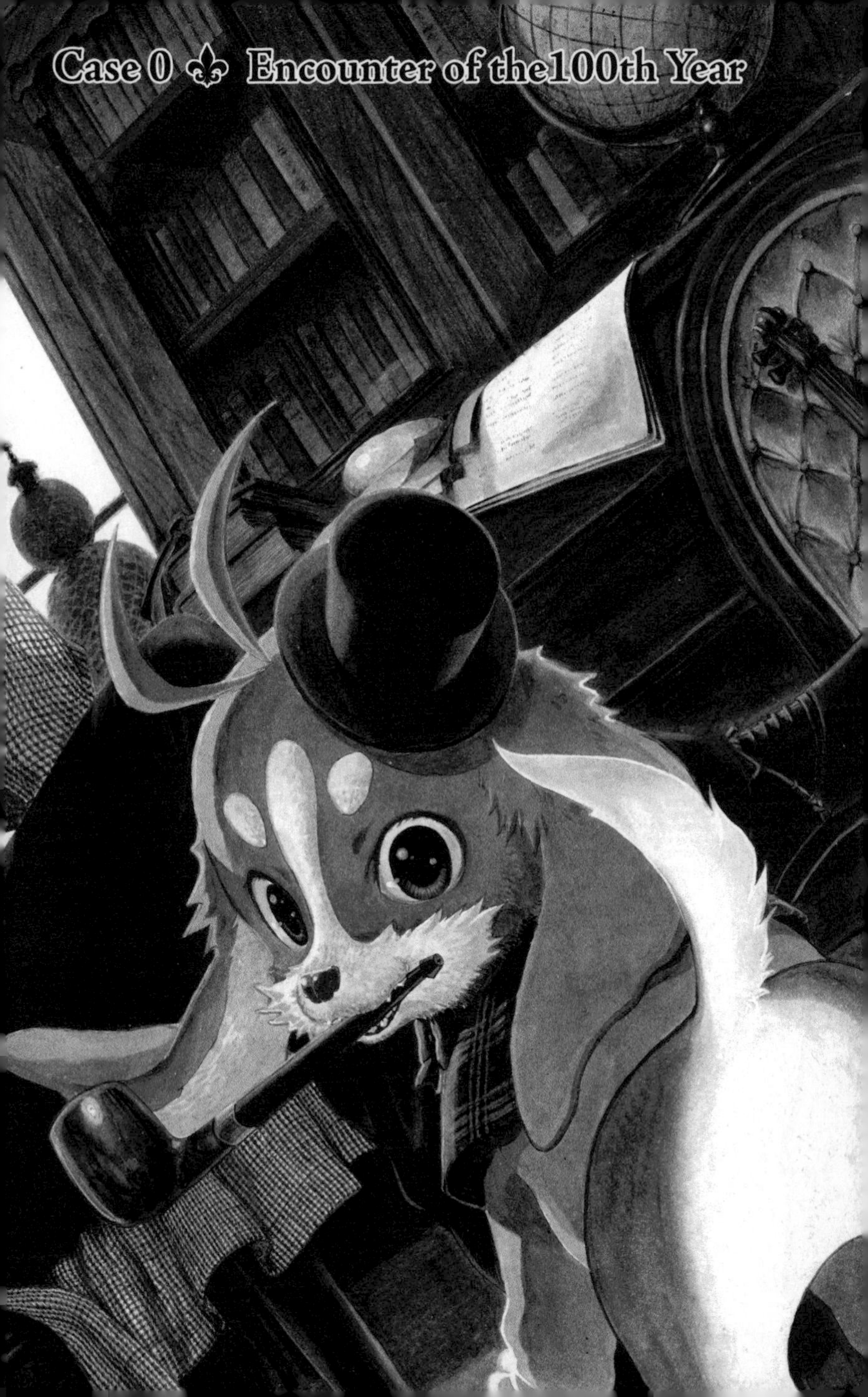

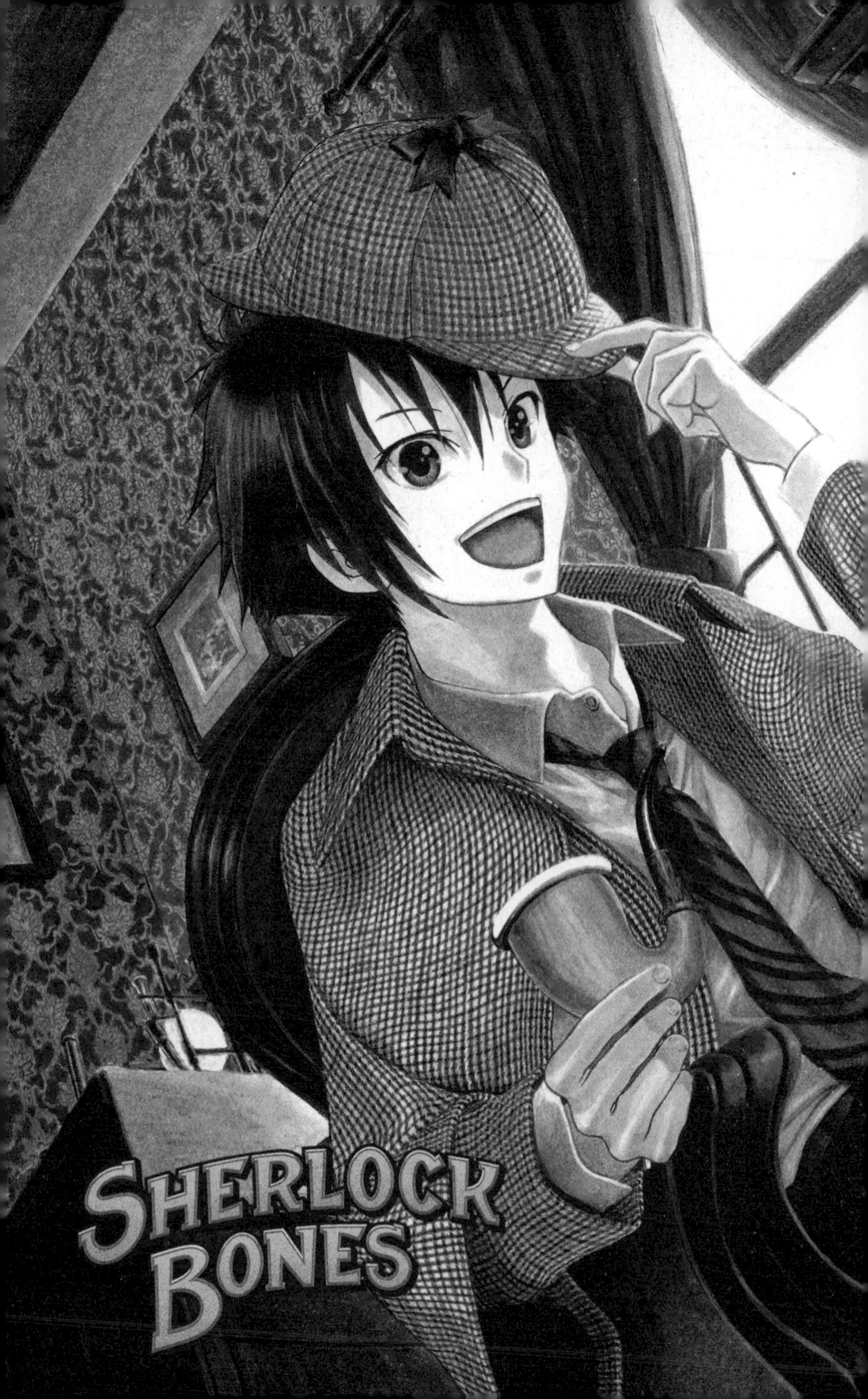
SHERLOCK
BONES

Volume.1

CONTENTS

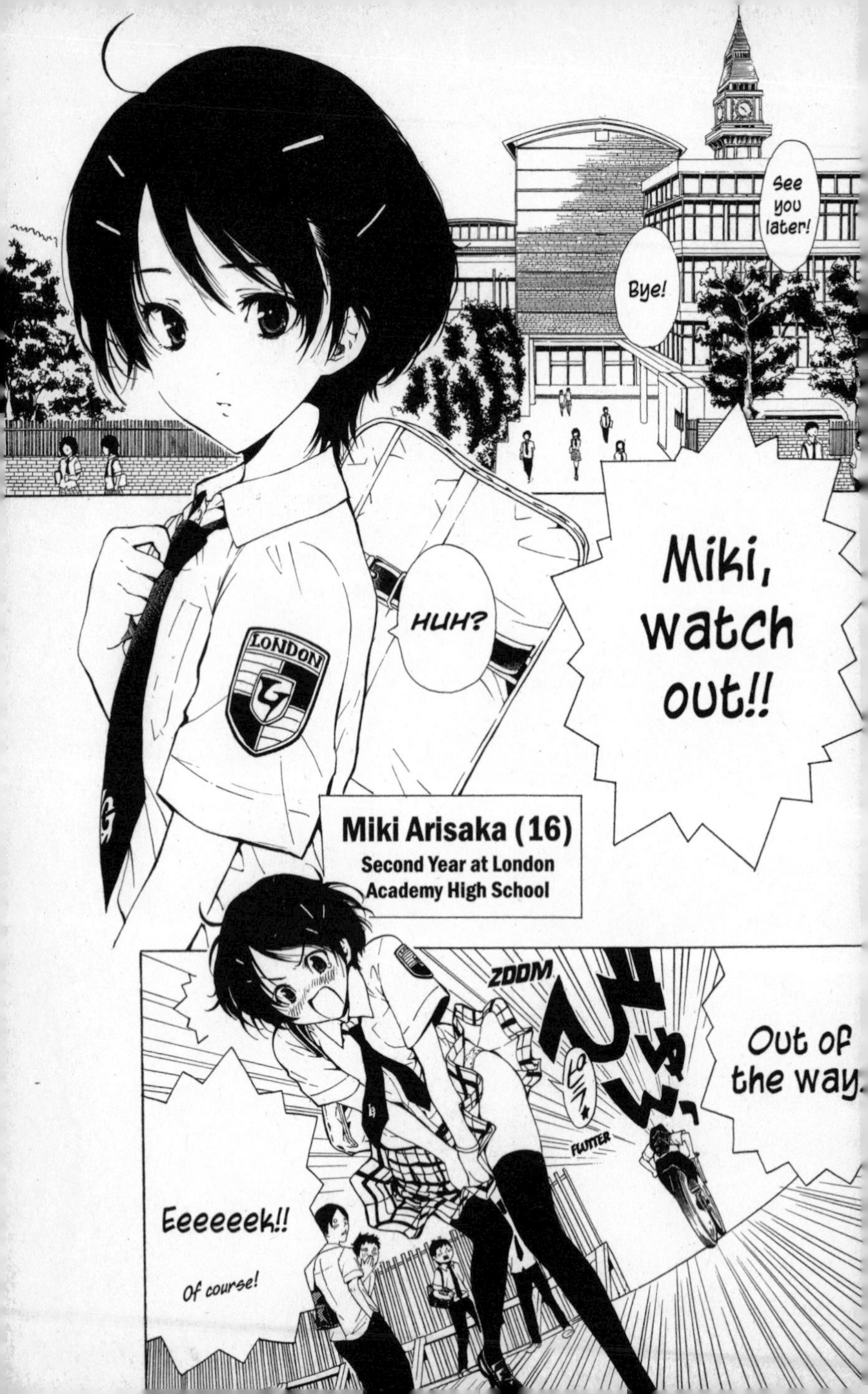
See you later!
Bye!
Miki, watch out!!
HUH?
Miki Arisaka (16)
Second Year at London Academy High School
Out of the way.
ZOOM
FLUTTER
Eeeeeek!!
Of course!

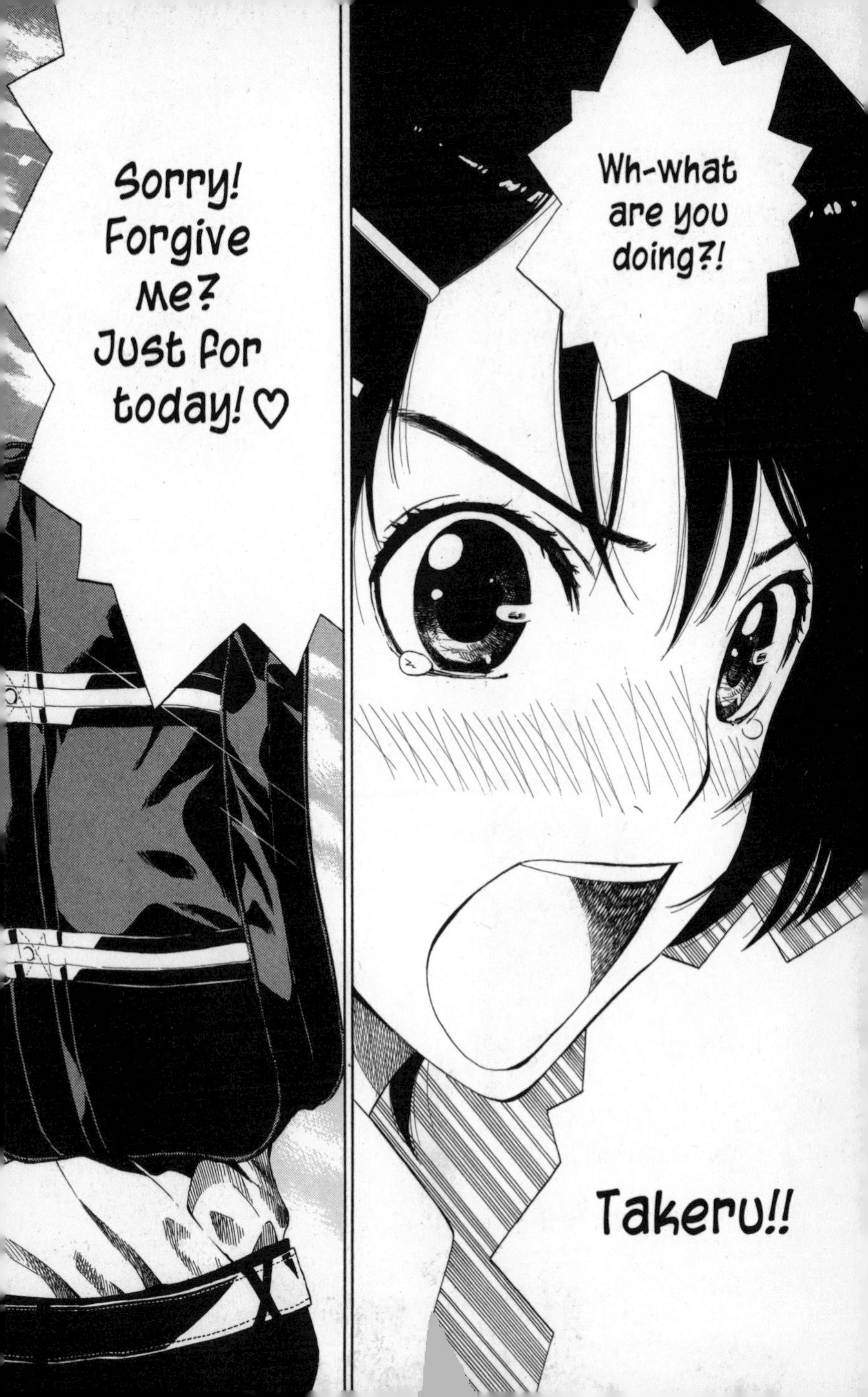
Wh-what are you doing?!
Takeru!!
Sorry! Forgive me? Just for today! ♡

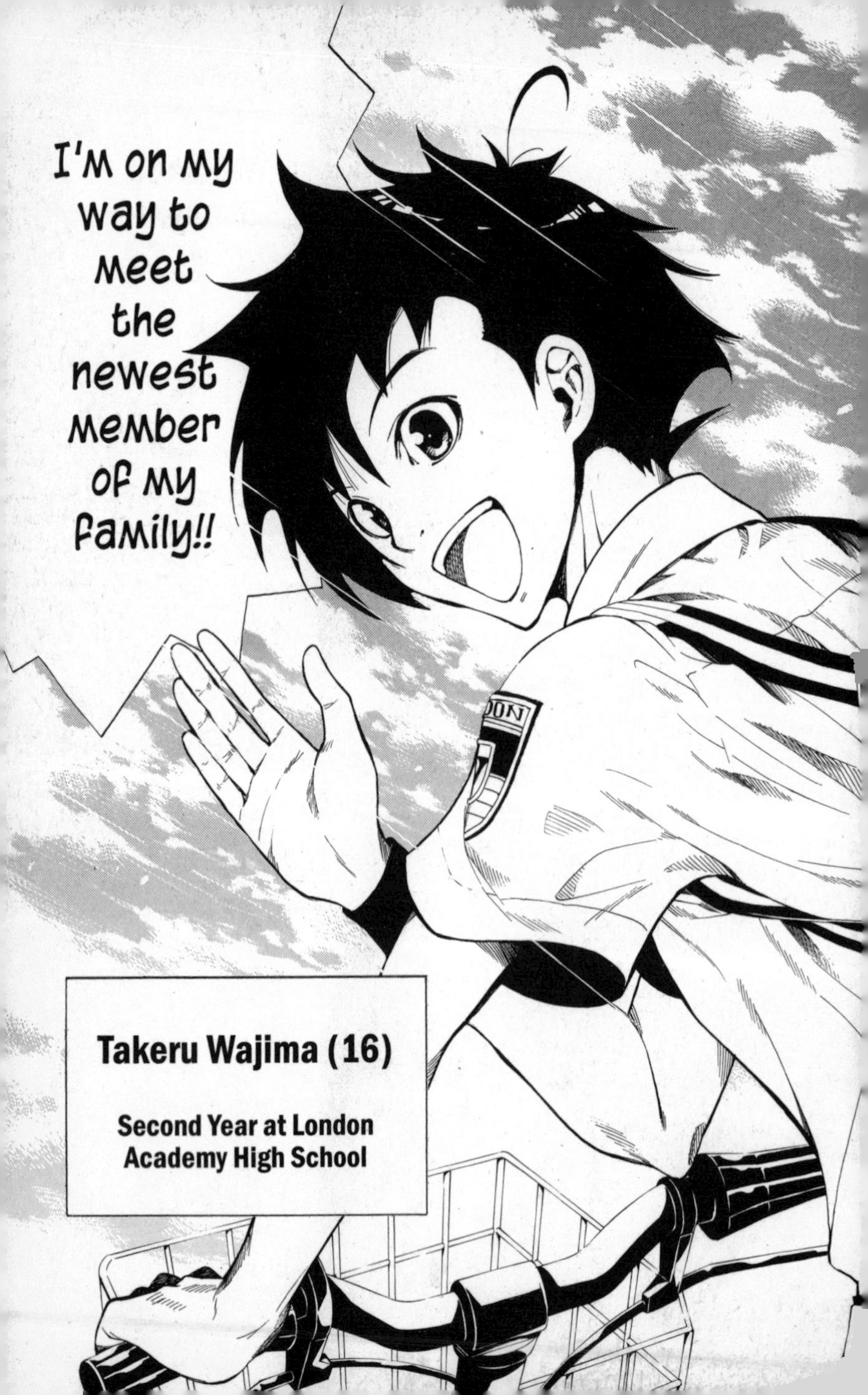
I'm on my way to meet the newest member of my family!!
Takeru Wajima (16)
Second Year at London Academy High School

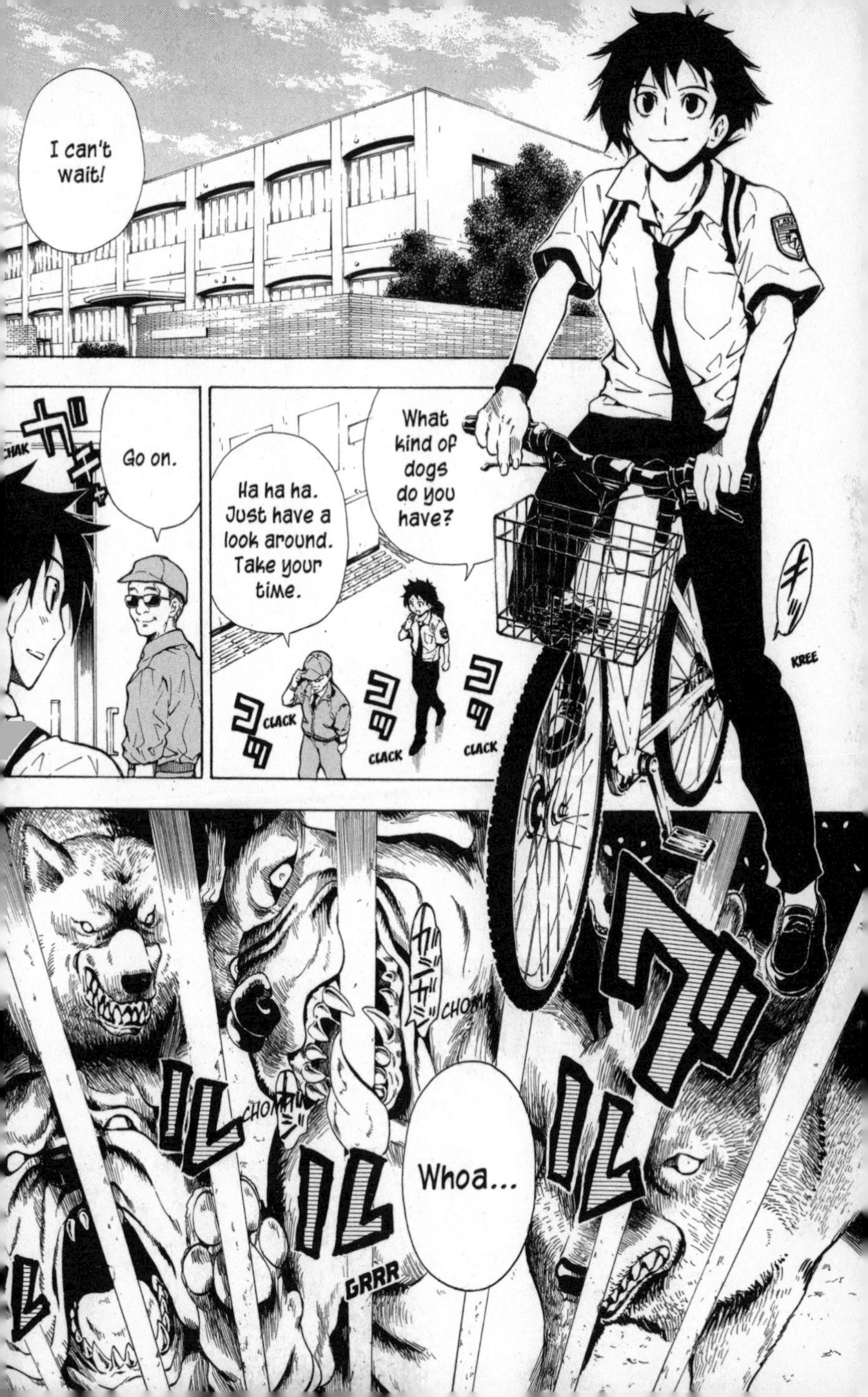
I can't wait!
KREE
What kind of dogs do you have?
Ha ha ha. Just have a look around. Take your time.
CLACK
CLACK
CLACK
Go on.
CHAK
CHOM
CHOM
Whoa...
GRRR

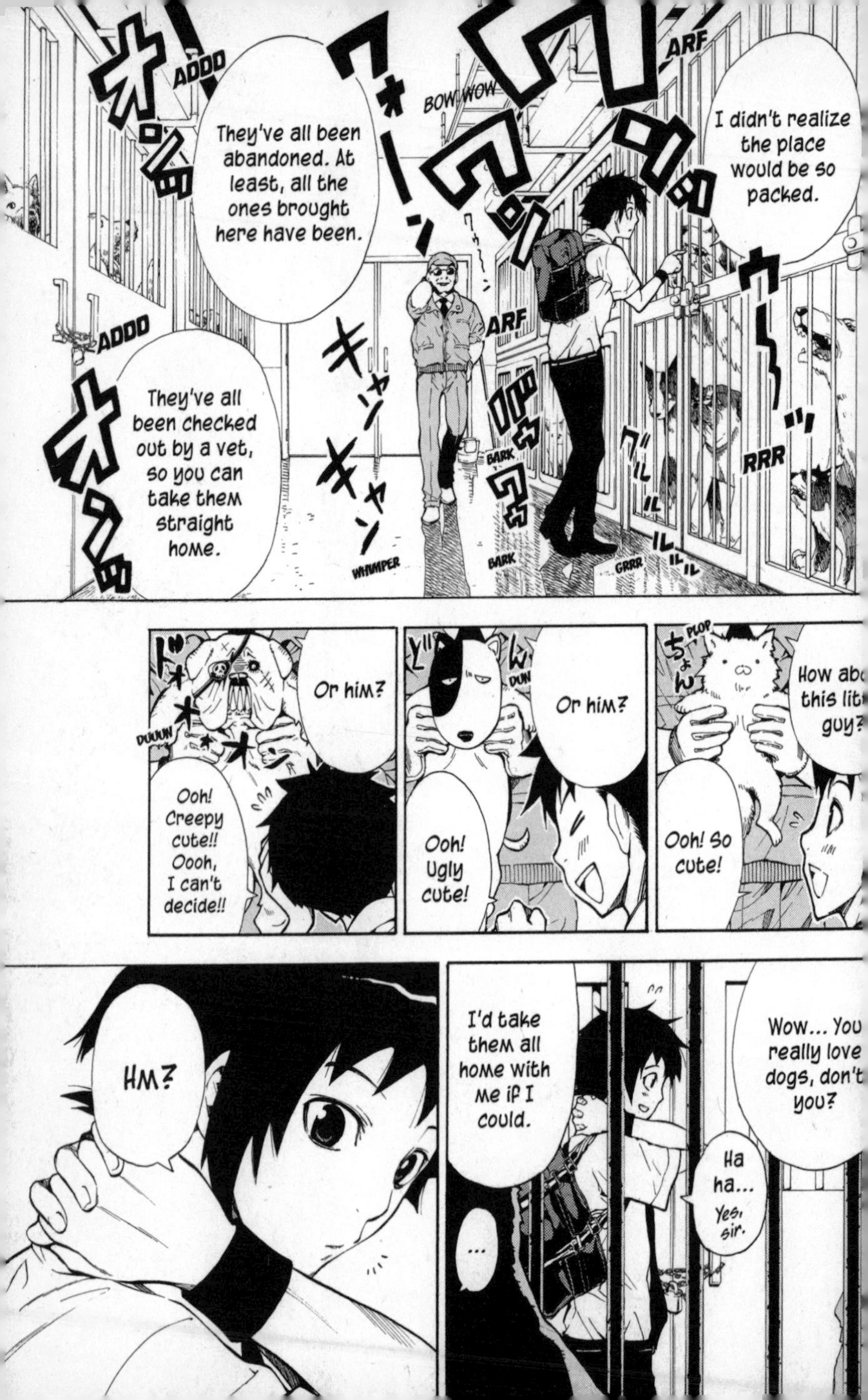
ARF
I didn't realize the place would be so packed.
BOW WOW
They've all been abandoned. At least, all the ones brought here have been.
ADDD
RRR
GRRR
BARK
BARK
ARF
WHIMPER
They've all been checked out by a vet, so you can take them straight home.
ADDD
PLOP
How abo this lit guy?
Ooh! So cute!
DUN
Or him?
Ooh! Ugly cute!
DUUUN
Or him?
Ooh! Creepy cute!! Oooh, I can't decide!!
Wow... You really love dogs, don't you?
Ha ha... Yes, sir.
I'd take them all home with me if I could.
...
HM?

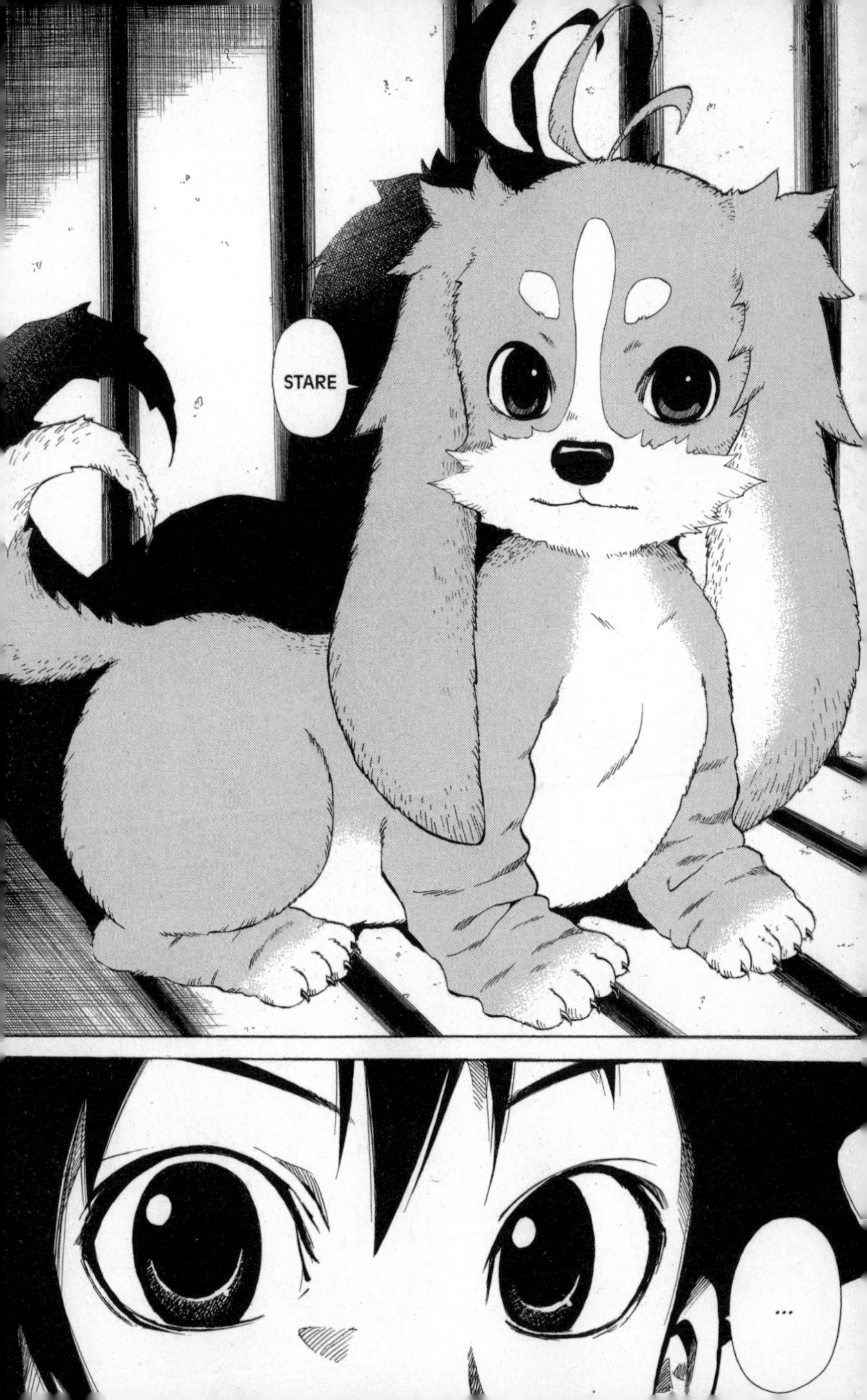
STARE
...

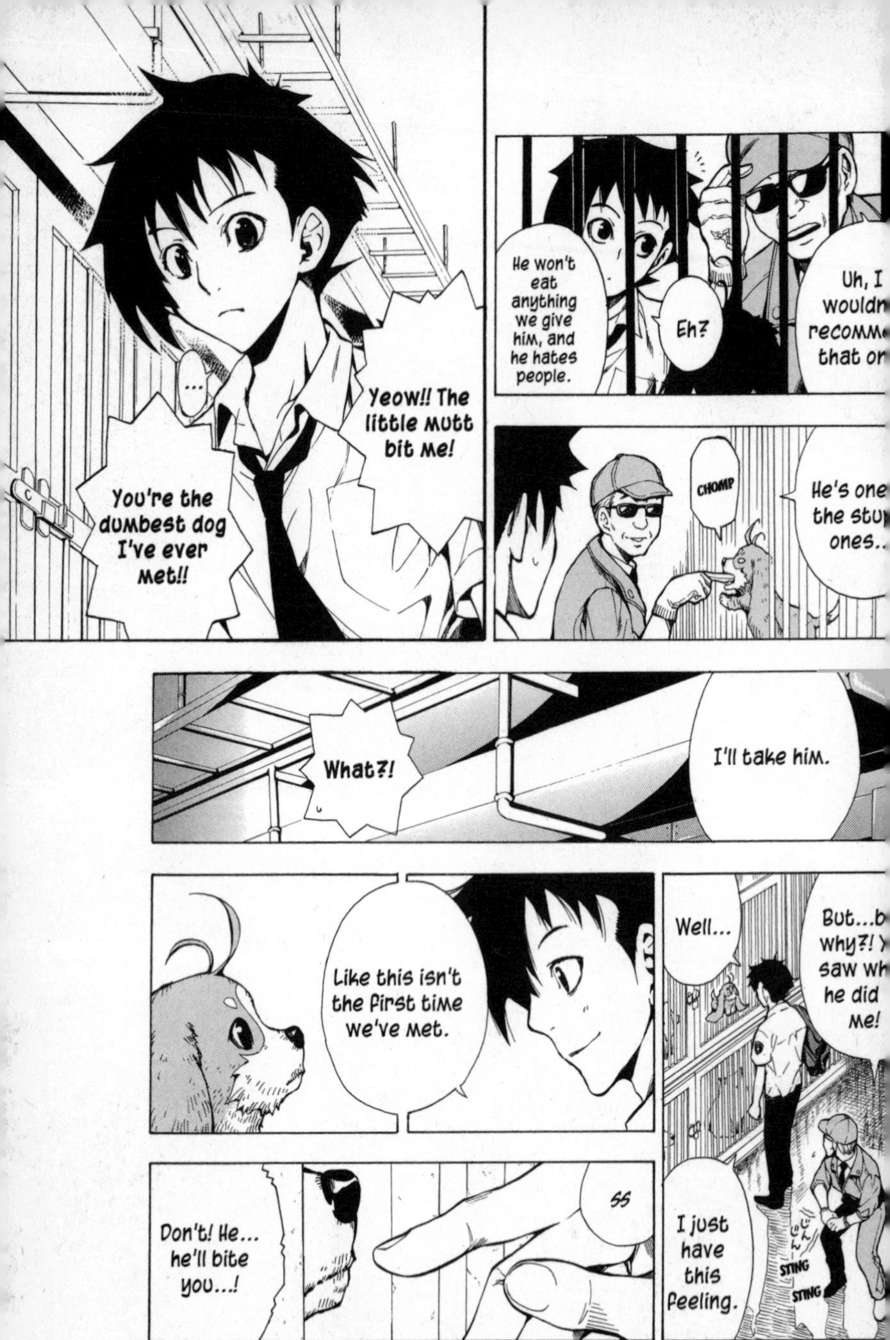

Uh, I wouldn recomm that on
Eh?
He won't eat anything we give him, and he hates people.
He's one the stu ones..
CHOMP
Yeow!! The little mutt bit me!
You're the dumbest dog I've ever met!!
...
I'll take him.
What?!
But...b why?! saw wh he did me!
Well...
I just have this feeling.
STING
STING
Like this isn't the first time we've met.
SS
Don't! He... he'll bite you...!

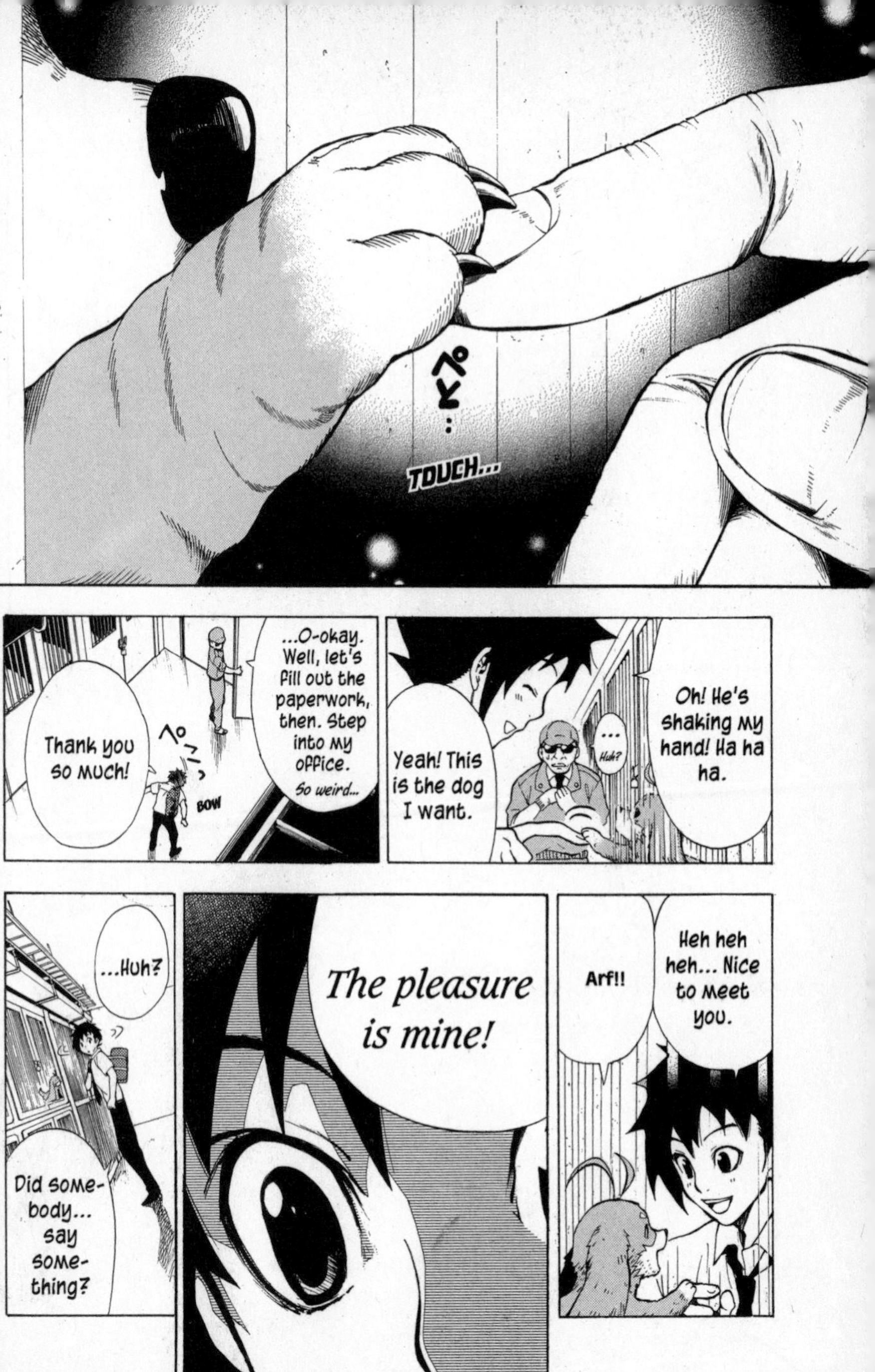
ペト…
TOUCH...
Oh! He's shaking my hand! Ha ha ha.
...
Huh?
Yeah! This is the dog I want.
...O-okay. Well, let's fill out the paperwork, then. Step into my office.
So weird...
BOW
Thank you so much!
Heh heh heh... Nice to meet you.
Arf!!
The pleasure is mine!
...Huh?
Did somebody... say something?

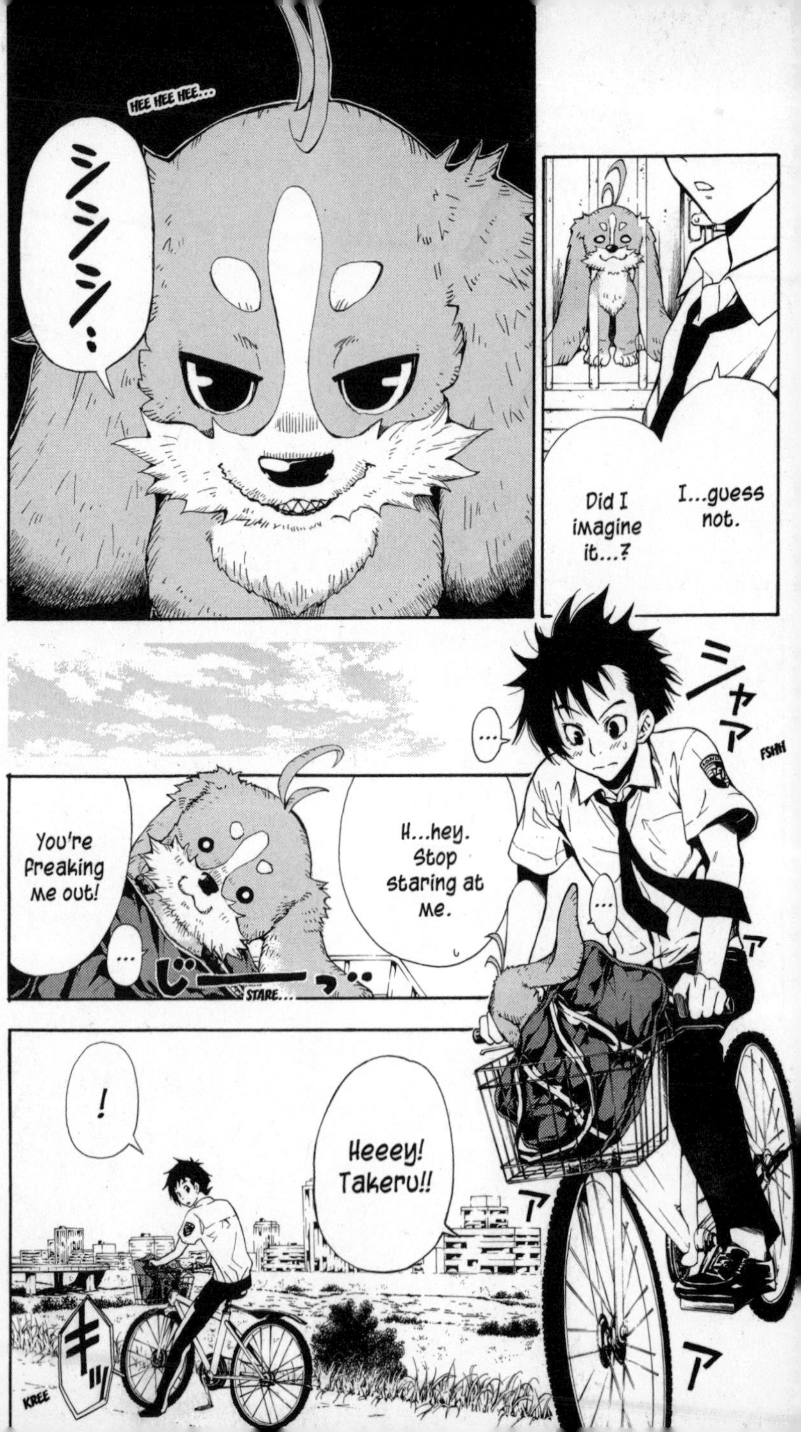
Did I imagine it...? I...guess not.
HEE HEE HEE...
シシシシ…
...
シャアアア
FSHH
...
H...hey. Stop staring at me.
You're freaking me out!
...
じーっ
STARE...
Heeey! Takeru!!
!
キッ
KREE

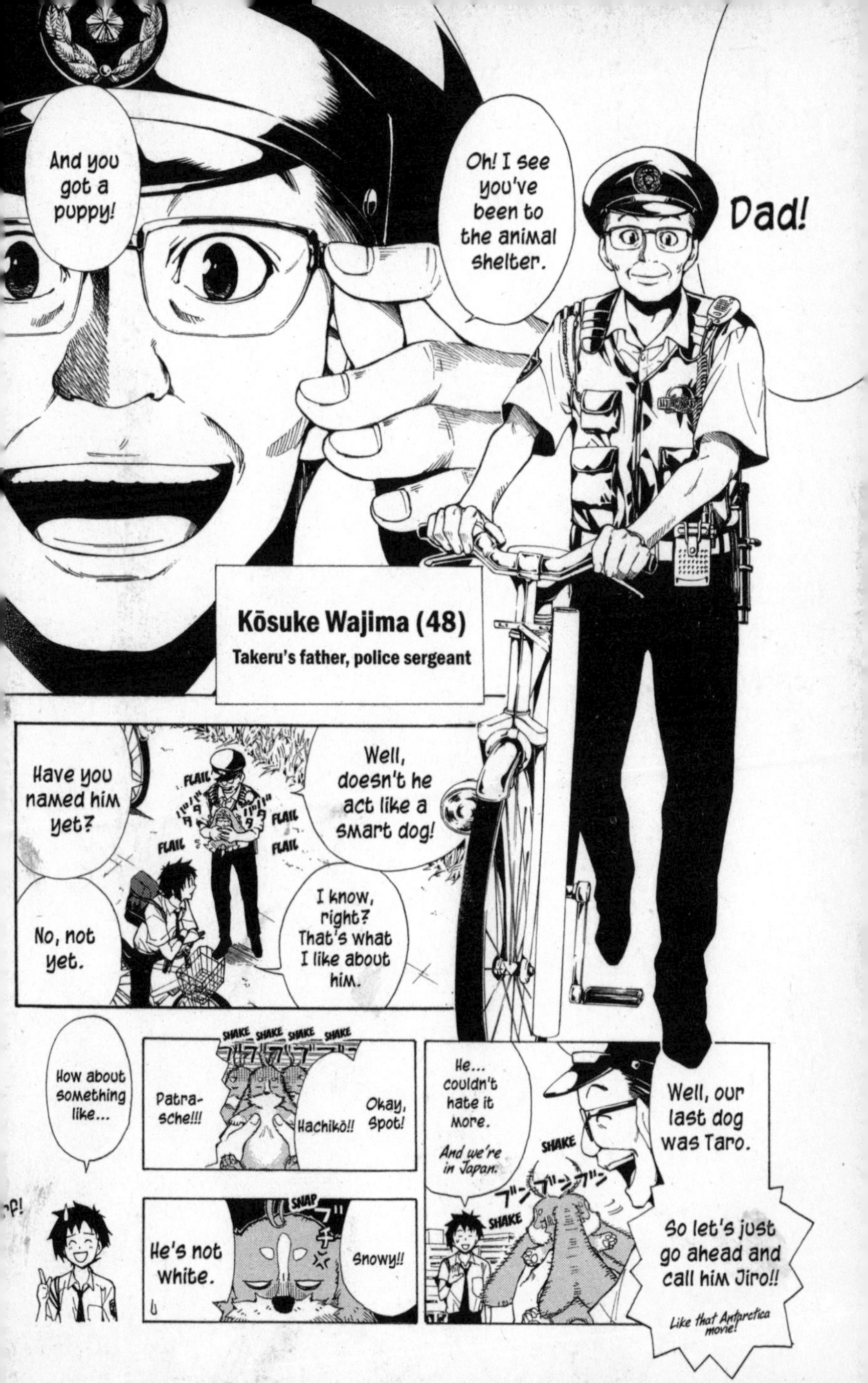

Dad!
Oh! I see you've been to the animal shelter.
And you got a puppy!
Kōsuke Wajima (48)
Takeru's father, police sergeant
Well, doesn't he act like a smart dog!
FLAIL
FLAIL
FLAIL
FLAIL
I know, right? That's what I like about him.
Have you named him yet?
No, not yet.
Well, our last dog was Taro.
So let's just go ahead and call him Jiro!!
Like that Antarctica movie!
SHAKE
SHAKE
He... couldn't hate it more.
And we're in Japan.
SHAKE SHAKE SHAKE SHAKE
Okay, Spot!
Hachikō!!
Patrasche!!!
Snowy!!
SNAP
He's not white.
How about something like...

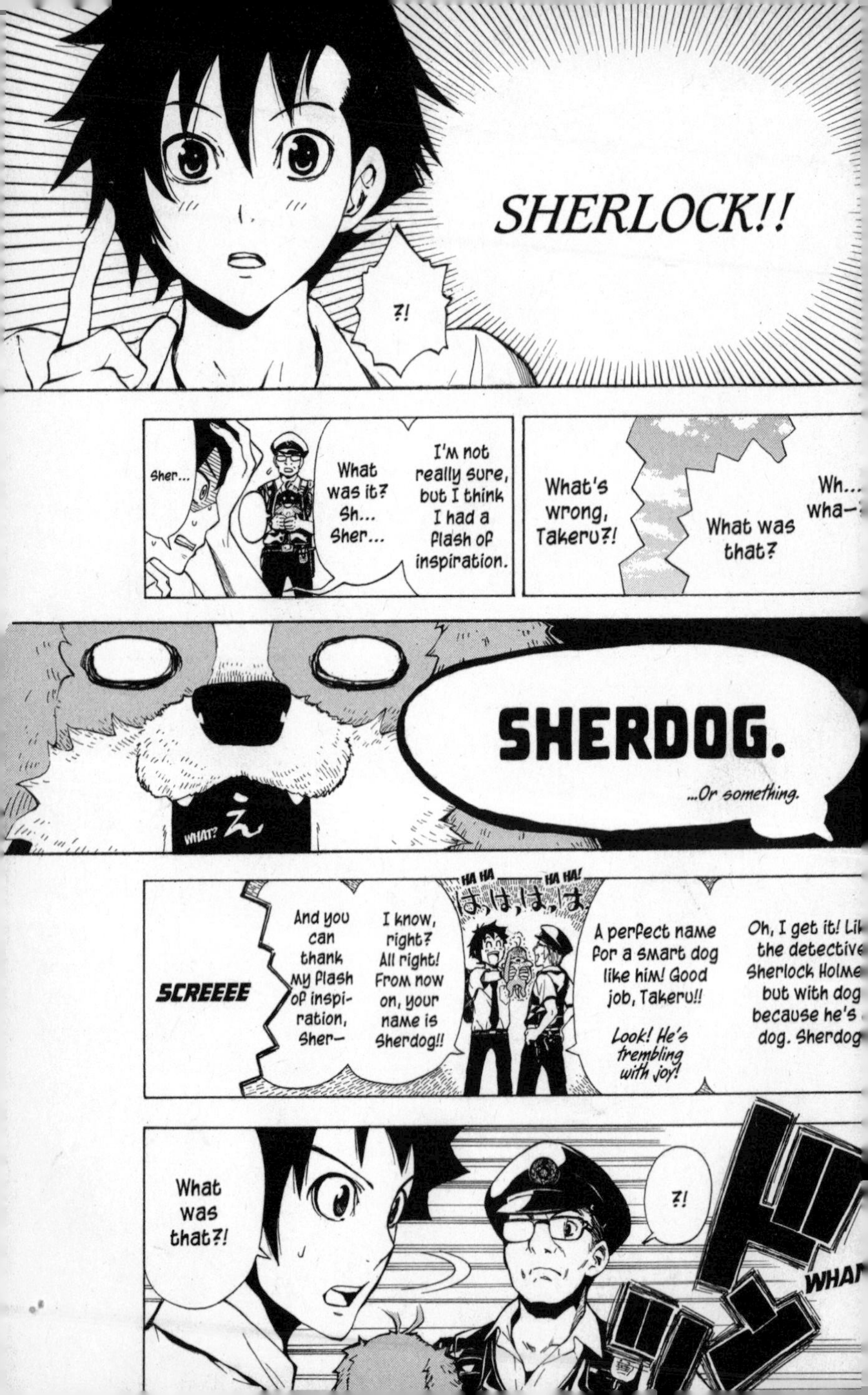
SHERLOCK!!
?!
Wh... wha–
What was that?
What's wrong, Takeru?!
I'm not really sure, but I think I had a flash of inspiration.
What was it? Sh... Sher...
Sher...
SHERDOG.
...Or something.
WHAT? え
Oh, I get it! Lik the detective Sherlock Holme but with dog because he's dog. Sherdog
A perfect name for a smart dog like him! Good job, Takeru!!
Look! He's trembling with joy!
HA HA HA HA!
はっはっはっは
I know, right? All right! From now on, your name is Sherdog!!
And you can thank my flash of inspiration, Sher–
SCREEEE
WHA
?!
What was that?!

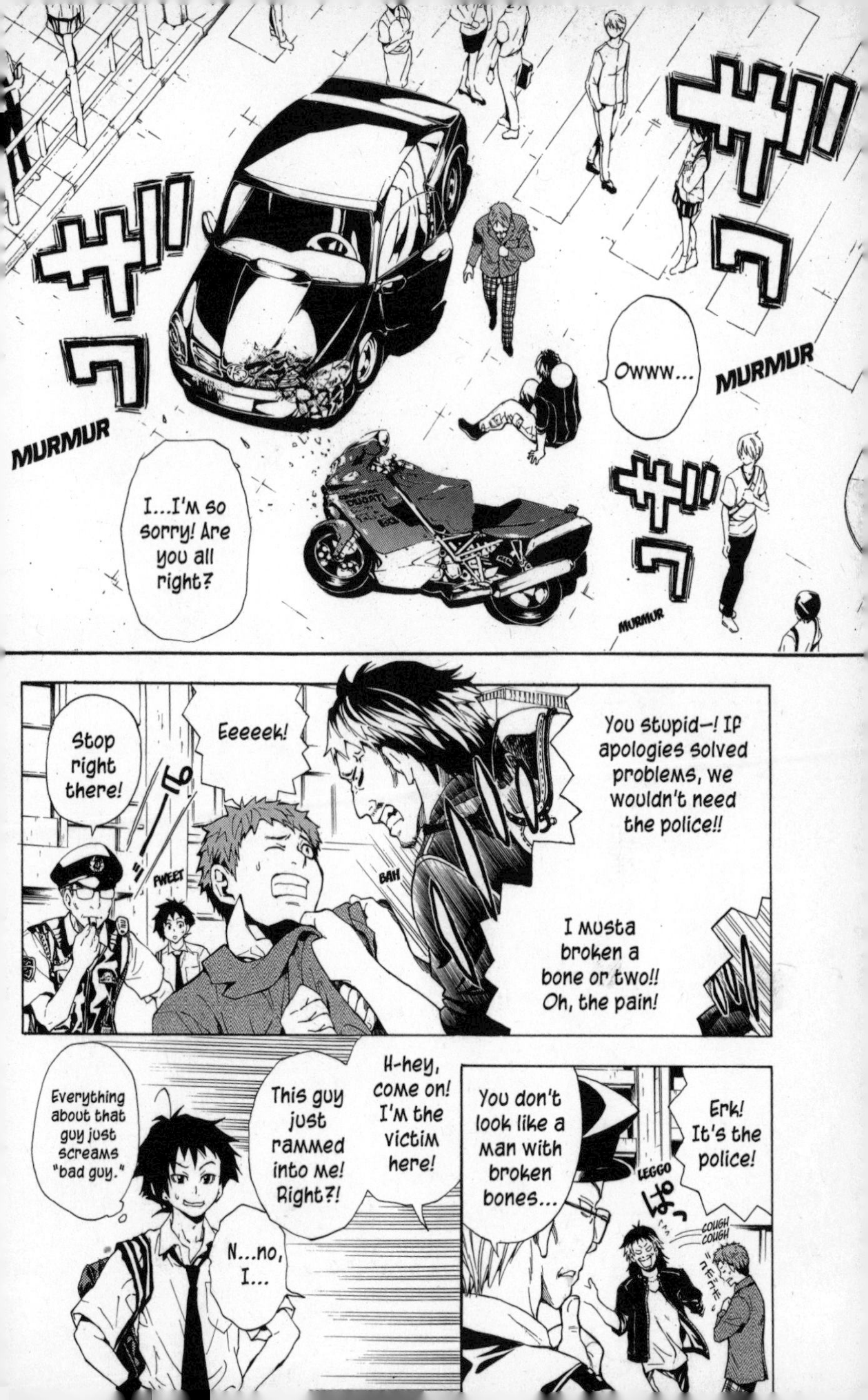
MURMUR
Owww...
MURMUR
I...I'm so sorry! Are you all right?
MURMUR
You stupid—! If apologies solved problems, we wouldn't need the police!!
I musta broken a bone or two!! Oh, the pain!
BAH
Eeeeek!
Stop right there!
PWEET
Erk! It's the police!
You don't look like a man with broken bones...
LEGGO
COUGH COUGH
H-hey, come on! I'm the victim here!
This guy just rammed into me! Right?!
N...no, I...
Everything about that guy just screams "bad guy."

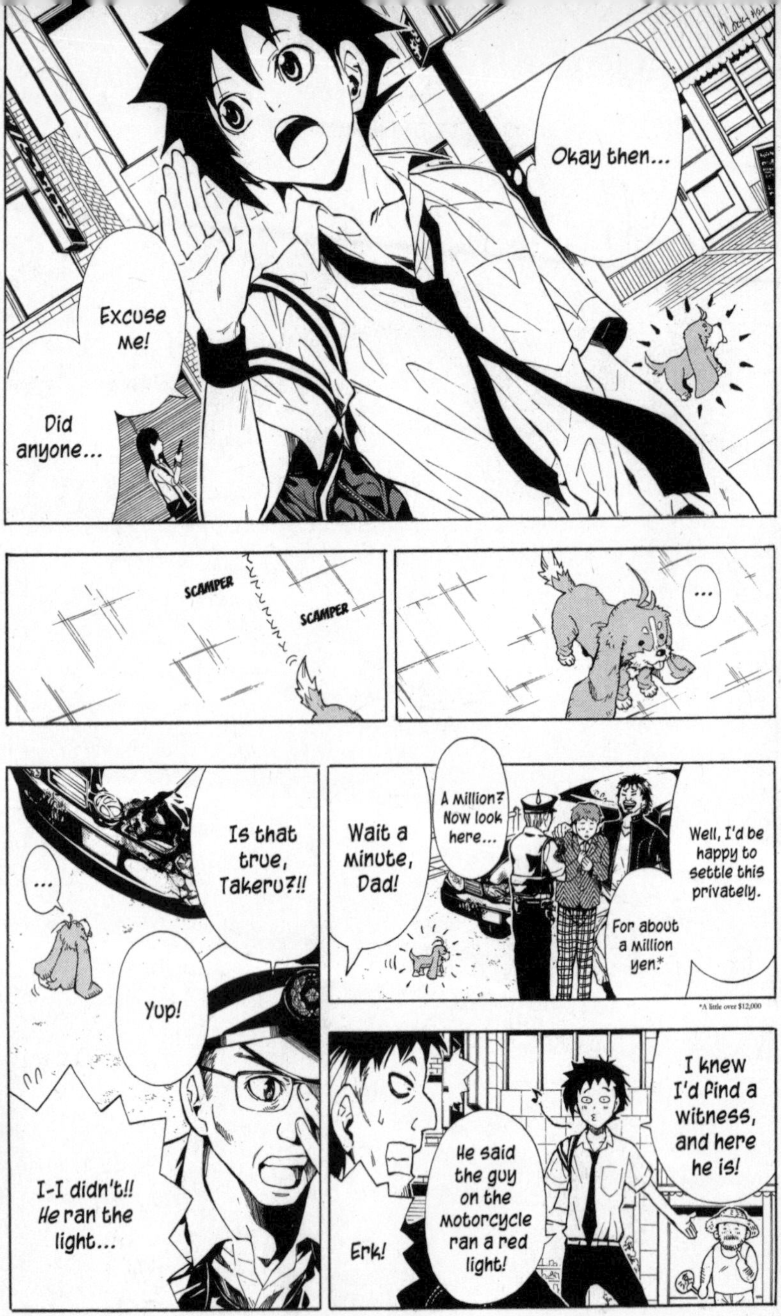
Okay then...
Excuse me!
Did anyone...
...
SCAMPER
SCAMPER
Well, I'd be happy to settle this privately.
For about a million yen.*
A Million? Now look here...
Wait a minute, Dad!
I knew I'd find a witness, and here he is!
He said the guy on the motorcycle ran a red light!
Erk!
Is that true, Takeru?!!
...
Yup!
I-I didn't!! He ran the light...

*A little over $12,000

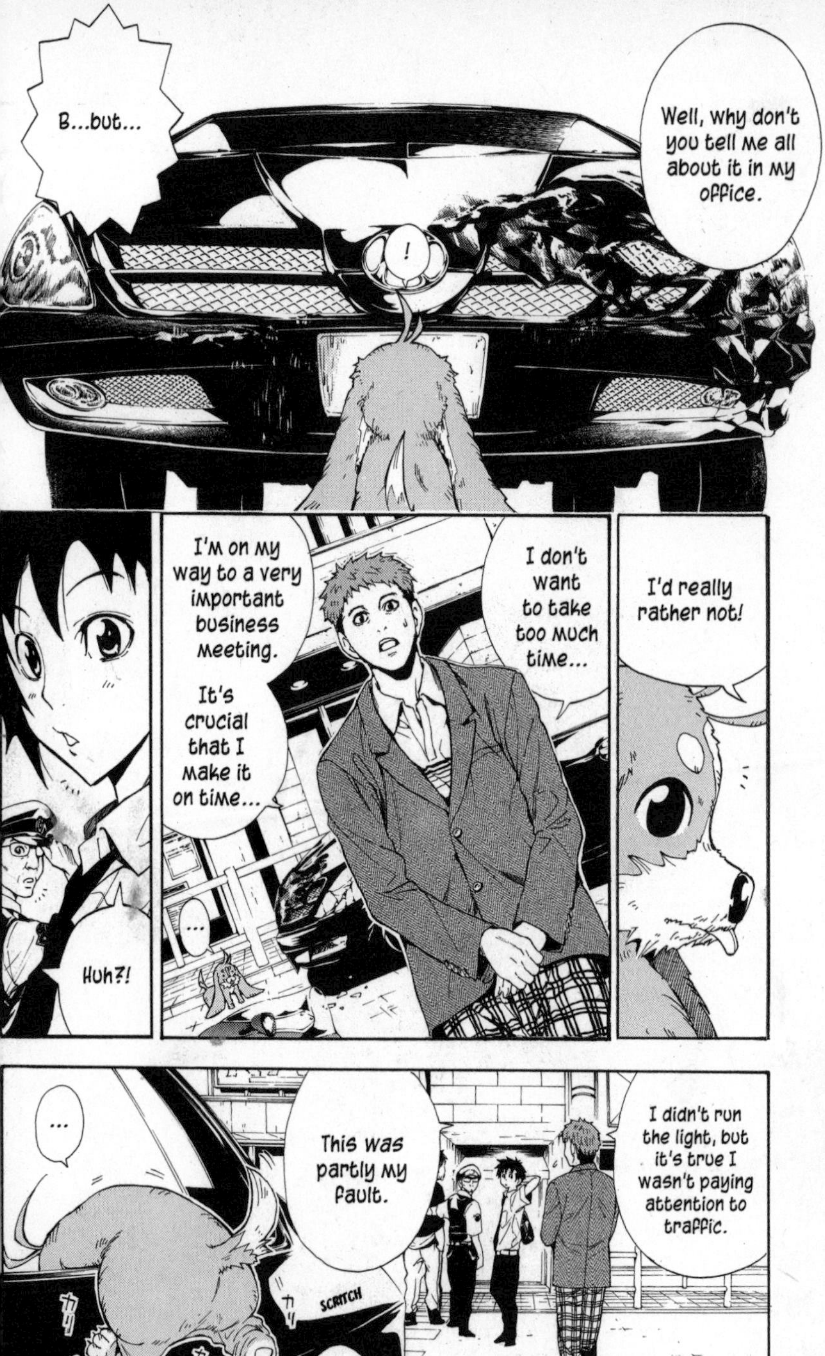
Well, why don't you tell me all about it in my office.
!
B...but...
I'd really rather not!
I don't want to take too much time...
I'm on my way to a very important business meeting.
It's crucial that I make it on time...
...
Huh?!
I didn't run the light, but it's true I wasn't paying attention to traffic.
This was partly my fault.
...
SCRITCH
SCRITCH
SCRITCH

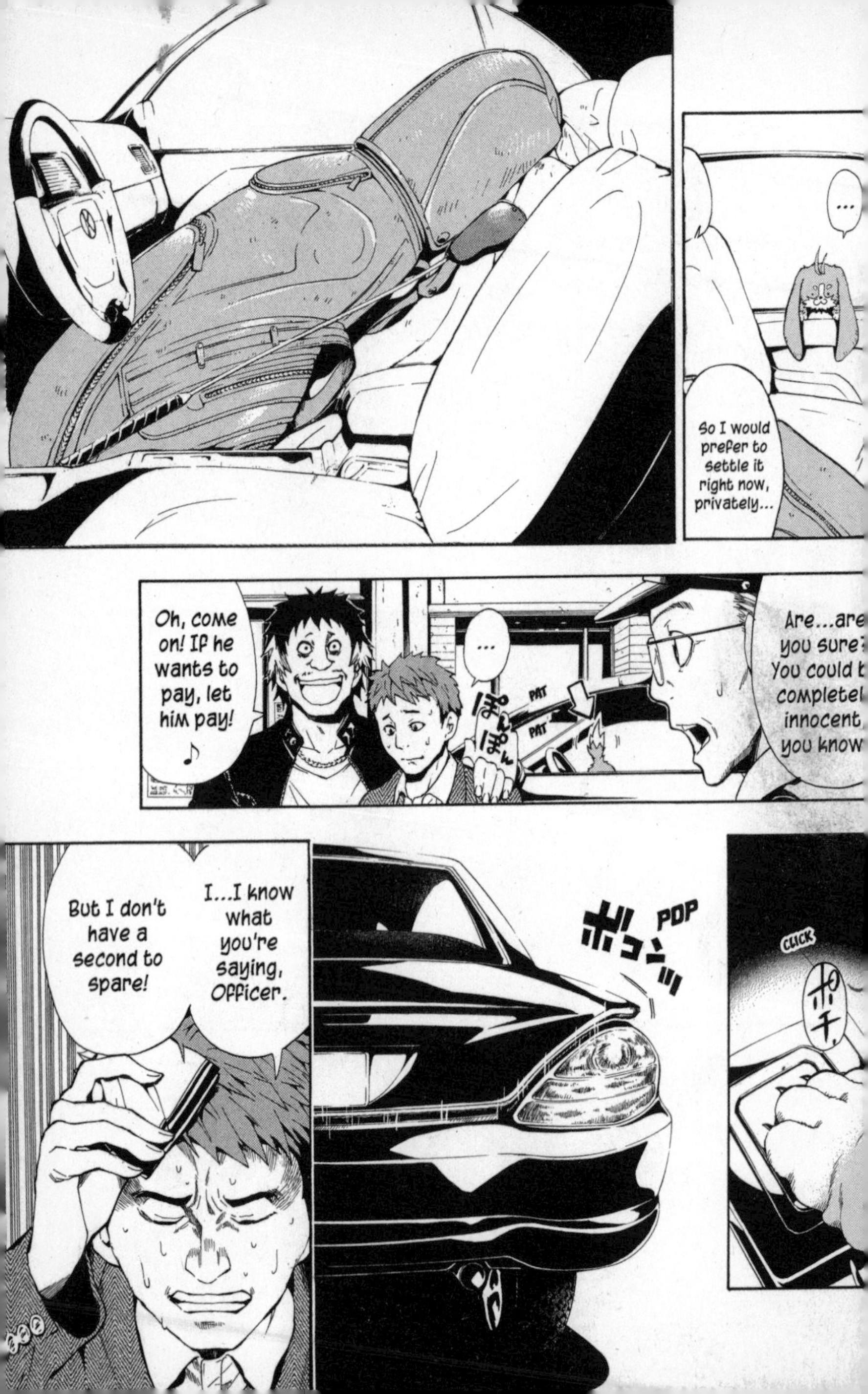
...
So I would prefer to settle it right now, privately...
Are...are you sure? You could b completel innocent, you know
...
ぽんぽん
PAT PAT
Oh, come on! If he wants to pay, let him pay! ♪
ポチ
CLICK
ボコンッ
POP
I...I know what you're saying, Officer.
But I don't have a second to spare!

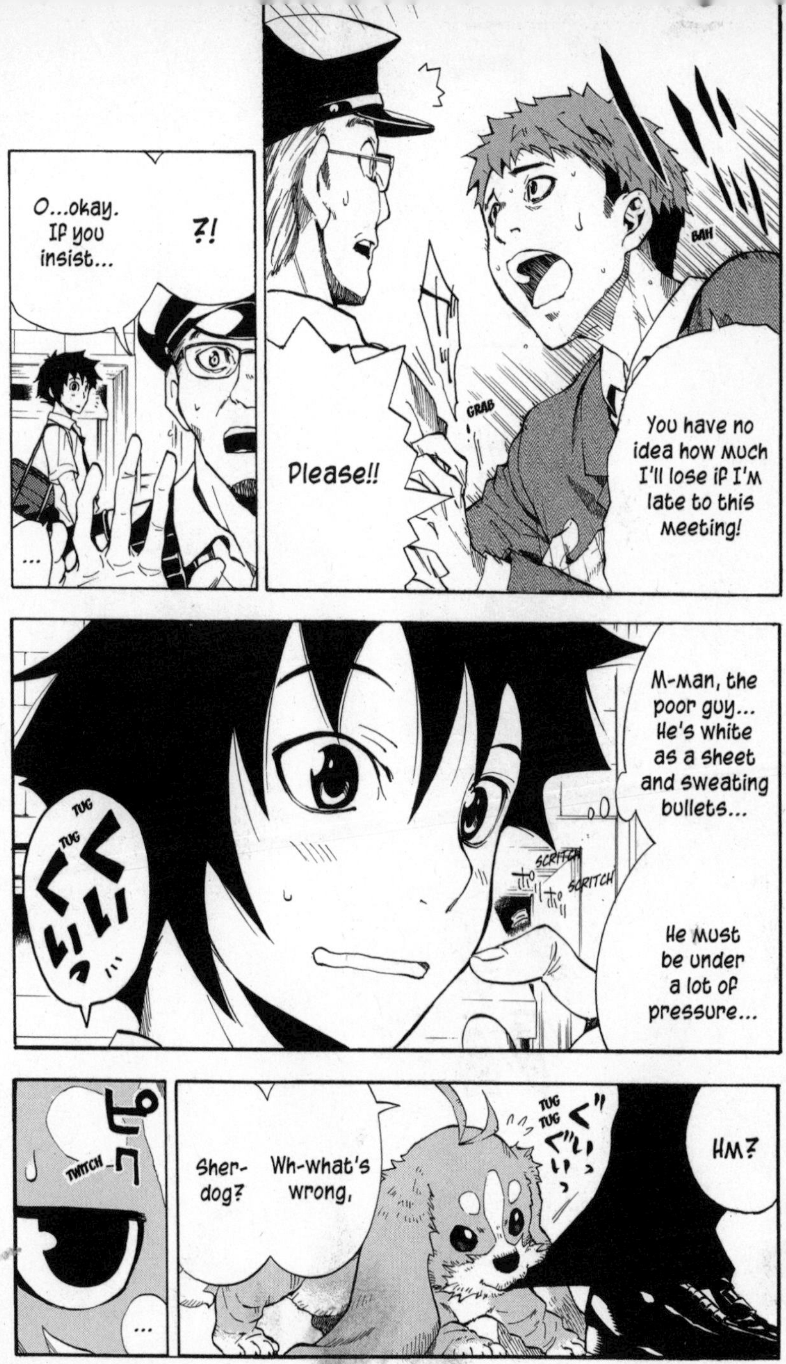
BAH
You have no idea how much I'll lose if I'm late to this meeting!
GRAB
Please!!
?!
O...okay. If you insist...
...
M-man, the poor guy... He's white as a sheet and sweating bullets...
He must be under a lot of pressure...
SCRITCH SCRITCH
TUG TUG
HM?
TUG TUG
Wh-what's wrong, Sher-dog?
TWITCH
...

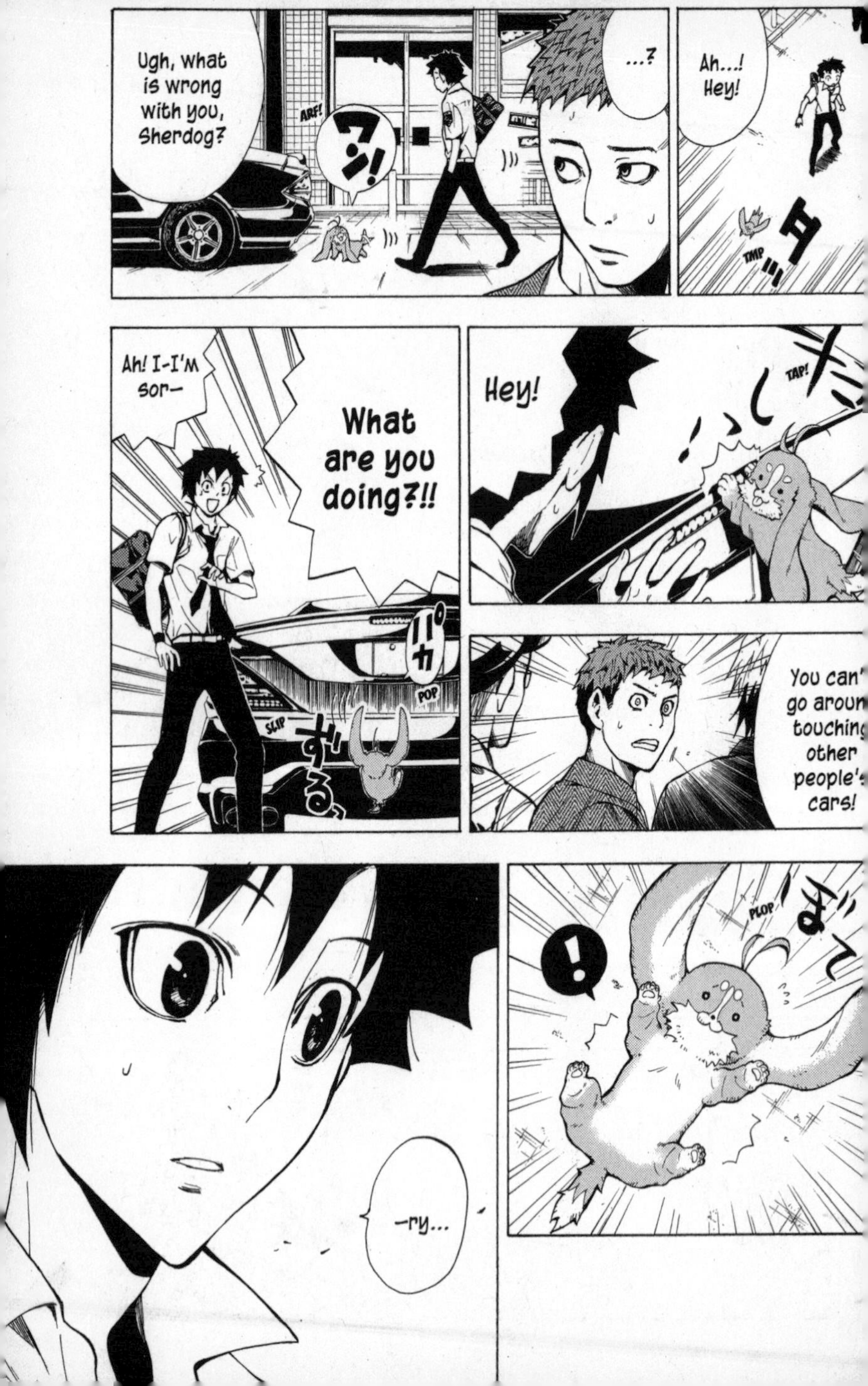
Ah...! Hey!
TMP
...?
Ugh, what is wrong with you, Sherdog?
ARF!
Hey!
TAP!
You can' go aroun touching other people' cars!
What are you doing?!!
Ah! I-I'm sor—
POP
SLIP
!
PLOP
—ry...

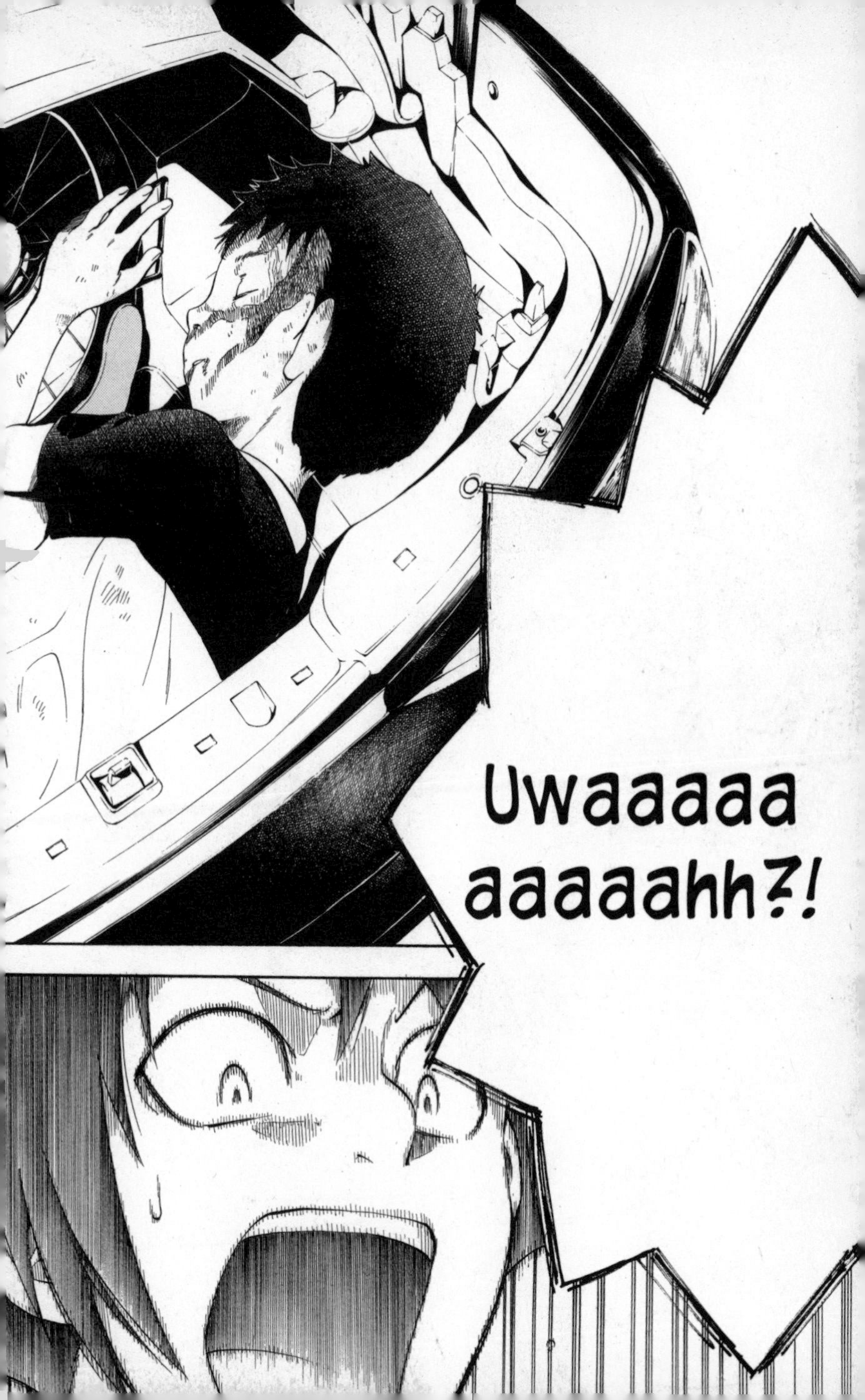
Uwaaaaaa aaaaaahh?!

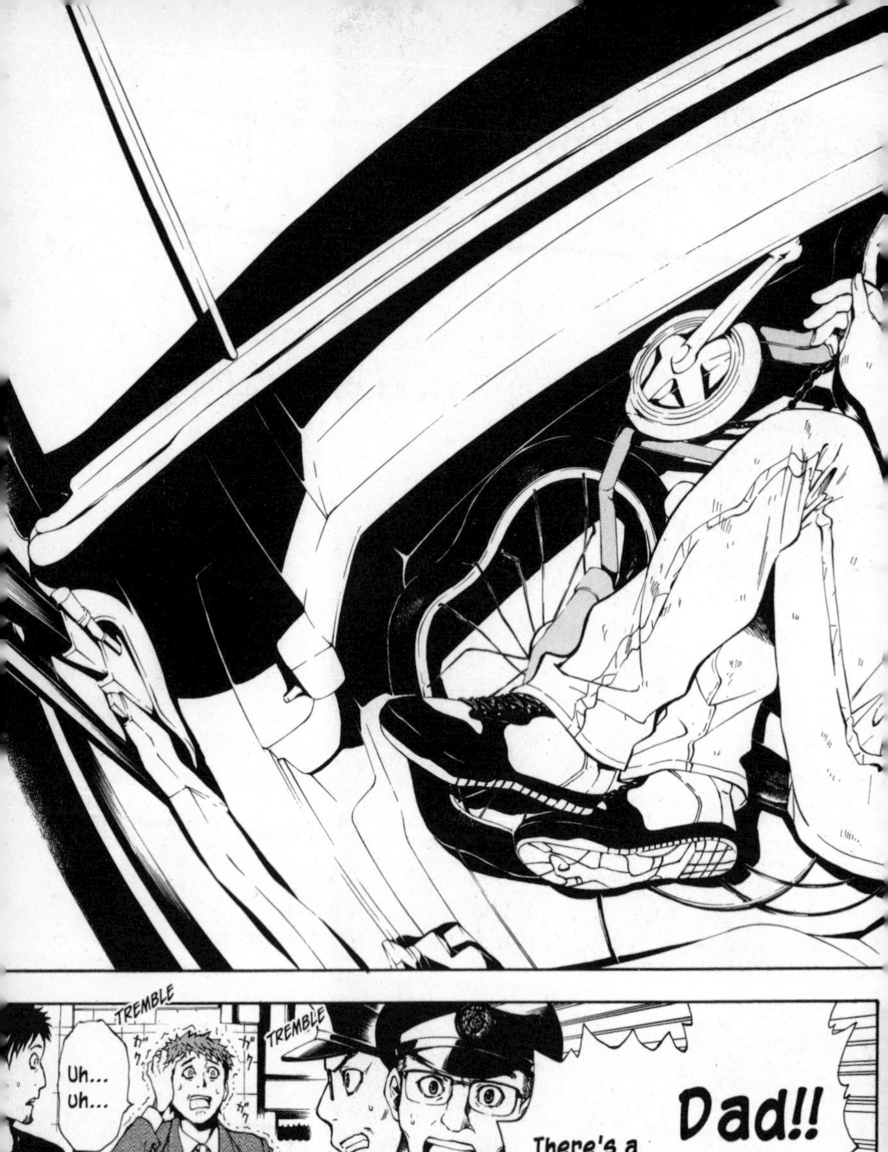

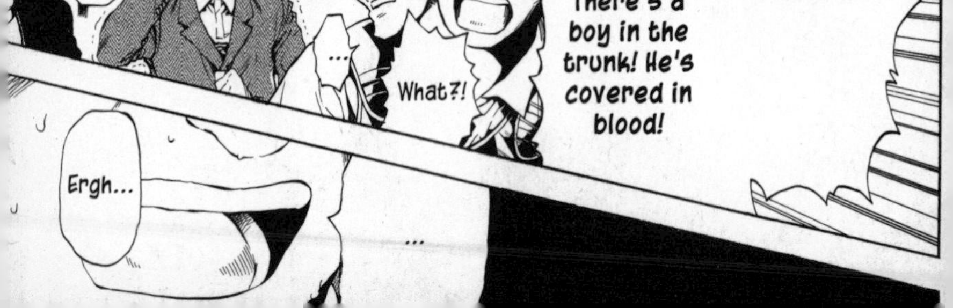
Dad!!
There's a boy in the trunk! He's covered in blood!
What?!
...
TREMBLE
TREMBLE
Uh... uh...
Ergh...
...

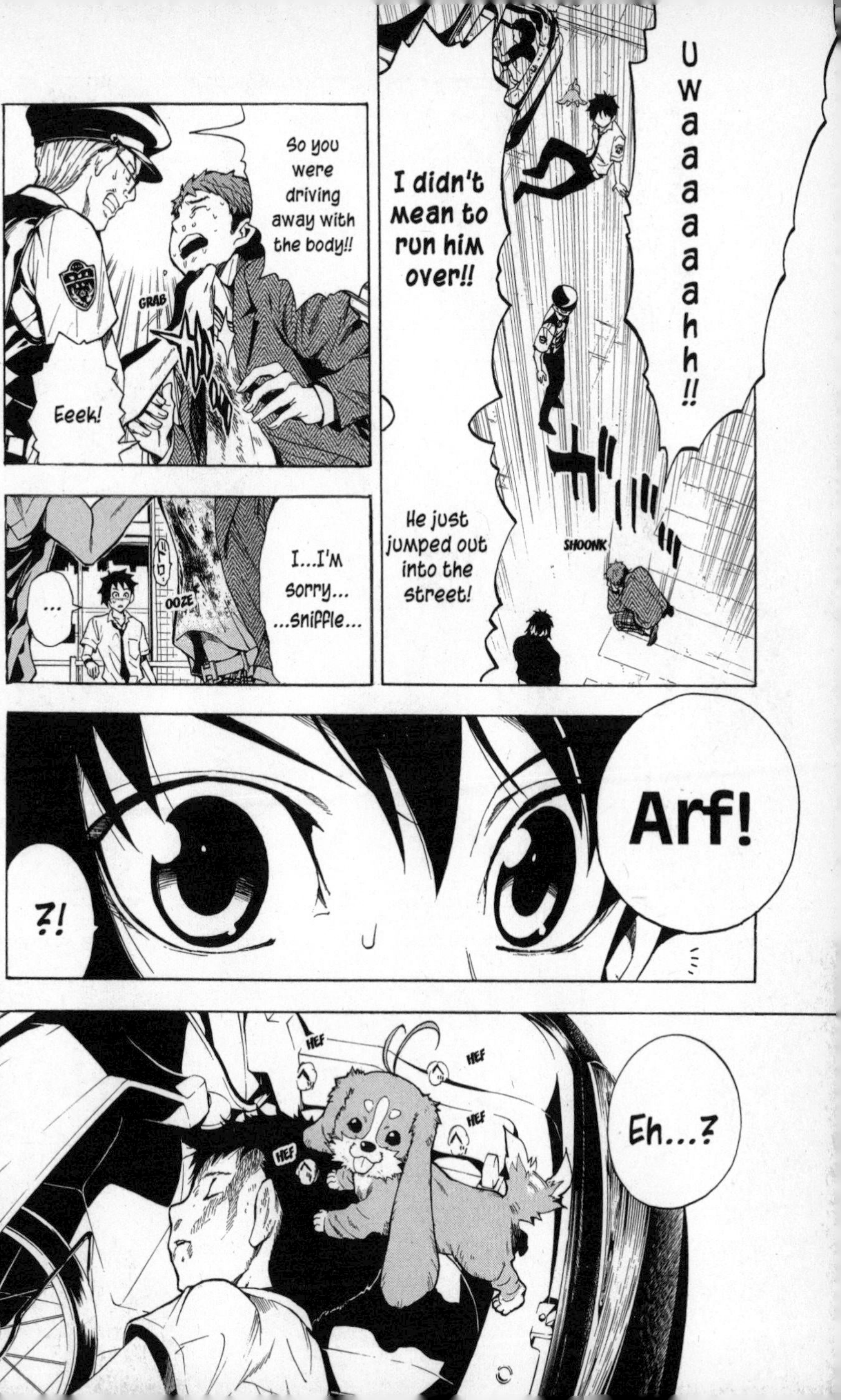
Uwaaaaaaahh!!
I didn't mean to run him over!!
He just jumped out into the street!
SHOONK
So you were driving away with the body!!
GRAB
Eeek!
I...I'm sorry... ...sniffle...
OOZE
...
Arf!
?!
Eh...?
HEF
HEF
HEF
HEF

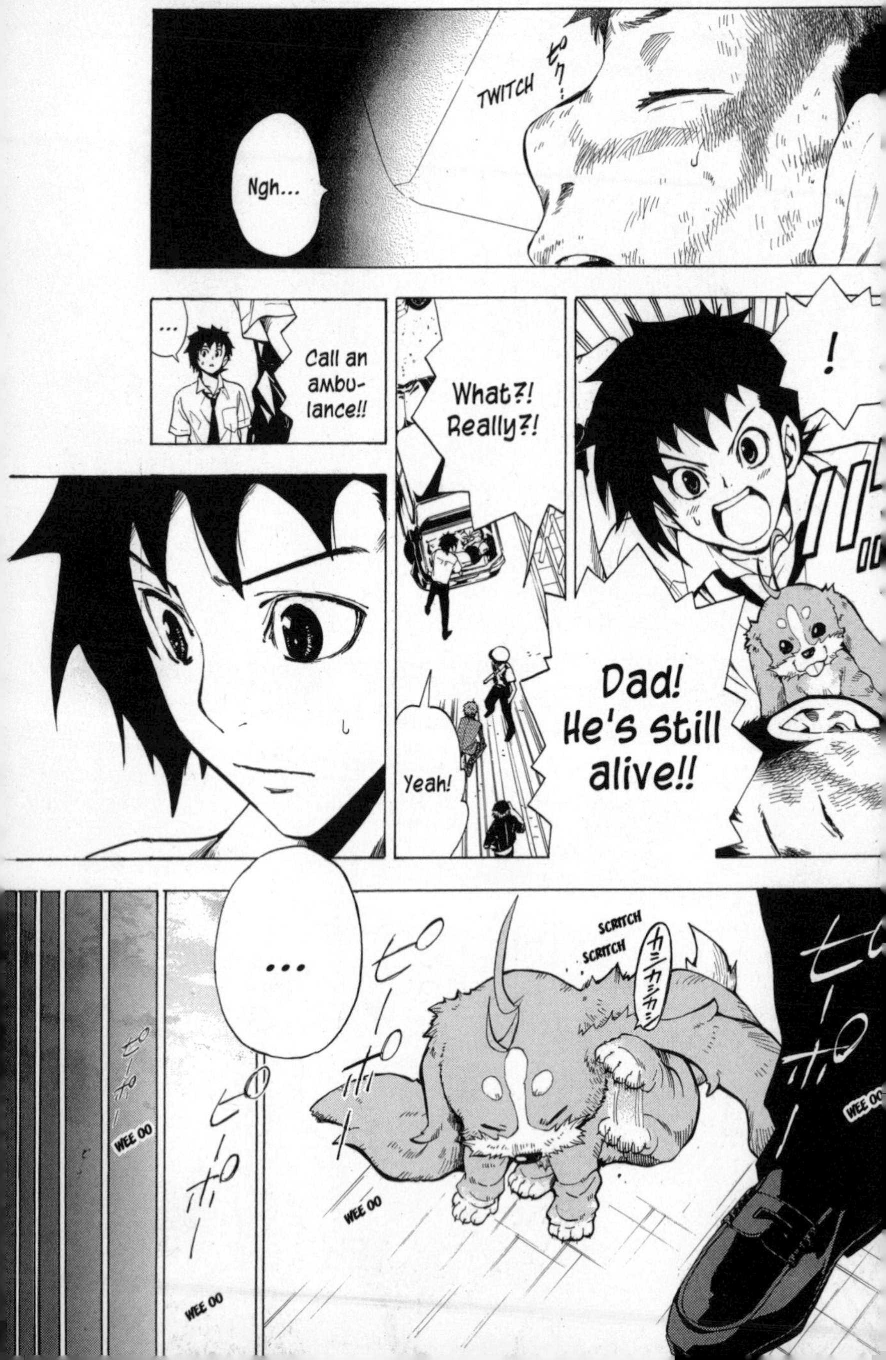

TWITCH
Ngh...
!
Dad! He's still alive!!
What?! Really?!
Yeah!
...
Call an ambulance!!
WEE OO
SCRITCH SCRITCH
WEE OO
...
WEE OO
WEE OO

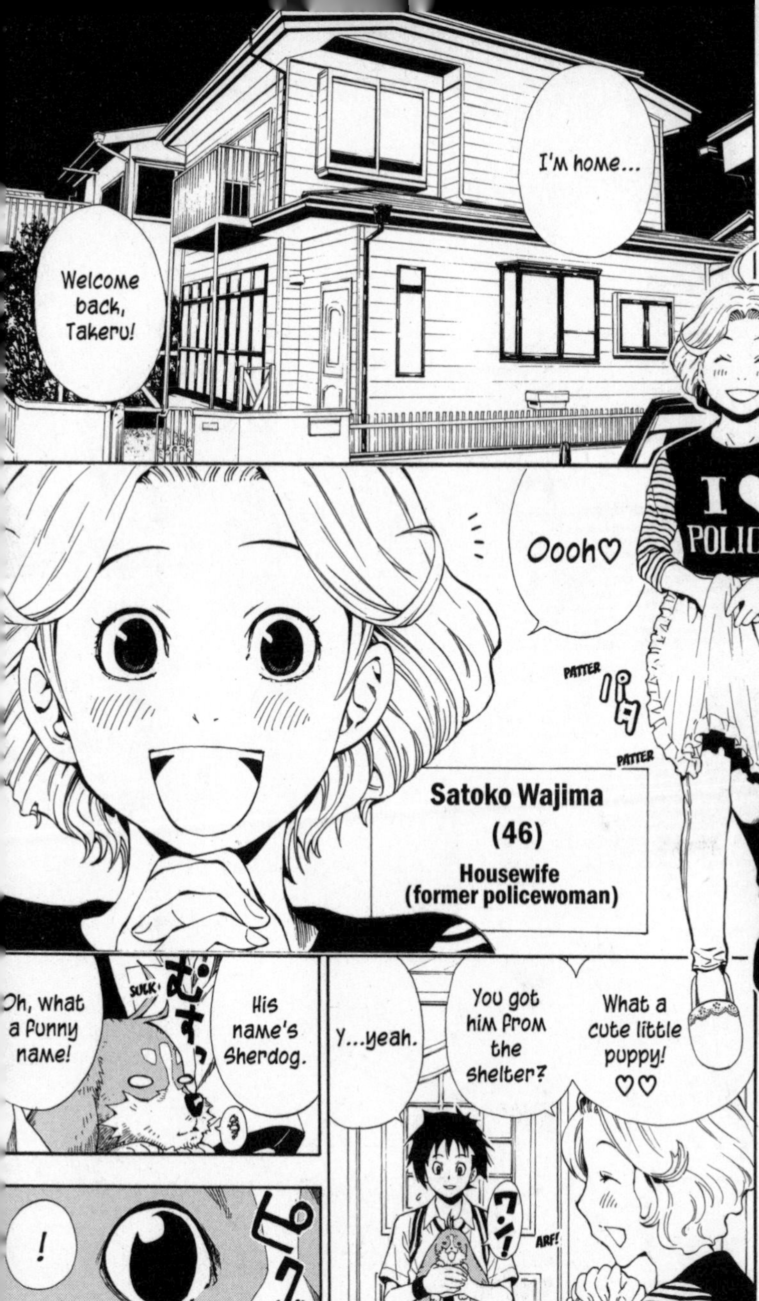
I'm home...
Welcome back, Takeru!
PATTER
パタ
PATTER
パタ
PATTER
パタ
PATTER
Oooh♡
Satoko Wajima
(46)
Housewife
(former policewoman)
I ♥ POLICE
What a cute little puppy! ♡♡
You got him from the shelter?
Y...yeah.
ワン!
ARF!
His name's Sherdog.
むすっ
SULK
Oh, what a funny name!
!
ピクッ
TWITCH

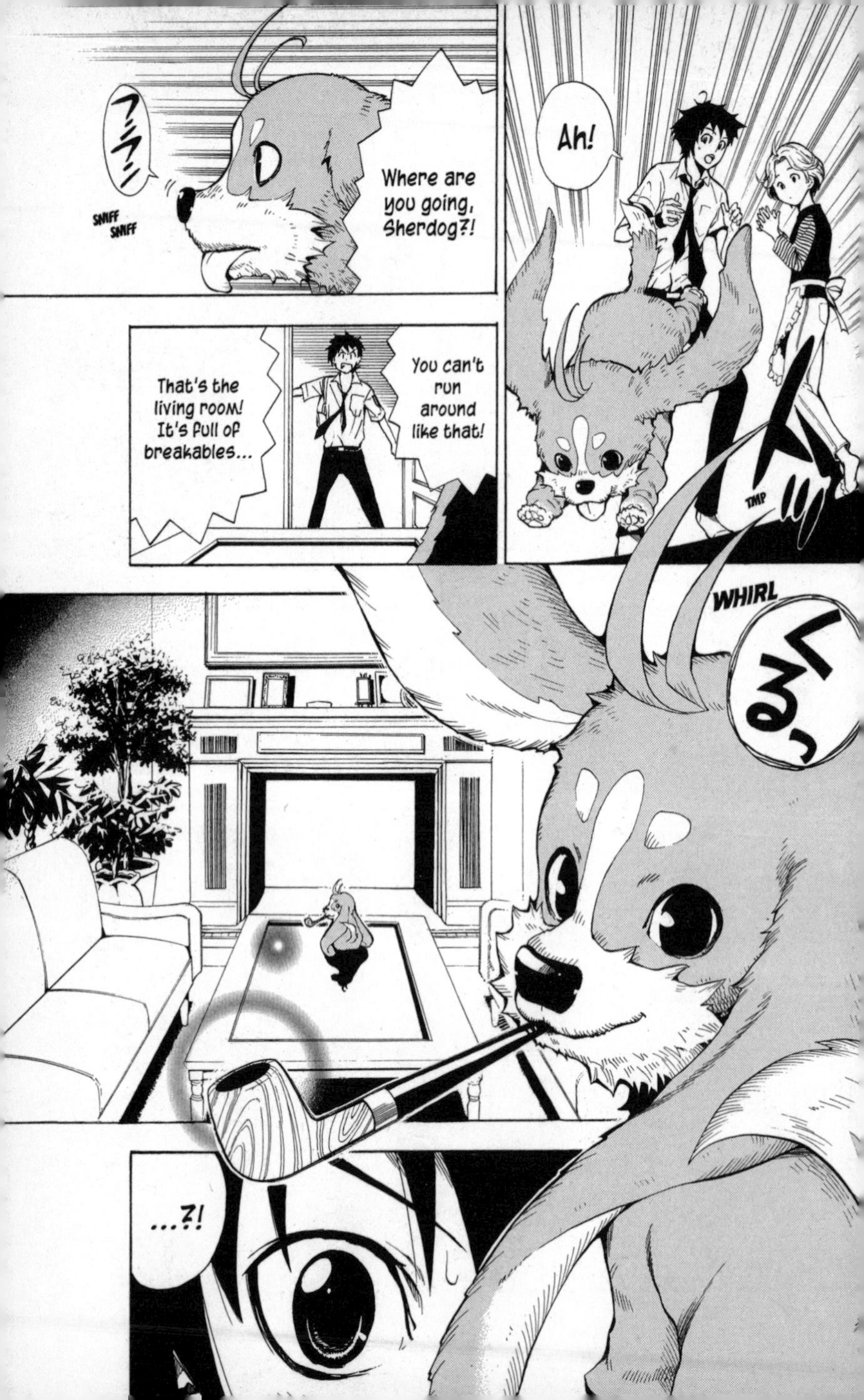

Ah!
TMP
Where are you going, Sherdog?!
フンフン
SNIFF SNIFF
You can't run around like that!
That's the living room! It's full of breakables...
WHIRL
くるっ
...?!

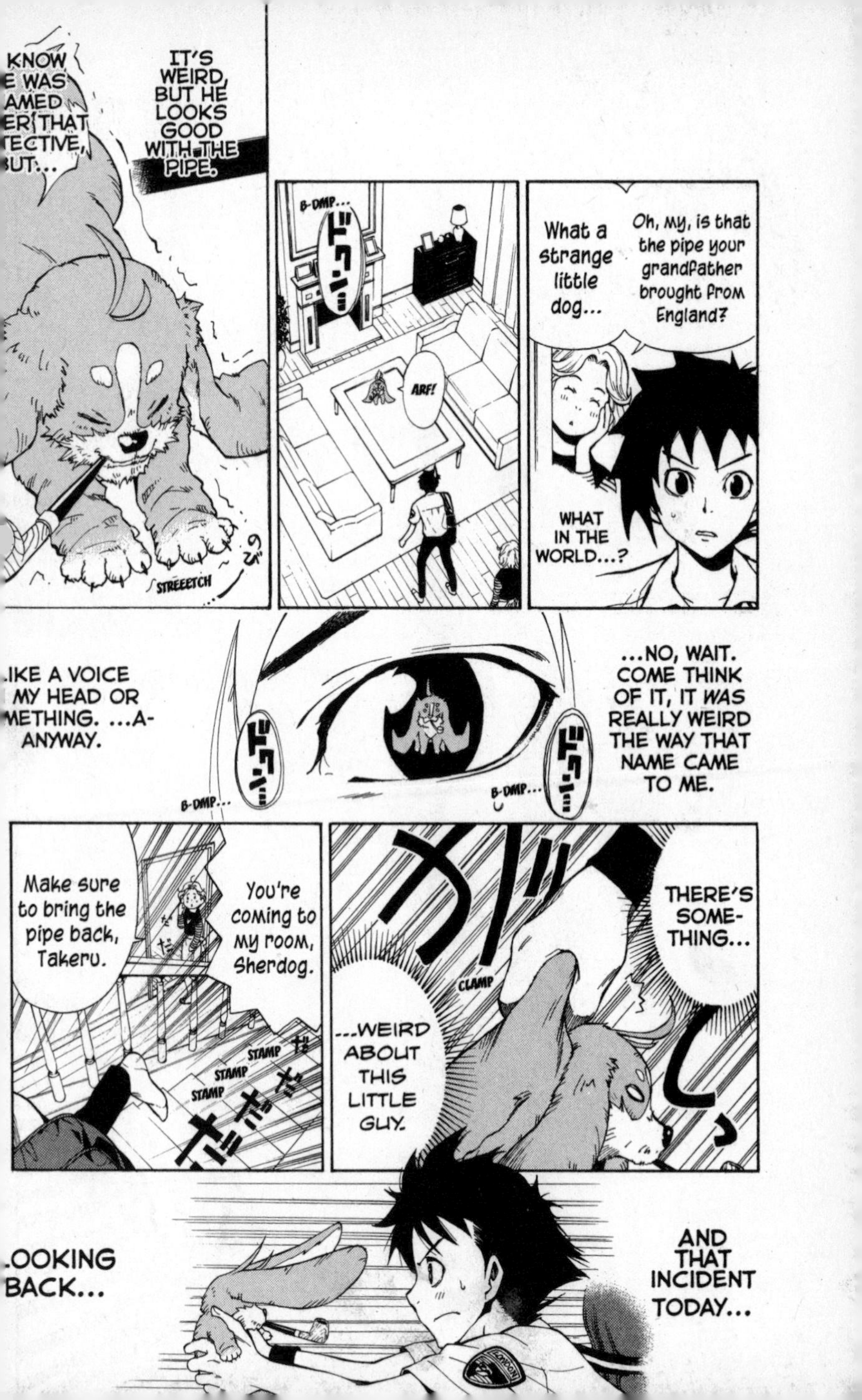
KNOW
E WAS
AMED
ER THAT
ECTIVE,
UT...
IT'S WEIRD, BUT HE LOOKS GOOD WITH THE PIPE.
STREEETCH
Oh, my, is that the pipe your grandfather brought from England?
What a strange little dog...
WHAT IN THE WORLD...?
B-DMP...
ARF!
...NO, WAIT. COME THINK OF IT, IT WAS REALLY WEIRD THE WAY THAT NAME CAME TO ME.
B-DMP...
IKE A VOICE
MY HEAD OR
METHING. ...A-
ANYWAY.
B-DMP...
THERE'S SOME-THING...
CLAMP
...WEIRD ABOUT THIS LITTLE GUY.
You're coming to my room, Sherdog.
Make sure to bring the pipe back, Takeru.
STAMP
STAMP
STAMP
AND THAT INCIDENT TODAY...
OOKING
BACK...

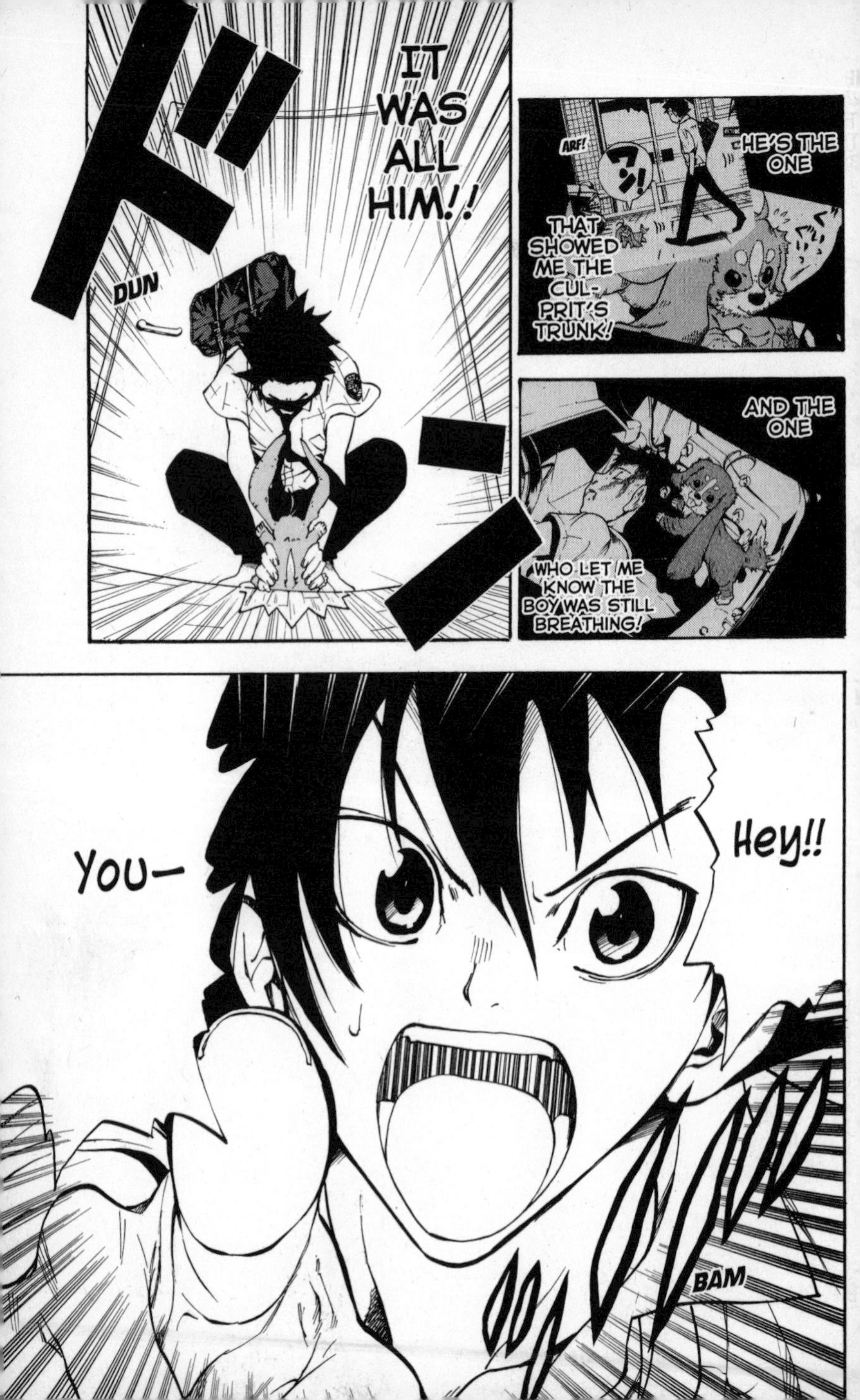
HE'S THE ONE
ARF!
THAT SHOWED ME THE CUL-PRIT'S TRUNK!
AND THE ONE
WHO LET ME KNOW THE BOY WAS STILL BREATHING!
IT WAS ALL HIM!!
DUN
Hey!!
YOU-
BAM

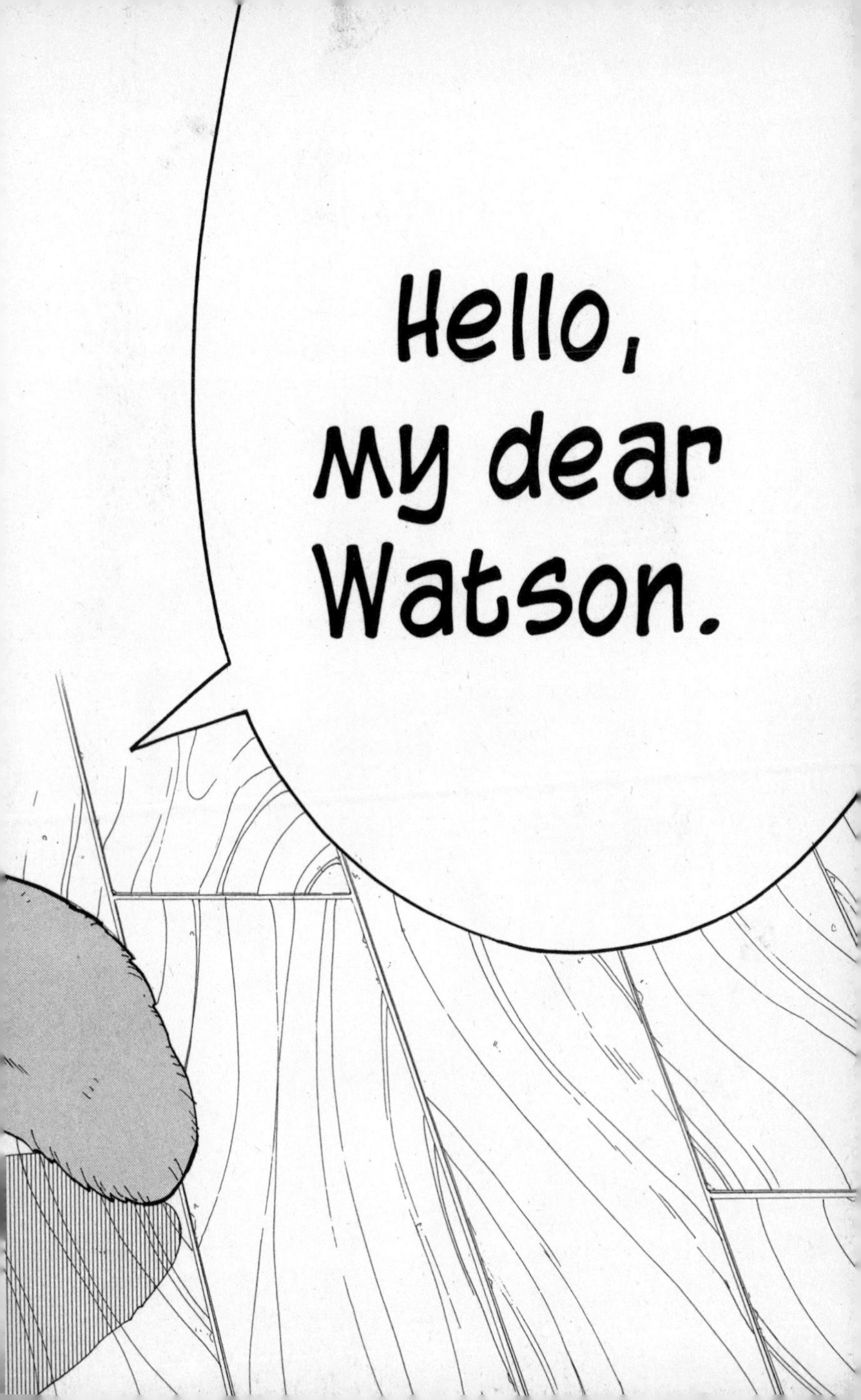
Hello, my dear Watson.

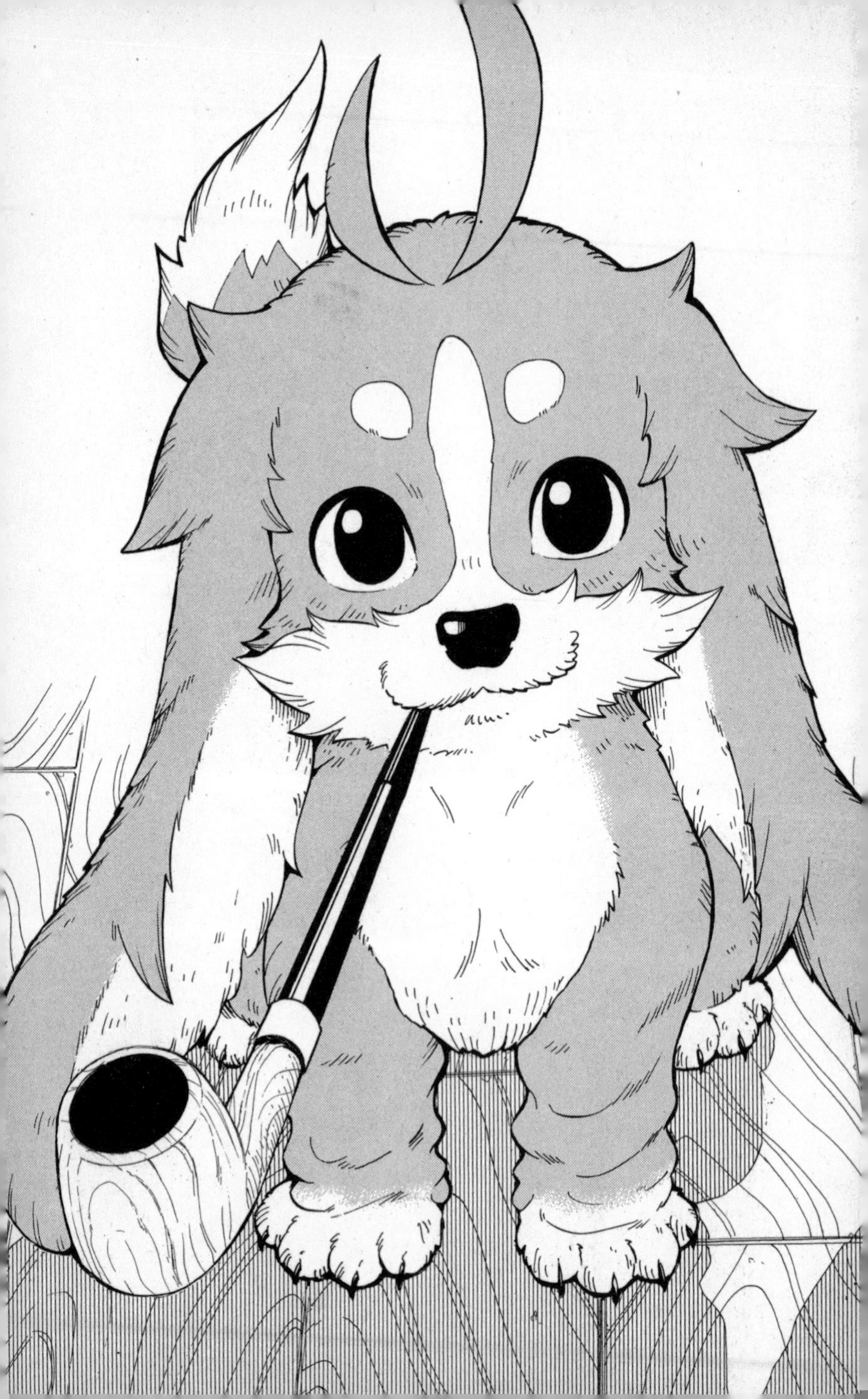

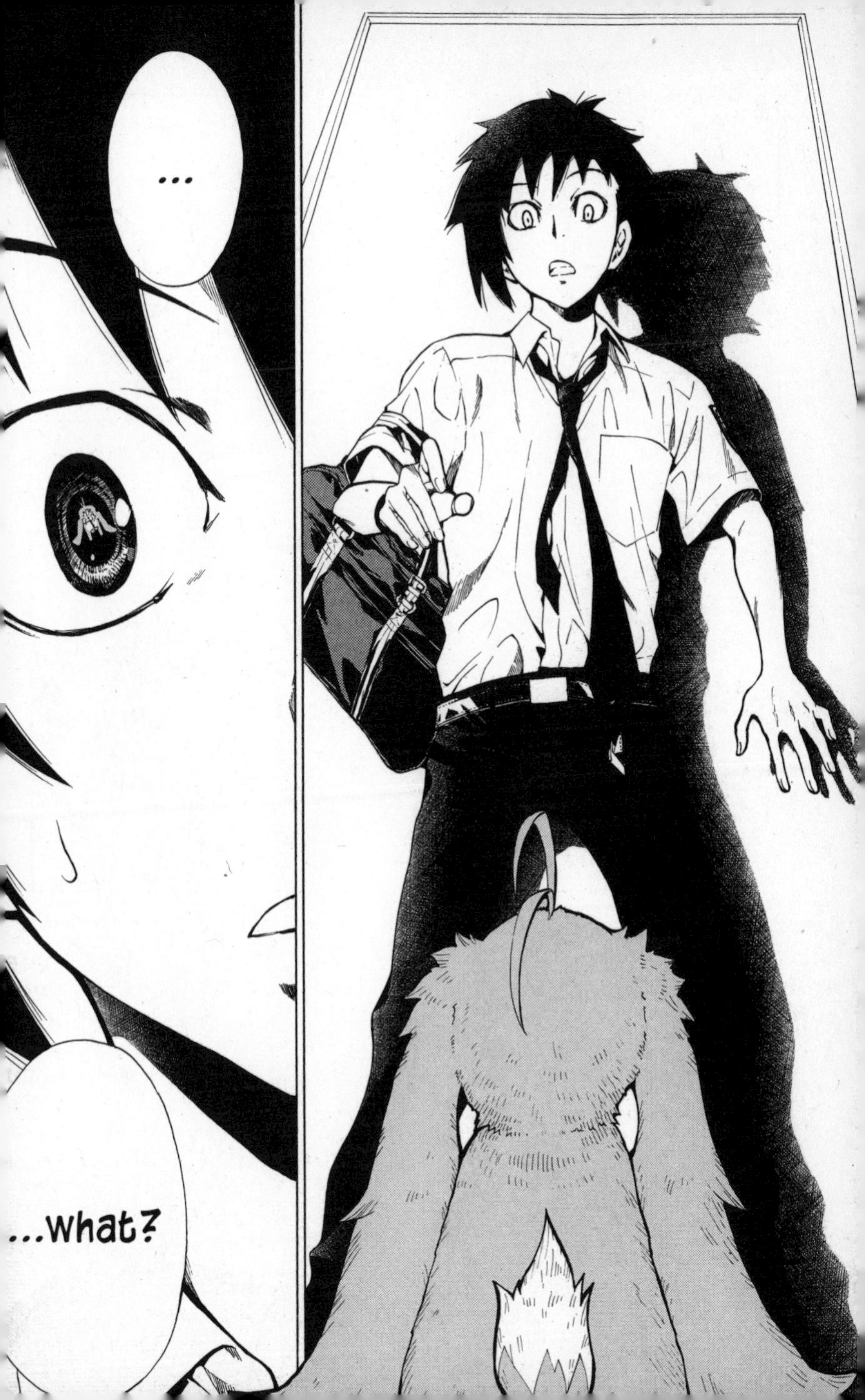
...
...what?

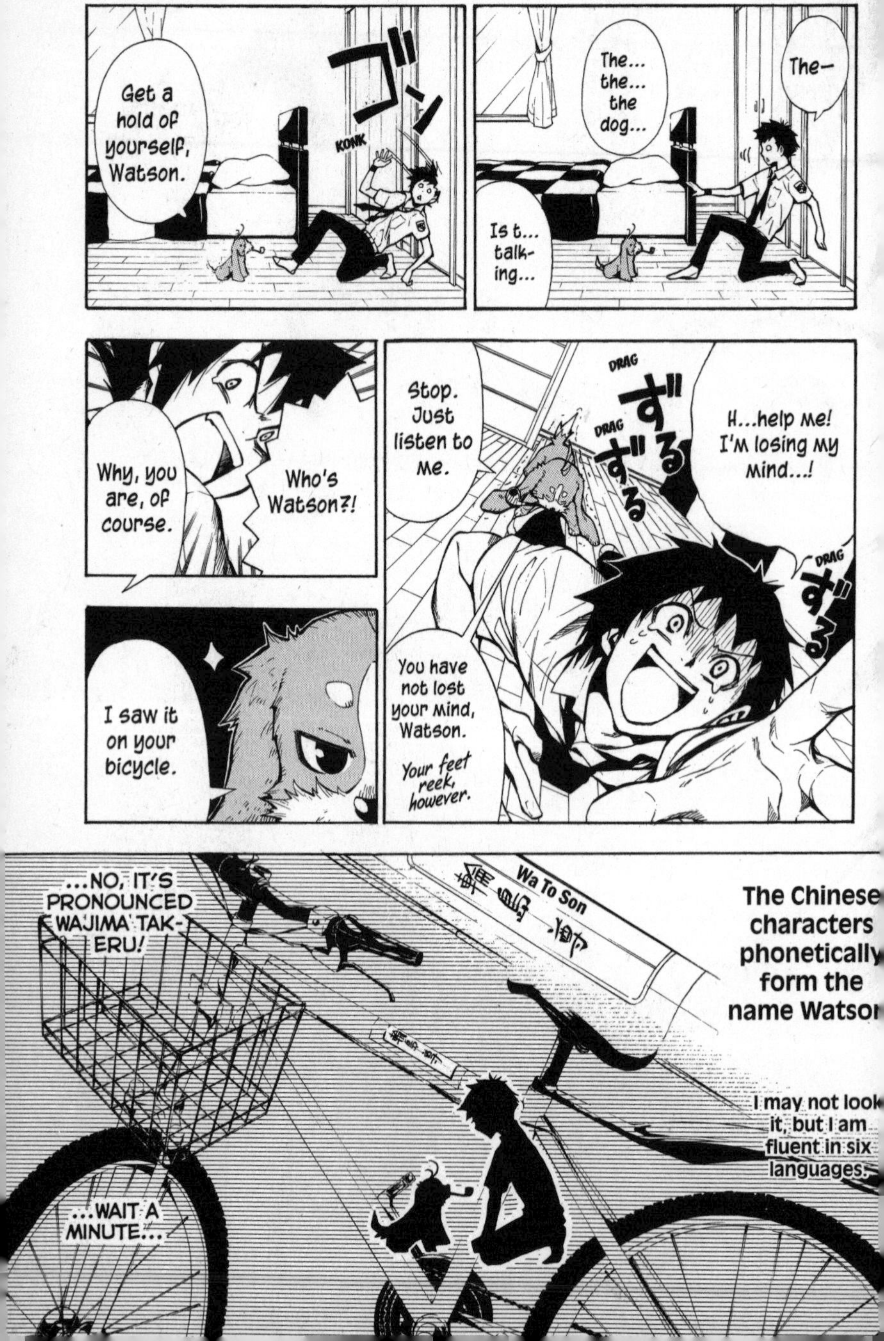

The—
The... the... the dog...
Is t... talking...
ゴン
KONK
Get a hold of yourself, Watson.
H...help me! I'm losing my mind...!
ずる
DRAG
ずる
DRAG
Stop. Just listen to me.
ずる
DRAG
You have not lost your mind, Watson. Your feet reek, however.
Who's Watson?!
Why, you are, of course.
I saw it on your bicycle.
The Chinese characters phonetically form the name Watson
I may not look it, but I am fluent in six languages.
Wa To Son
...NO, IT'S PRONOUNCED WAJIMA TAKERU!
...WAIT A MINUTE...

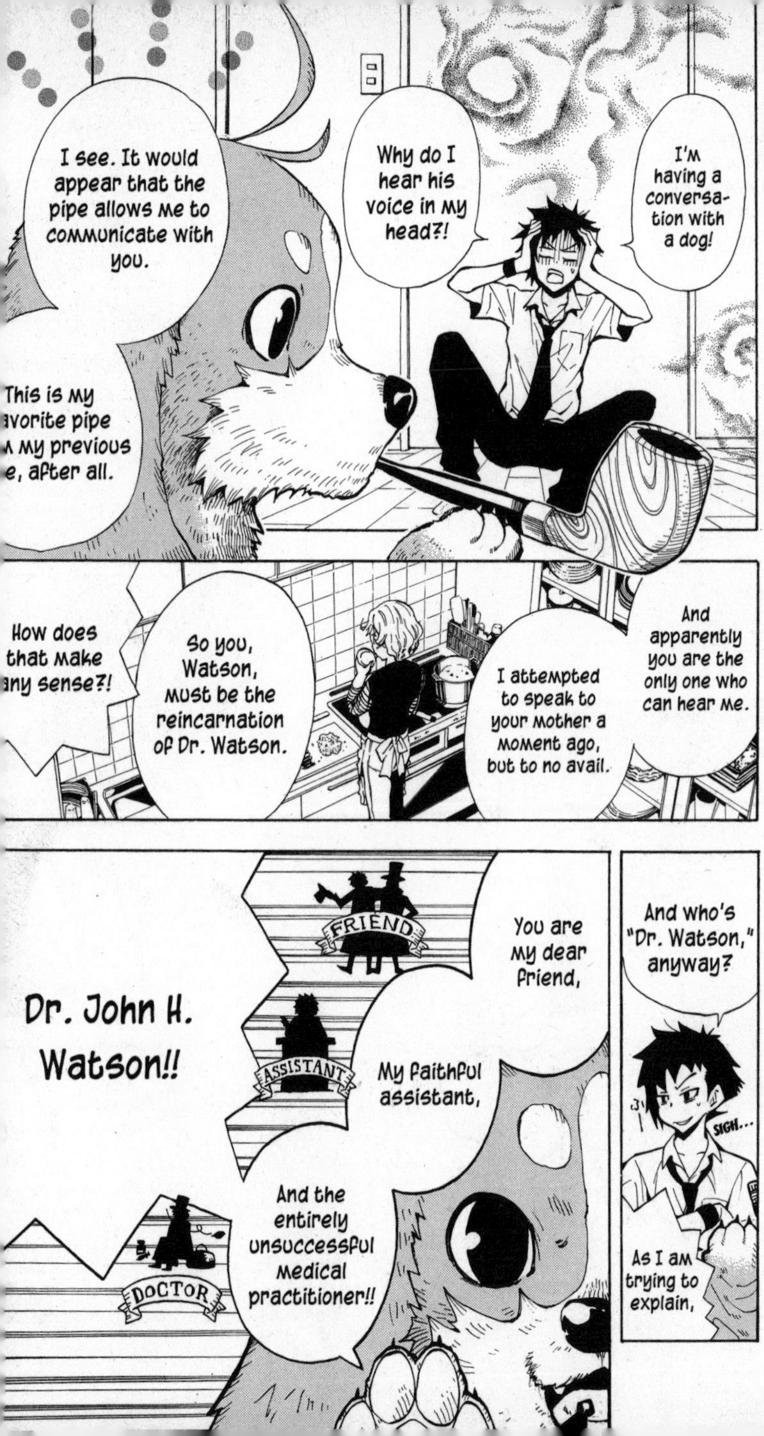
I'm having a conversation with a dog!
Why do I hear his voice in my head?!
I see. It would appear that the pipe allows me to communicate with you.
This is my avorite pipe my previous e, after all.
And apparently you are the only one who can hear me.
I attempted to speak to your mother a moment ago, but to no avail.
So you, Watson, must be the reincarnation of Dr. Watson.
How does that make ny sense?!
And who's "Dr. Watson," anyway?
SIGH...
As I am trying to explain,
You are my dear friend,
FRIEND
My faithful assistant,
ASSISTANT
And the entirely unsuccessful medical practitioner!!
DOCTOR
Dr. John H. Watson!!

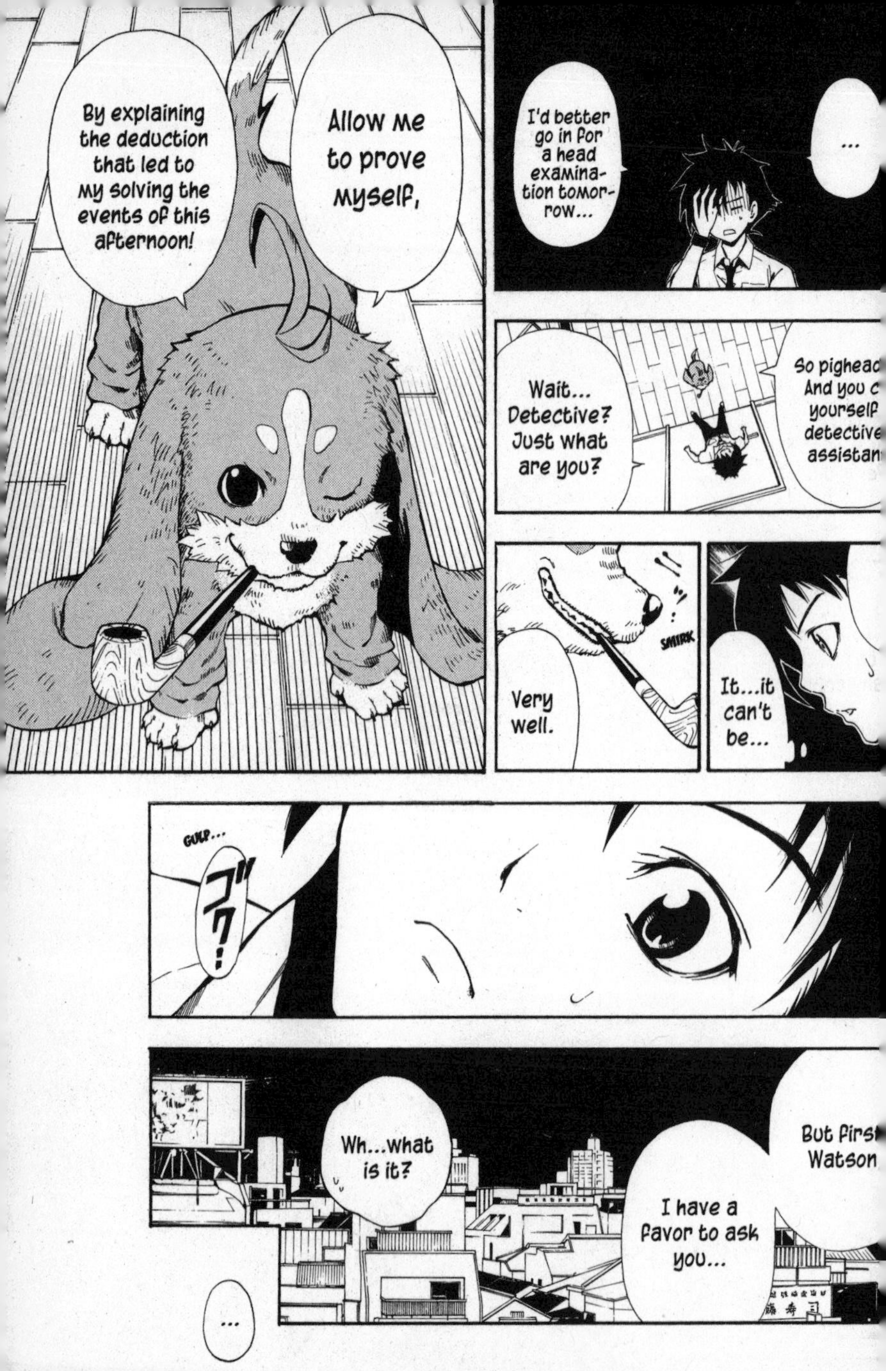
...
I'd better go in for a head examination tomorrow...
So pighead
And you c
yourself
detective
assistan
Wait... Detective? Just what are you?
It...it can't be...
SMIRK
Very well.
Allow me to prove myself,
By explaining the deduction that led to my solving the events of this afternoon!
GULP...
ゴク!
But firs
Watson
I have a favor to ask you...
Wh...what is it?
...

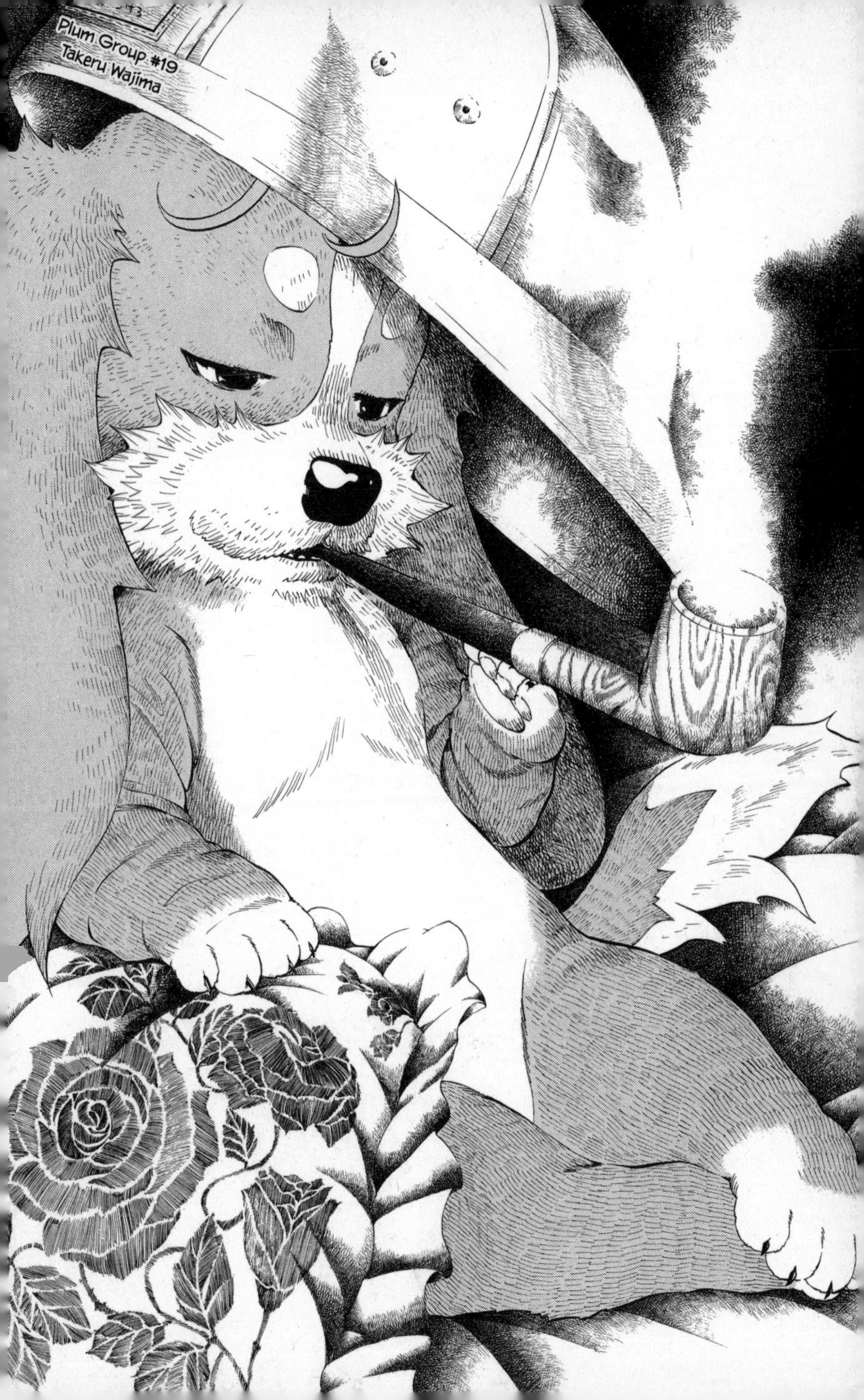
Plum Group #19
Takeru Wajima

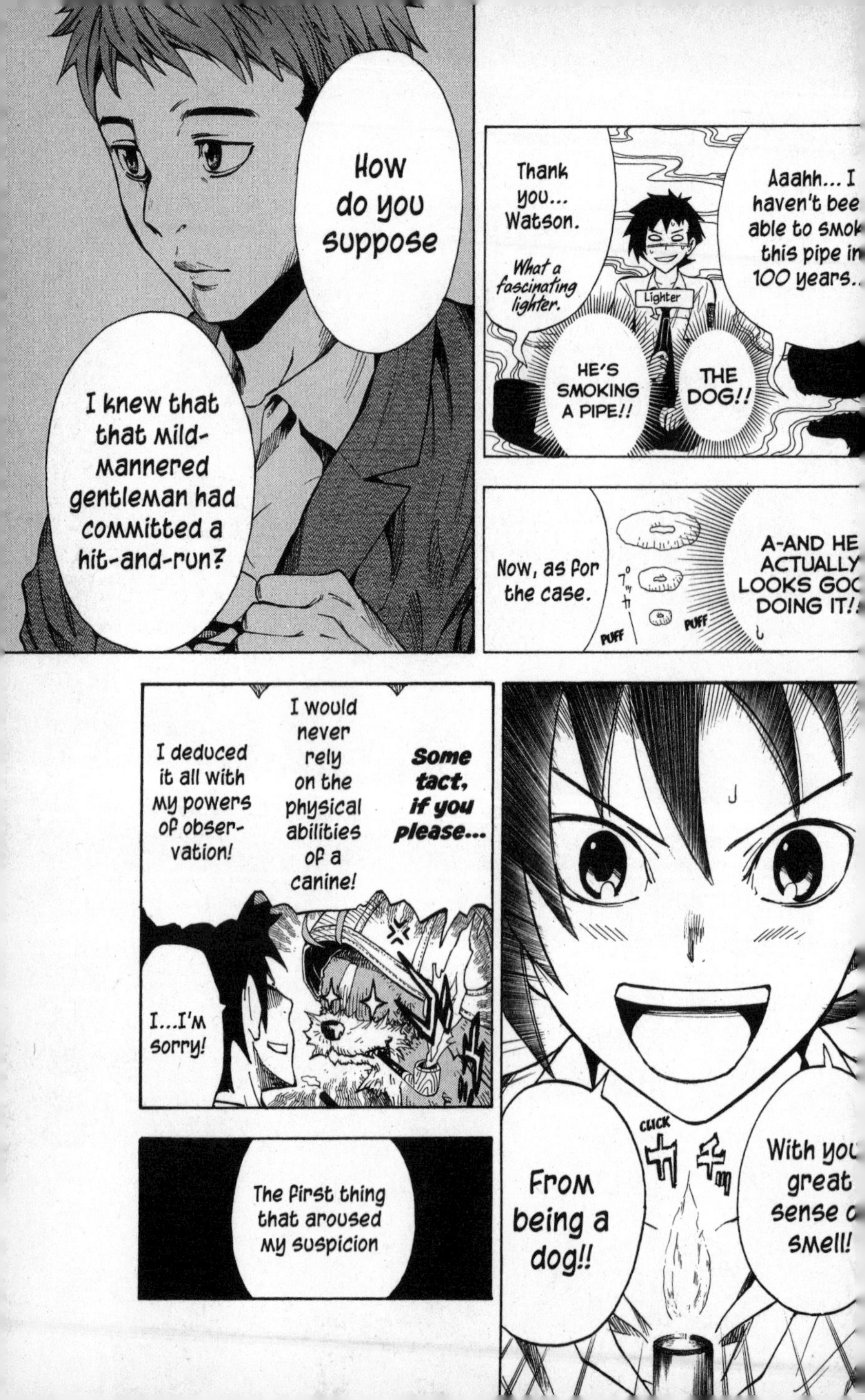
Aaahh... I haven't bee able to smok this pipe in 100 years...
Thank you... Watson.
What a fascinating lighter.
Lighter
THE DOG!!
HE'S SMOKING A PIPE!!
A-AND HE ACTUALLY LOOKS GOO DOING IT!!
PUFF
PUFF
Now, as for the case.
How do you suppose
I knew that that mild-mannered gentleman had committed a hit-and-run?
With you great sense o smell!
CLICK
From being a dog!!
Some tact, if you please...
I would never rely on the physical abilities of a canine!
I deduced it all with my powers of observation!
I...I'm sorry!
The first thing that aroused my suspicion

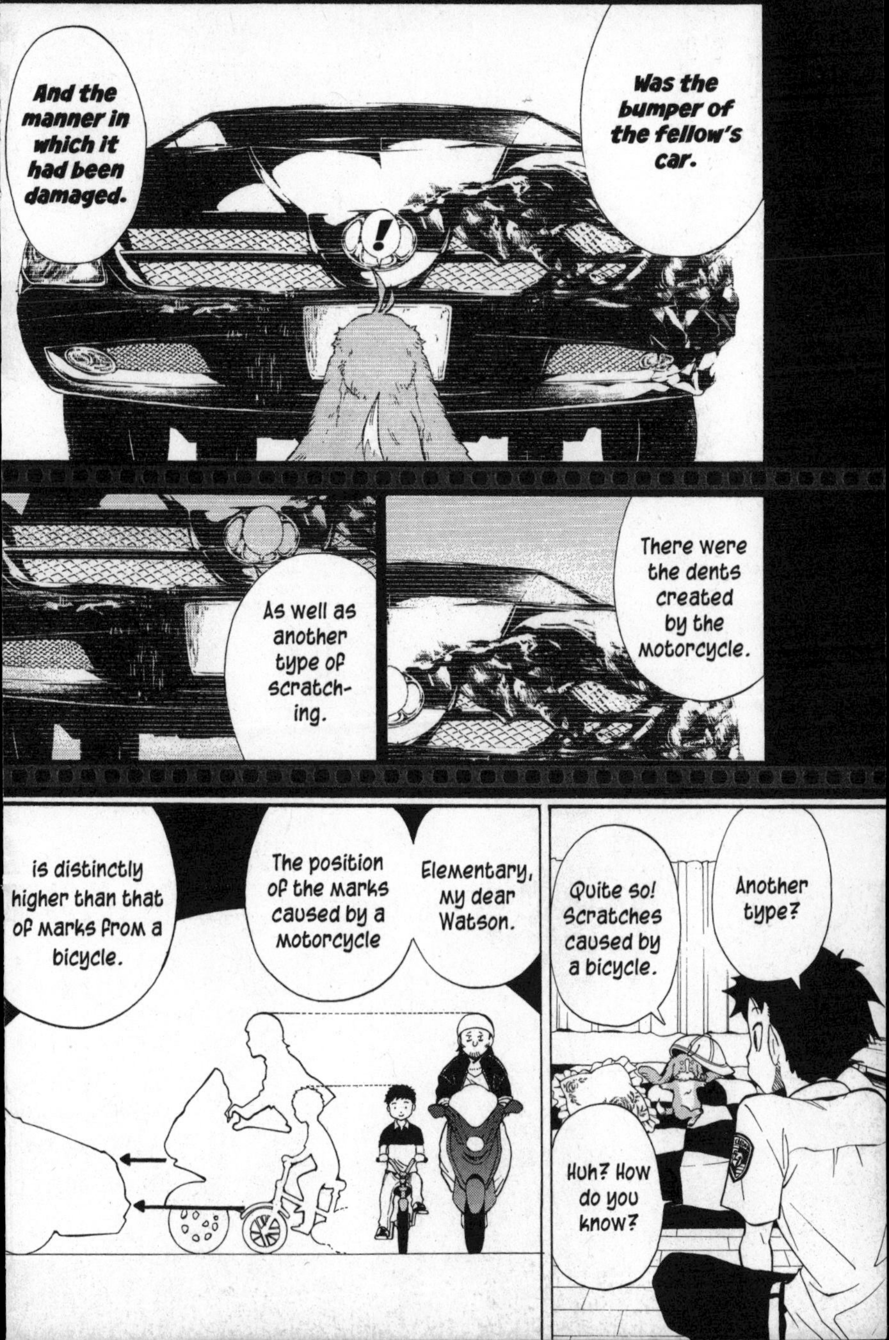
Was the bumper of the fellow's car.
And the manner in which it had been damaged.
There were the dents created by the motorcycle.
As well as another type of scratching.
Another type?
Quite so! Scratches caused by a bicycle.
Huh? How do you know?
Elementary, my dear Watson.
The position of the marks caused by a motorcycle
is distinctly higher than that of marks from a bicycle.

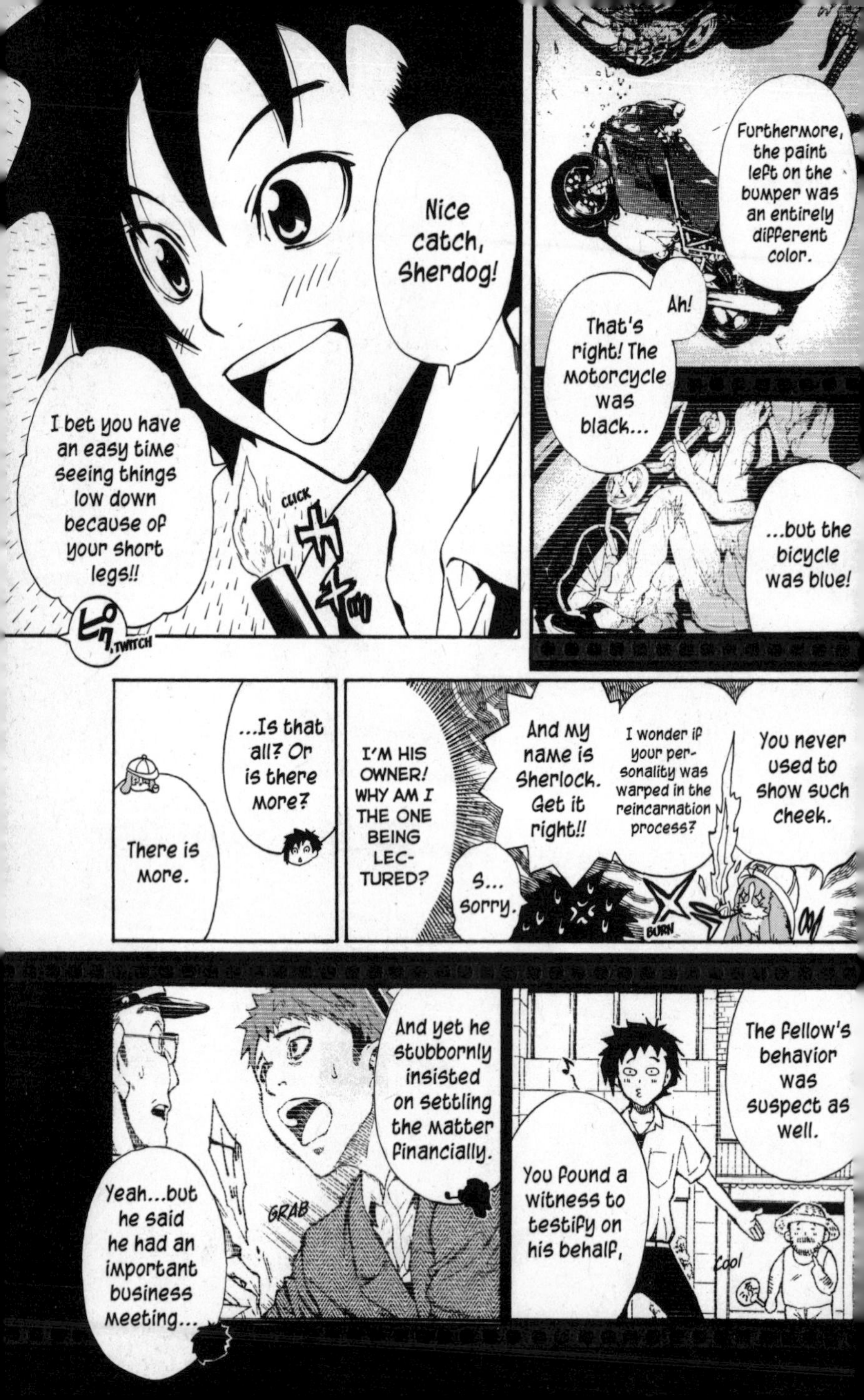
Furthermore, the paint left on the bumper was an entirely different color.
Ah!
That's right! The motorcycle was black...
...but the bicycle was blue!
Nice catch, Sherdog!
CLICK
I bet you have an easy time seeing things low down because of your short legs!!
TWITCH
You never used to show such cheek.
I wonder if your personality was warped in the reincarnation process?
And my name is Sherlock. Get it right!!
BURN
S... sorry.
I'M HIS OWNER! WHY AM I THE ONE BEING LECTURED?
...Is that all? Or is there more?
There is more.
The fellow's behavior was suspect as well.
You found a witness to testify on his behalf,
Cool
And yet he stubbornly insisted on settling the matter financially.
GRAB
Yeah...but he said he had an important business meeting...

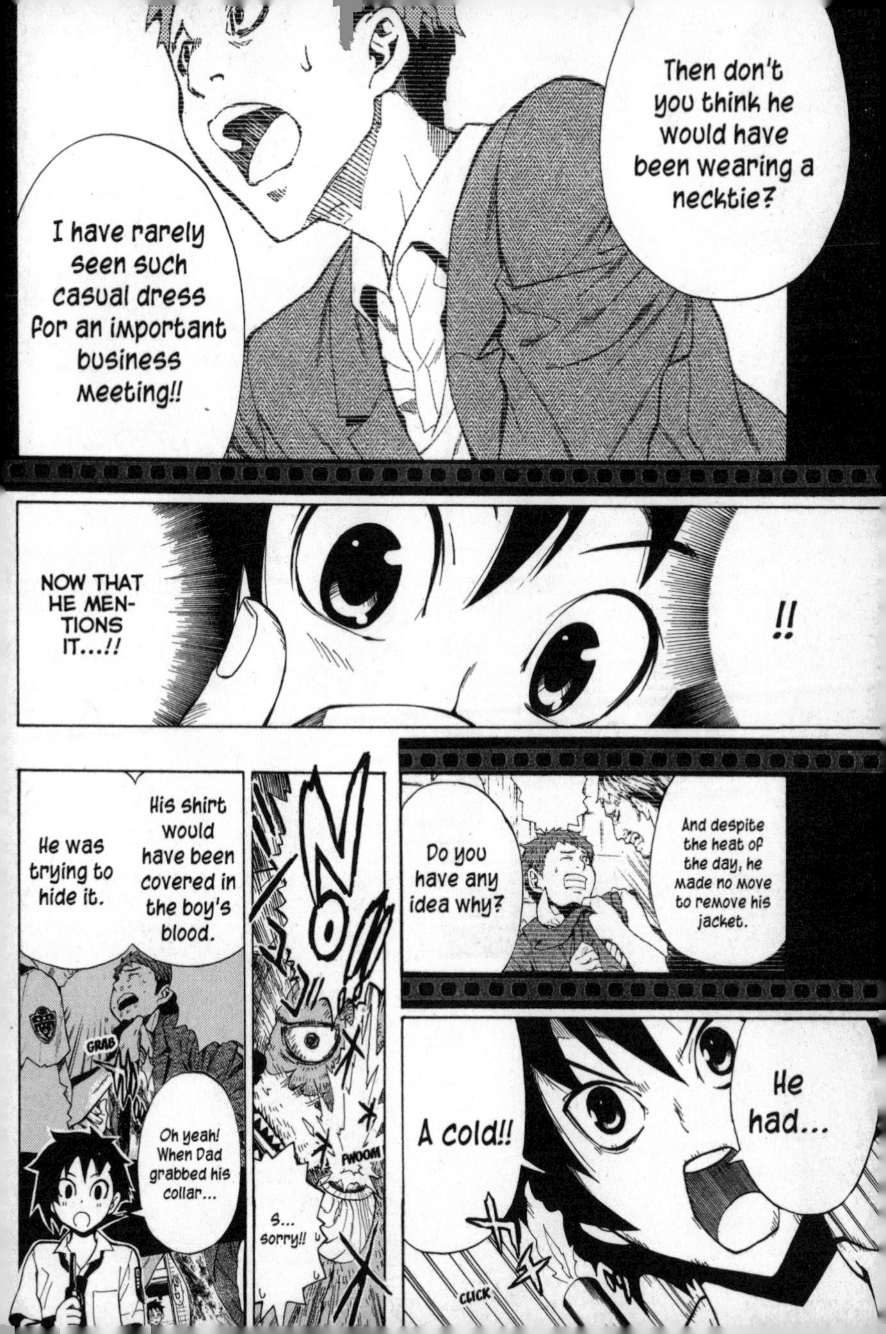
Then don't you think he would have been wearing a necktie?
I have rarely seen such casual dress for an important business meeting!!
!!
NOW THAT HE MENTIONS IT...!!
And despite the heat of the day, he made no move to remove his jacket.
Do you have any idea why?
He had...
A cold!!
CLICK
PWOOM
S... sorry!!
His shirt would have been covered in the boy's blood.
He was trying to hide it.
GRAB
Oh yeah! When Dad grabbed his collar...

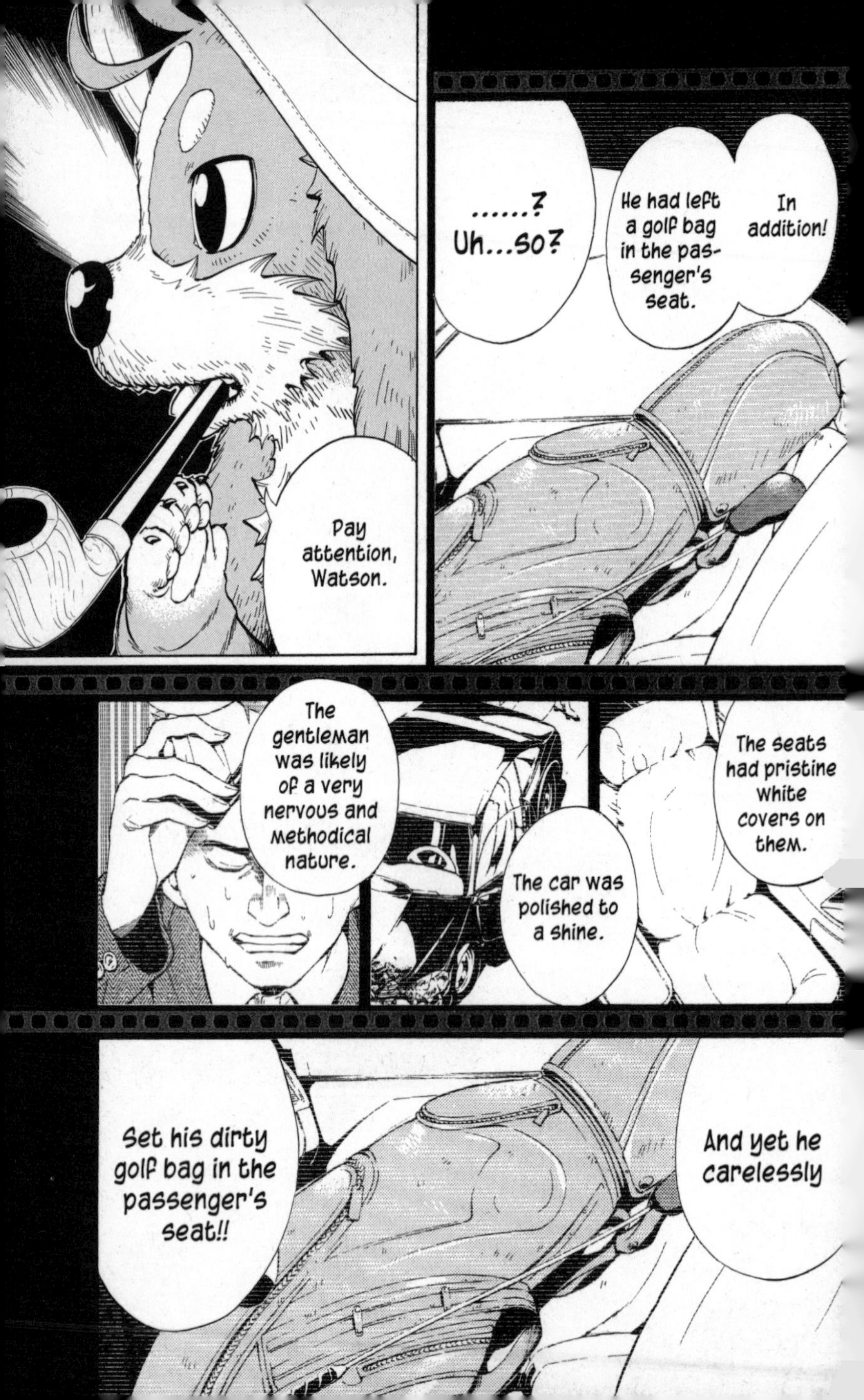
In addition!
He had left a golf bag in the passenger's seat.
......? Uh...so?
Pay attention, Watson.
The seats had pristine white covers on them.
The car was polished to a shine.
The gentleman was likely of a very nervous and methodical nature.
And yet he carelessly
Set his dirty golf bag in the passenger's seat!!

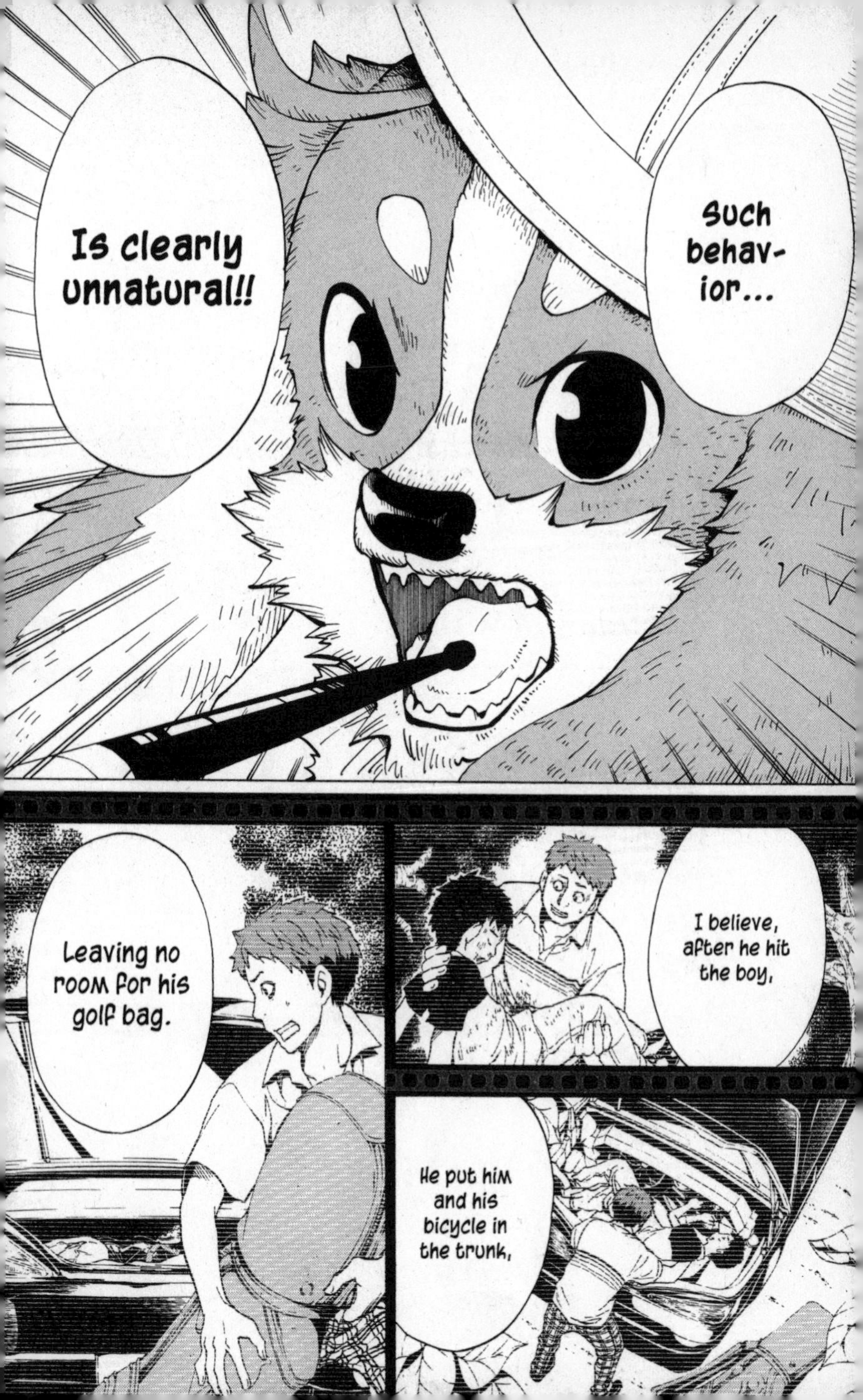
Such behav-ior...
Is clearly unnatural!!
I believe, after he hit the boy,
He put him and his bicycle in the trunk,
Leaving no room for his golf bag.

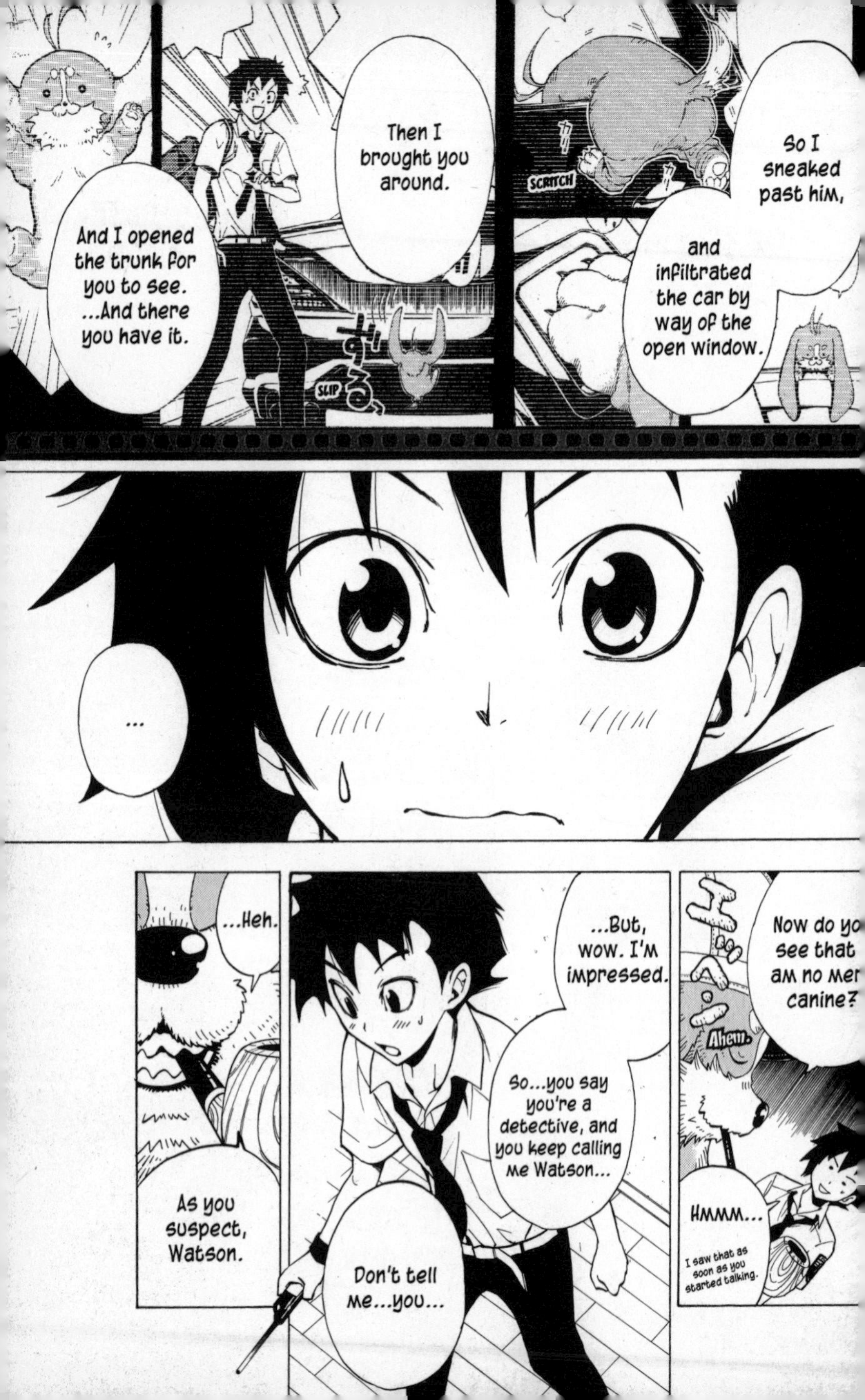
So I sneaked past him,
SCRITCH
and infiltrated the car by way of the open window.
Then I brought you around.
SLIP
And I opened the trunk for you to see. ...And there you have it.
...
Now do yo see that am no mer canine?
Ahem.
HMMM...
I saw that as soon as you started talking.
...But, wow. I'm impressed.
So...you say you're a detective, and you keep calling me Watson...
Don't tell me...you...
...Heh.
As you suspect, Watson.

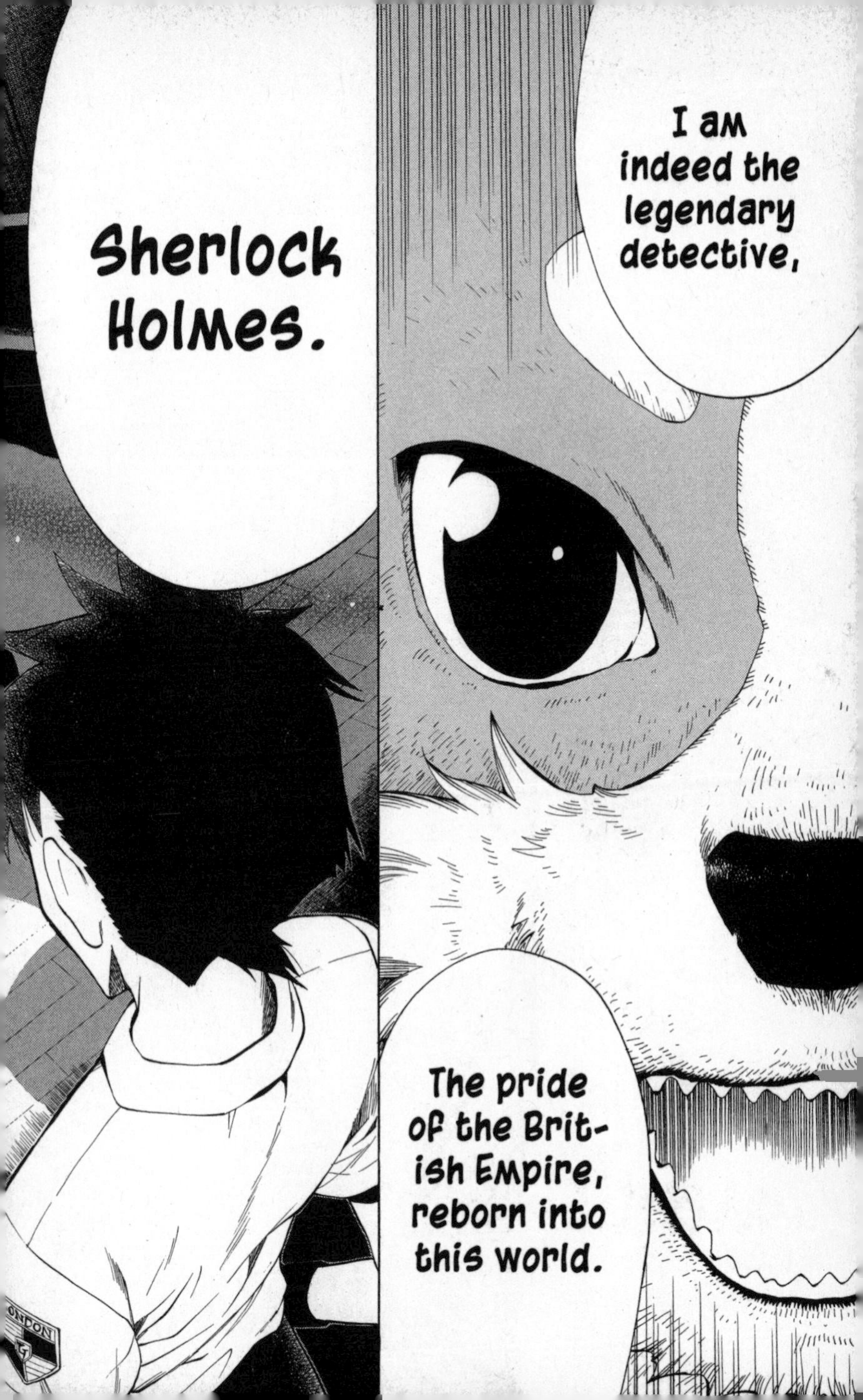
I am indeed the legendary detective,
The pride of the Brit-ish Empire, reborn into this world.
Sherlock Holmes.

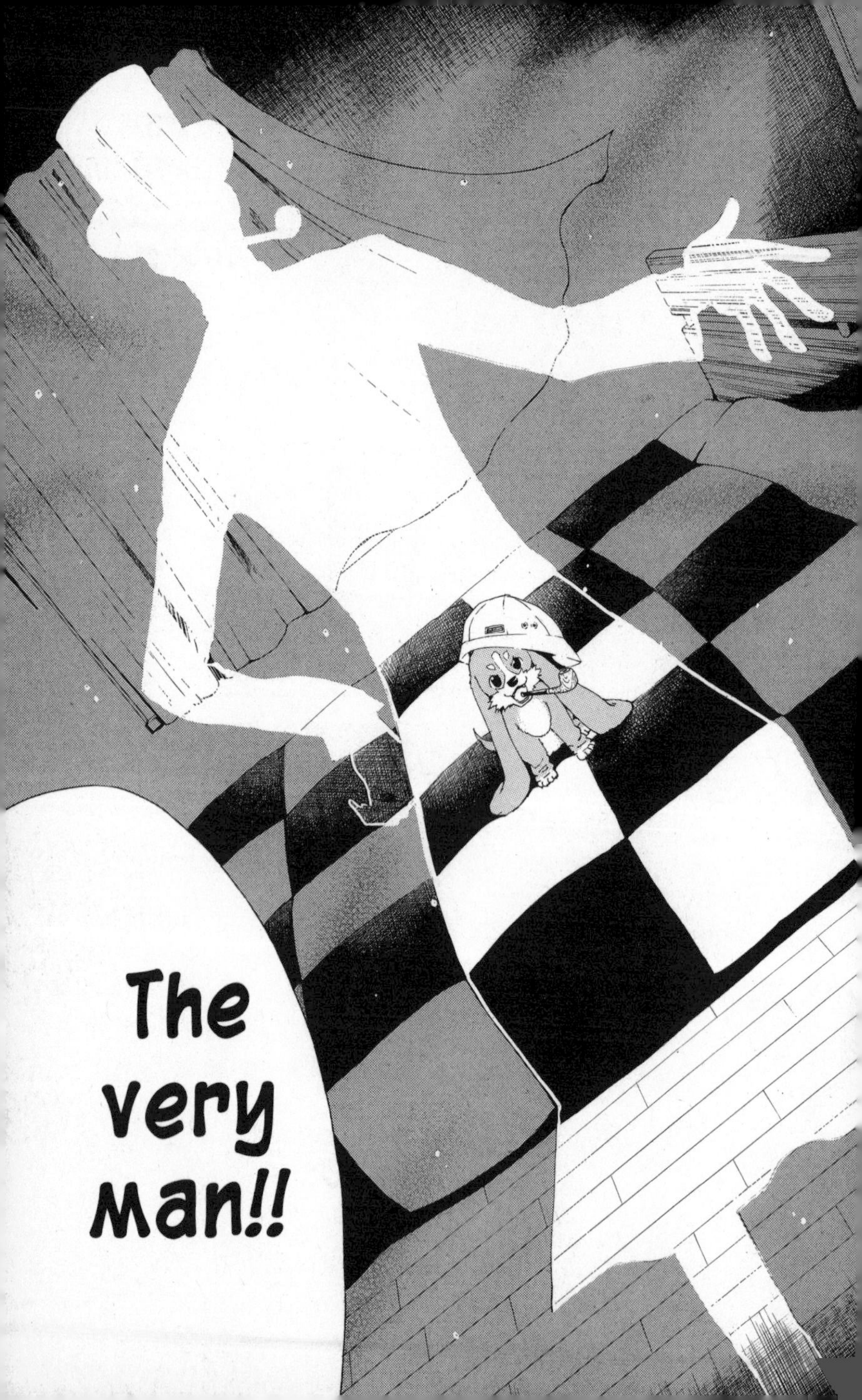
The very man!!

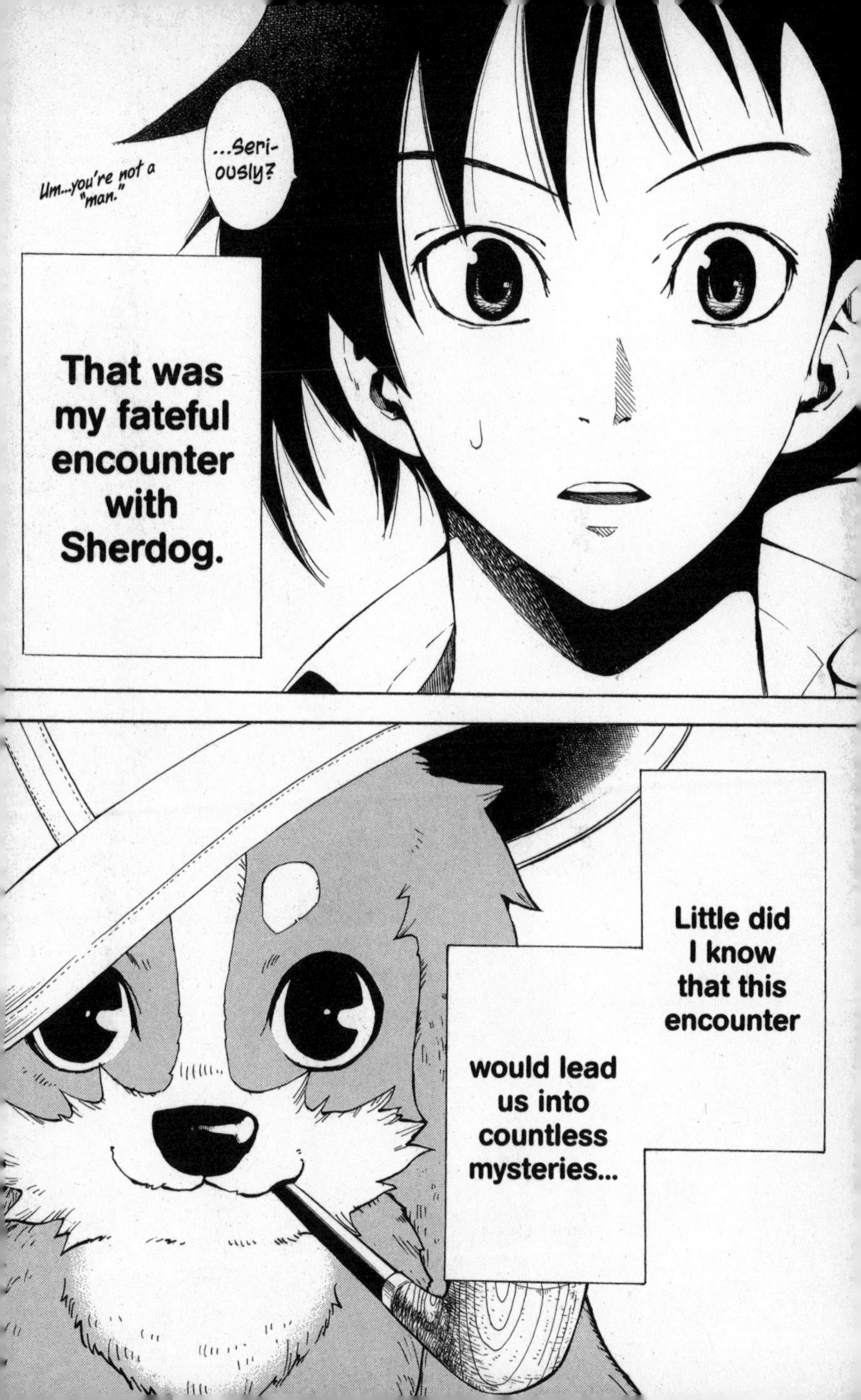
...Seriously?
Um...you're not a "man."
That was my fateful encounter with Sherdog.
Little did I know that this encounter
would lead us into countless mysteries...

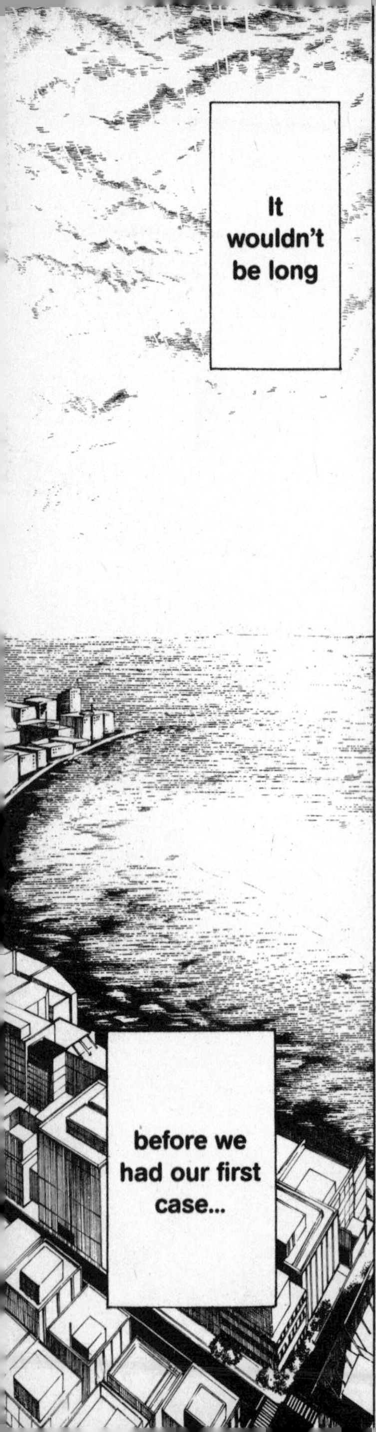
It wouldn't be long
before we had our first case...

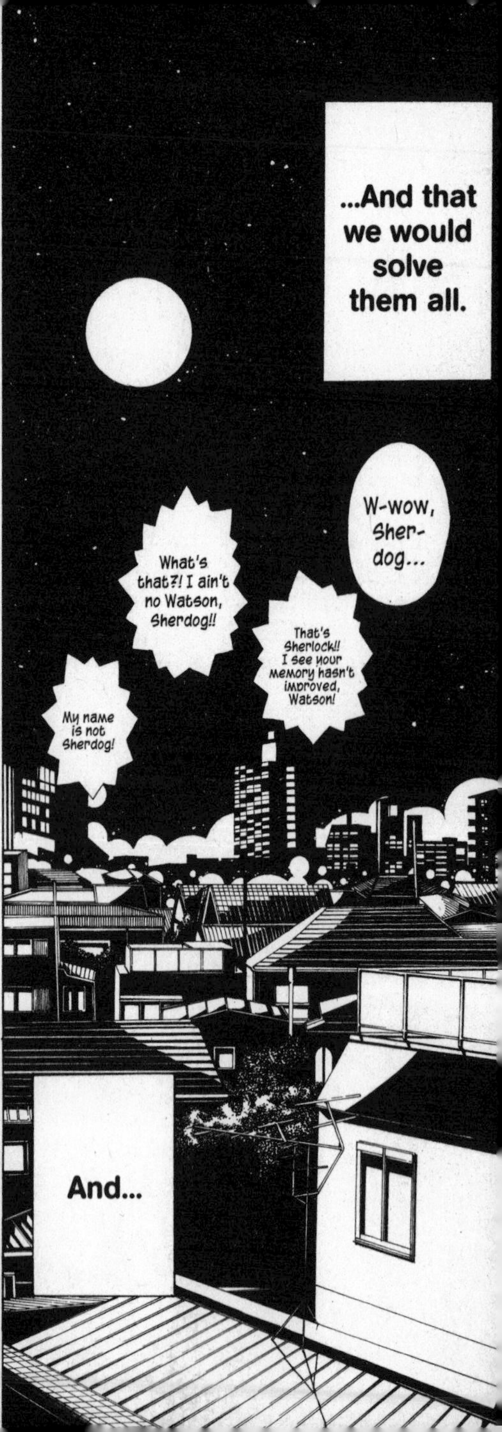
...And that we would solve them all.
W-wow, Sher-dog...
That's Sherlock!! I see your memory hasn't improved, Watson!
What's that?! I ain't no Watson, Sherdog!!
My name is not Sherdog!
And...

SHERLOCK BONES

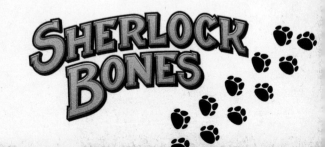

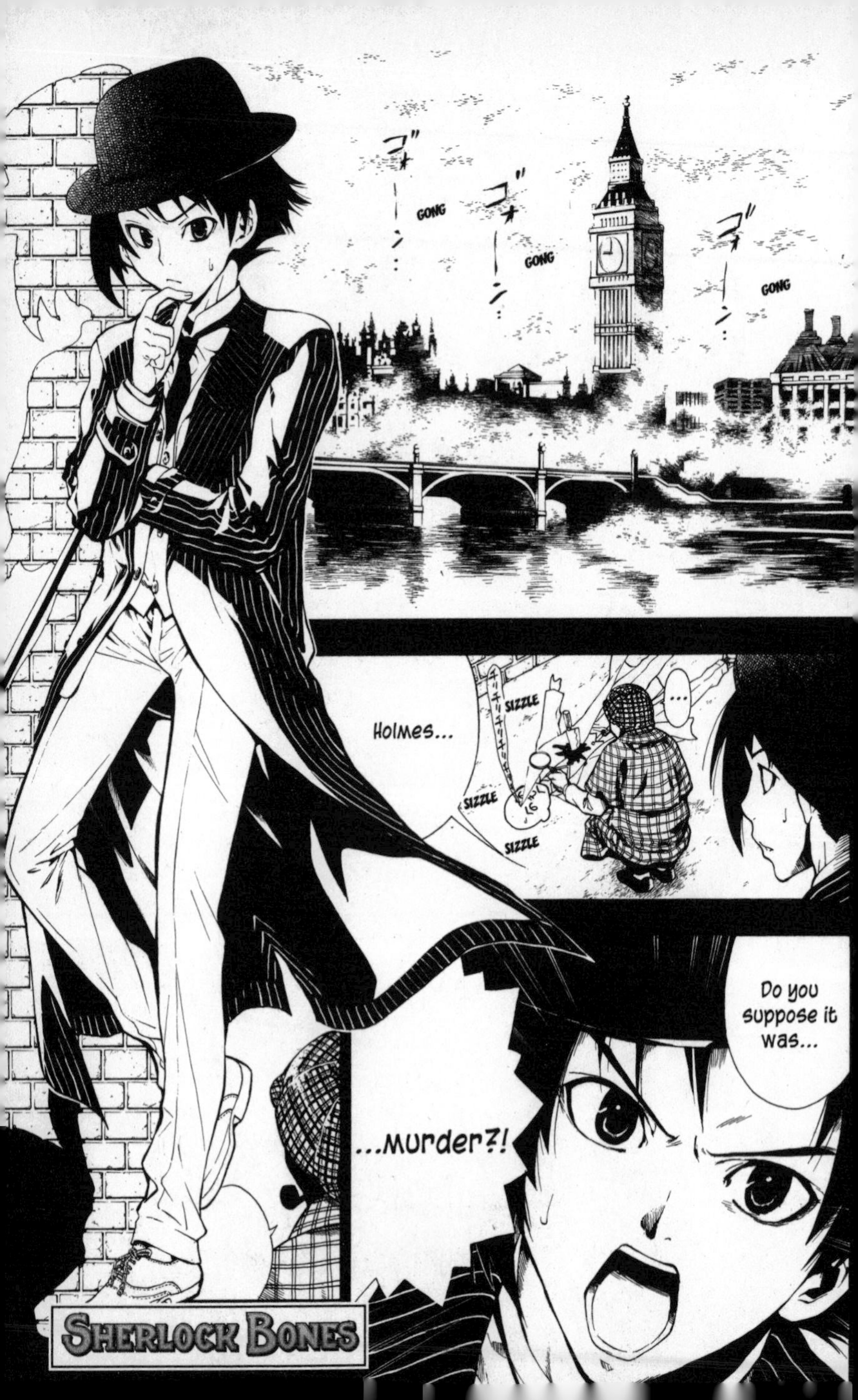

ゴォーン…
GONG
ゴォーン…
GONG
ゴォーン…
GONG
...
SIZZLE
SIZZLE
SIZZLE
Holmes...
Do you suppose it was...
...murder?!
SHERLOCK BONES

Case 1 ⚜ The 12:20 Witness, Part 1

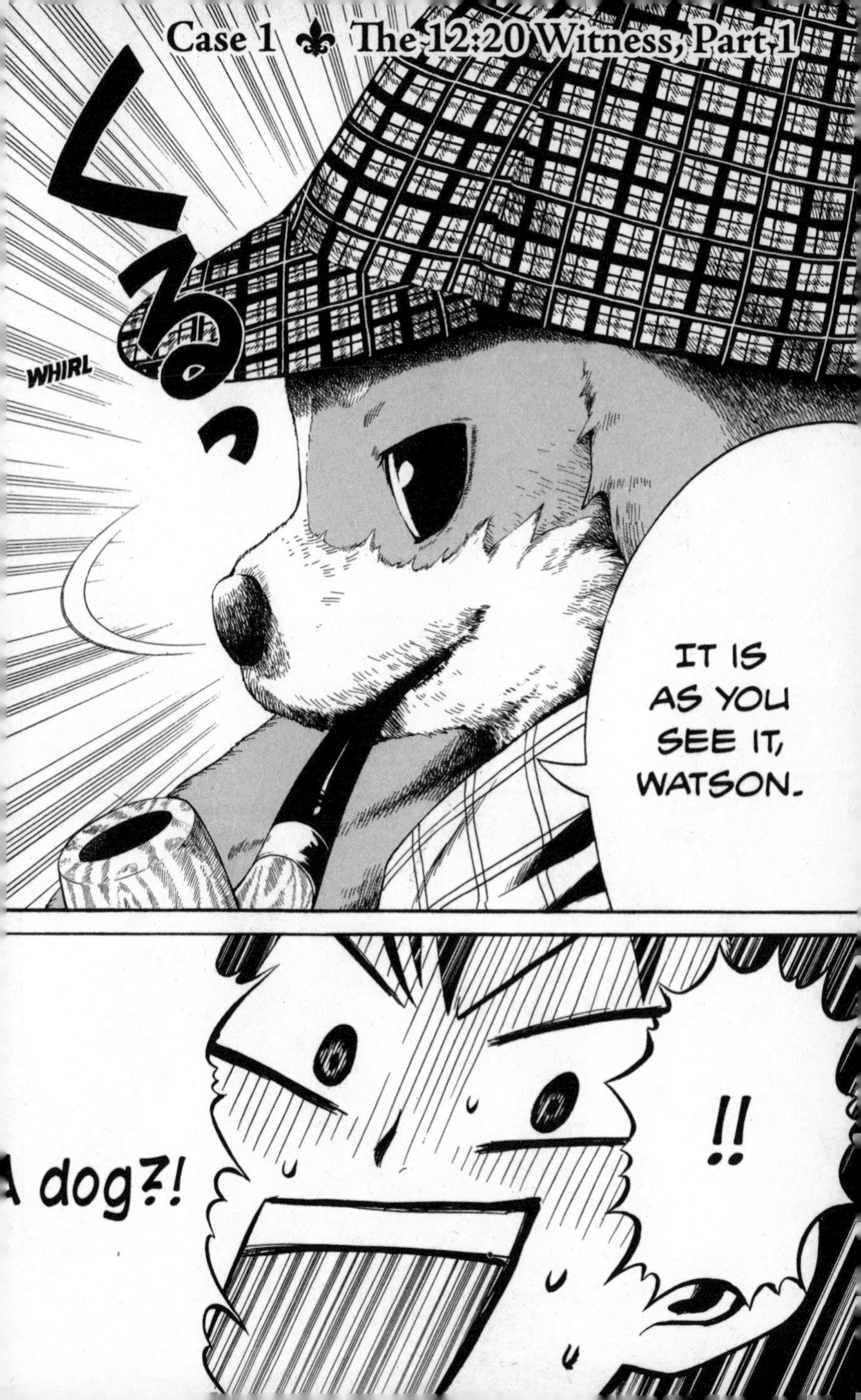
WHIRL
IT IS AS YOU SEE IT, WATSON.
!!
A dog?!

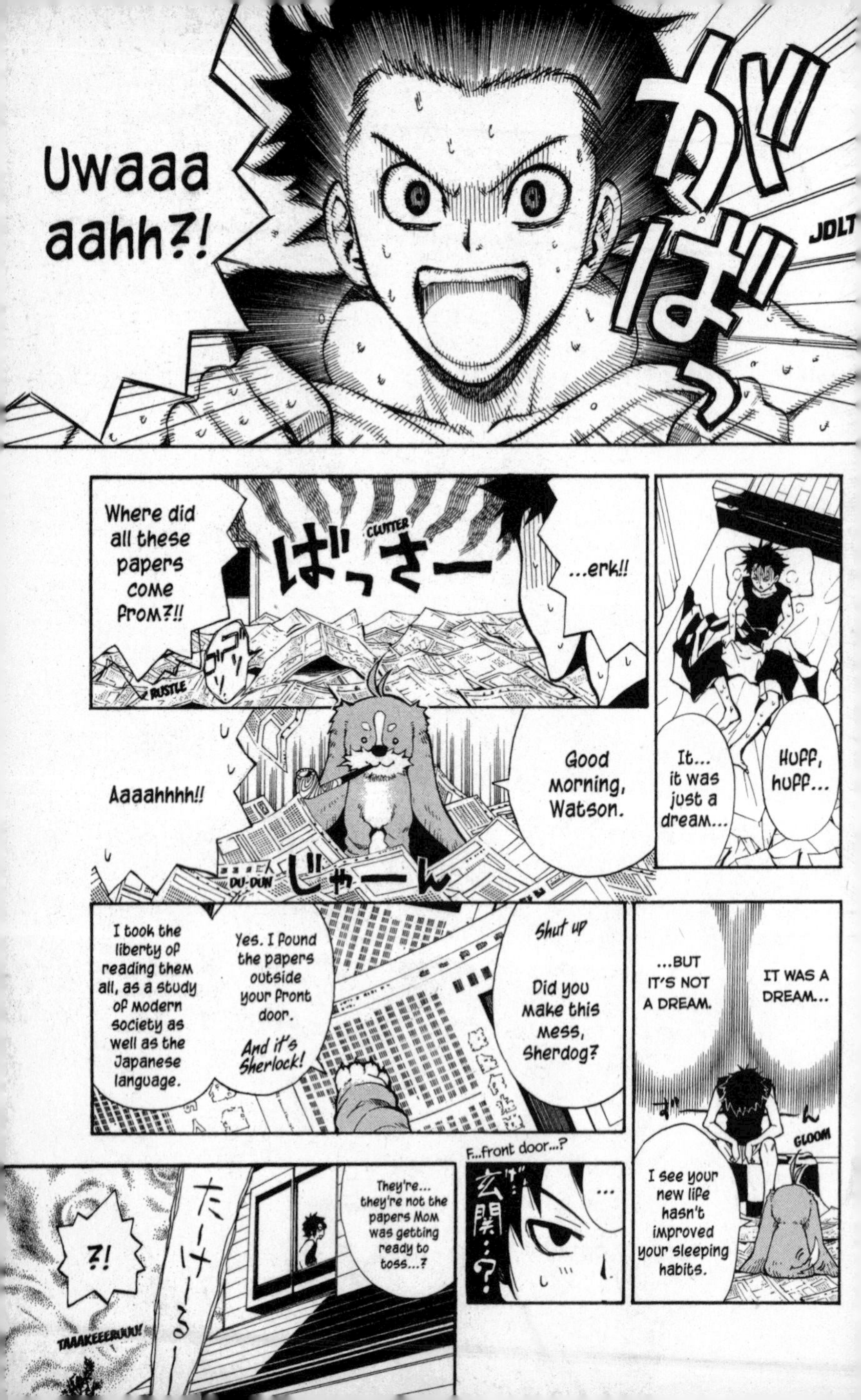

がばっ
JOLT
Uwaaa aahh?!
Huff, huff...
It... it was just a dream...
...erk!!
ばっさー
CLUTTER
Where did all these papers come from?!!
RUSTLE
Good morning, Watson.
Aaaahhh!!
じゃーん
DU-DUN
IT WAS A DREAM...
...BUT IT'S NOT A DREAM.
GLOOM
Shut up
Did you make this mess, Sherdog?
Yes. I found the papers outside your front door.
And it's Sherlock!
I took the liberty of reading them all, as a study of modern society as well as the Japanese language.
I see your new life hasn't improved your sleeping habits.
...
F...front door...?
玄関…?
They're... they're not the papers Mom was getting ready to toss...?
?!
たーけーるー
TAAAKEEERUUU!

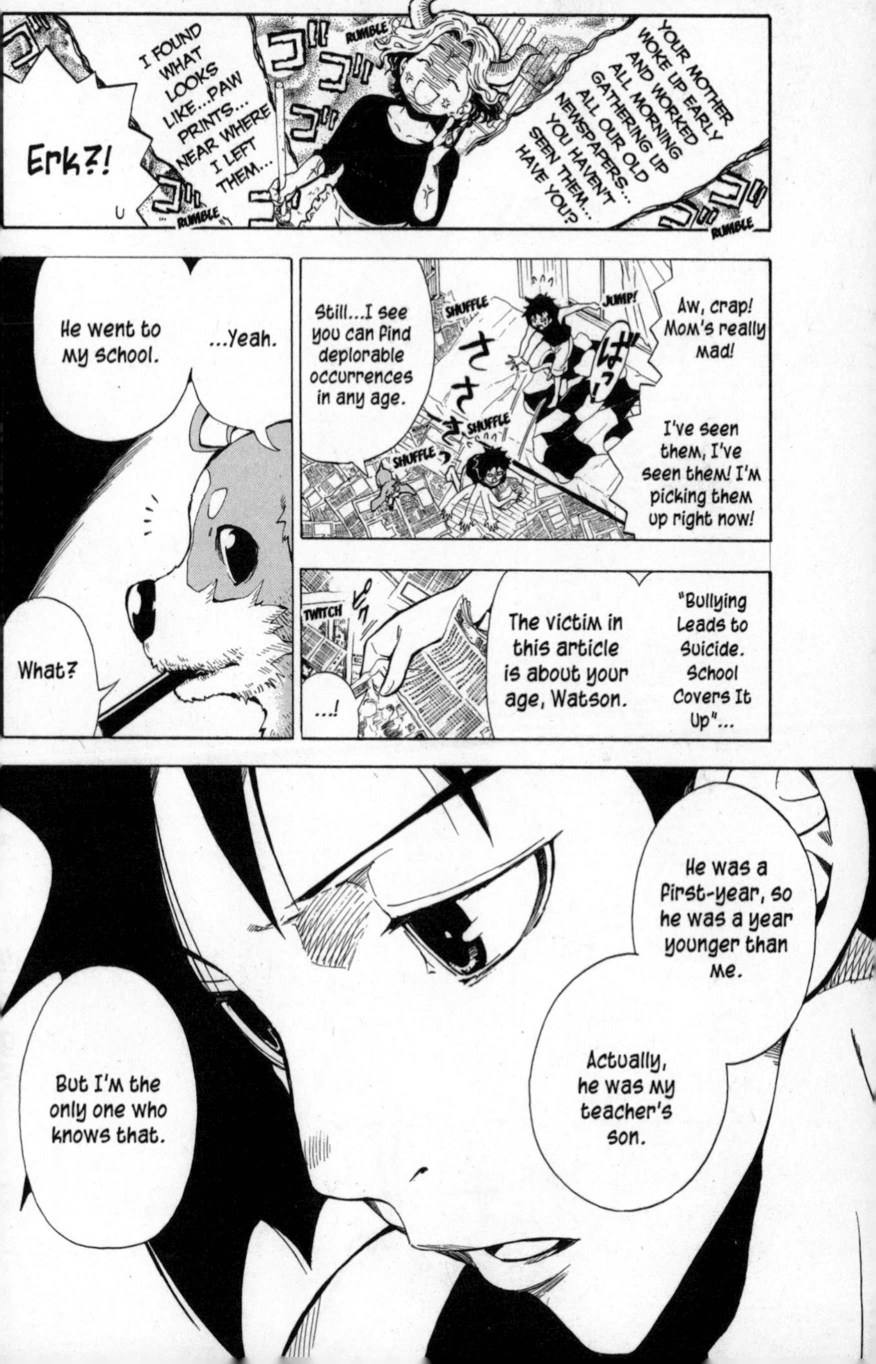
RUMBLE
YOUR MOTHER WOKE UP EARLY AND WORKED ALL MORNING GATHERING UP ALL OUR OLD NEWSPAPERS... YOU HAVEN'T SEEN THEM... HAVE YOU?
RUMBLE
I FOUND WHAT LOOKS LIKE...PAW PRINTS... NEAR WHERE I LEFT THEM...
RUMBLE
Erk?!
Aw, crap! Mom's really mad!
JUMP!
ばっ!
I've seen them, I've seen them! I'm picking them up right now!
SHUFFLE
さささ
SHUFFLE
SHUFFLE
Still...I see you can find deplorable occurrences in any age.
"Bullying Leads to Suicide. School Covers It Up"...
The victim in this article is about your age, Watson.
TWITCH
...!
...Yeah.
He went to my school.
What?
He was a first-year, so he was a year younger than me.
Actually, he was my teacher's son.
But I'm the only one who knows that.

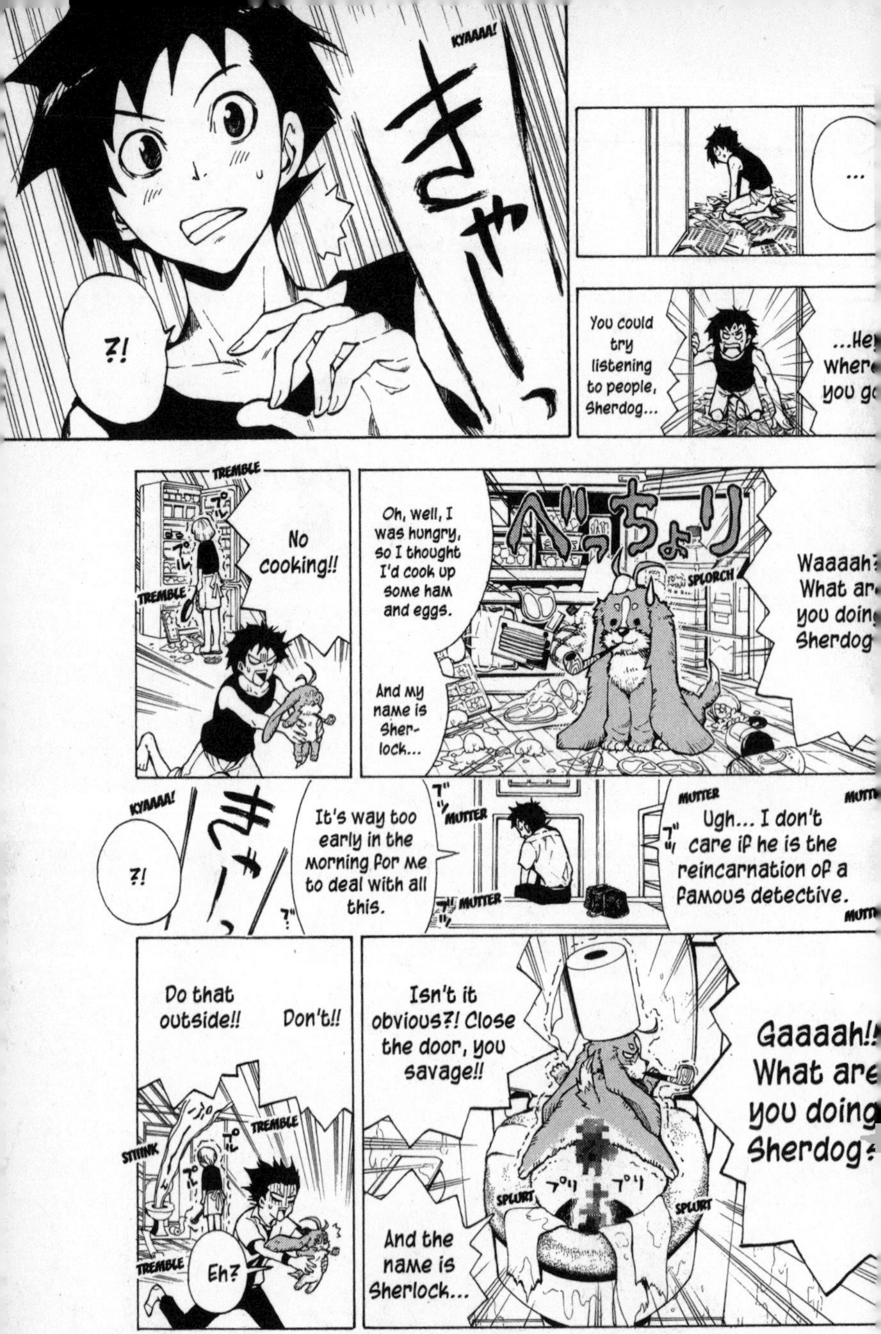
...
...He where you g
You could try listening to people, Sherdog...
KYAAAA!
?!
Waaaah? What are you doing Sherdog
SPLORCH
Oh, well, I was hungry, so I thought I'd cook up some ham and eggs.
And my name is Sherlock...
TREMBLE
No cooking!!
TREMBLE
MUTTER
Ugh... I don't care if he is the reincarnation of a famous detective.
MUTTER
It's way too early in the morning for me to deal with all this.
MUTTER
KYAAAA!
?!
Gaaaah!! What are you doing Sherdog
Isn't it obvious?! Close the door, you savage!!
SPLURT
SPLURT
And the name is Sherlock...
Don't!!
Do that outside!!
STIIINK
TREMBLE
Eh?
TREMBLE

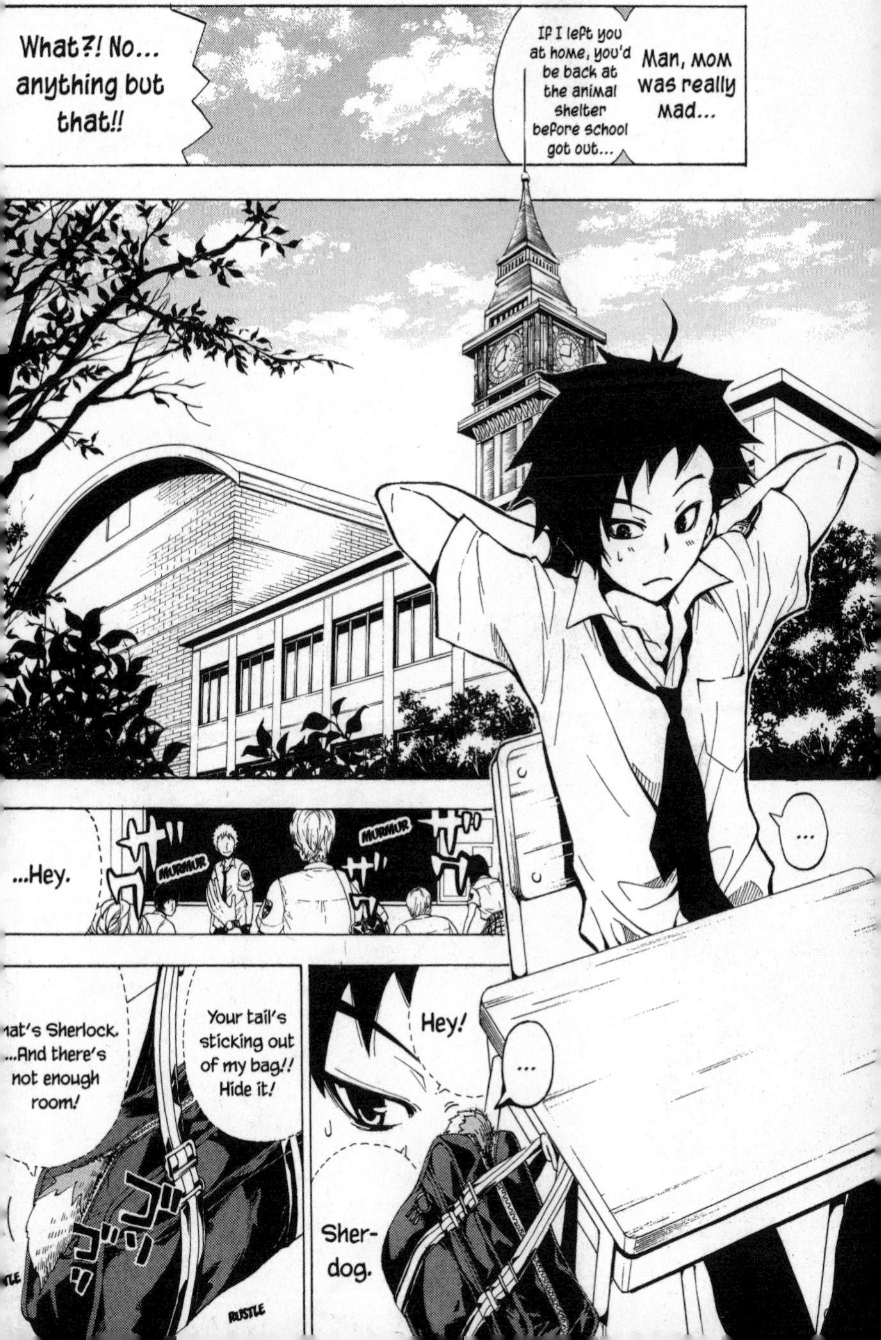

Man, mom was really mad...
If I left you at home, you'd be back at the animal shelter before school got out...
What?! No... anything but that!!
...
MURMUR
MURMUR
...Hey.
Hey!
...
Sher-dog.
RUSTLE
Your tail's sticking out of my bag!! Hide it!
...at's Sherlock. ...And there's not enough room!

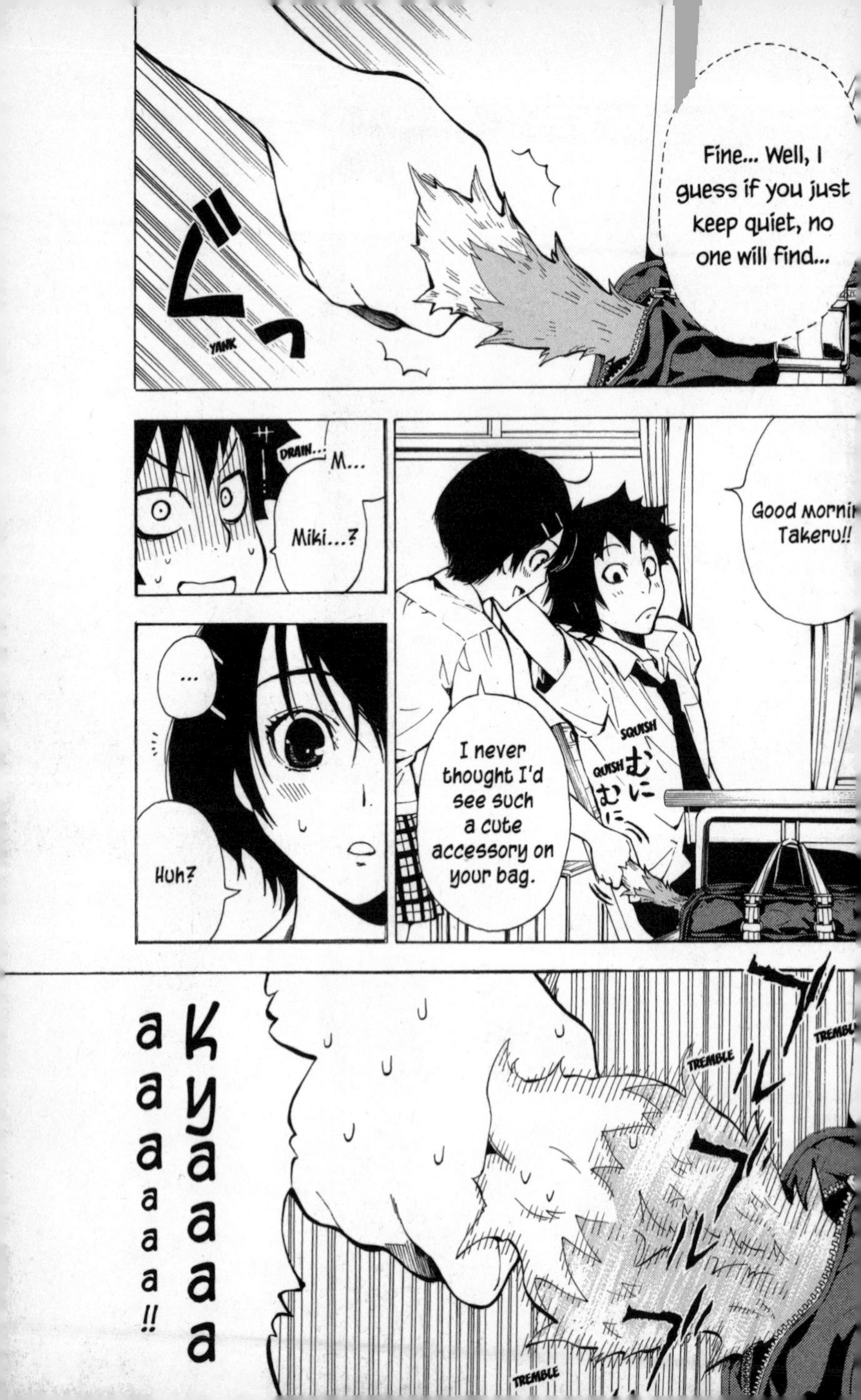

Fine... Well, I guess if you just keep quiet, no one will find...
ズッ
YANK
Good mornin Takeru!!
I never thought I'd see such a cute accessory on your bag.
むに むに
SQUISH SQUISH
DRAIN...
M...
Miki...?
...
Huh?
Kyaaaaa aaaaaa!!
ブル ブル
TREMBLE
TREMBLE
TREMBLE

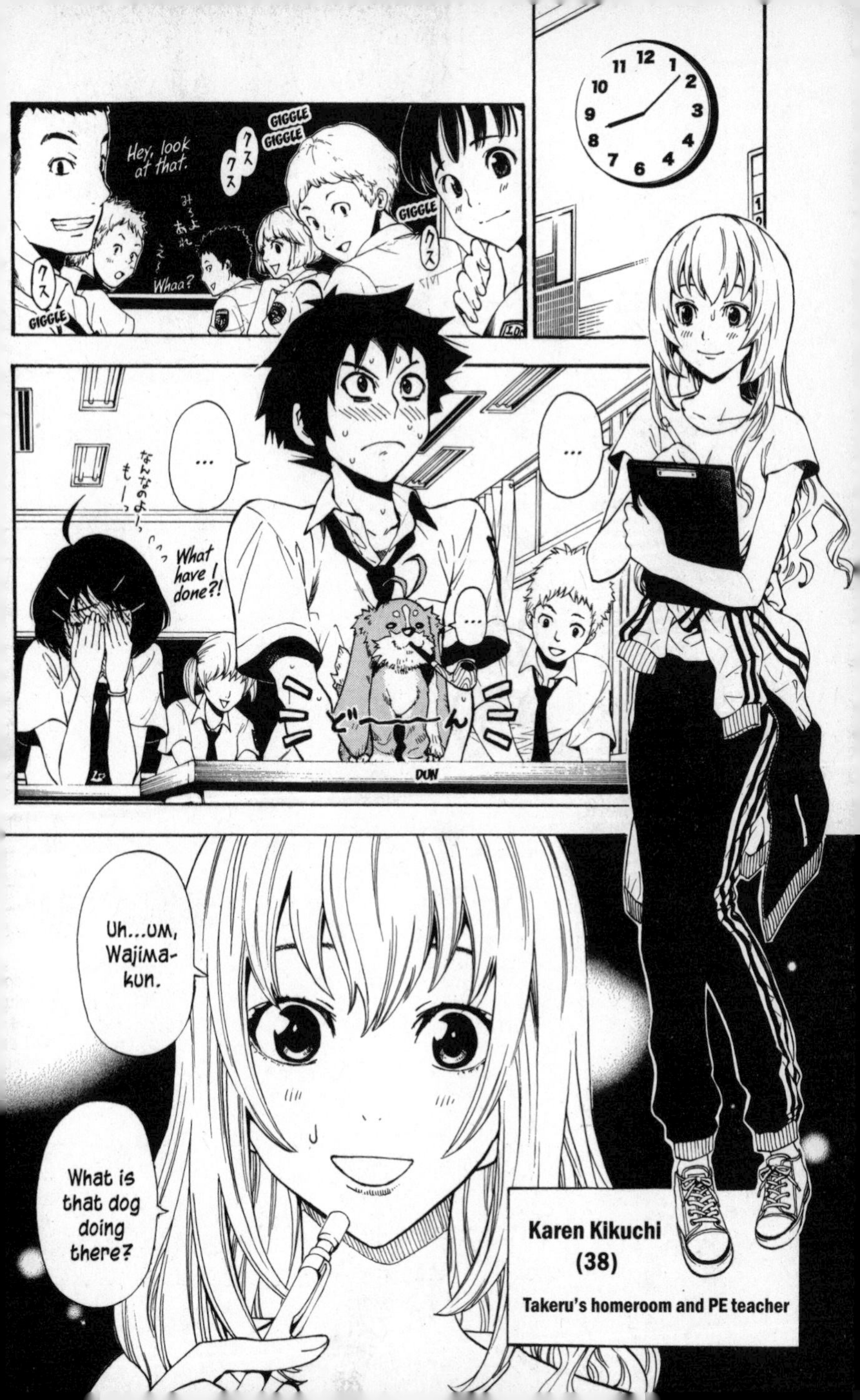

クスクス
GIGGLE GIGGLE
GIGGLE
クス
Hey, look at that.
Whaa?
クス
GIGGLE
...
...
What have I done?!
...
DUN
Uh...um, Wajima-kun.
What is that dog doing there?
Karen Kikuchi (38)
Takeru's homeroom and PE teacher

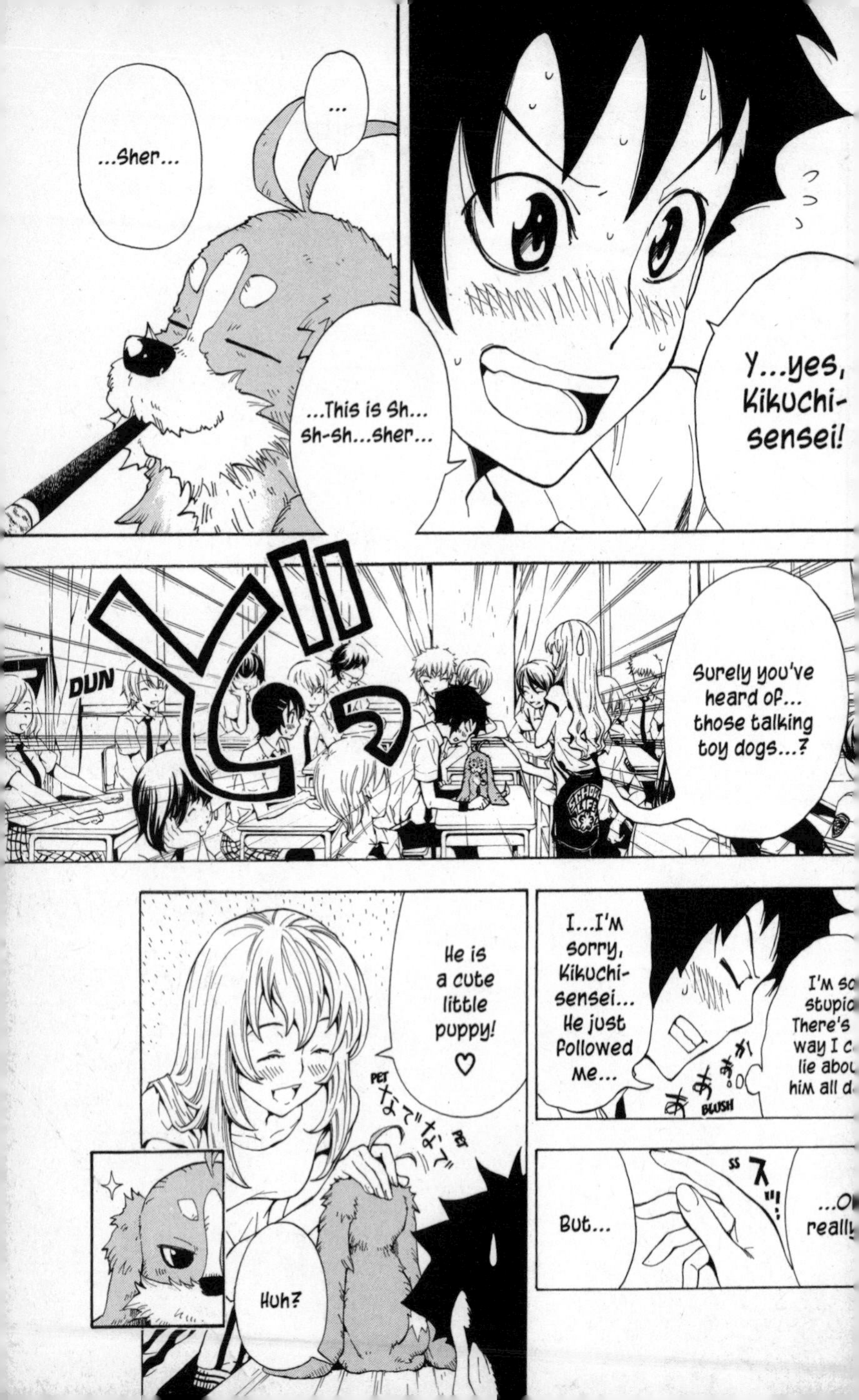

Y...yes, Kikuchi-sensei!
...This is Sh... sh-sh...sher...
...
...Sher...
Surely you've heard of... those talking toy dogs...?
DUN
I'm so stupid There's way I c lie abou him all d
I...I'm sorry, Kikuchi-sensei... He just followed me...
BLUSH
...O really
SS
But...
He is a cute little puppy! ♡
PET
PET
Huh?

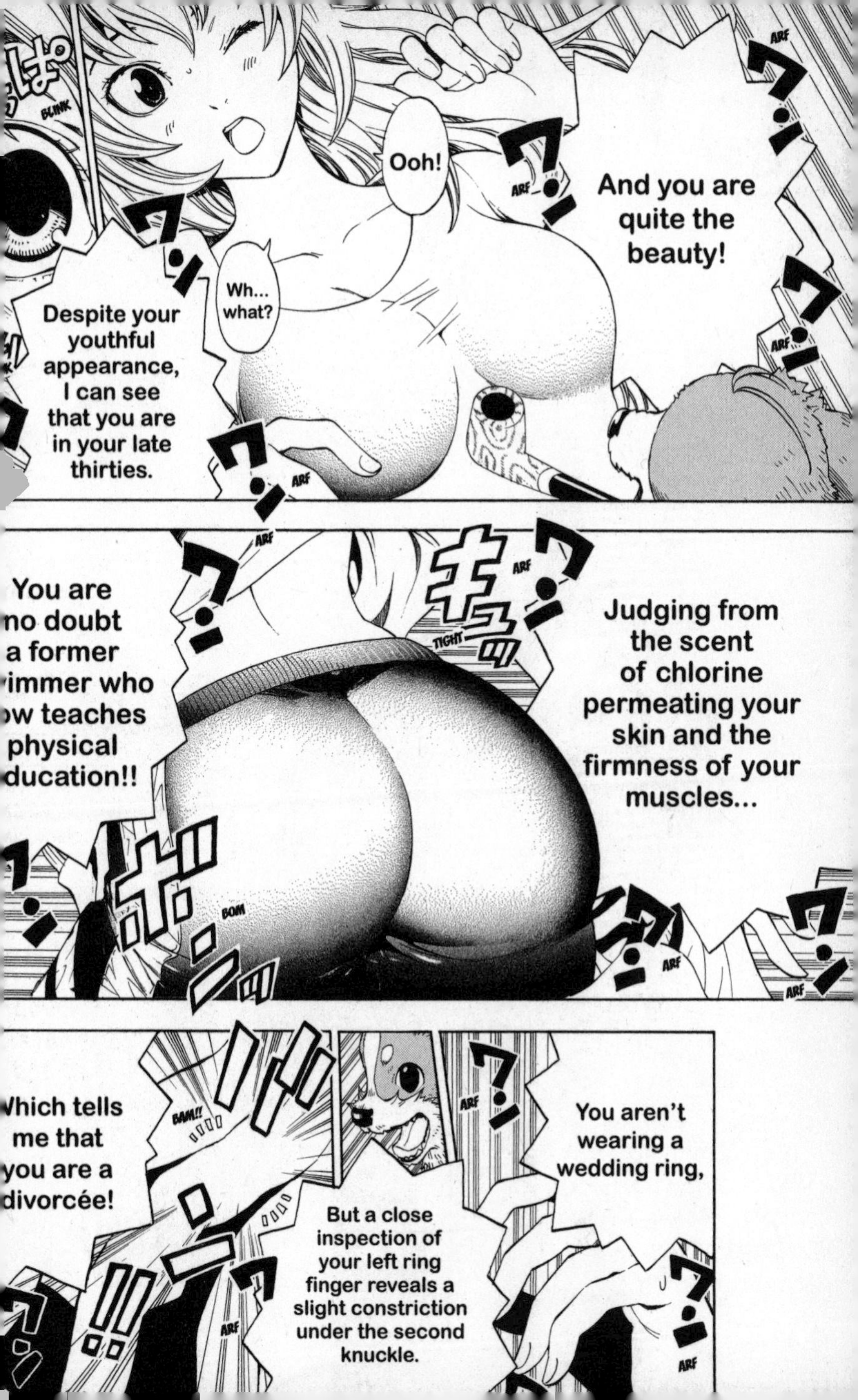
ARF
And you are quite the beauty!
ARF
Ooh!
BLINK
Wh... what?
ARF
Despite your youthful appearance, I can see that you are in your late thirties.
ARF
ARF
Judging from the scent of chlorine permeating your skin and the firmness of your muscles...
ARF
TIGHT
ARF
You are no doubt a former immer who w teaches physical ducation!!
ARF
ARF
BOM
ARF
You aren't wearing a wedding ring,
But a close inspection of your left ring finger reveals a slight constriction under the second knuckle.
ARF
BAM!!
hich tells me that you are a divorcée!
ARF

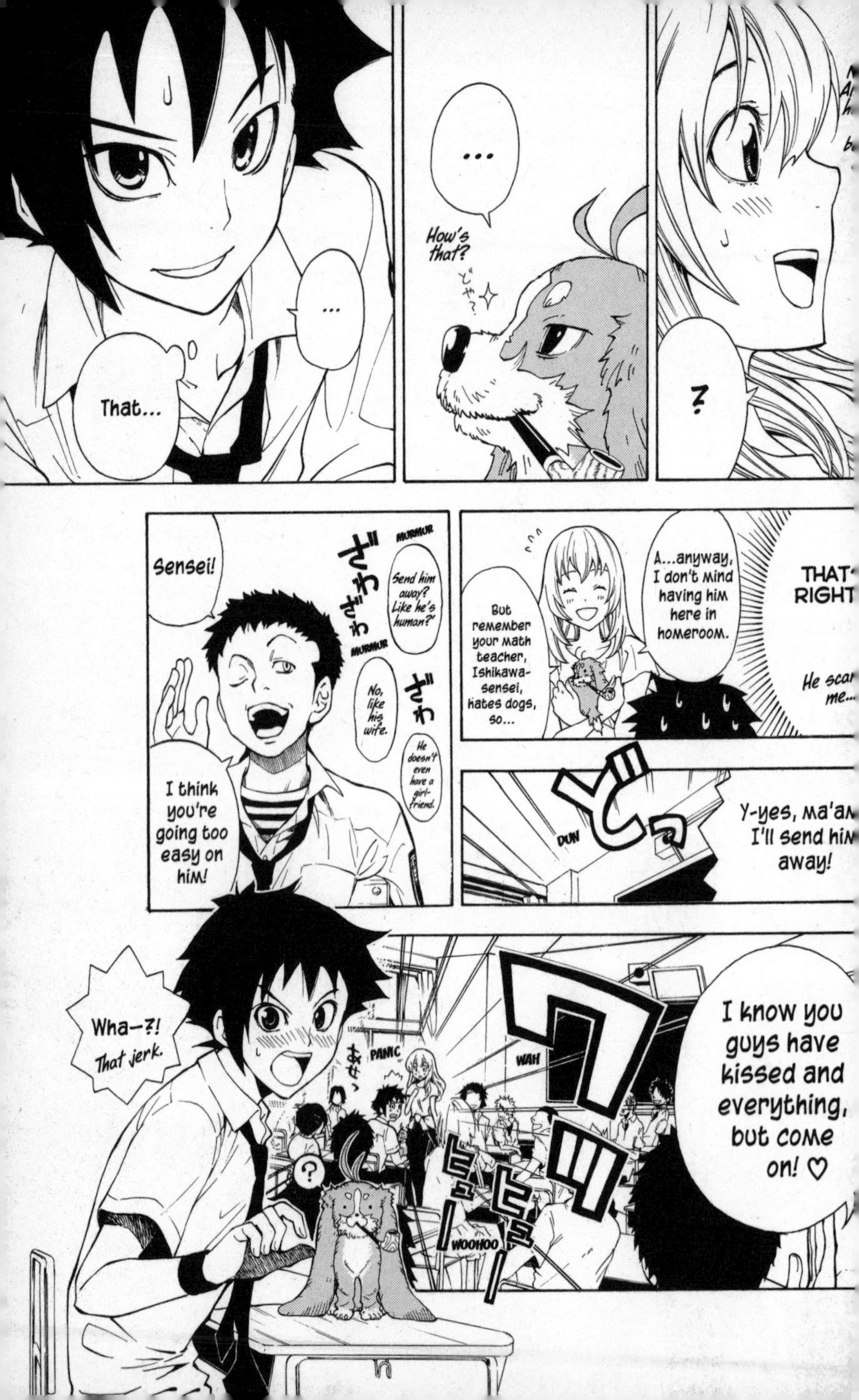
?
...
How's that?
どや?
...
That...
THAT'
RIGHT
He scar
me...
A...anyway, I don't mind having him here in homeroom.
But remember your math teacher, Ishikawa-sensei, hates dogs, so...
Y-yes, ma'am
I'll send hin
away!
どっ
DUN
Sensei!
ざわ ざわ
MURMUR
Send him away? Like he's human?
MURMUR
ざわ
No, like his wife.
He doesn't even have a girlfriend.
I think you're going too easy on him!
I know you guys have kissed and everything, but come on! ♡
ワッ
WAH
ヒューヒュー
WOOHOO
あせっ
PANIC
?
Wha-?! That jerk.

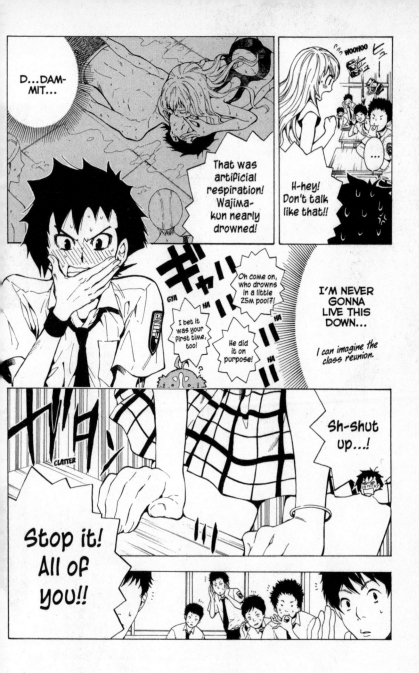

WOOHOO
...
H-hey! Don't talk like that!!
That was artificial respiration! Wajima-kun nearly drowned!
D...DAM-MIT...
I'M NEVER GONNA LIVE THIS DOWN...
I can imagine the class reunion.
Oh come on, who drowns in a little 25M pool?!
GYA HA HA HA
I bet it was your first time, too!
He did it on purpose!
Sh-shut up...!
CLATTER
Stop it! All of you!!

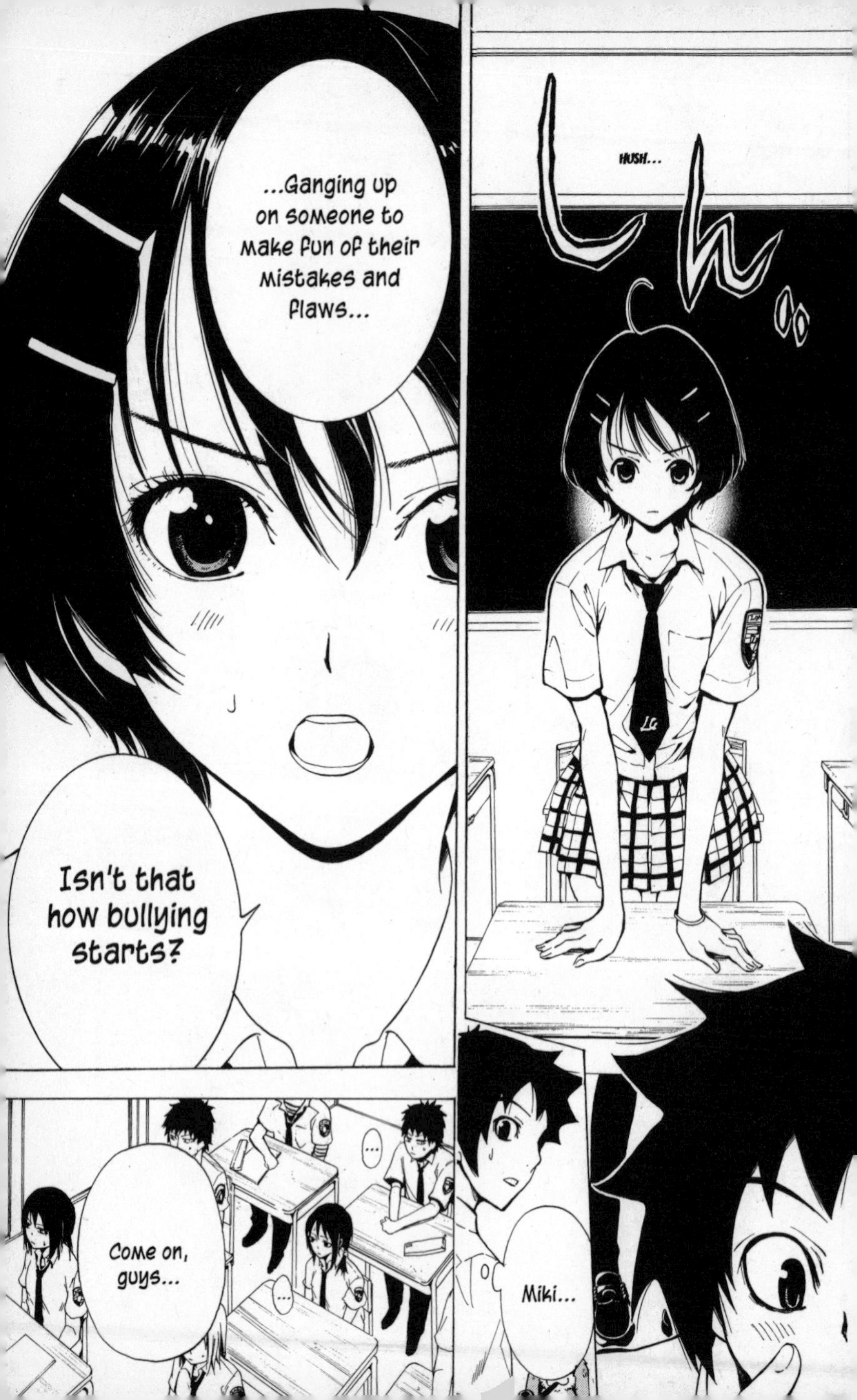
HUSH...
...Ganging up on someone to make fun of their mistakes and flaws...
Isn't that how bullying starts?
Miki...
...
Come on, guys...
...

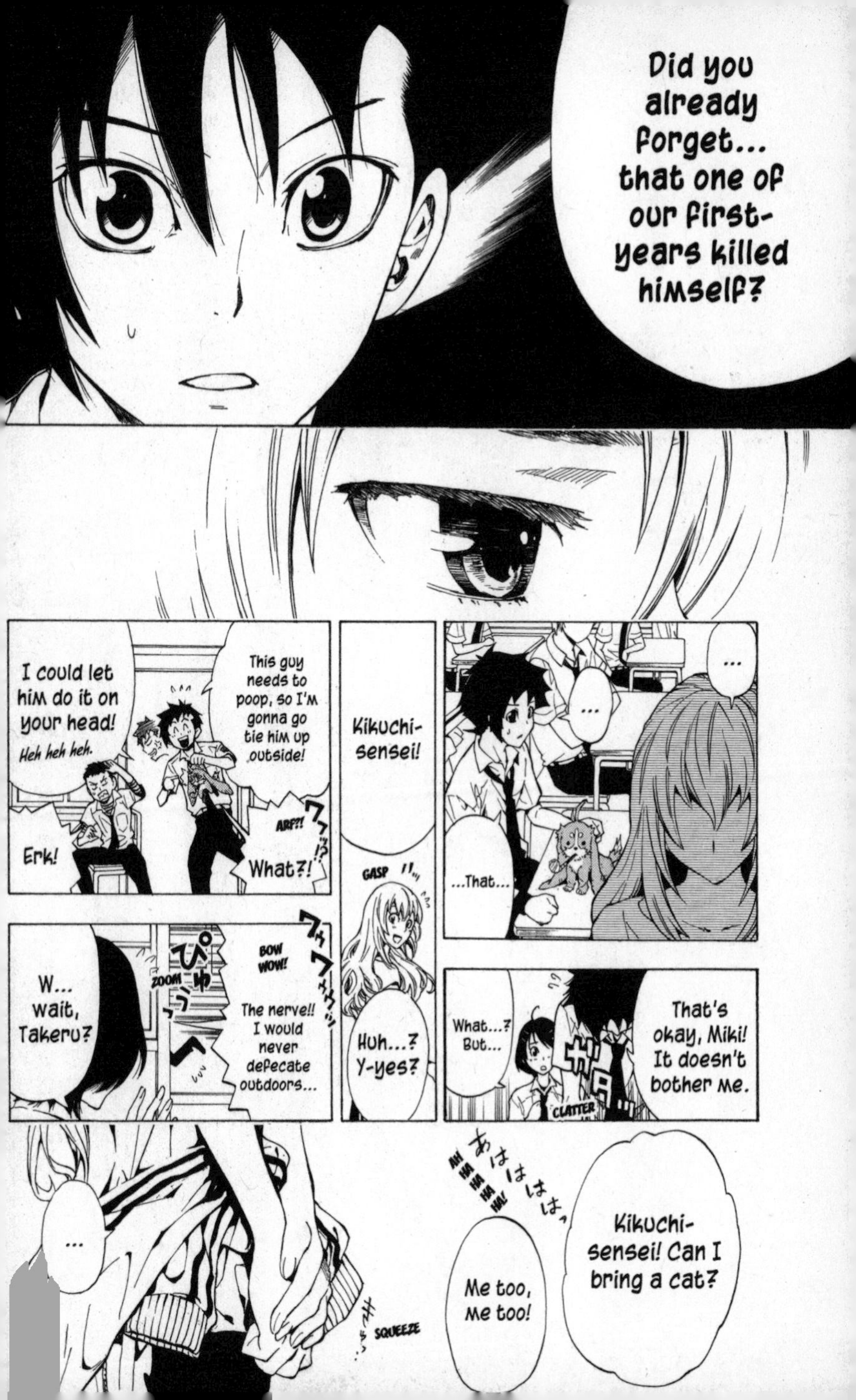
Did you already forget... that one of our first-years killed himself?
...
...
...That...
That's okay, Miki! It doesn't bother me.
What...? But...
CLATTER
Kikuchi-sensei!
GASP
Huh...? Y-yes?
This guy needs to poop, so I'm gonna go tie him up outside!
I could let him do it on your head!
Heh heh heh.
ARF?!
What?!
Erk!
BOW WOW!
The nerve!! I would never defecate outdoors...
ZOOM
W... wait, Takeru?
Kikuchi-sensei! Can I bring a cat?
AH HA HA HA HA!
あははは
Me too, me too!
...
SQUEEZE

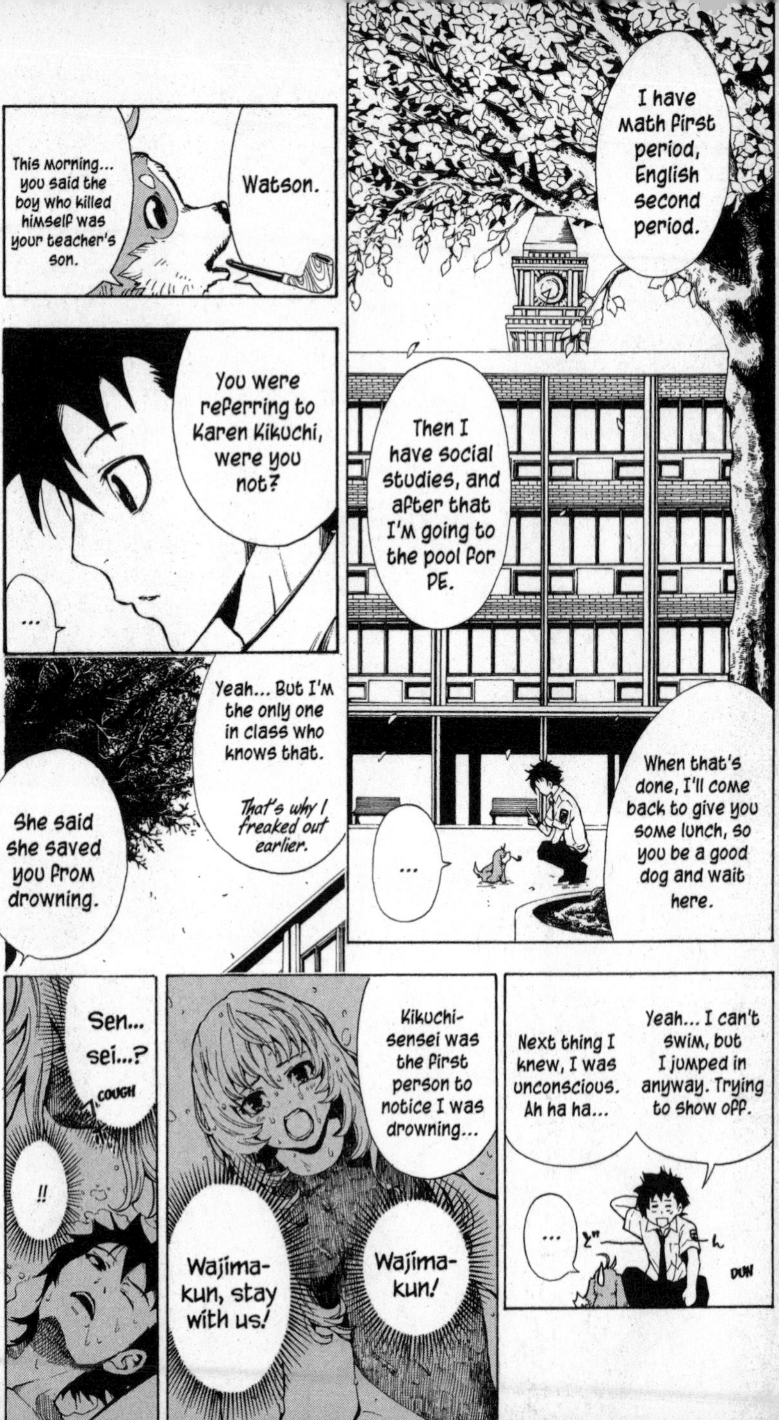

I have math first period, English second period.
Then I have social studies, and after that I'm going to the pool for PE.
When that's done, I'll come back to give you some lunch, so you be a good dog and wait here.
...
Watson.
This morning... you said the boy who killed himself was your teacher's son.
You were referring to Karen Kikuchi, were you not?
...
Yeah... But I'm the only one in class who knows that.
That's why I freaked out earlier.
She said she saved you from drowning.
Yeah... I can't swim, but I jumped in anyway. Trying to show off.
Next thing I knew, I was unconscious. Ah ha ha...
...
DUN
Kikuchi-sensei was the first person to notice I was drowning...
Wajima-kun!
Wajima-kun, stay with us!
Sen... sei...?
COUGH
!!

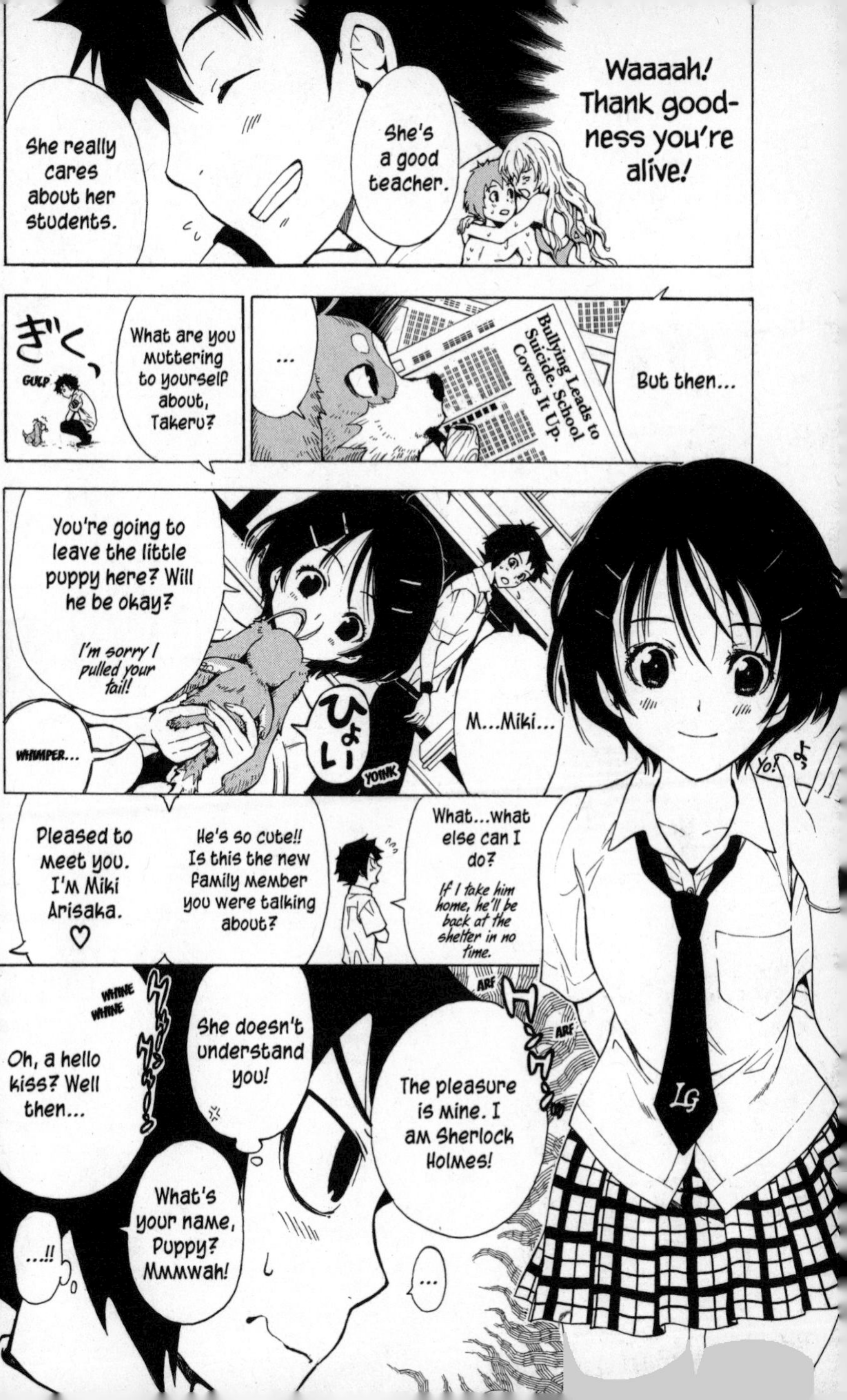

Waaaah! Thank goodness you're alive!
She's a good teacher.
She really cares about her students.
But then...
Bullying Leads to Suicide. School Covers It Up.
...
What are you muttering to yourself about, Takeru?
ぎく
GULP
よっ
Yo!
M...Miki...
ひょい
YOINK
You're going to leave the little puppy here? Will he be okay?
I'm sorry I pulled your tail!
WHIMPER...
What...what else can I do?
If I take him home, he'll be back at the shelter in no time.
He's so cute!! Is this the new family member you were talking about?
Pleased to meet you. I'm Miki Arisaka. ♡
ARF
ARF
The pleasure is mine. I am Sherlock Holmes!
She doesn't understand you!
WHINE
WHINE
Oh, a hello kiss? Well then...
What's your name, Puppy? Mmmwah!
...
...!!

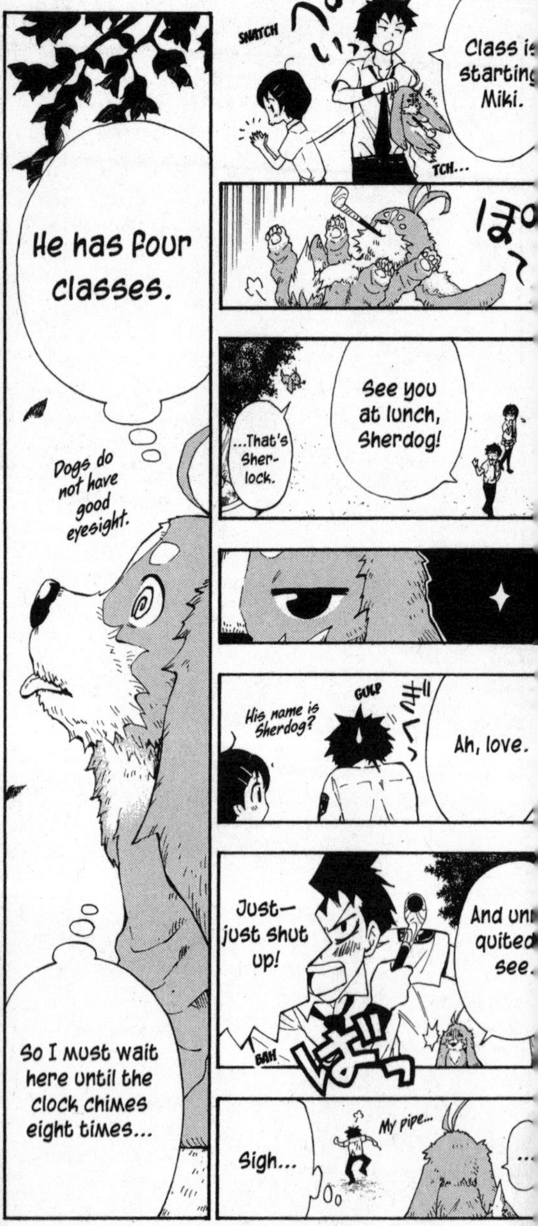
Class is starting Miki.
SNATCH
TCH...
See you at lunch, Sherdog!
...That's Sher-lock.
Ah, love.
GULP
His name is Sherdog?
And unr quited see.
Just— just shut up!
BAH
...
My pipe...
Sigh...
He has four classes.
Dogs do not have good eyesight.
So I must wait here until the clock chimes eight times...

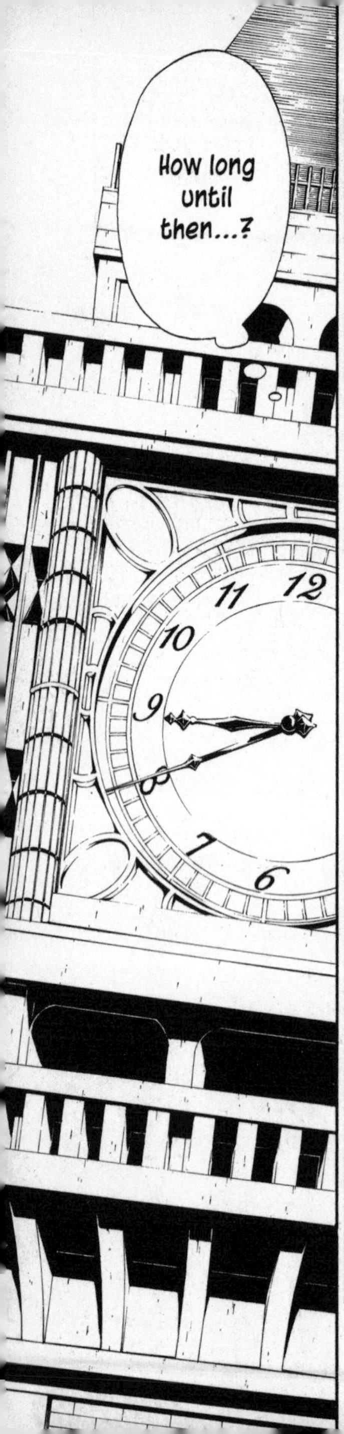
How long until then...?

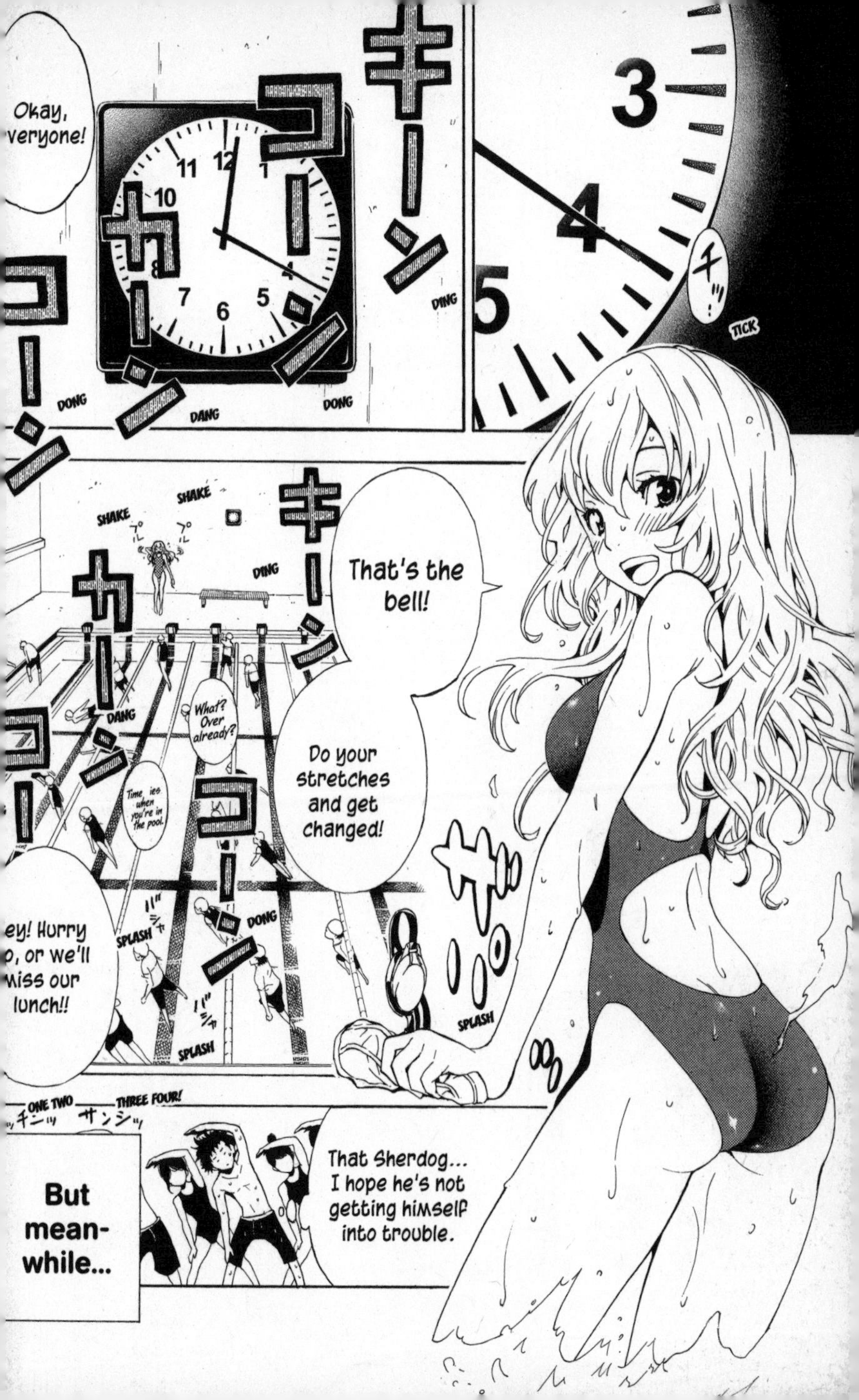

TICK
DING
DONG
DANG
DONG
veryone!
Okay,
That's the bell!
Do your stretches and get changed!
SPLASH
SHAKE
SHAKE
DING
What? Over already?
DANG
Time ies when you're in the pool.
DONG
SPLASH
SPLASH
ey! Hurry p, or we'll miss our lunch!!
That Sherdog... I hope he's not getting himself into trouble.
THREE FOUR!
ONE TWO
But mean-while...

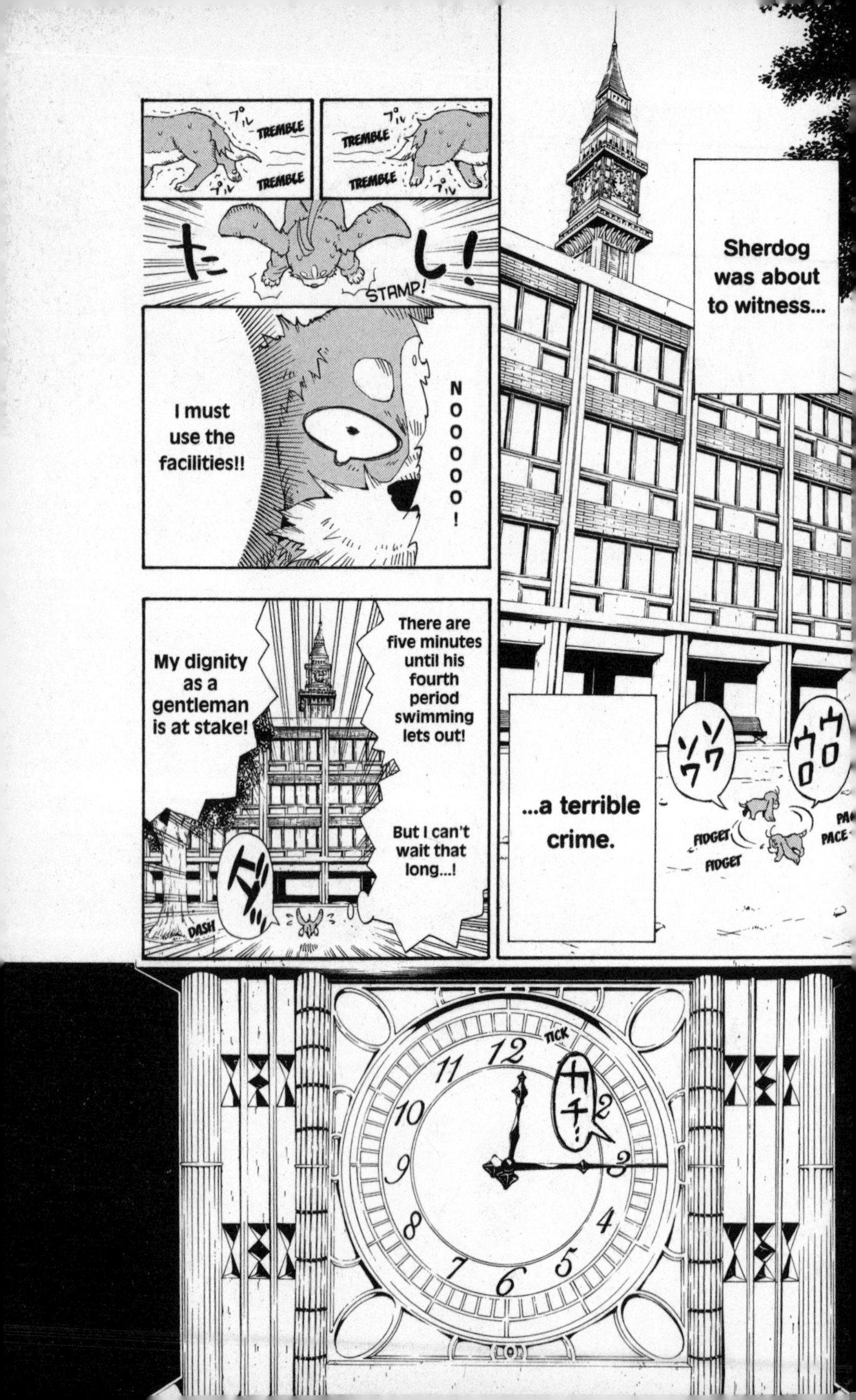

Sherdog was about to witness...
ウロウロ
PACE
ソワソワ
FIDGET
FIDGET
...a terrible crime.
プル
TREMBLE
TREMBLE
プル
プル
TREMBLE
TREMBLE
プル
たし!
STAMP!
NOOOOOO!
I must use the facilities!!
There are five minutes until his fourth period swimming lets out!
My dignity as a gentleman is at stake!
But I can't wait that long...!
ダッ
DASH
TICK
カチ!

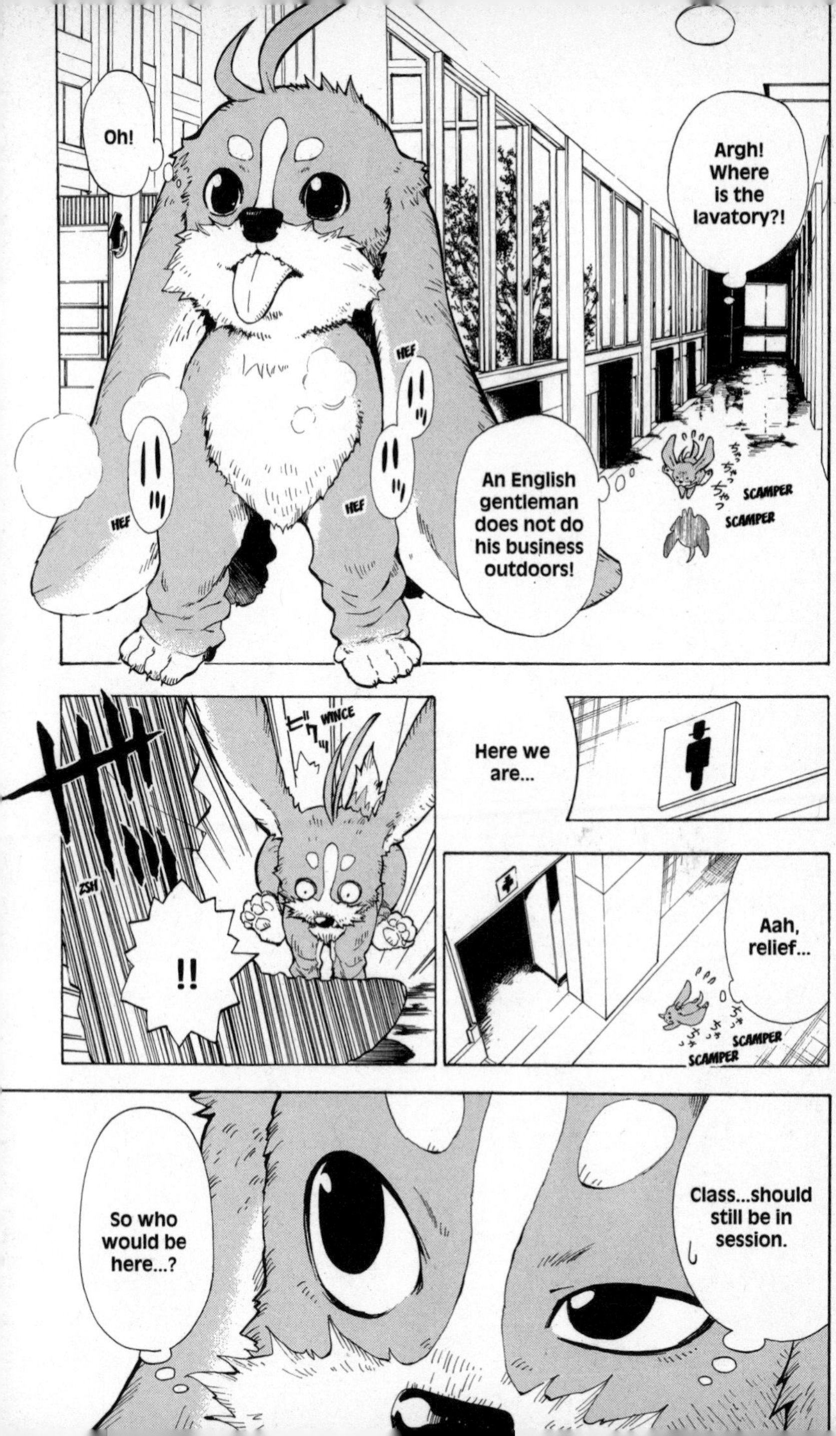
Argh! Where is the lavatory?!
An English gentleman does not do his business outdoors!
SCAMPER
SCAMPER
HEF
HEF
HEF
Oh!
Here we are...
Aah, relief...
SCAMPER
SCAMPER
WINCE
ZSH
!!
Class...should still be in session.
So who would be here...?

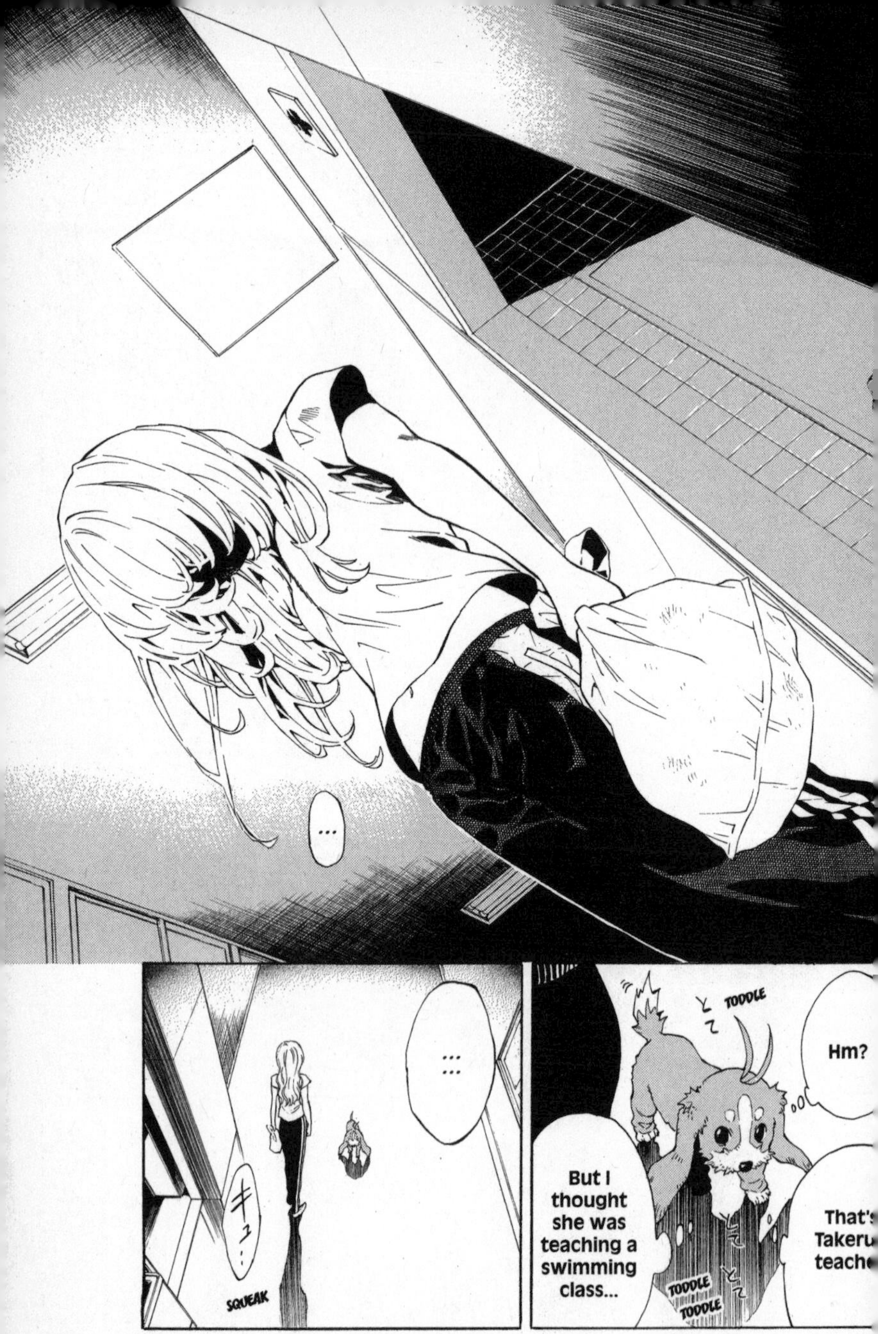
...
Hm?
TODDLE
That's Takeru teache
But I thought she was teaching a swimming class...
TODDLE TODDLE
... ...
キュ…
SQUEAK

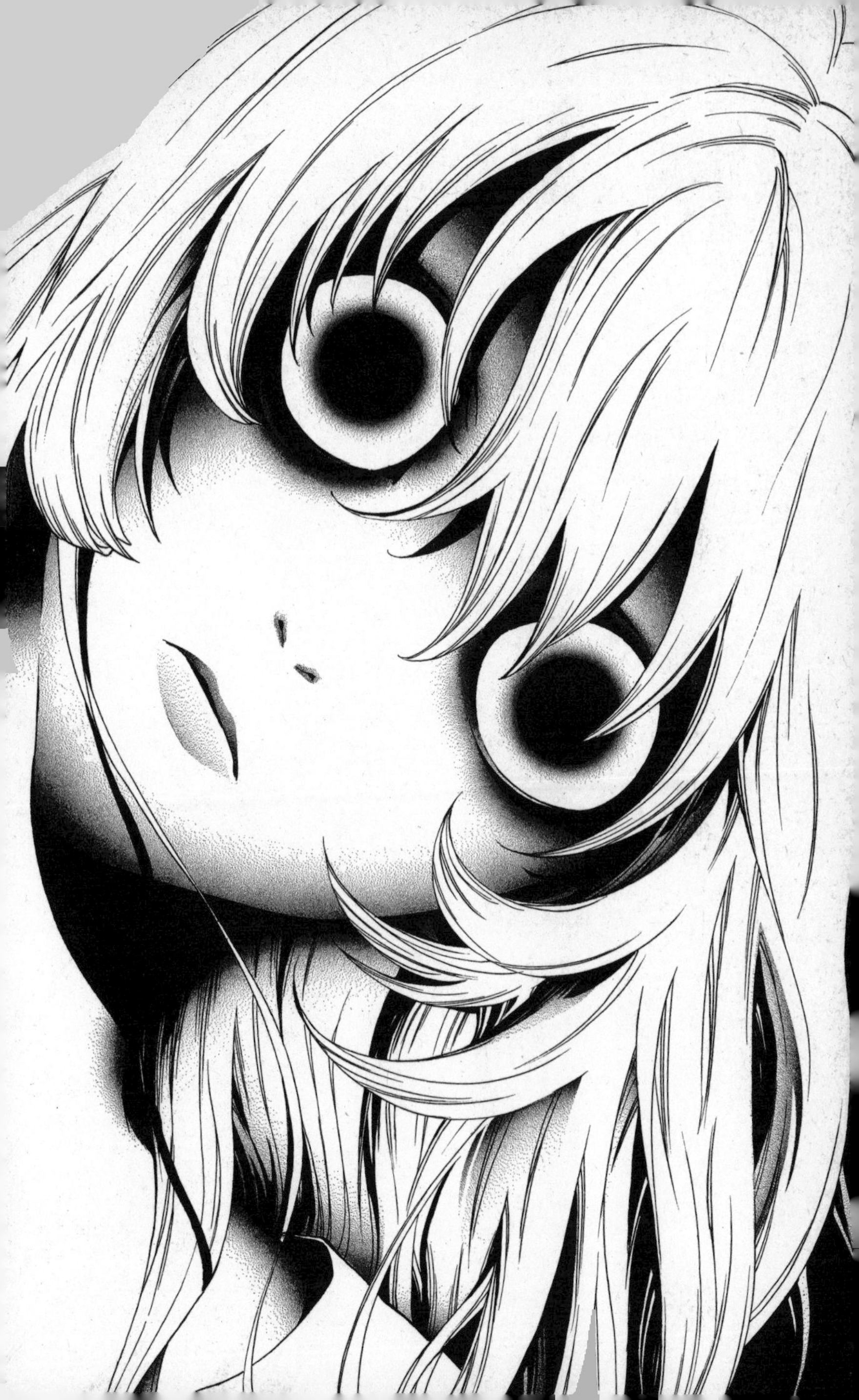

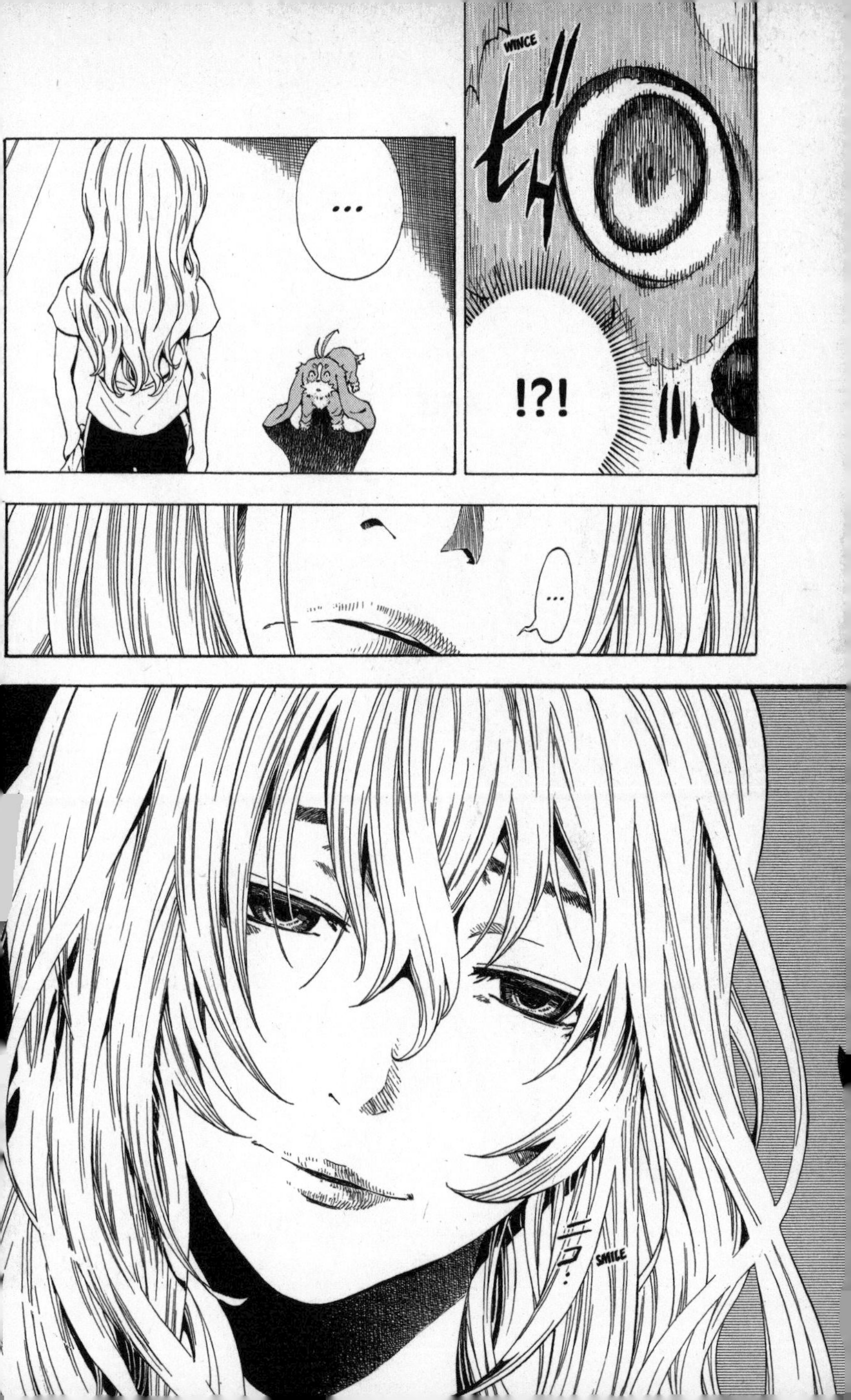
WINCE
!?!
...
...
SMILE

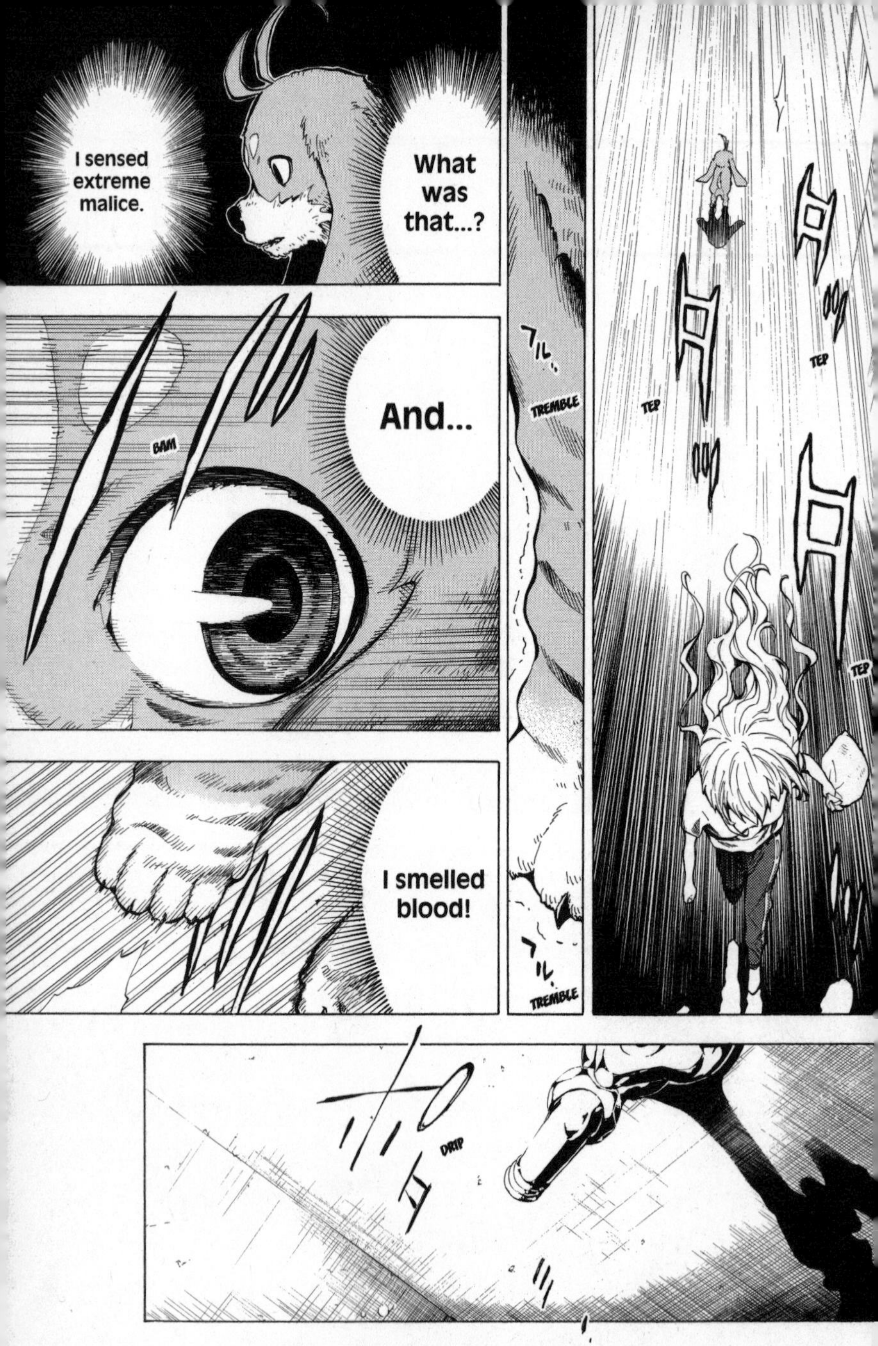

TEP
TEP
TEP
TREMBLE
TREMBLE
What was that...?
I sensed extreme malice.
And...
BAM
I smelled blood!
DRIP

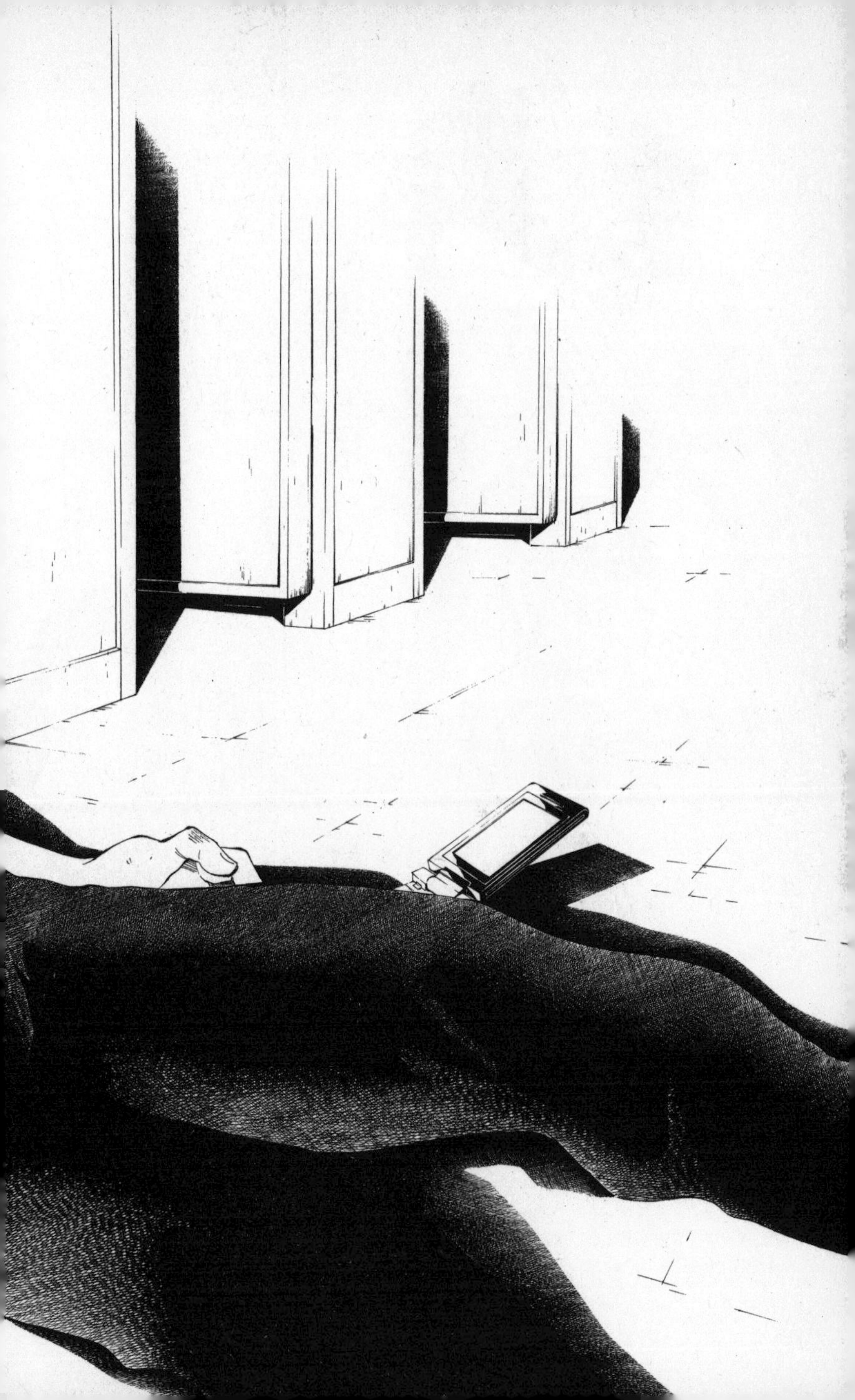

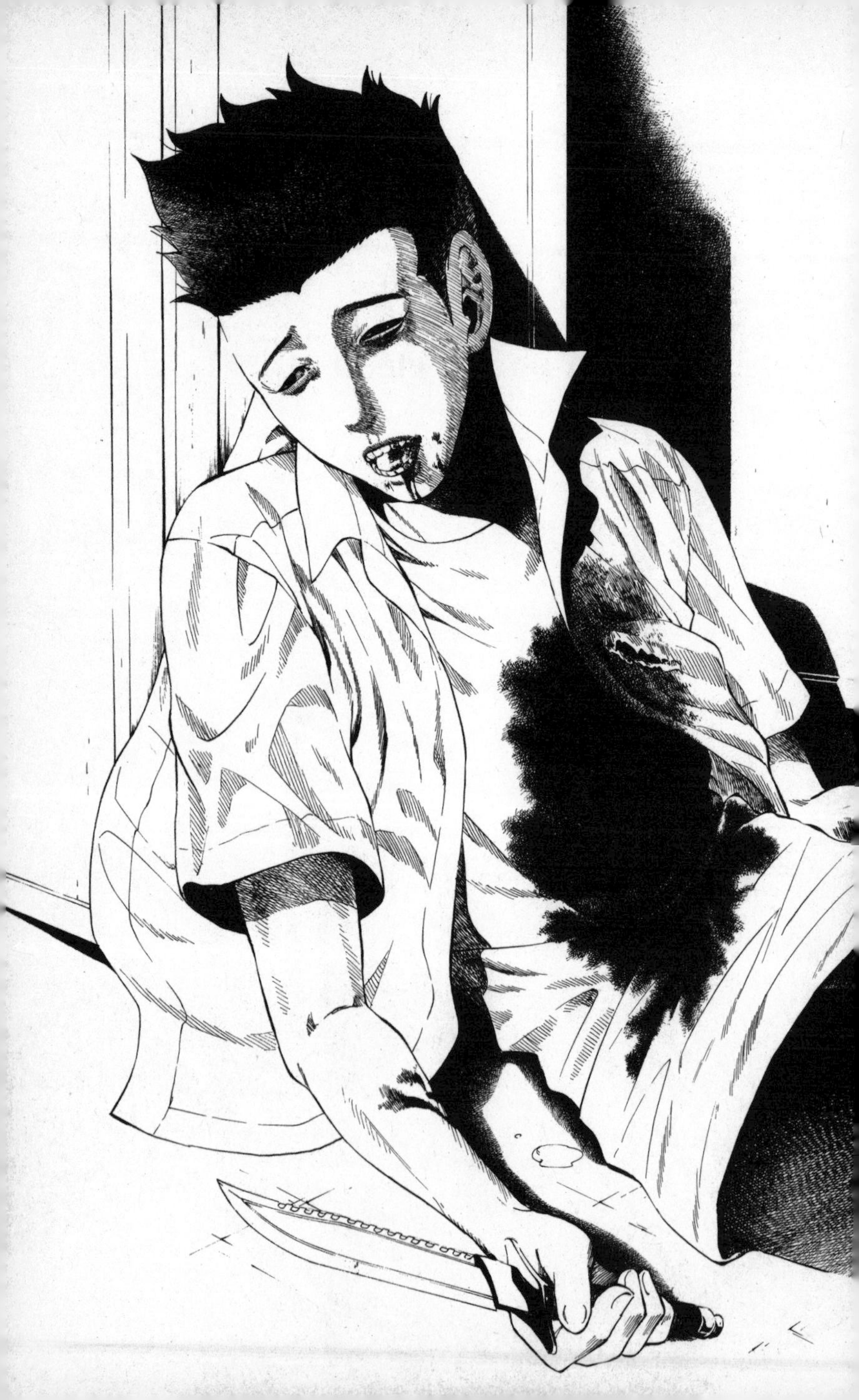

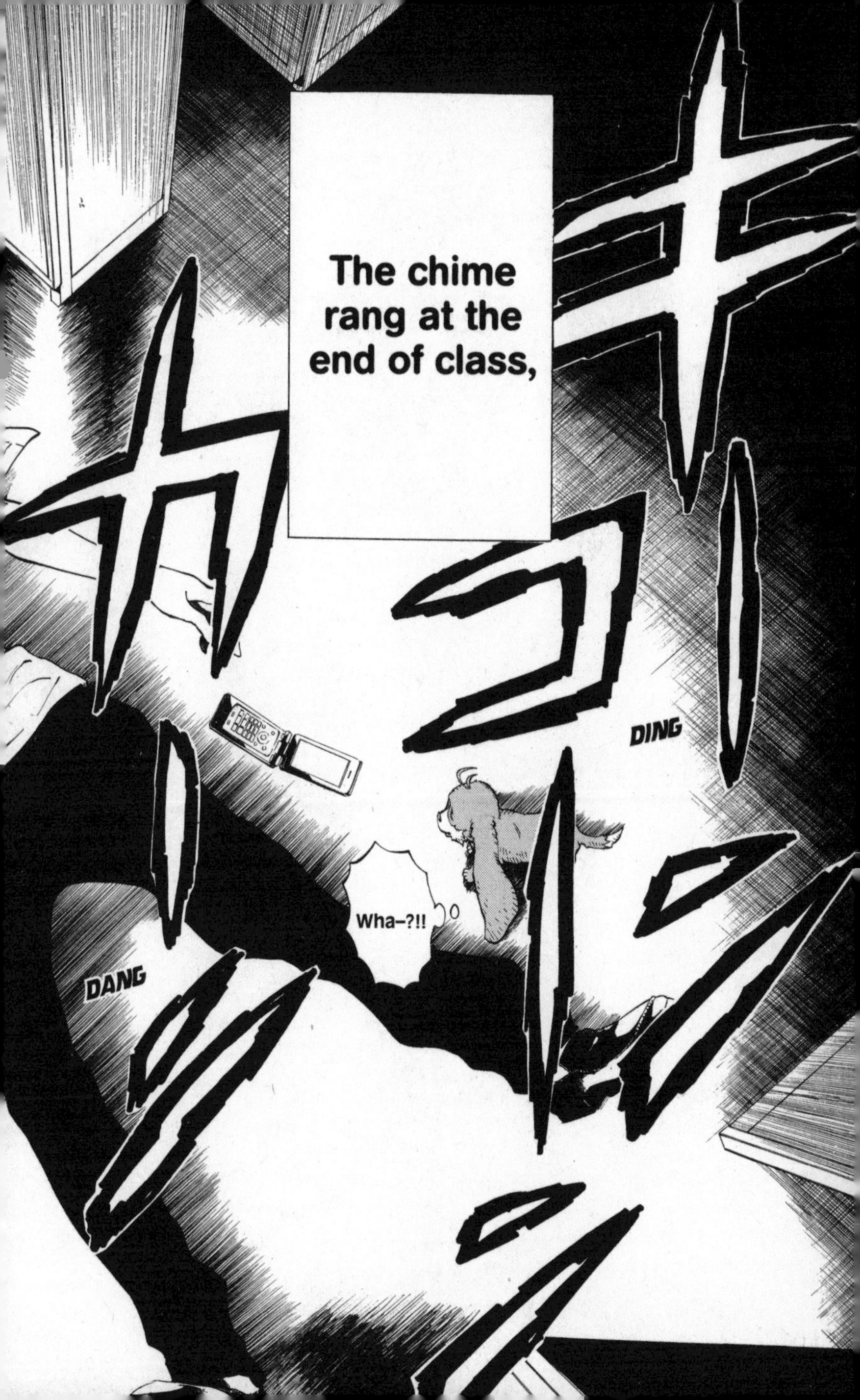
The chime rang at the end of class,
DING
Wha-?!!
DANG

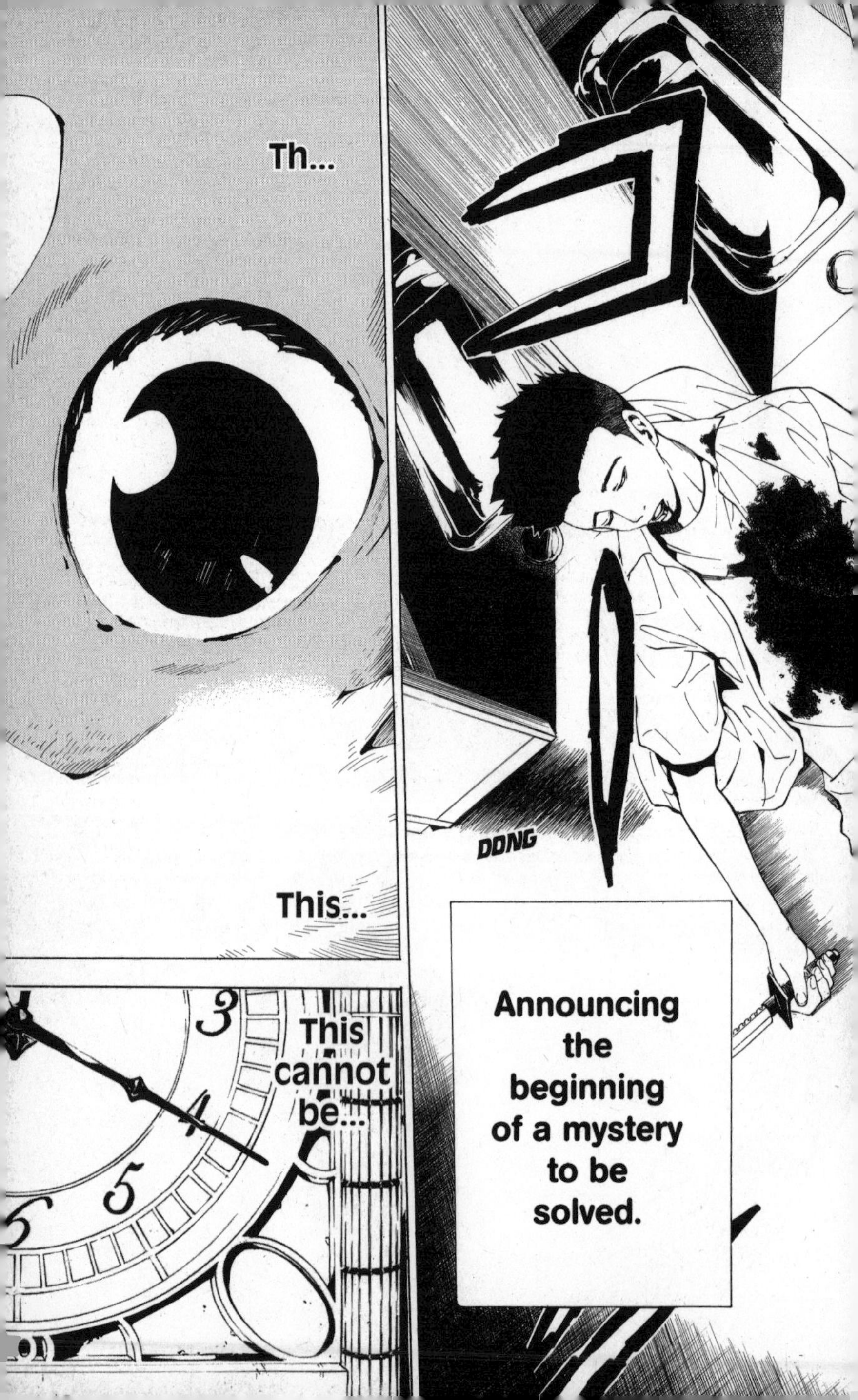
DONG
Announcing the beginning of a mystery to be solved.
Th...
This...
This cannot be...

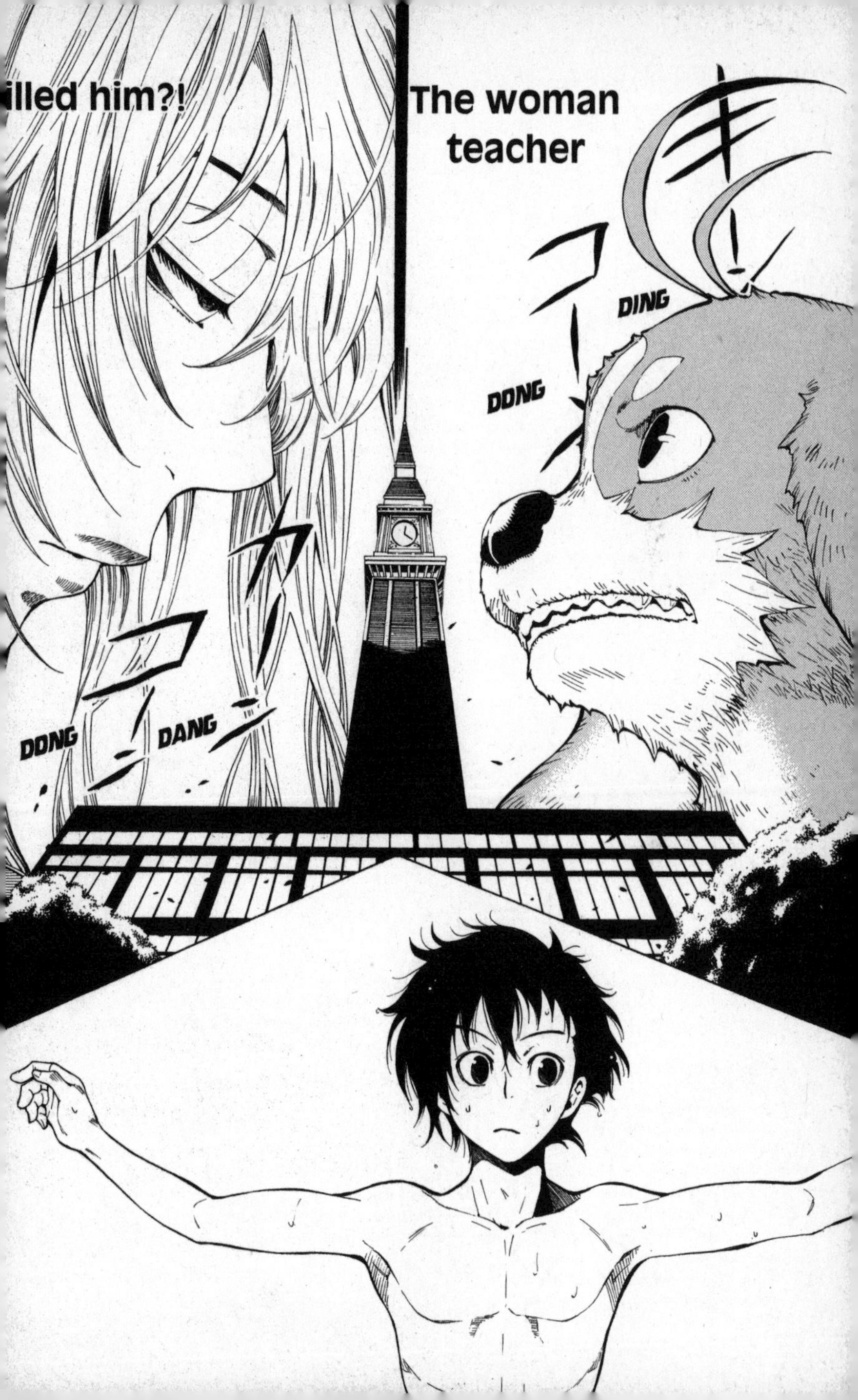
The woman teacher
DING
DONG
illed him?!
DONG
DANG

SHERLOCK BONES

SHERLOCK
BONES

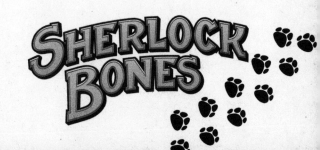

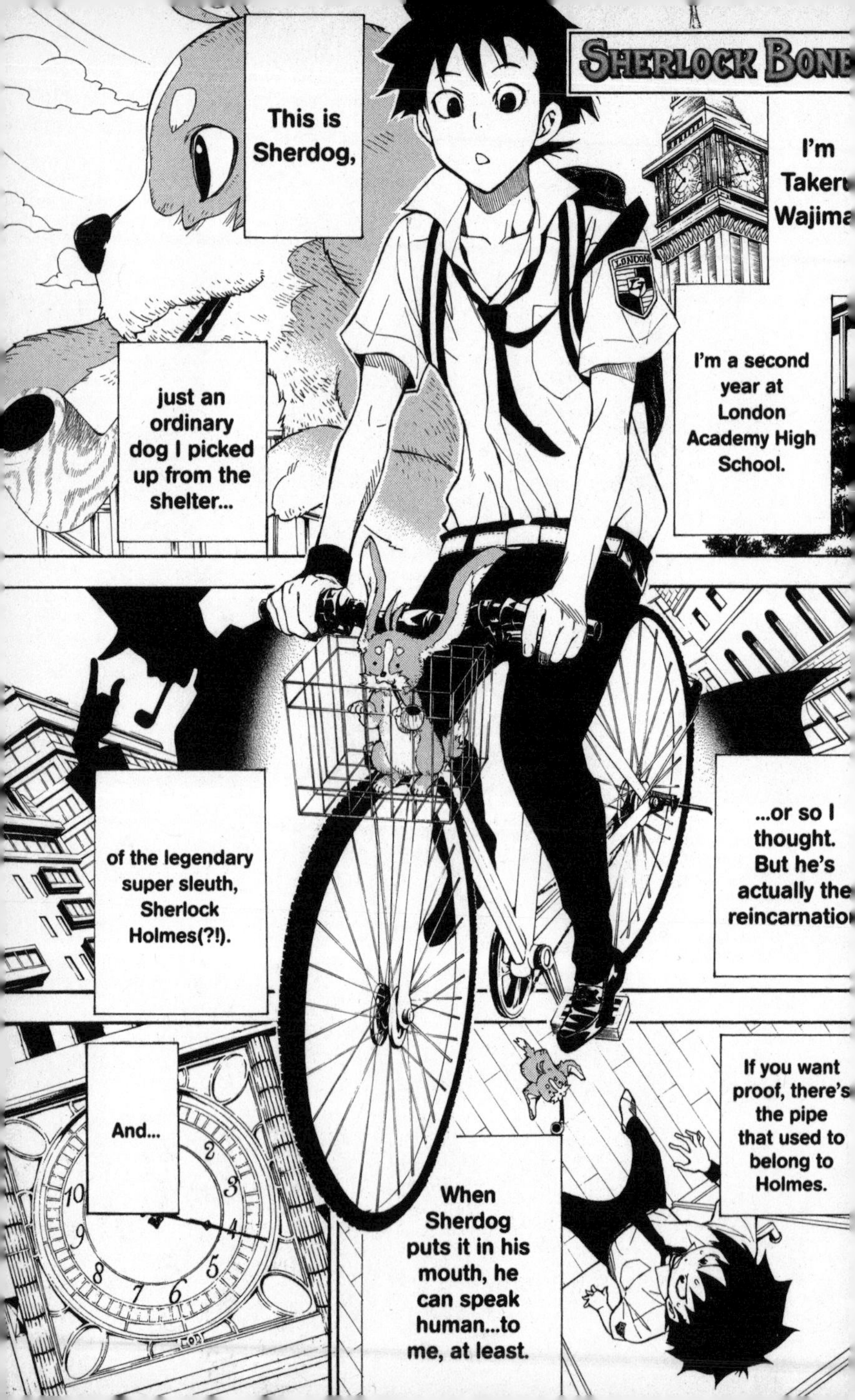
SHERLOCK BONE
I'm Takeru Wajima
I'm a second year at London Academy High School.
This is Sherdog,
just an ordinary dog I picked up from the shelter...
...or so I thought. But he's actually the reincarnation
of the legendary super sleuth, Sherlock Holmes(?!).
If you want proof, there's the pipe that used to belong to Holmes.
When Sherdog puts it in his mouth, he can speak human...to me, at least.
And...

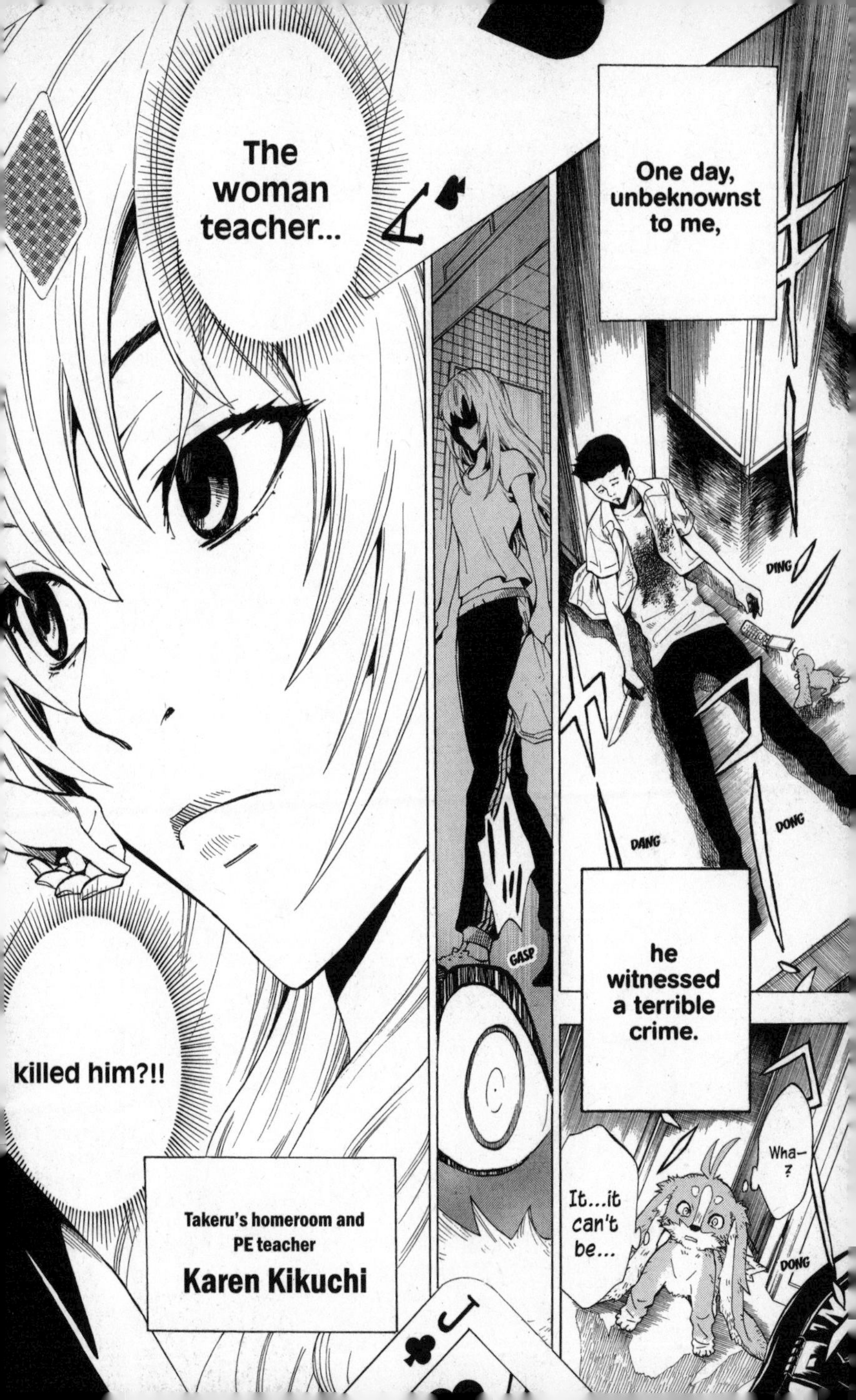
One day, unbeknownst to me,
DING
DONG
DANG
he witnessed a terrible crime.
Wha-?
It...it can't be...
DONG
GASP
The woman teacher...
killed him?!!
Takeru's homeroom and PE teacher
Karen Kikuchi

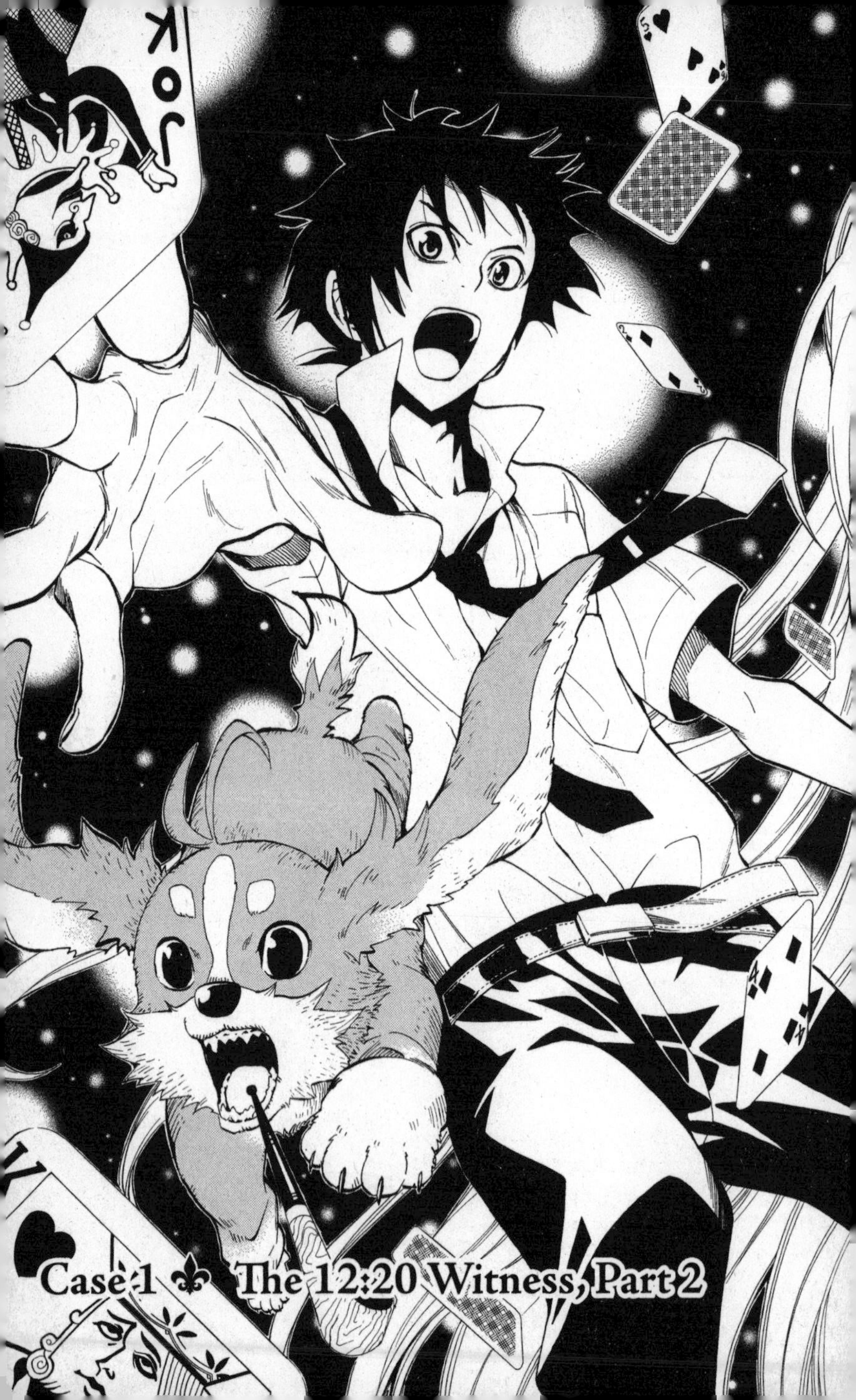

Case 1 ⚜ The 12:20 Witness, Part 2

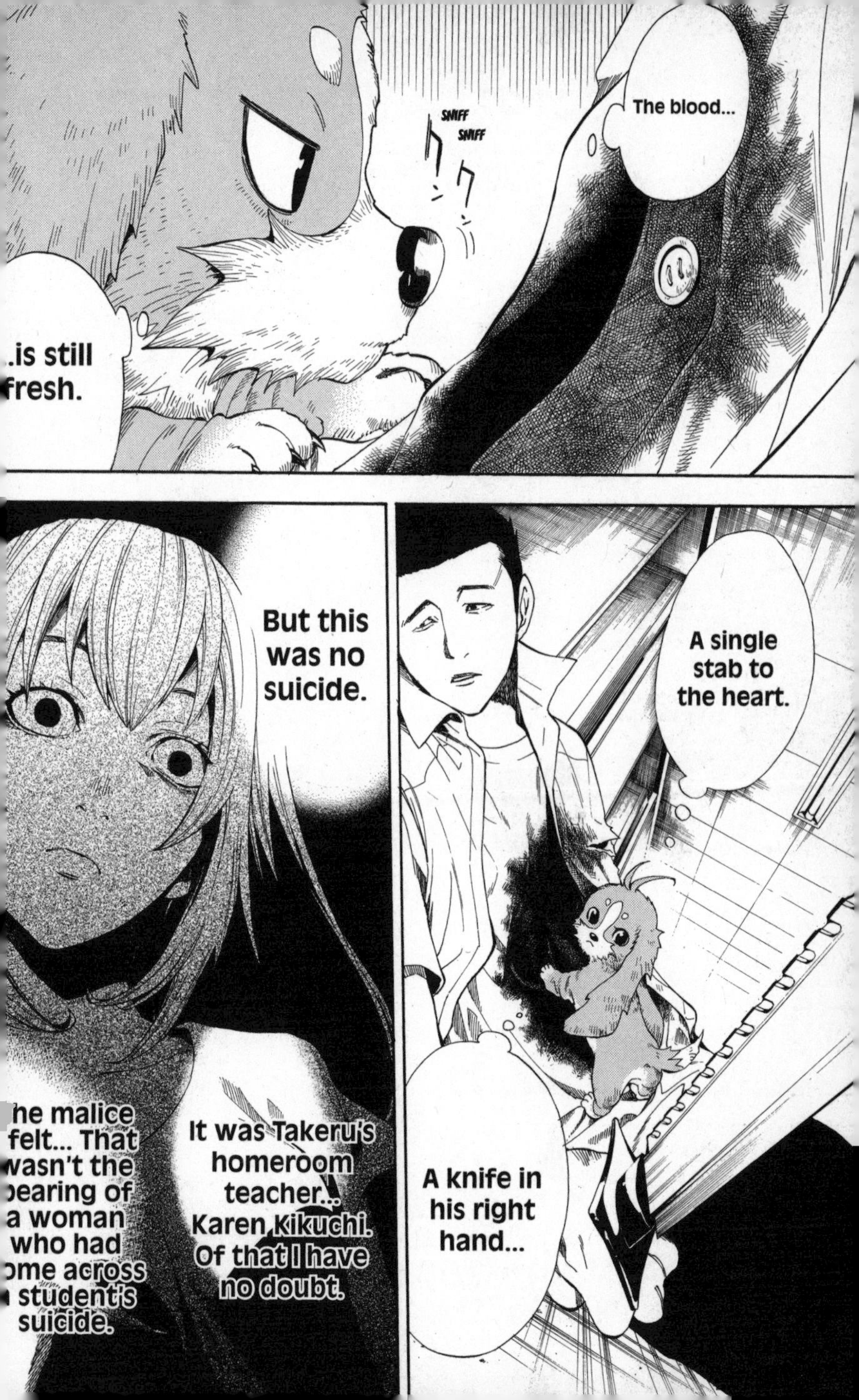
The blood...
SNIFF
SNIFF
.is still fresh.
A single stab to the heart.
A knife in his right hand...
But this was no suicide.
It was Takeru's homeroom teacher... Karen Kikuchi. Of that I have no doubt.
he malice felt... That vasn't the earing of a woman who had ome across student's suicide.

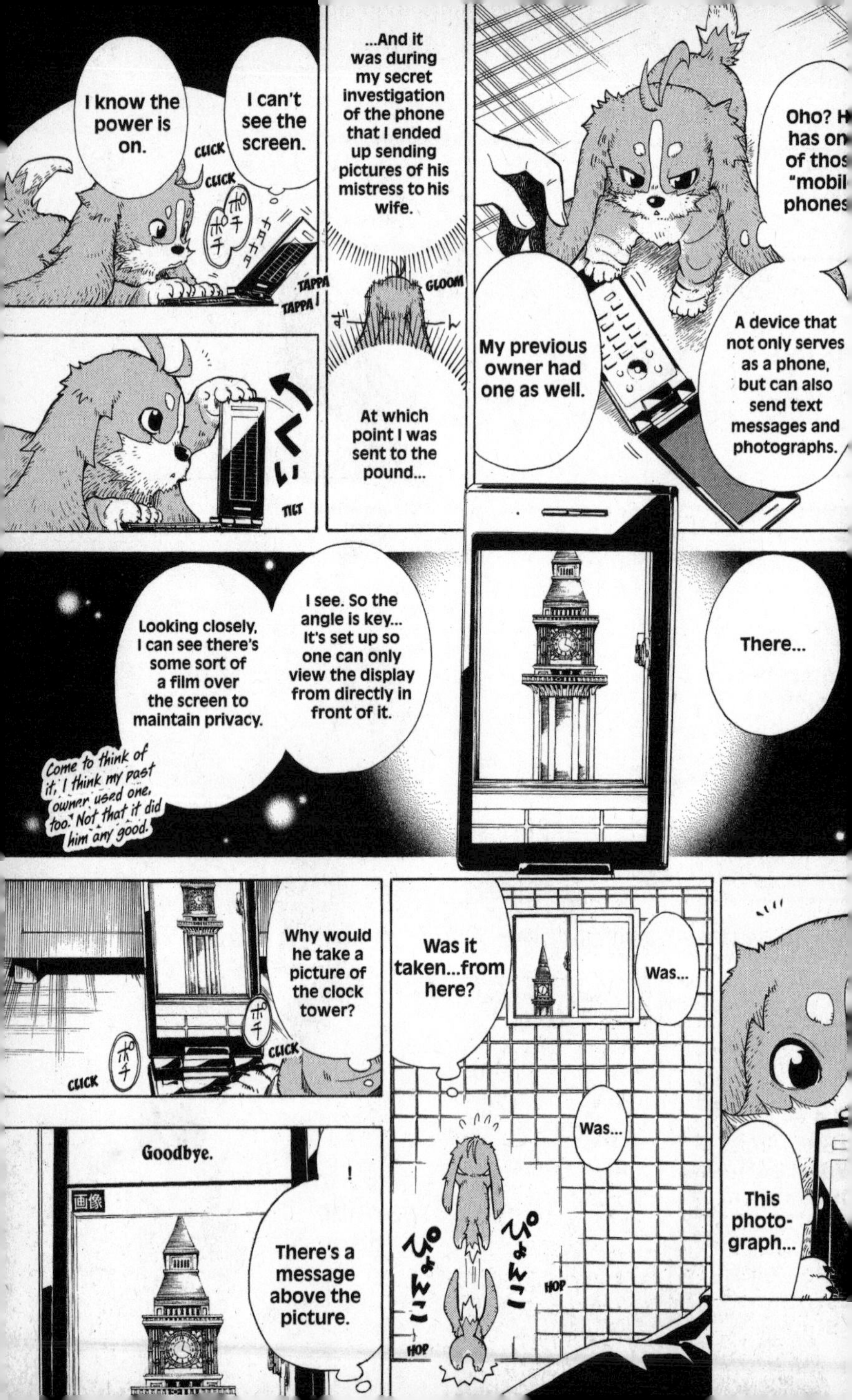
Oho? H
has on
of thos
"mobil
phones
A device that not only serves as a phone, but can also send text messages and photographs.
My previous owner had one as well.
...And it was during my secret investigation of the phone that I ended up sending pictures of his mistress to his wife.
GLOOM
At which point I was sent to the pound...
I can't see the screen.
I know the power is on.
CLICK
CLICK
TAPPA
TAPPA
TILT
There...
I see. So the angle is key... It's set up so one can only view the display from directly in front of it.
Looking closely, I can see there's some sort of a film over the screen to maintain privacy.
Come to think of it, I think my past owner used one, too. Not that it did him any good.
This photo-graph...
Was...
Was...
Was it taken...from here?
HOP
HOP
Why would he take a picture of the clock tower?
CLICK
CLICK
Goodbye.
画像
!
There's a message above the picture.

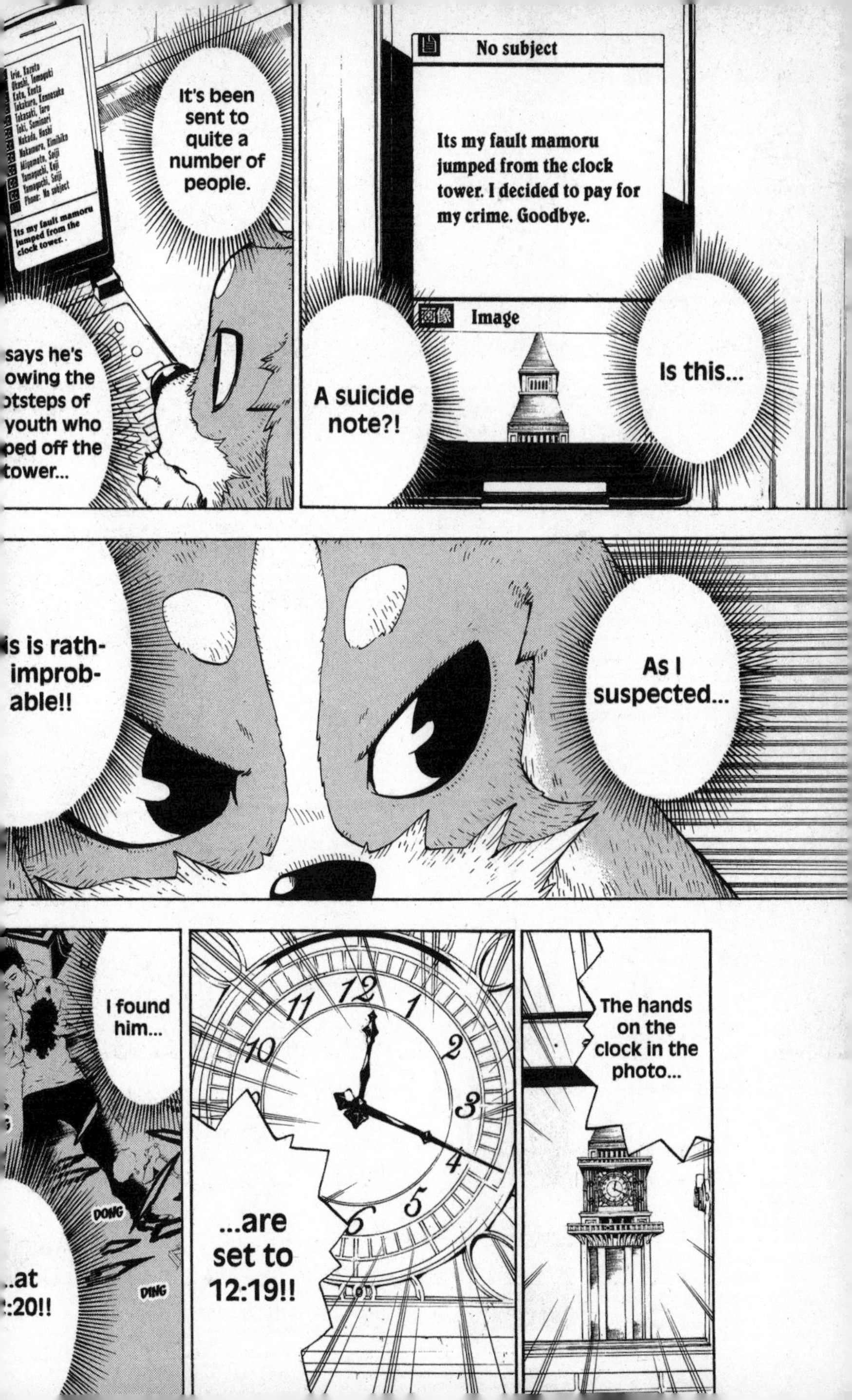
No subject
Its my fault mamoru jumped from the clock tower. I decided to pay for my crime. Goodbye.
Image
Is this...
A suicide note?!
It's been sent to quite a number of people.
Its my fault mamoru jumped from the clock tower. .
says he's
owing the
otsteps of
youth who
oped off the
tower...
As I suspected...
is is rath-
improb-
able!!
The hands on the clock in the photo...
...are set to 12:19!!
I found him...
DONG
DING
..at
:20!!

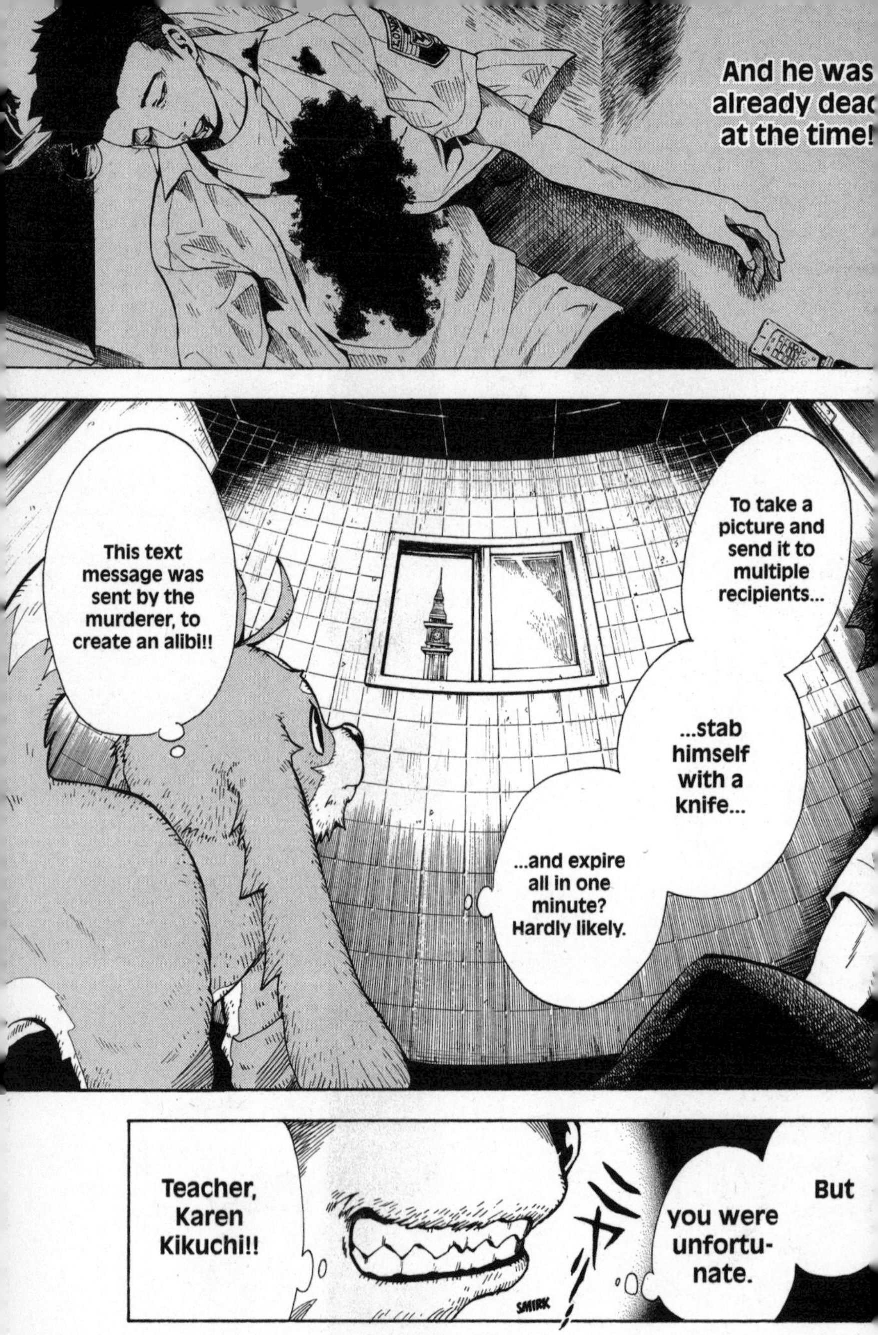
And he was already dea at the time!
To take a picture and send it to multiple recipients...
...stab himself with a knife...
...and expire all in one minute? Hardly likely.
This text message was sent by the murderer, to create an alibi!!
But you were unfortu- nate.
SMIRK
Teacher, Karen Kikuchi!!

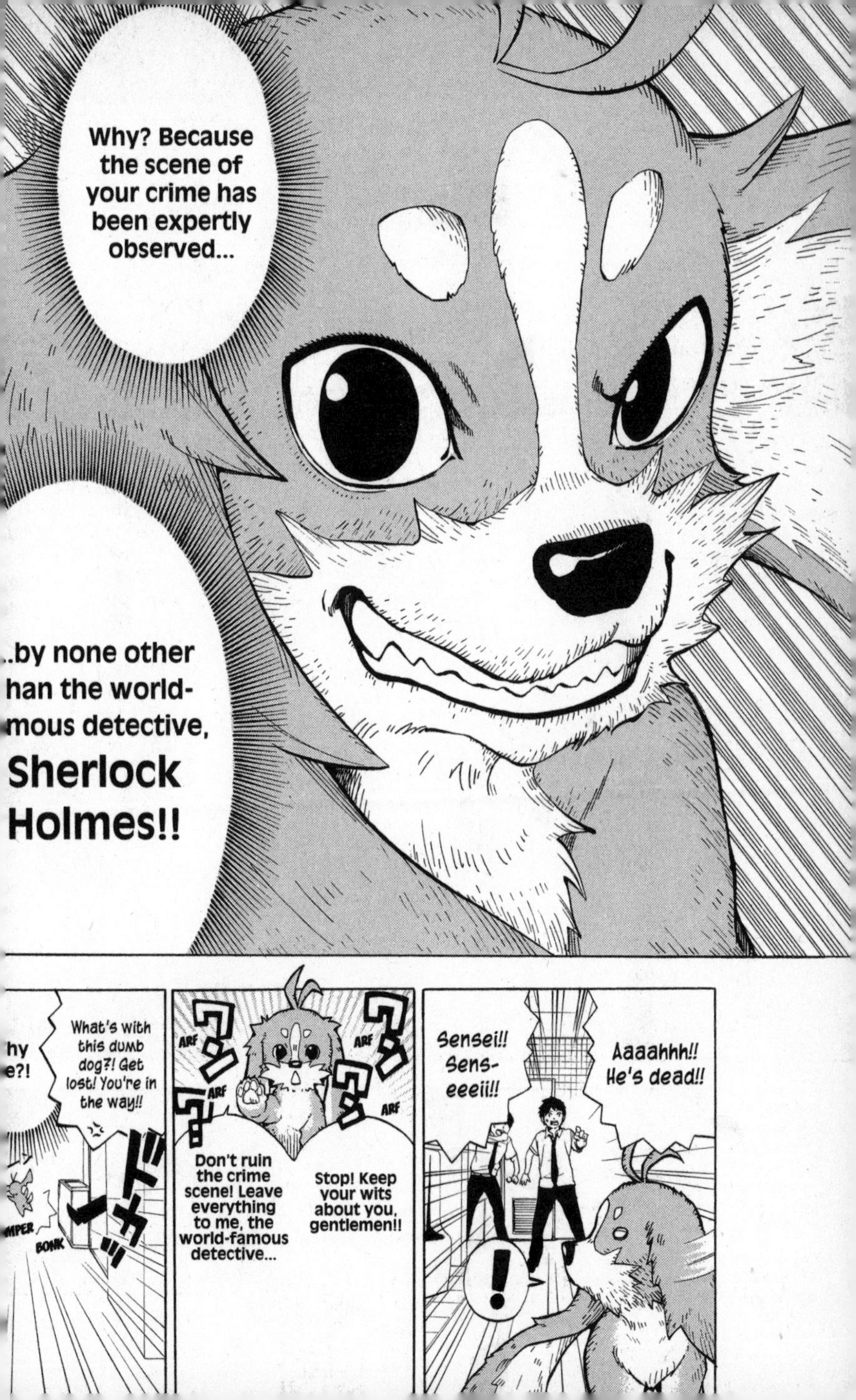
Why? Because the scene of your crime has been expertly observed...
..by none other han the world-mous detective, Sherlock Holmes!!
Aaaahhh!! He's dead!!
Sensei!! Sens-eeeii!!
!
ARF
ARF
ARF
ARF
Stop! Keep your wits about you, gentlemen!!
Don't ruin the crime scene! Leave everything to me, the world-famous detective...
What's with this dumb dog?! Get lost! You're in the way!!
hy e?!
MPER
BONK

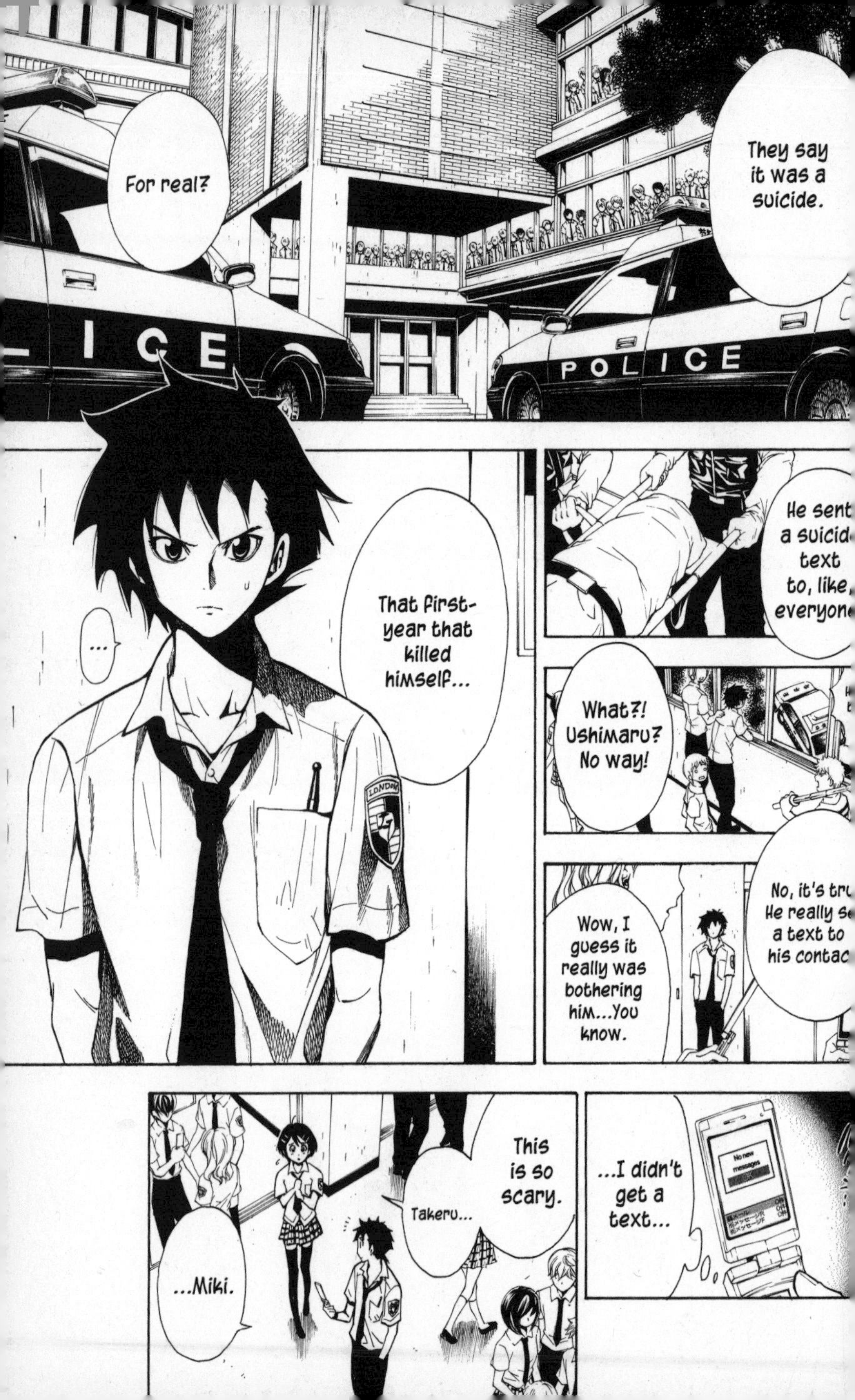
They say it was a suicide.
For real?
He sent a suicid text to, like, everyon
What?! Ushimaru? No way!
No, it's tru He really s a text to his contac
Wow, I guess it really was bothering him...You know.
That first-year that killed himself...
...
...I didn't get a text...
No new messages
This is so scary.
Takeru...
...Miki.

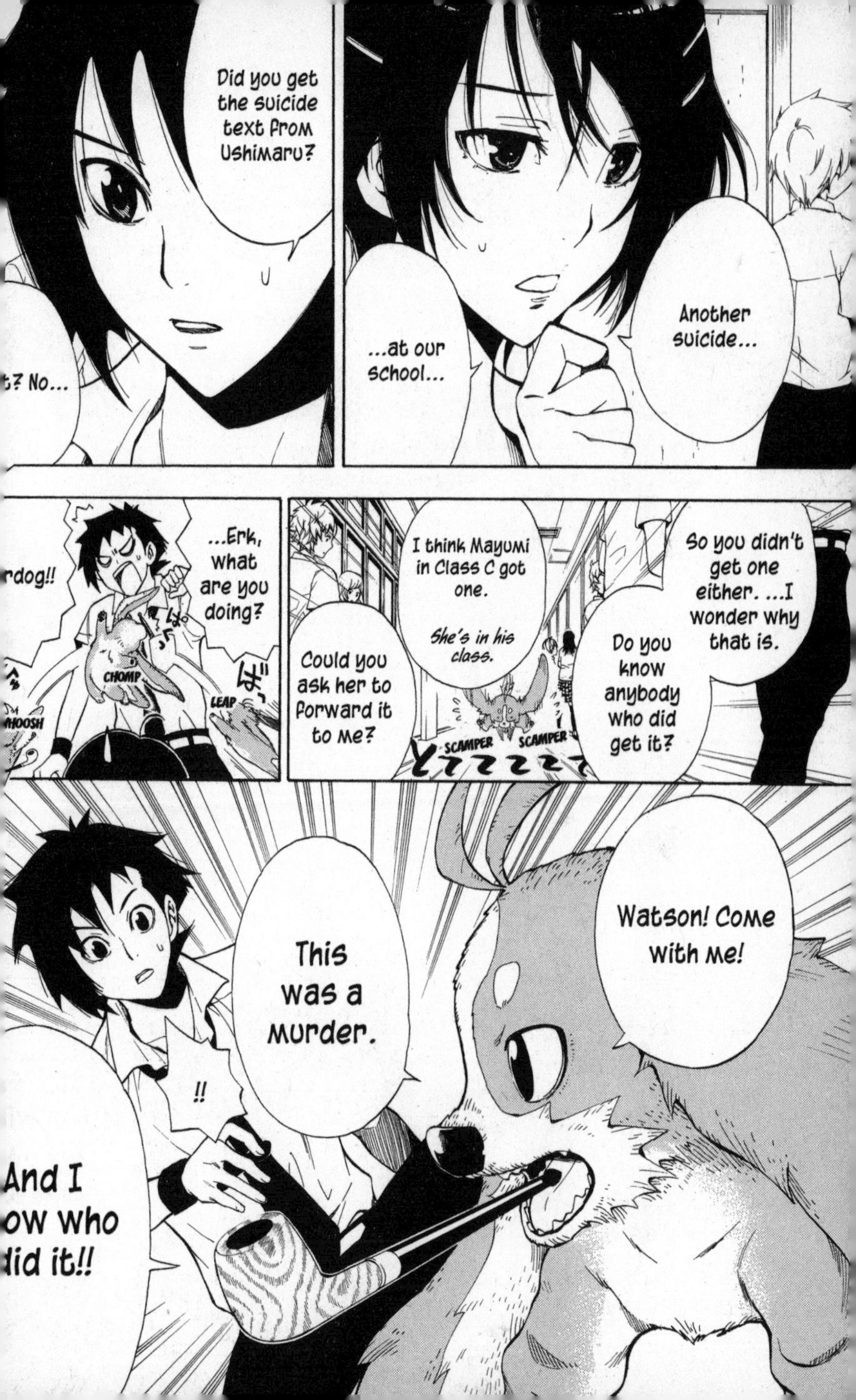

Another suicide...
...at our school...
Did you get the suicide text from Ushimaru?
t? No...
So you didn't get one either. ...I wonder why that is.
Do you know anybody who did get it?
I think Mayumi in Class C got one.
She's in his class.
Could you ask her to forward it to me?
SCAMPER
SCAMPER
...Erk, what are you doing?
rdog!!
LEAP
CHOMP
WHOOSH
Watson! Come with me!
This was a murder.
!!
And I
ow who
lid it!!

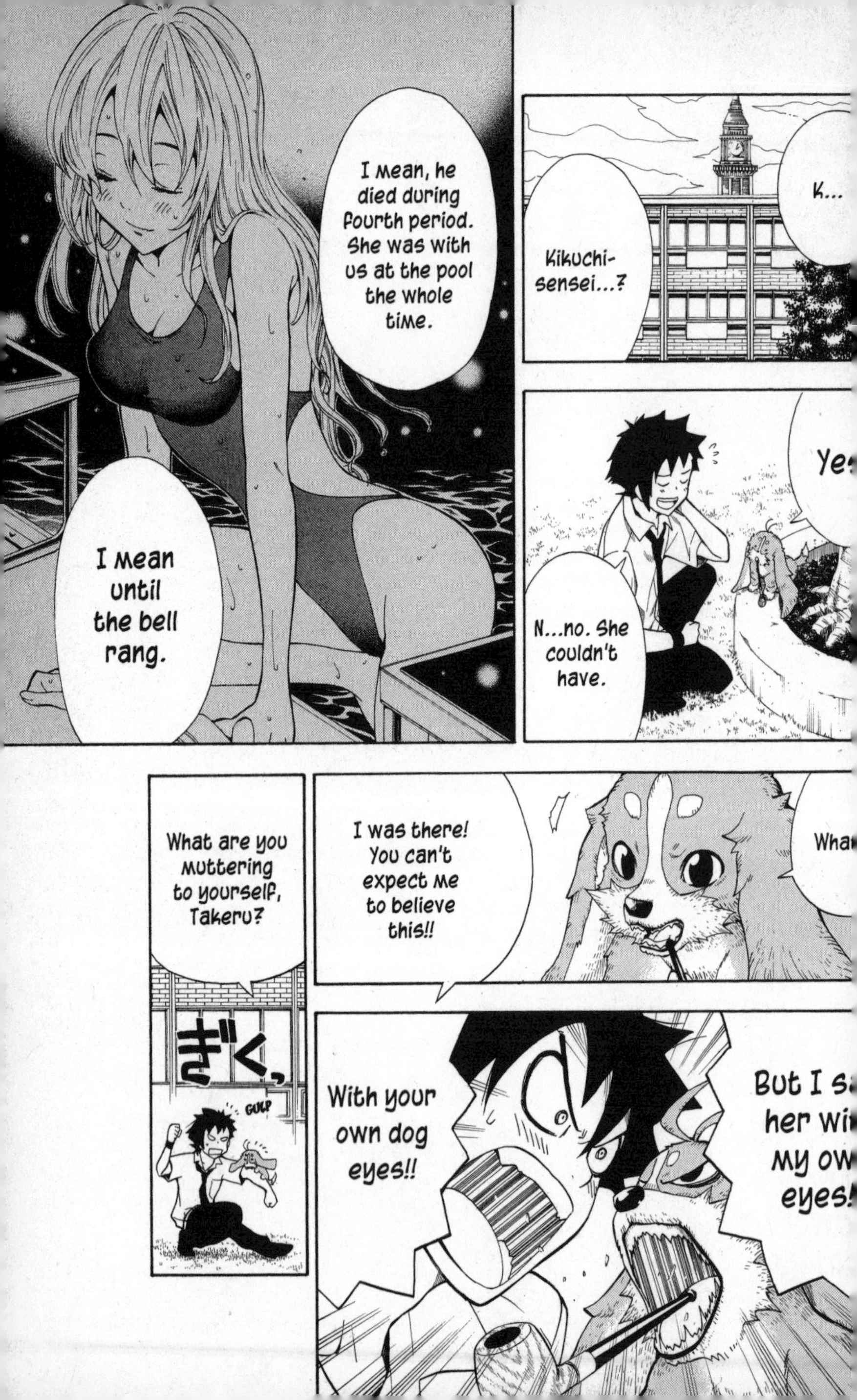
K...
Kikuchi-sensei...?
Ye
N...no. She couldn't have.
I mean, he died during fourth period. She was with us at the pool the whole time.
I mean until the bell rang.
Wha
I was there! You can't expect me to believe this!!
But I s her wi my ow eyes!
With your own dog eyes!!
What are you muttering to yourself, Takeru?
ぎく
GULP

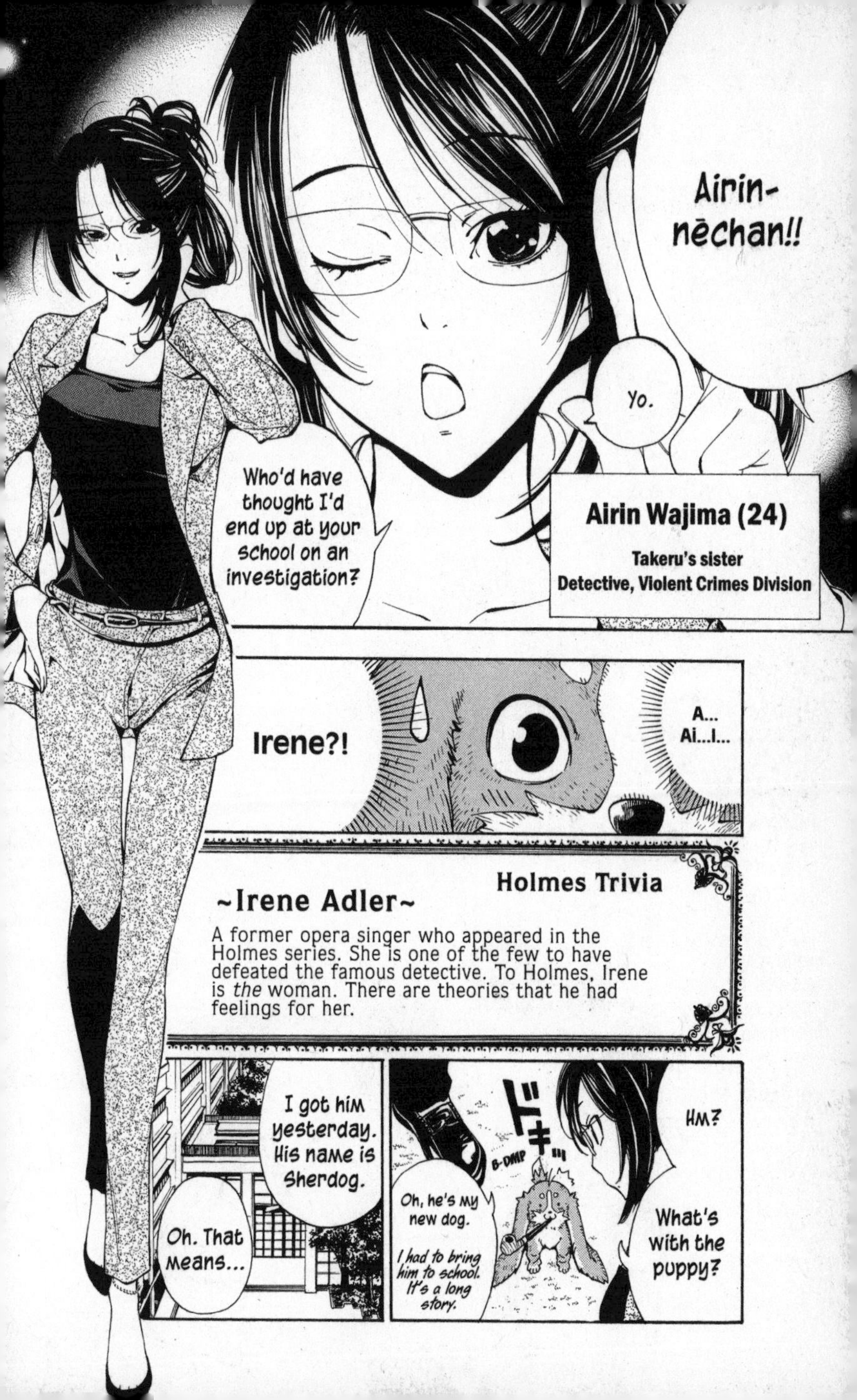
Airin-nēchan!!
Yo.
Who'd have thought I'd end up at your school on an investigation?
Airin Wajima (24)
Takeru's sister
Detective, Violent Crimes Division
A... Ai...I...
Irene?!
Holmes Trivia
~Irene Adler~
A former opera singer who appeared in the Holmes series. She is one of the few to have defeated the famous detective. To Holmes, Irene is *the* woman. There are theories that he had feelings for her.
Hm?
What's with the puppy?
B-DMP
Oh, he's my new dog.
I had to bring him to school. It's a long story.
I got him yesterday. His name is Sherdog.
Oh. That means...

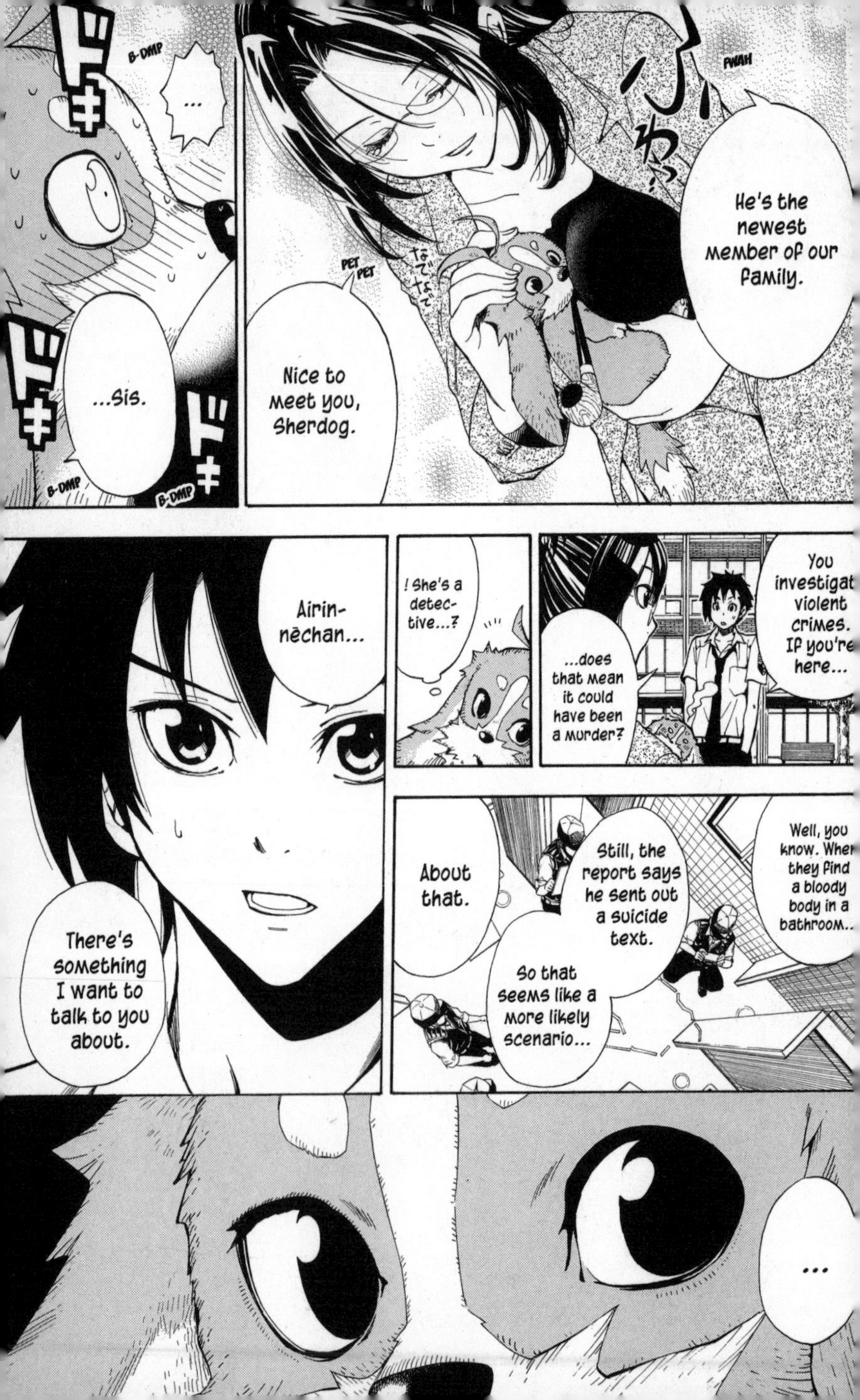
PWAH
ふわっ
He's the newest member of our family.
PET PET
なでなで
Nice to meet you, Sherdog.
B-DMP
ドキ
...
...Sis.
ドキ
B-DMP
ドキ
B-DMP
You investigat violent crimes. If you'r here...
...does that mean it could have been a murder?
! She's a detective...?
Well, you know. Whe they find a bloody body in a bathroom..
Still, the report says he sent out a suicide text.
About that.
So that seems like a more likely scenario...
Airin-nēchan...
There's something I want to talk to you about.
...

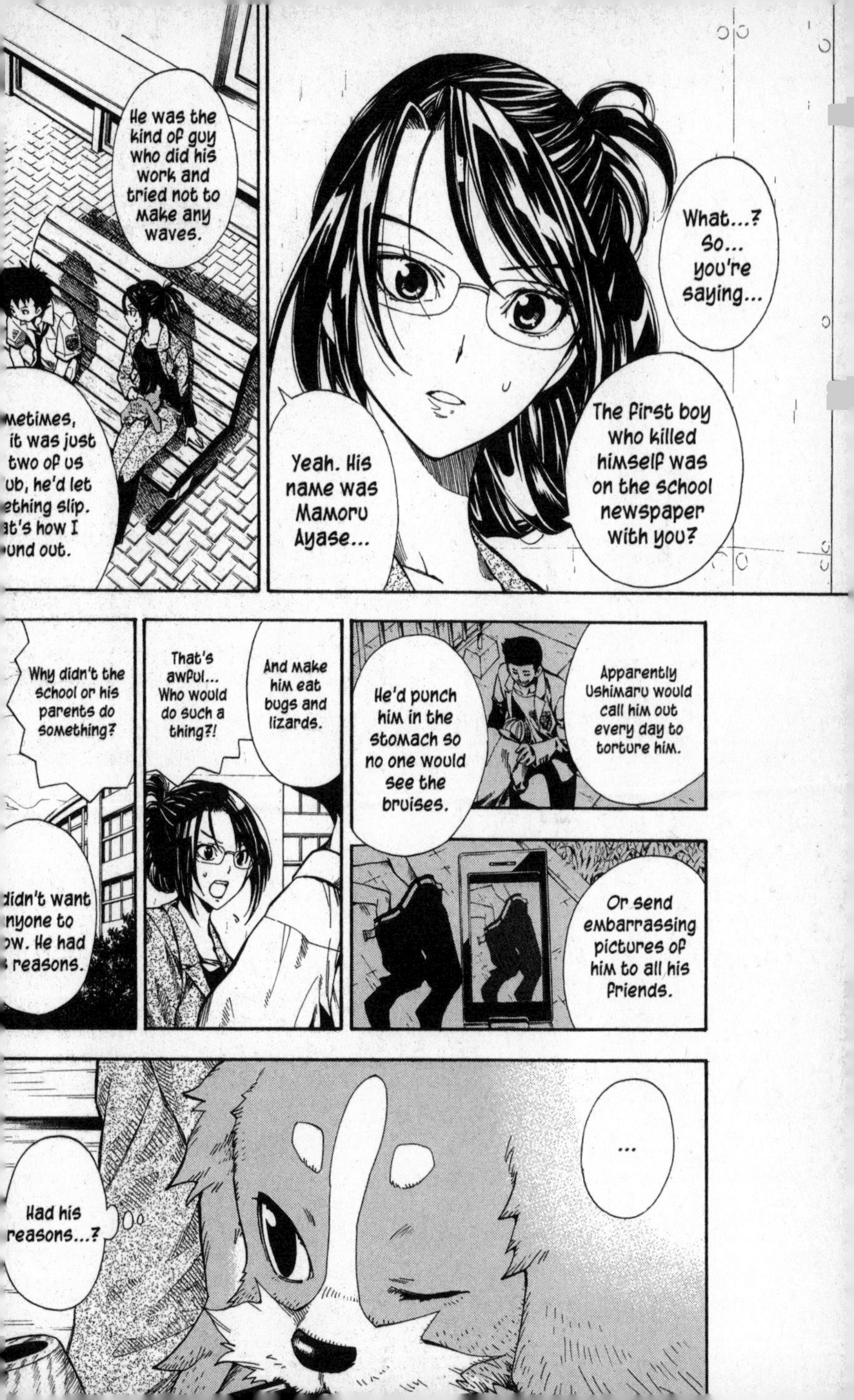
What...? So... you're saying...
The first boy who killed himself was on the school newspaper with you?
Yeah. His name was Mamoru Ayase...
He was the kind of guy who did his work and tried not to make any waves.
metimes, it was just two of us ub, he'd let ething slip. at's how I ound out.
Apparently Ushimaru would call him out every day to torture him.
He'd punch him in the stomach so no one would see the bruises.
Or send embarrassing pictures of him to all his friends.
And make him eat bugs and lizards.
That's awful... Who would do such a thing?!
Why didn't the school or his parents do something?
didn't want nyone to ow. He had reasons.
...
Had his reasons...?

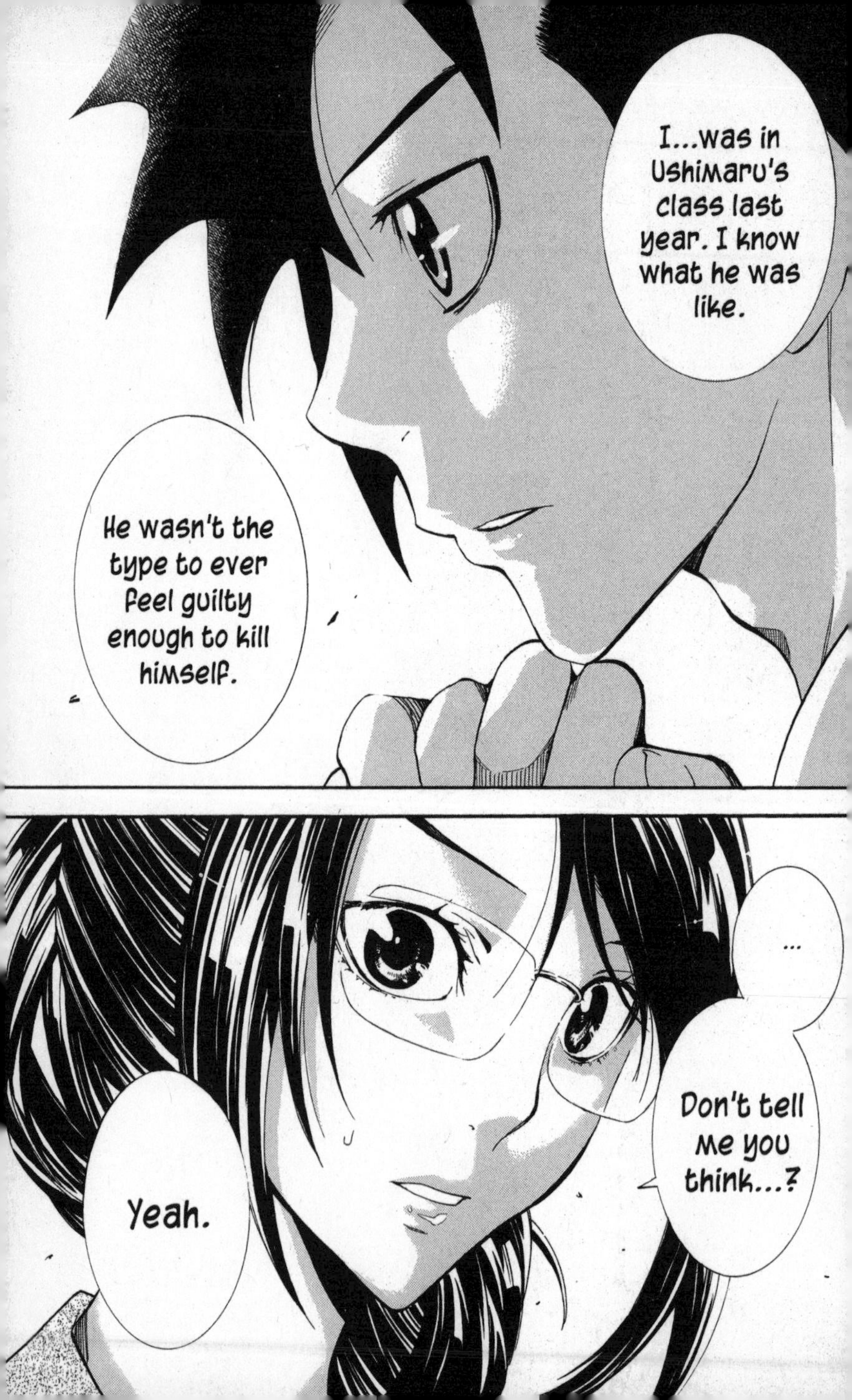
I...was in Ushimaru's class last year. I know what he was like.
He wasn't the type to ever feel guilty enough to kill himself.
...
Don't tell me you think...?
Yeah.

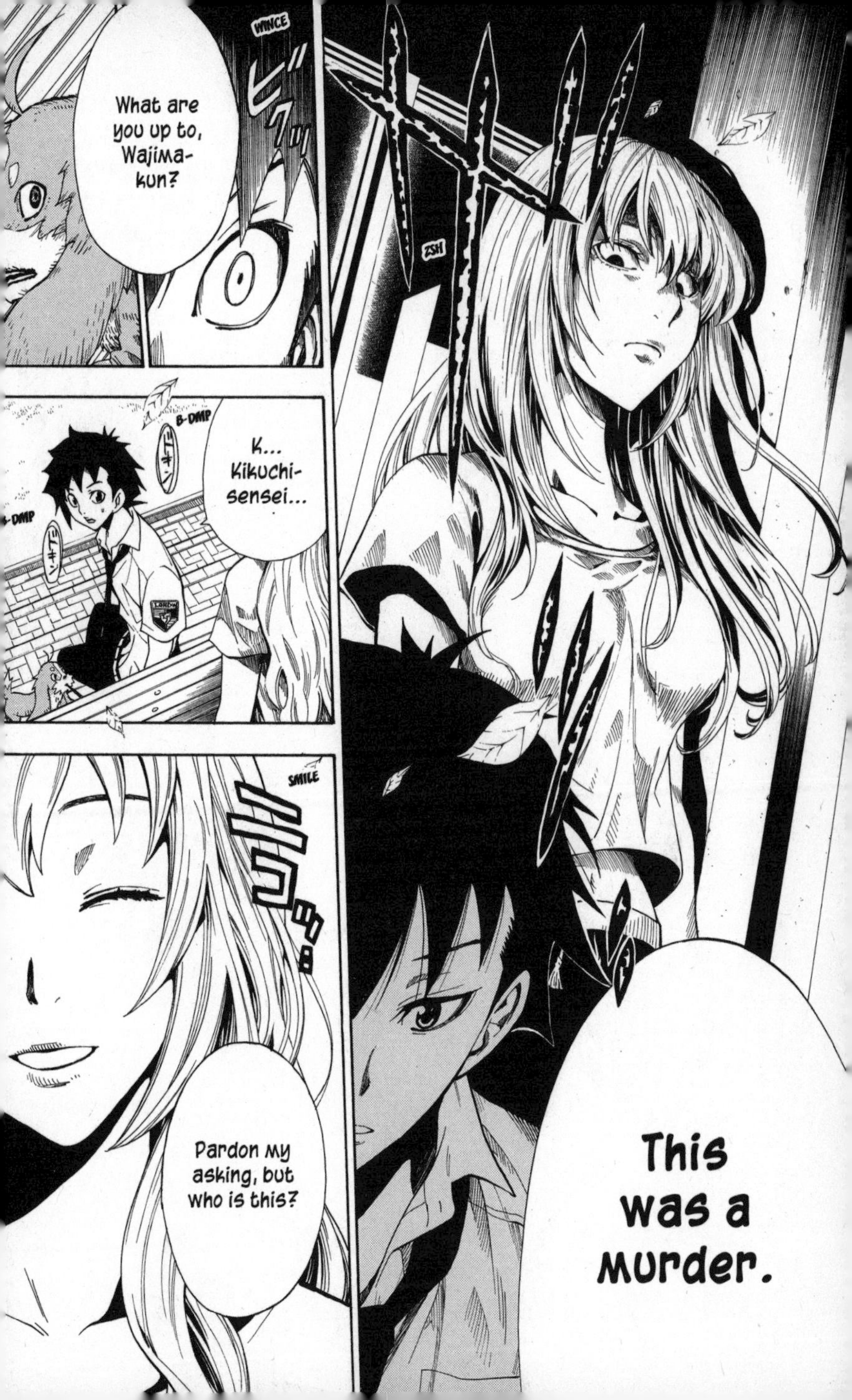
ZSH
This was a murder.
WINCE
What are you up to, Wajima-kun?
B-DMP
K... Kikuchi-sensei...
SMILE
Pardon my asking, but who is this?

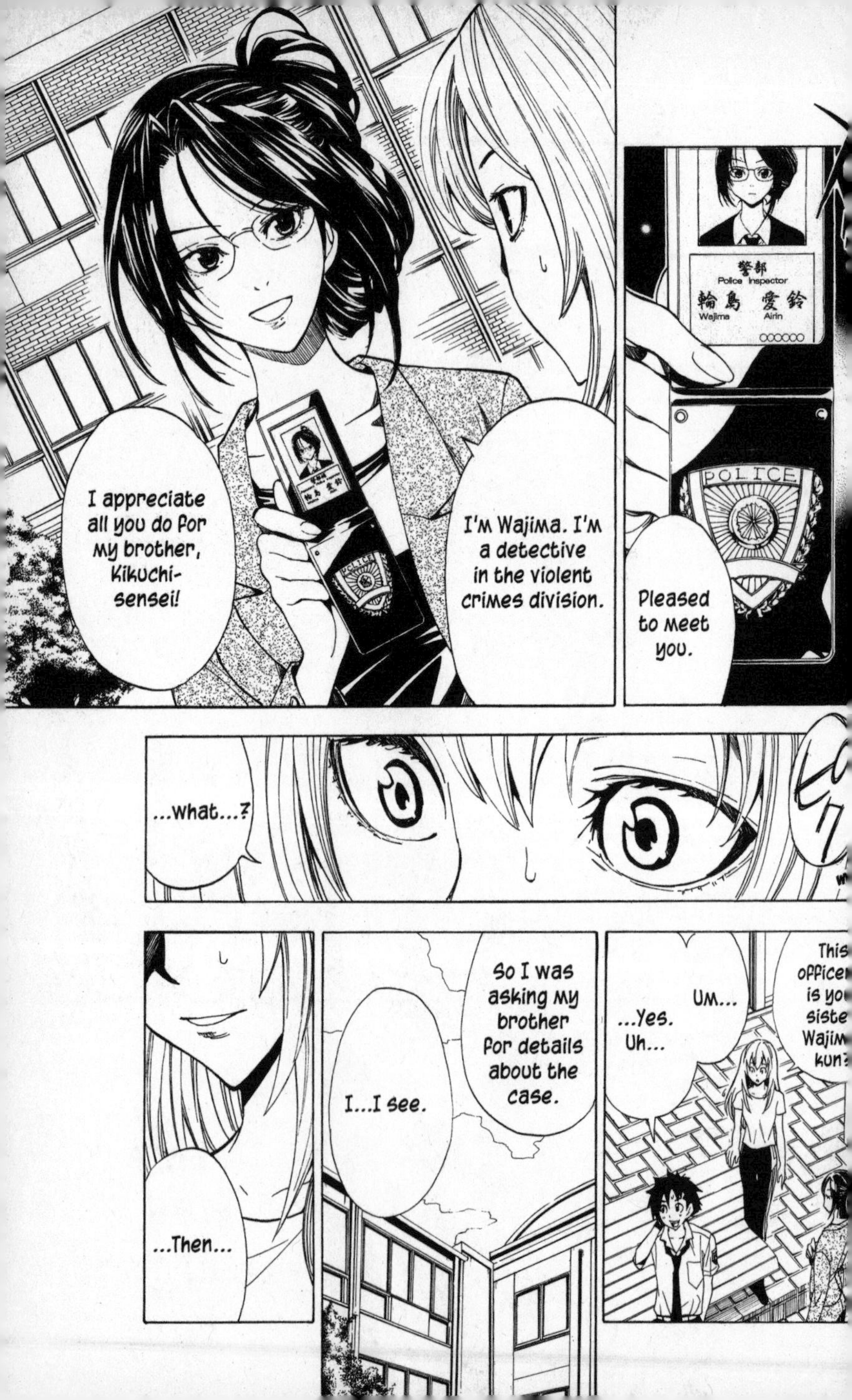
警部
Police Inspector
輪島 愛鈴
Wajima Airin
Pleased to meet you.
I'm Wajima. I'm a detective in the violent crimes division.
I appreciate all you do for my brother, Kikuchi-sensei!
...what...?
This office is yo siste Wajim kun
Um...
...Yes. Uh...
So I was asking my brother for details about the case.
I...I see.
...Then...

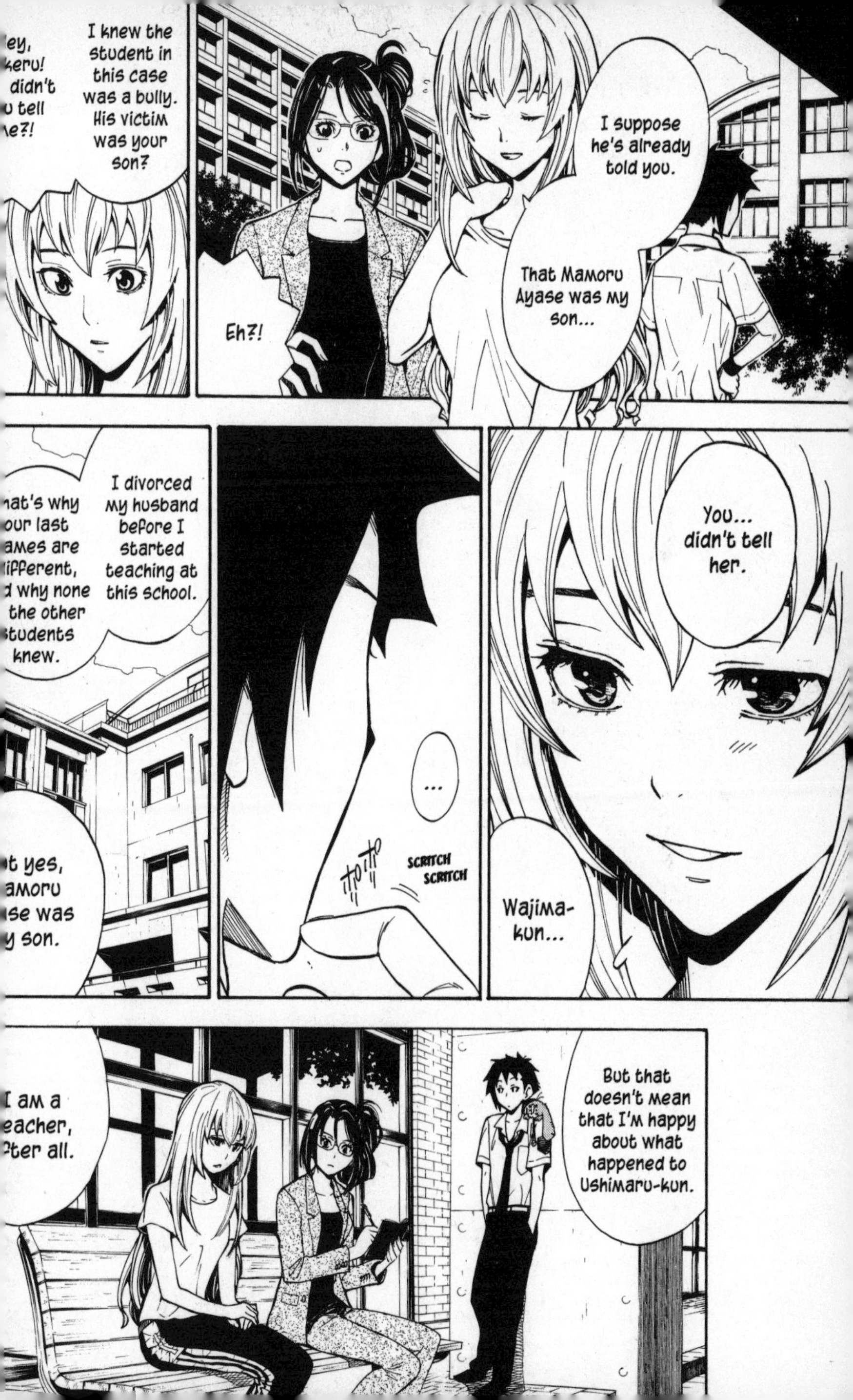

I suppose he's already told you.
That Mamoru Ayase was my son...
Eh?!
I knew the student in this case was a bully. His victim was your son?
ey, keru! didn't u tell e?!
You... didn't tell her.
Wajima-kun...
...
SCRITCH SCRITCH
I divorced my husband before I started teaching at this school.
hat's why our last ames are ifferent, d why none the other students knew.
t yes, amoru se was y son.
But that doesn't mean that I'm happy about what happened to Ushimaru-kun.
I am a eacher, fter all.

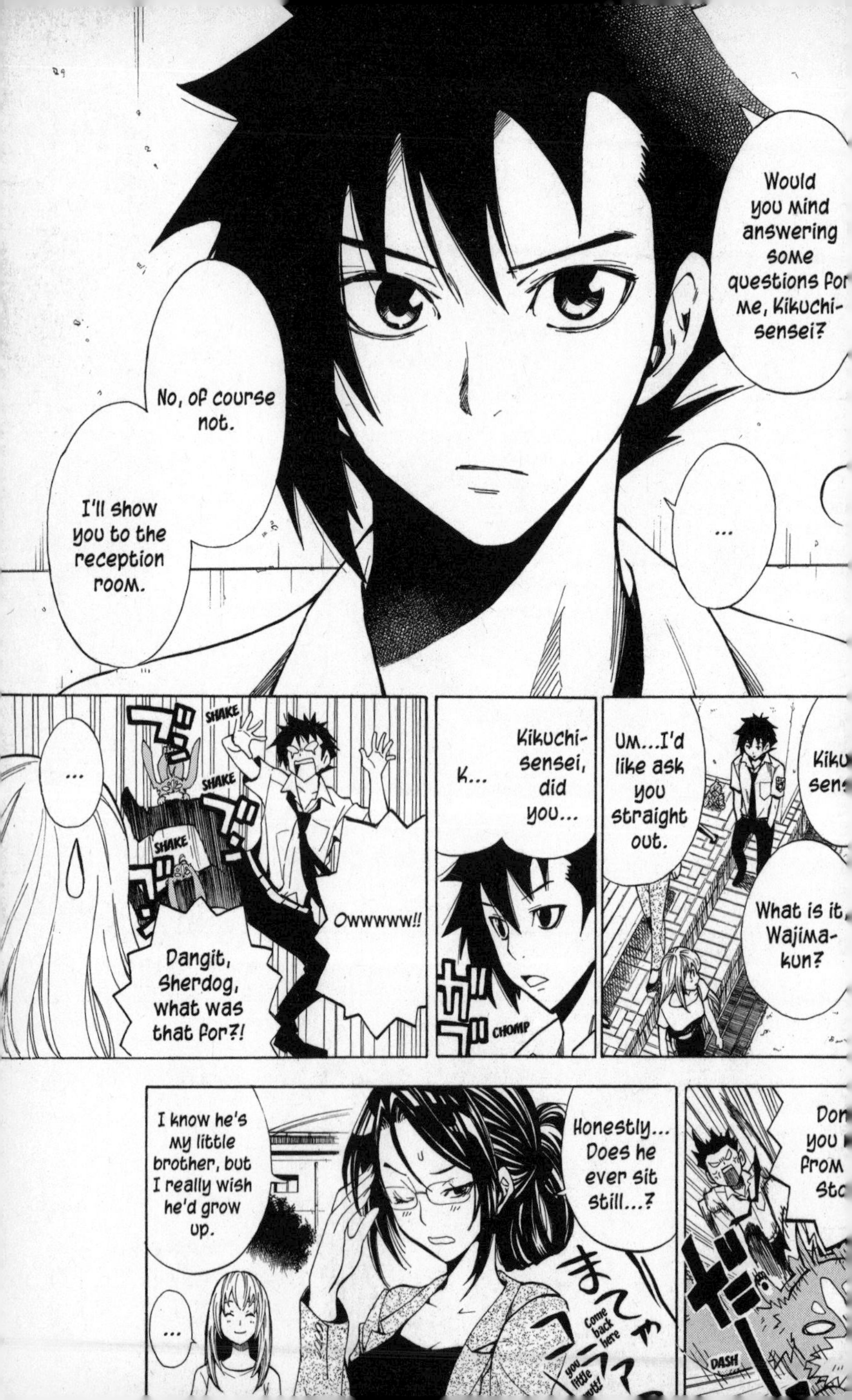

Would you mind answering some questions for me, Kikuchi-sensei?
...
No, of course not.
I'll show you to the reception room.
Kiku sen
What is it, Wajima-kun?
Um...I'd like ask you straight out.
Kikuchi-sensei, did you...
K...
CHOMP
SHAKE
SHAKE
SHAKE
Owwwww!!
Dangit, Sherdog, what was that for?!
...
Don you from Sto
DASH
Honestly... Does he ever sit still...?
Come back here you little mutt!
I know he's my little brother, but I really wish he'd grow up.
...

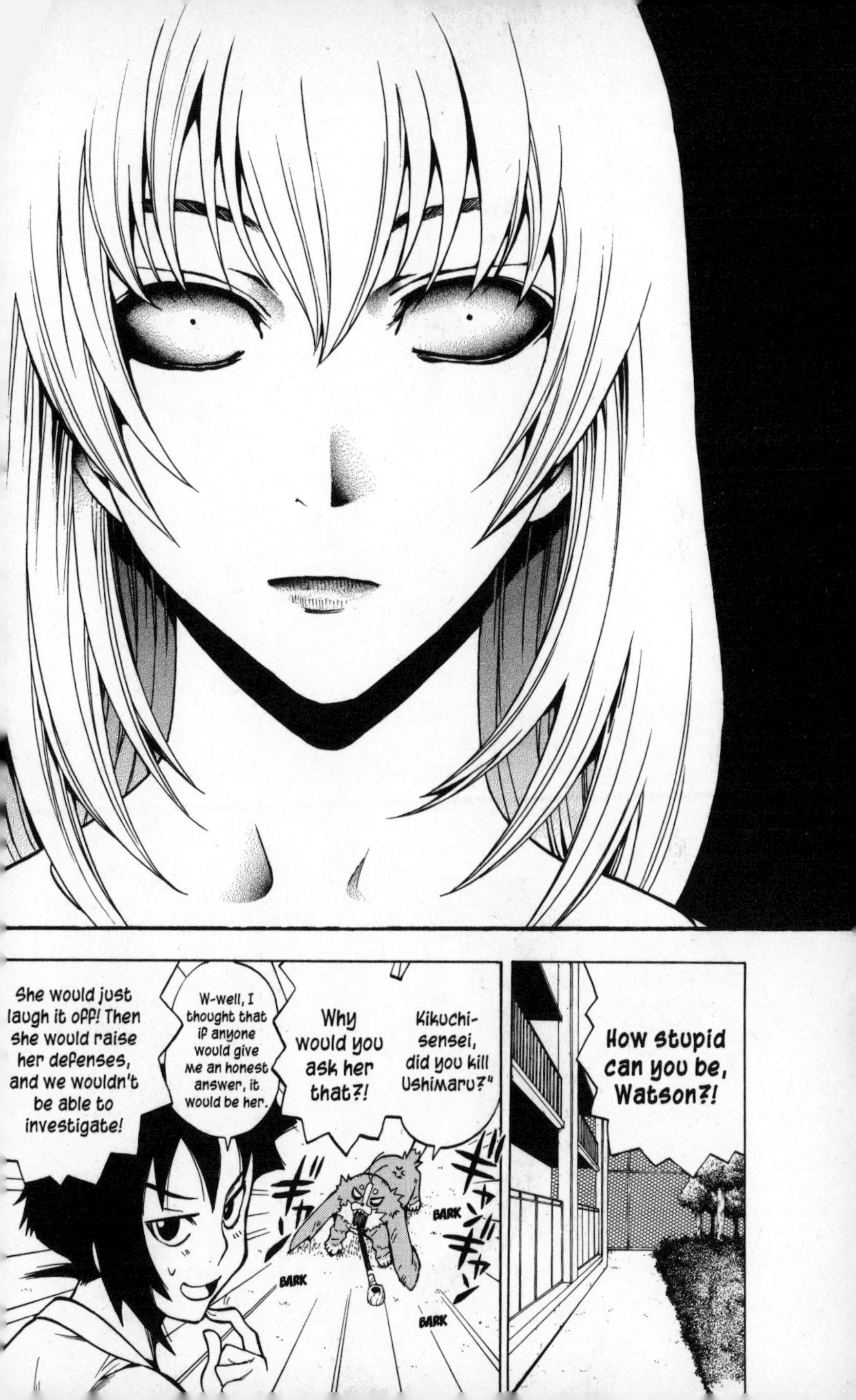
How stupid can you be, Watson?!
Kikuchi-sensei, did you kill Ushimaru?"
Why would you ask her that?!
W-well, I thought that if anyone would give me an honest answer, it would be her.
She would just laugh it off! Then she would raise her defenses, and we wouldn't be able to investigate!
BARK
BARK
BARK

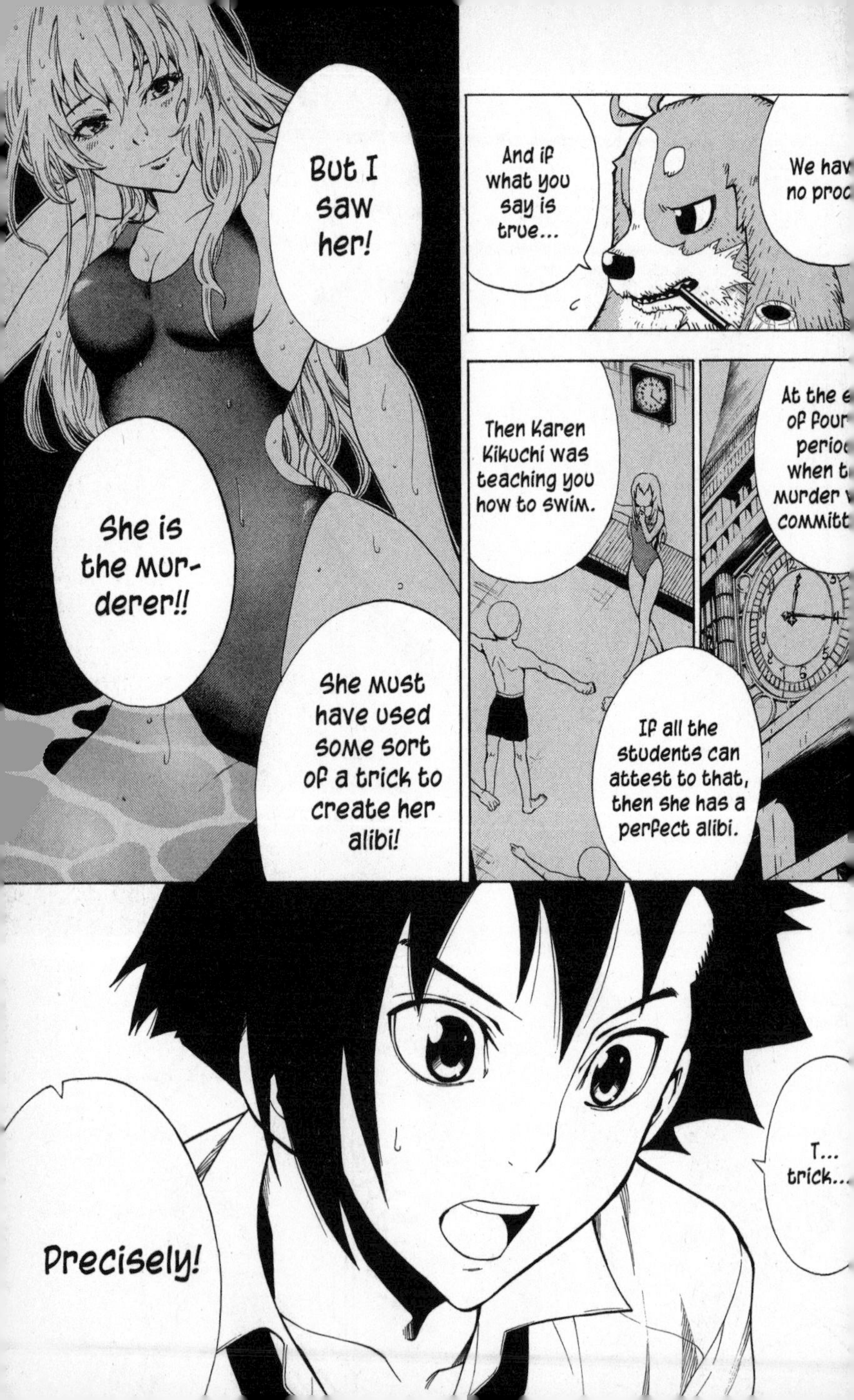

We hav no proc
And if what you say is true...
At the e of four perio when t murder w committ
Then Karen Kikuchi was teaching you how to swim.
If all the students can attest to that, then she has a perfect alibi.
But I saw her!
She is the mur-derer!!
She must have used some sort of a trick to create her alibi!
T... trick...
Precisely!

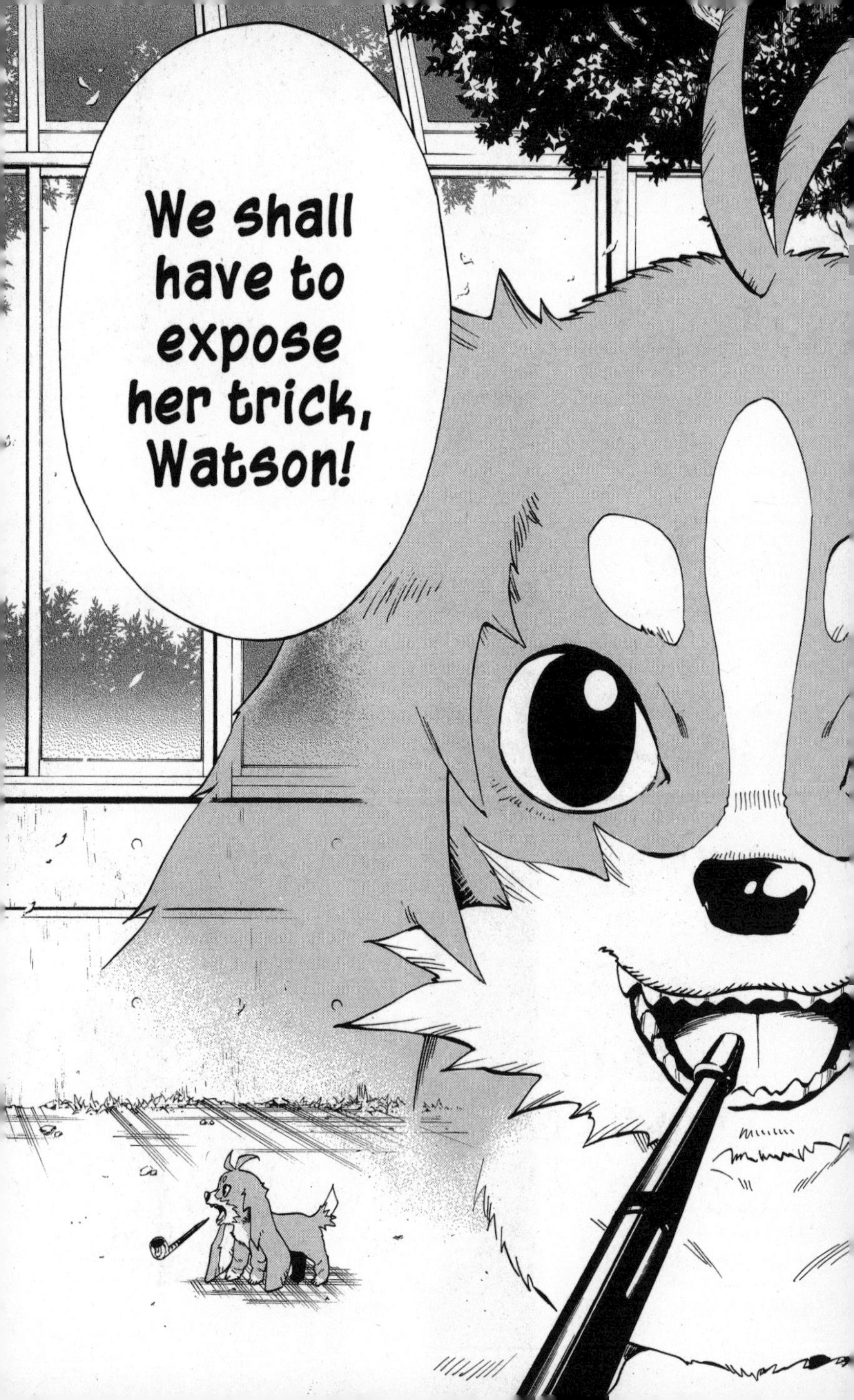
We shall have to expose her trick, Watson!

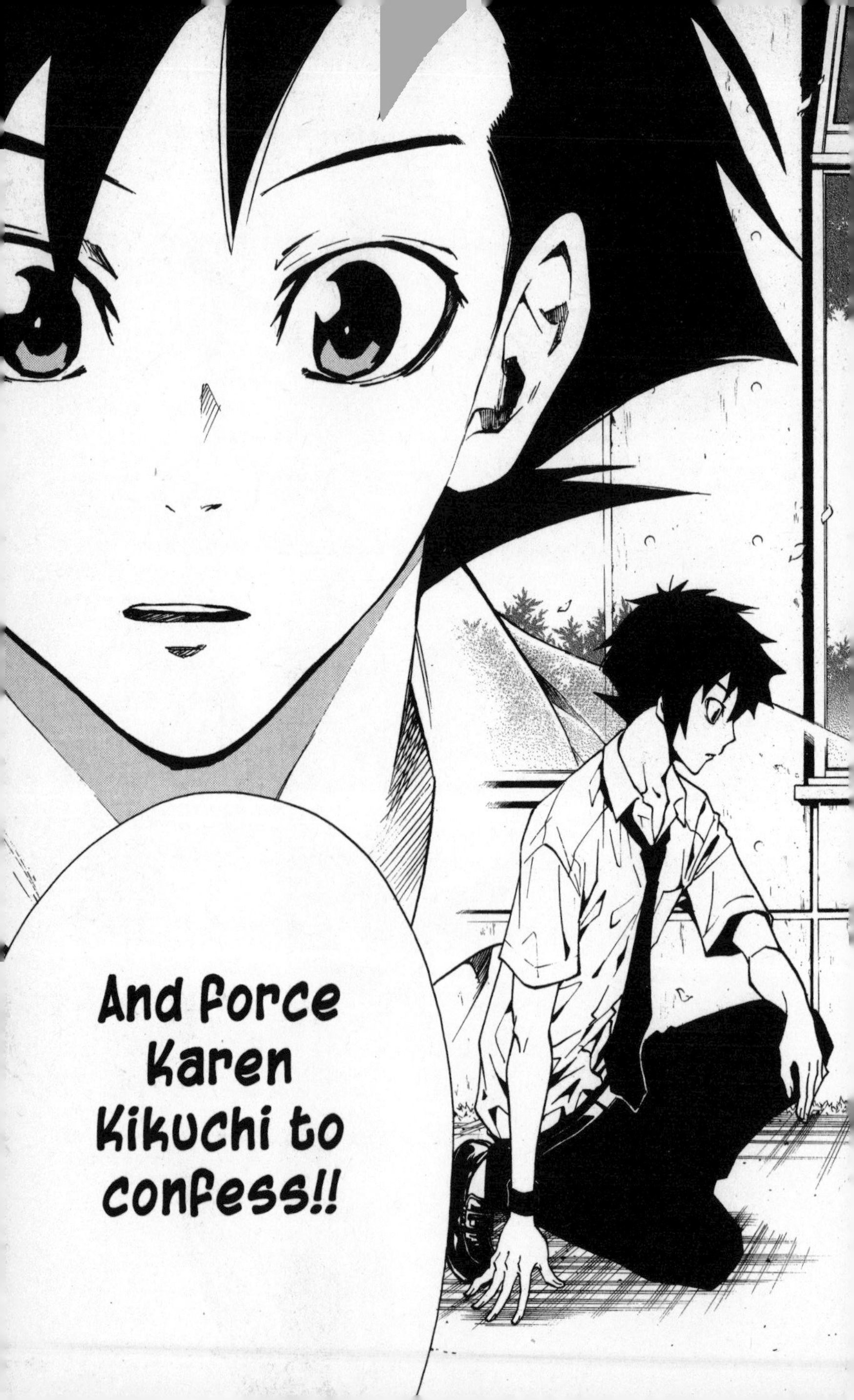
And force Karen Kikuchi to confess!!

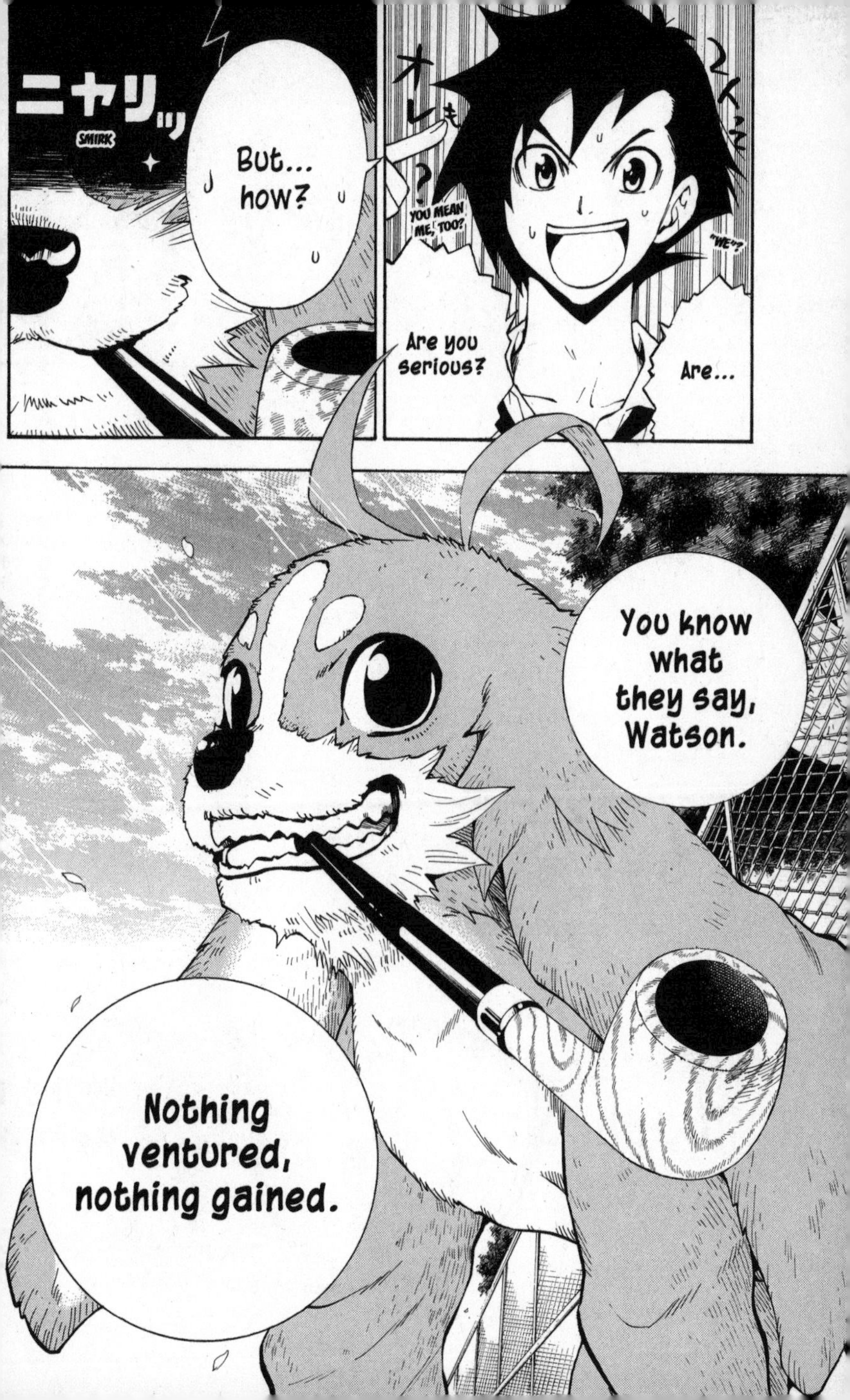
"WE"?
YOU MEAN ME, TOO?
Are...
Are you serious?
ニヤリッ
SMIRK
But... how?
You know what they say, Watson.
Nothing ventured, nothing gained.

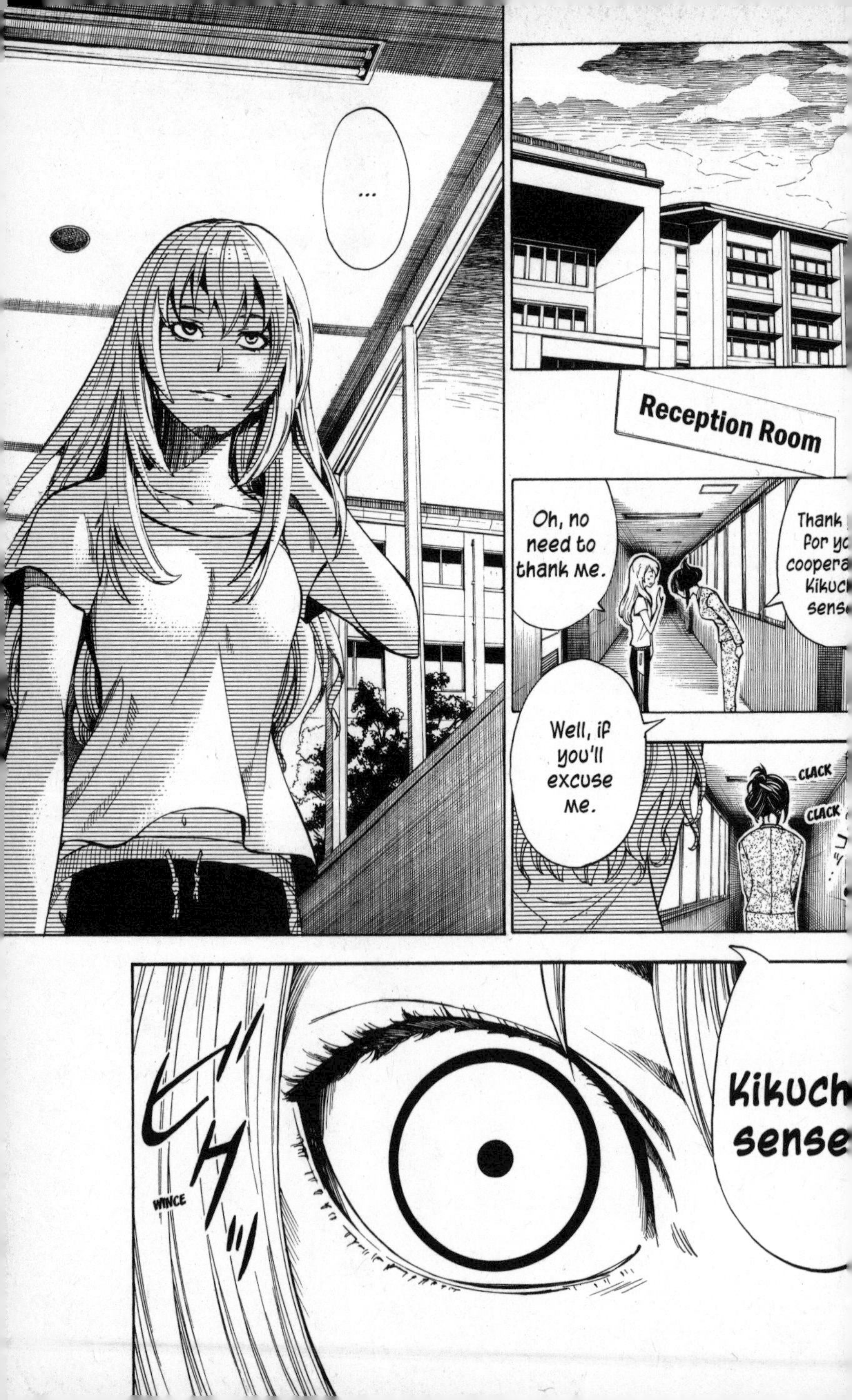
Reception Room
Thank for yo coopera Kikuch sens
Oh, no need to thank me.
Well, if you'll excuse me.
CLACK
CLACK
...
Kikuch sense
WINCE

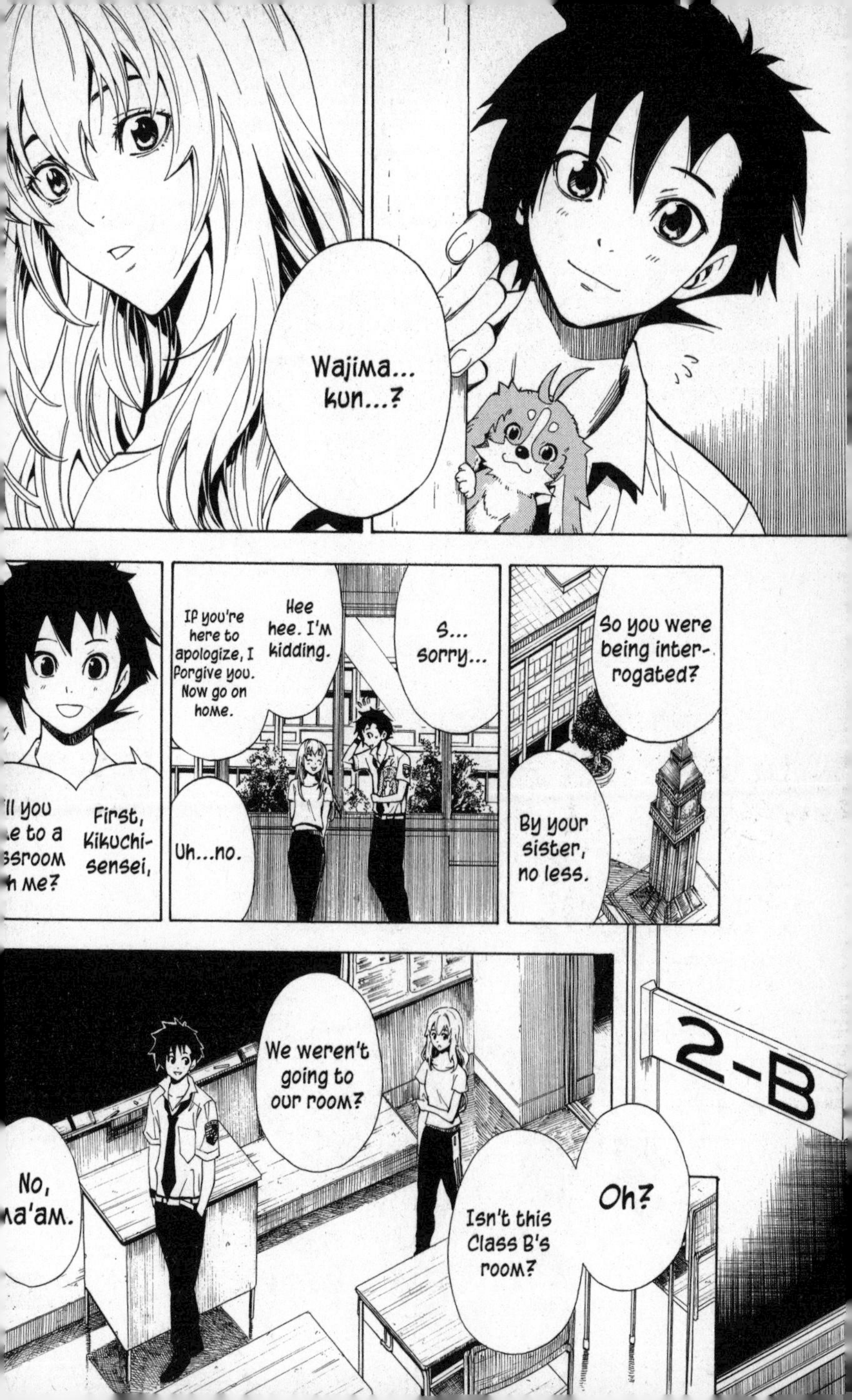

Wajima... kun...?
So you were being inter-rogated?
By your sister, no less.
S... sorry...
Hee hee. I'm kidding.
If you're here to apologize, I forgive you. Now go on home.
Uh...no.
First, Kikuchi-sensei,
ll you e to a ssroom h me?
2-B
Oh?
Isn't this Class B's room?
We weren't going to our room?
No, a'am.

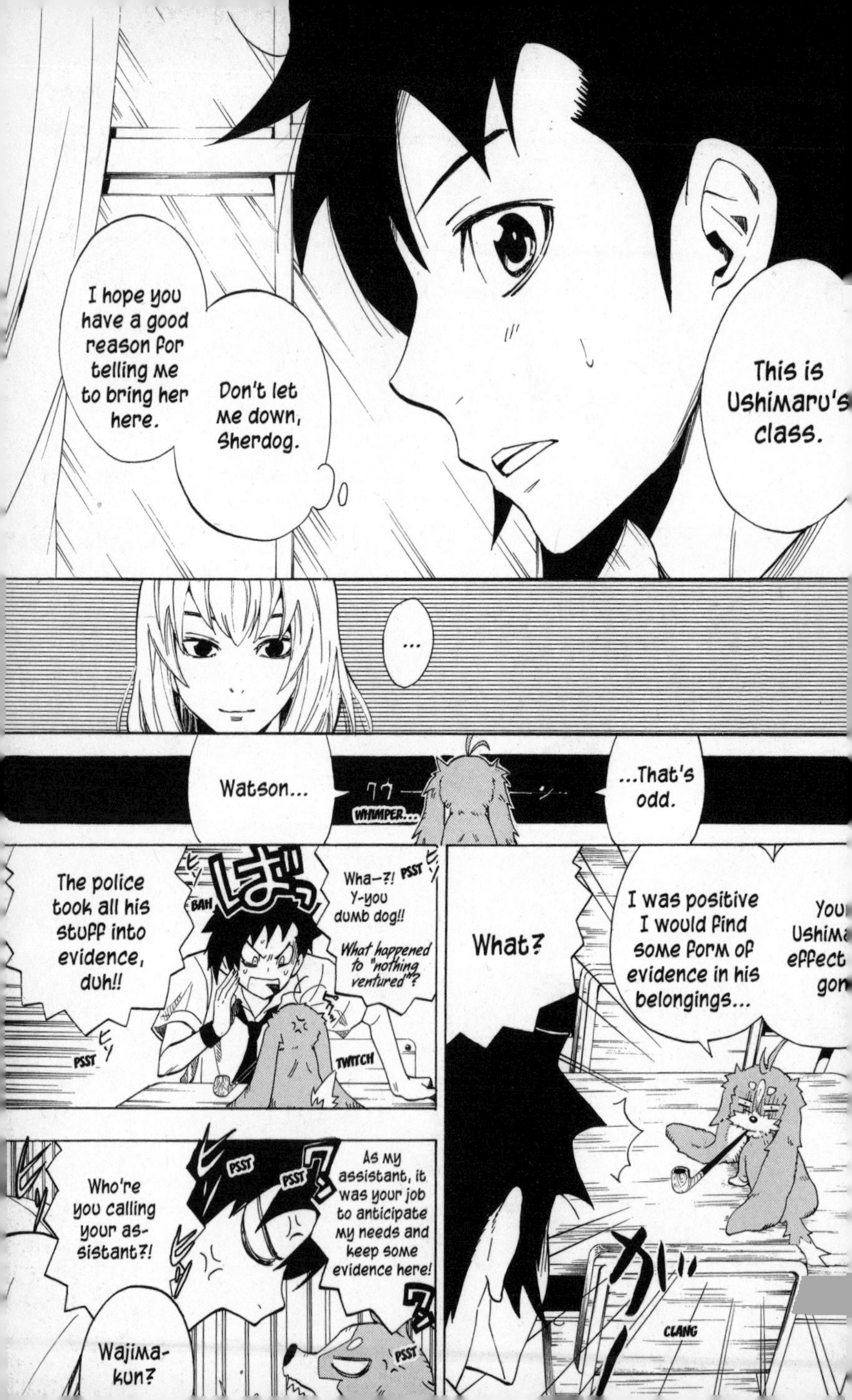

This is Ushimaru's class.
Don't let me down, Sherdog.
I hope you have a good reason for telling me to bring her here.
...
...That's odd.
WHIMPER...
Watson...
You Ushima effect gon
I was positive I would find some form of evidence in his belongings...
What?
CLANG
PSST
Wha-?! Y-you dumb dog!!
What happened to "nothing ventured"?
BAH
The police took all his stuff into evidence, duh!!
TWITCH
PSST
As my assistant, it was your job to anticipate my needs and keep some evidence here!
PSST
PSST
Who're you calling your as-sistant?!
PSST
Wajima-kun?

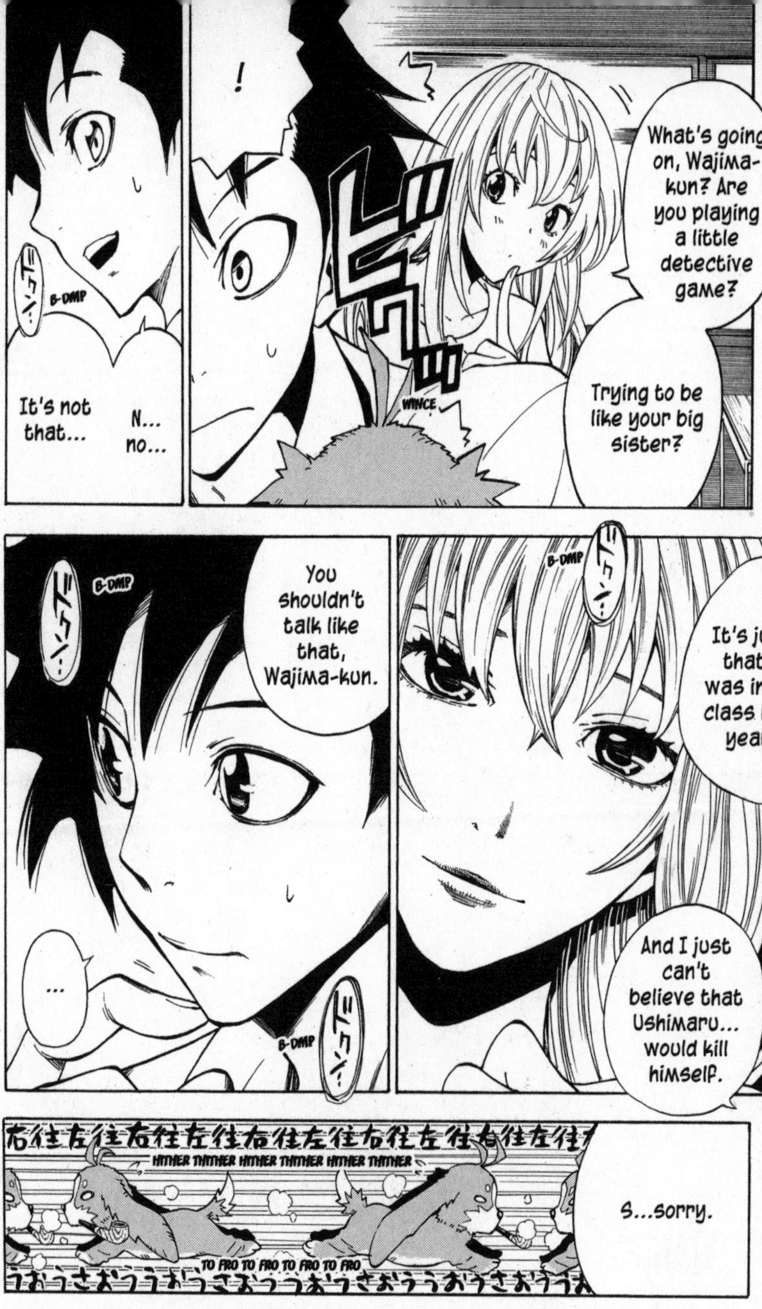
!
What's going on, Wajima-kun? Are you playing a little detective game?
WINCE
Trying to be like your big sister?
B-DMP
N... no...
It's not that...
B-DMP
It's just that I was in his class last year.
And I just can't believe that Ushimaru... would kill himself.
B-DMP
You shouldn't talk like that, Wajima-kun.
...
B-DMP
S...sorry.
HITHER THITHER HITHER THITHER HITHER THITHER
TO FRO TO FRO TO FRO TO FRO

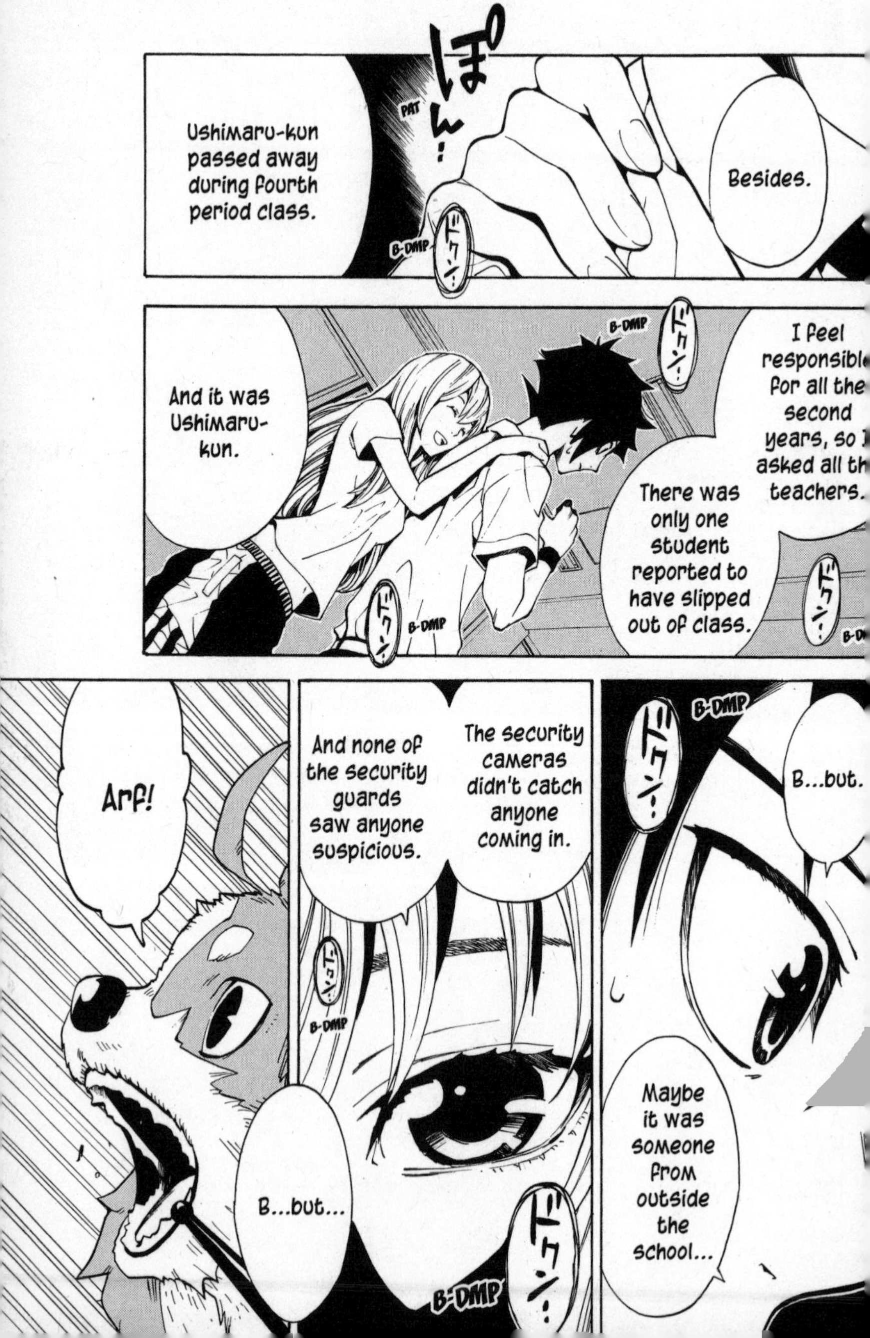

Besides.
PAT
B-DMP
Ushimaru-kun passed away during fourth period class.
I feel responsibl for all the second years, so I asked all th teachers.
B-DMP
There was only one student reported to have slipped out of class.
And it was Ushimaru-kun.
B-DMP
B...but.
B-DMP
Maybe it was someone from outside the school...
The security cameras didn't catch anyone coming in.
And none of the security guards saw anyone suspicious.
B-DMP
B...but...
B-DMP
Arf!

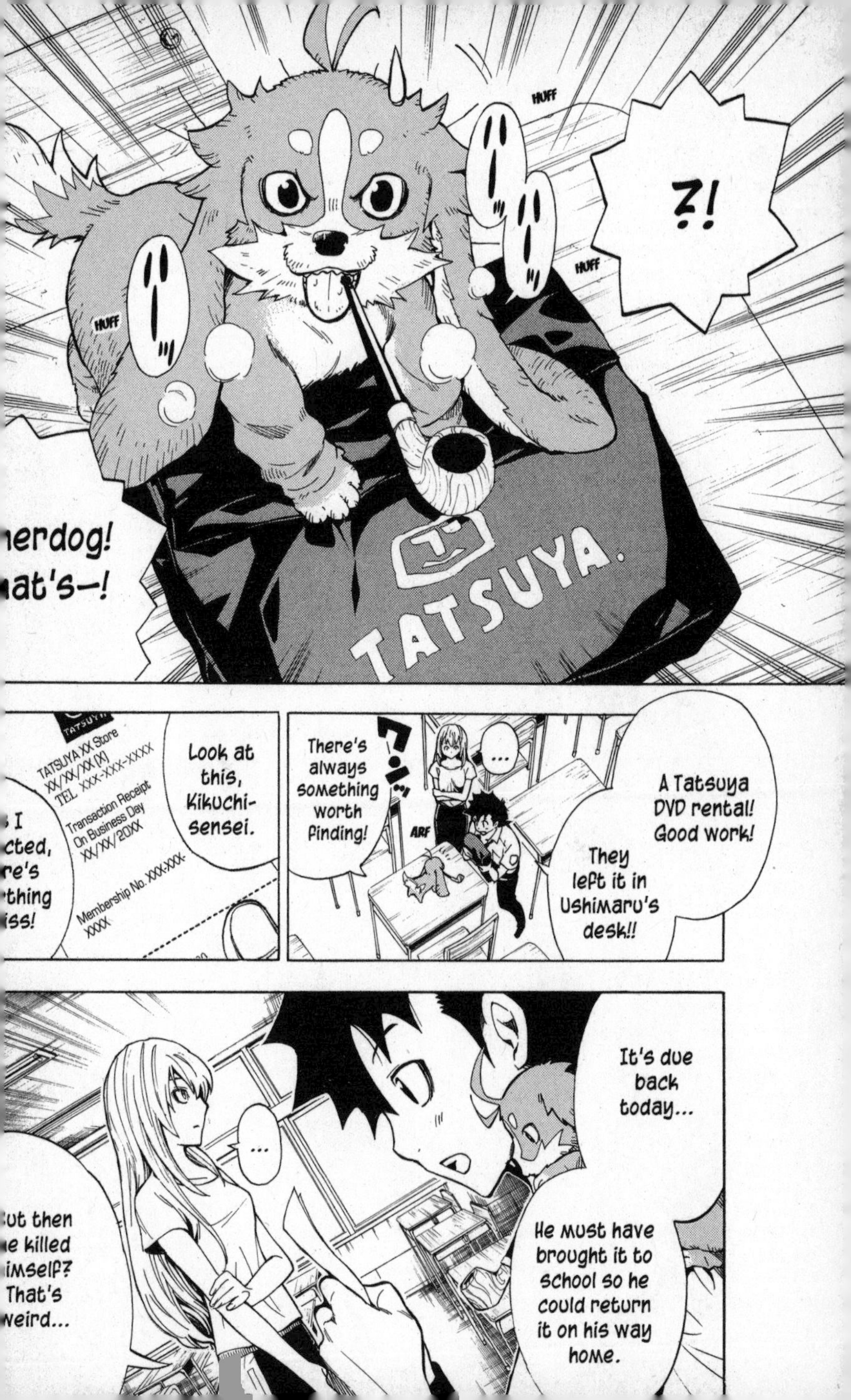
?!
HUFF
HUFF
HUFF
erdog!
at's—!
A Tatsuya DVD rental! Good work!
They left it in Ushimaru's desk!!
...
There's always something worth finding!
ARF
Look at this, Kikuchi-sensei.
TATSUYA
TATSUYA XX Store
XX/XX/XX (X)
TEL XXX-XXX-XXXX
Transaction Receipt
On Business Day
XX/XX/20XX
Membership No. XXX-XXX-XXXX
It's due back today...
He must have brought it to school so he could return it on his way home.
...
That's

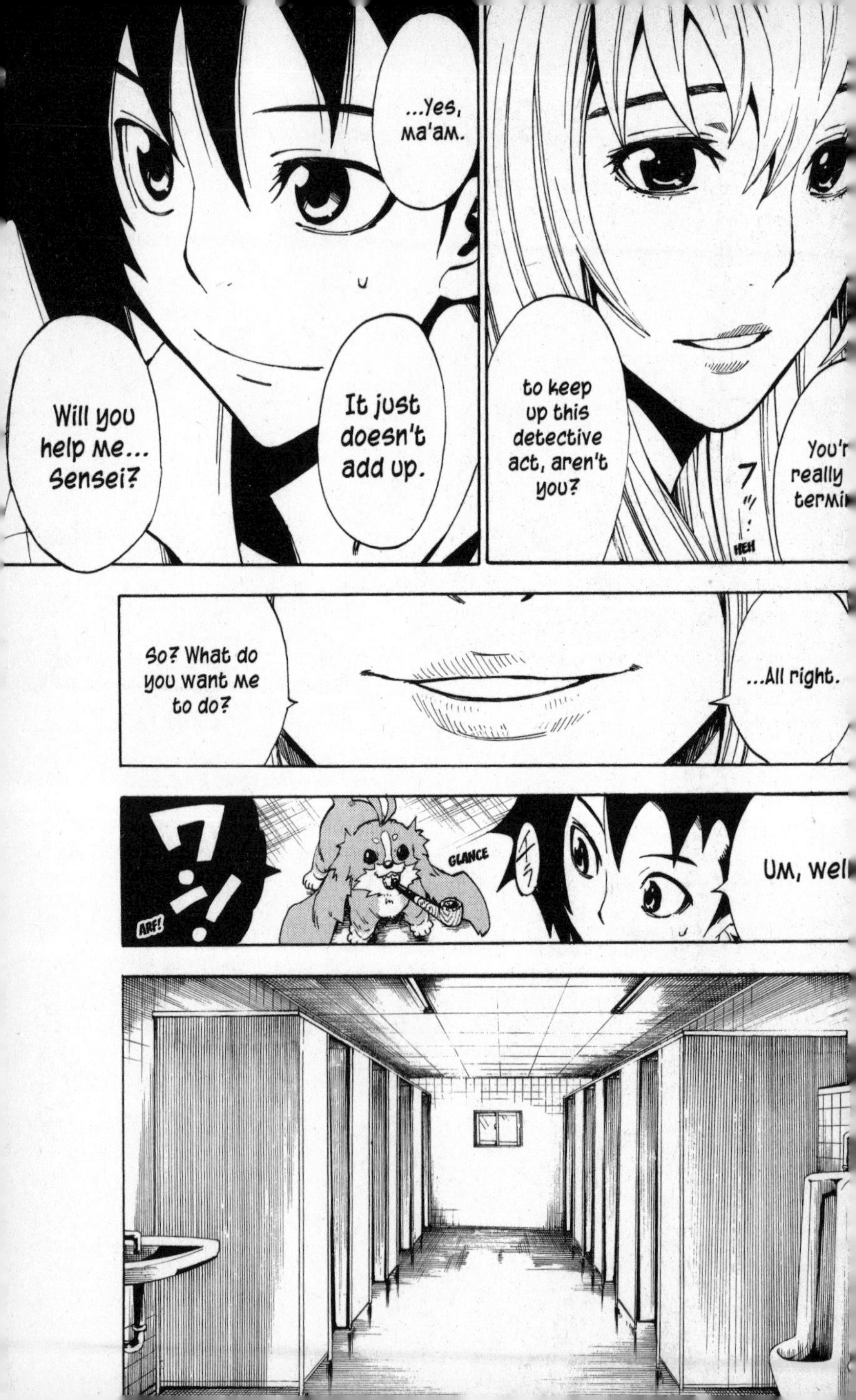
You'r really termi
HEH
to keep up this detective act, aren't you?
...Yes, ma'am.
It just doesn't add up.
Will you help me... Sensei?
...All right.
So? What do you want me to do?
Um, well
GLANCE
ARF!

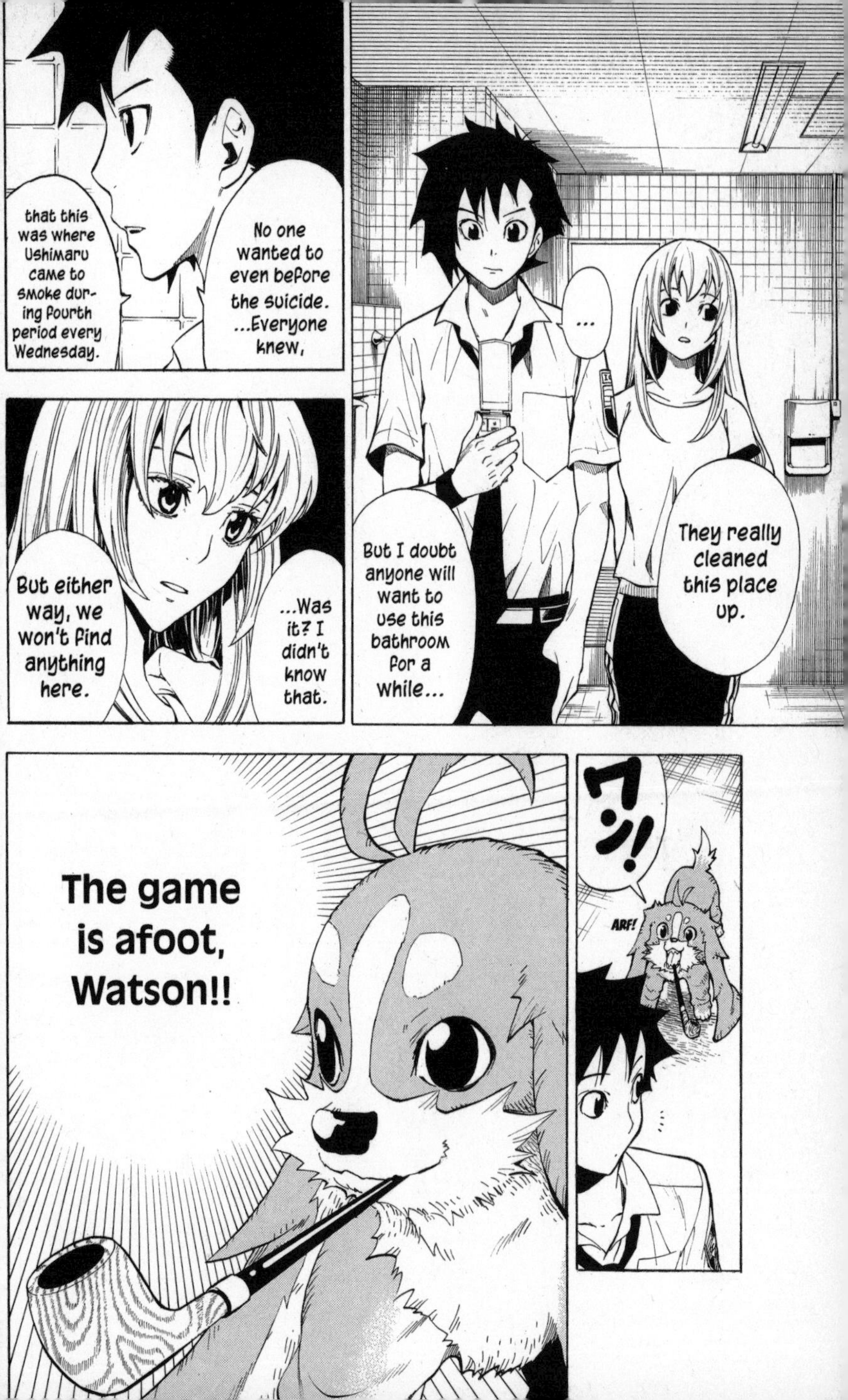
...
They really cleaned this place up.
But I doubt anyone will want to use this bathroom for a while...
No one wanted to even before the suicide. ...Everyone knew,
that this was where Ushimaru came to smoke during fourth period every Wednesday.
...Was it? I didn't know that.
But either way, we won't find anything here.
ワン!
ARF!
The game is afoot, Watson!!

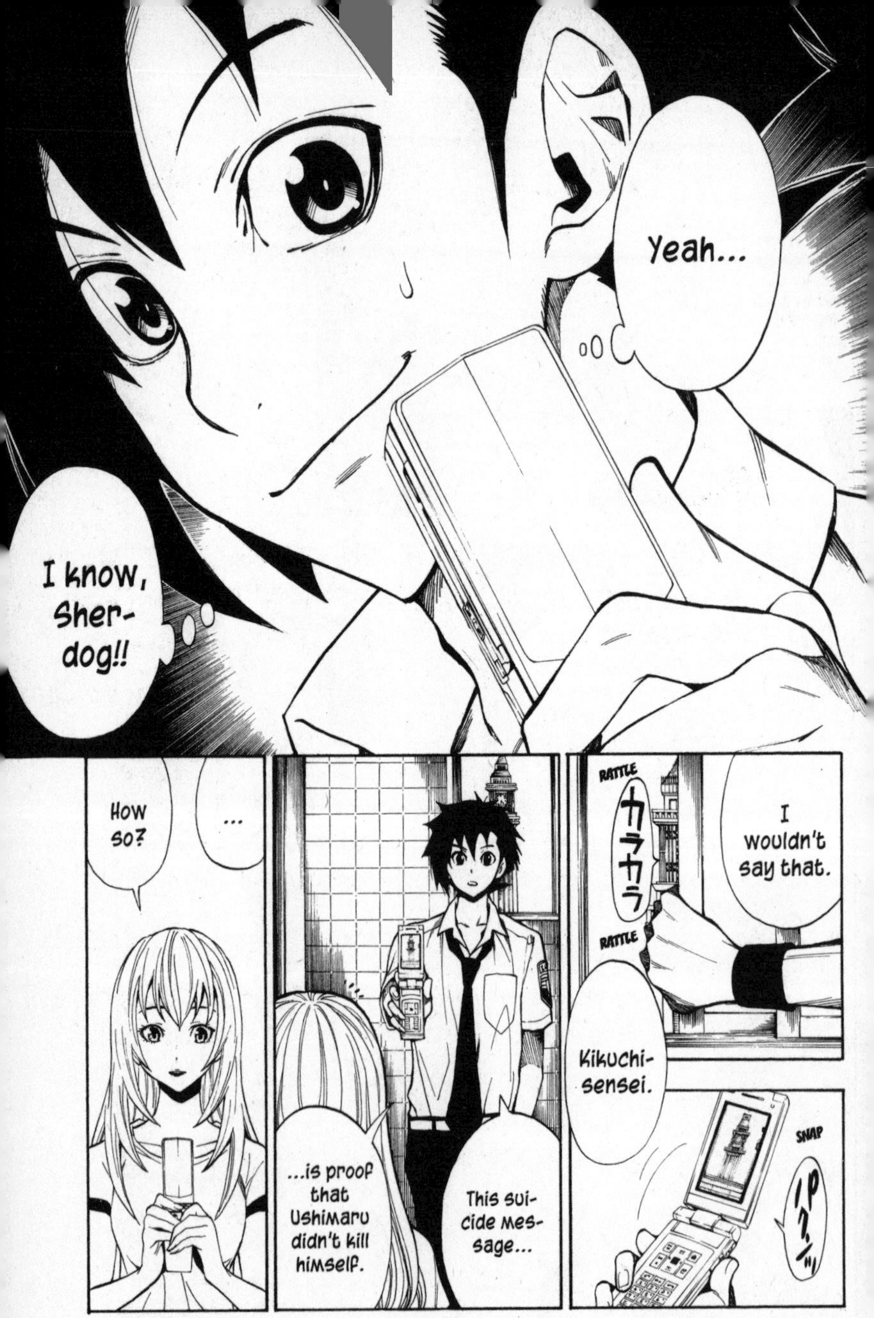
Yeah...
I know, Sher-dog!!
I wouldn't say that.
RATTLE
カラカラ
RATTLE
Kikuchi-sensei.
SNAP
This suicide message...
...is proof that Ushimaru didn't kill himself.
...
How so?

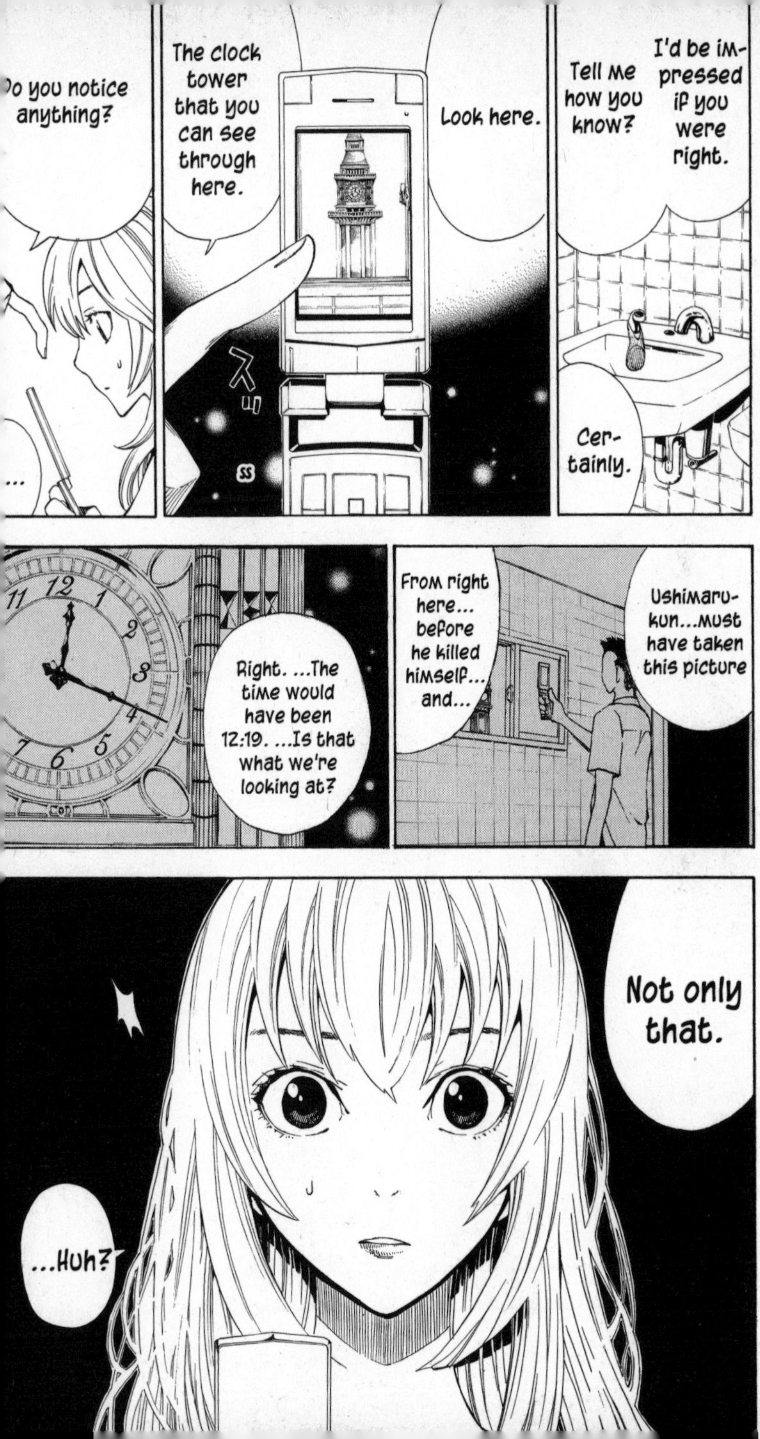
I'd be impressed if you were right.
Tell me how you know?
Certainly.
Look here.
The clock tower that you can see through here.
スッ
ss
Do you notice anything?
...
Ushimaru-kun...must have taken this picture
From right here... before he killed himself... and...
Right. ...The time would have been 12:19. ...Is that what we're looking at?
Not only that.
...Huh?

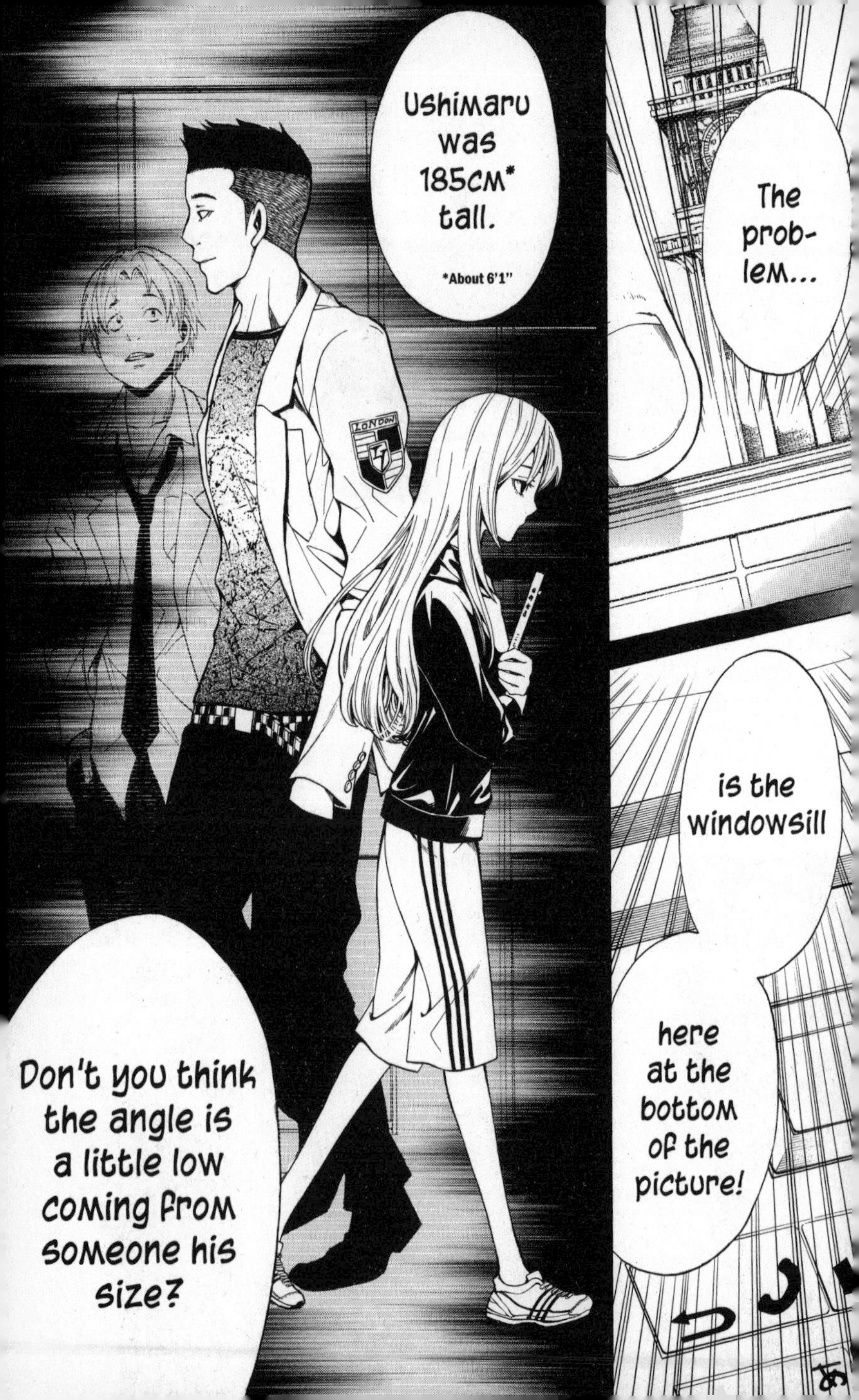
The prob-lem...
is the windowsill
here at the bottom of the picture!
Ushimaru was 185cm* tall.
*About 6'1"
Don't you think the angle is a little low coming from someone his size?

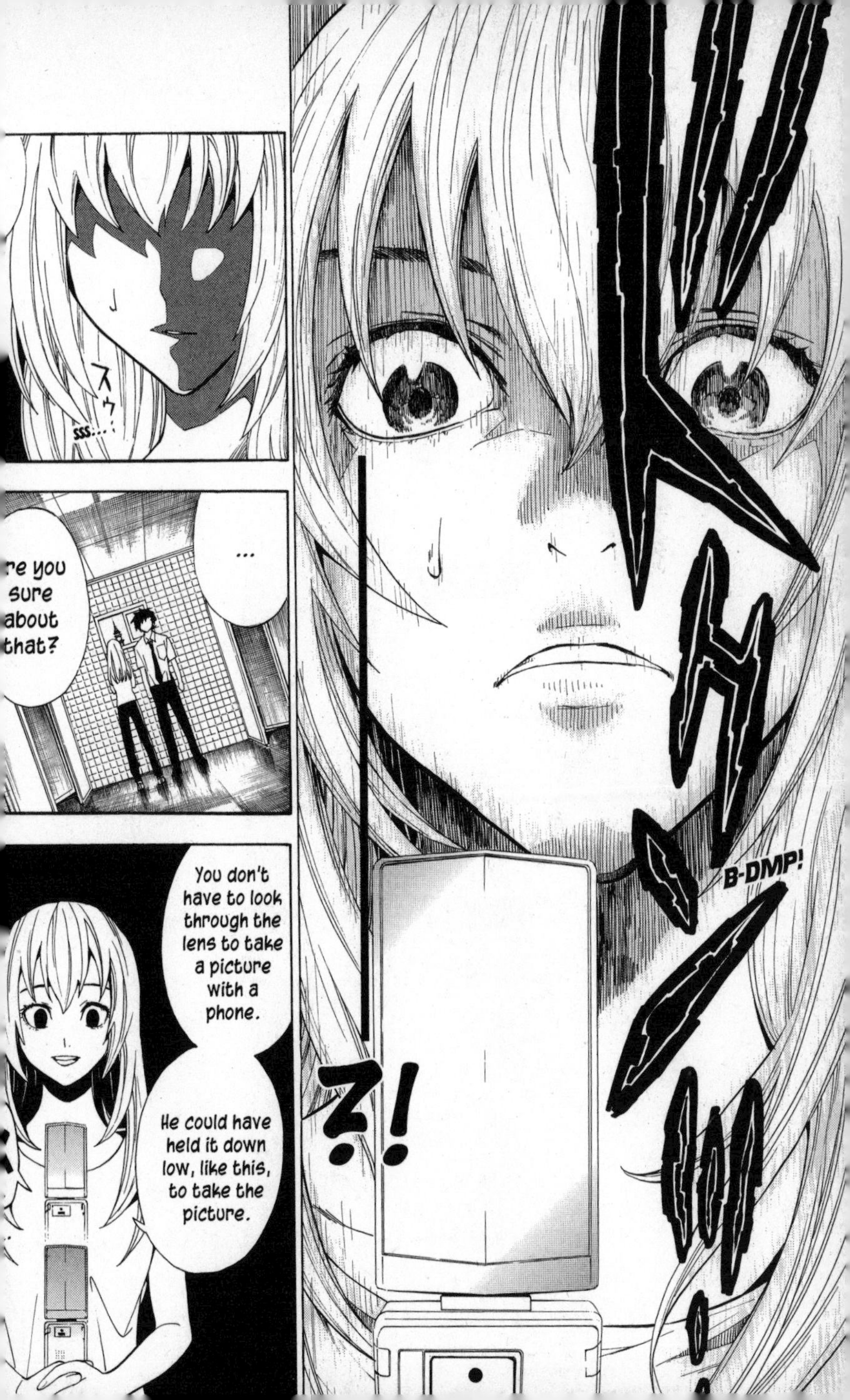
B-DMP!
?!
スゥ
SSS...
...
re you sure about that?
You don't have to look through the lens to take a picture with a phone.
He could have held it down low, like this, to take the picture.

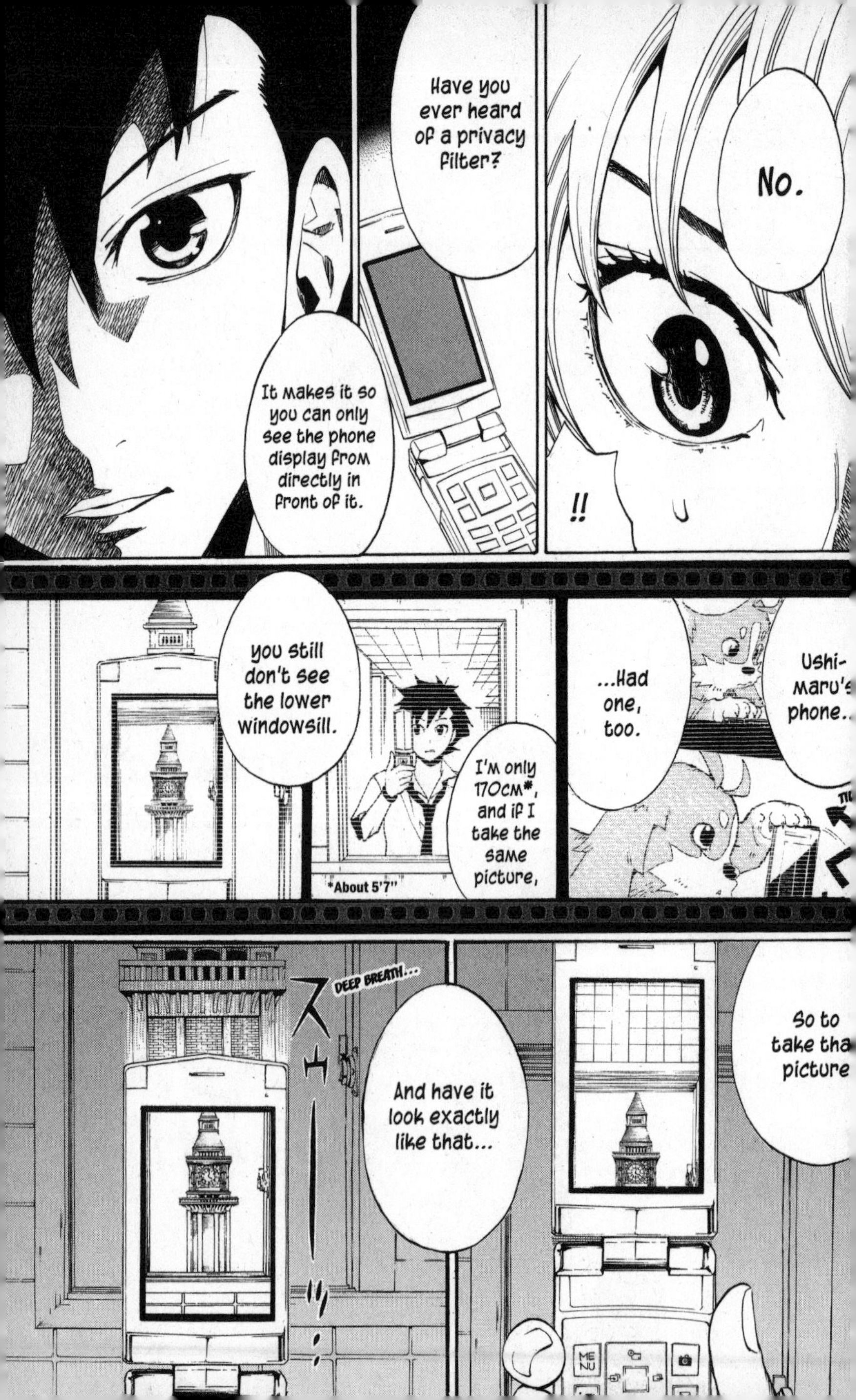
No.
!!
Have you ever heard of a privacy filter?
It makes it so you can only see the phone display from directly in front of it.
Ushi-maru's phone...
...Had one, too.
I'm only 170cm*, and if I take the same picture,
you still don't see the lower windowsill.
*About 5'7"
So to take that picture
And have it look exactly like that...
DEEP BREATH...

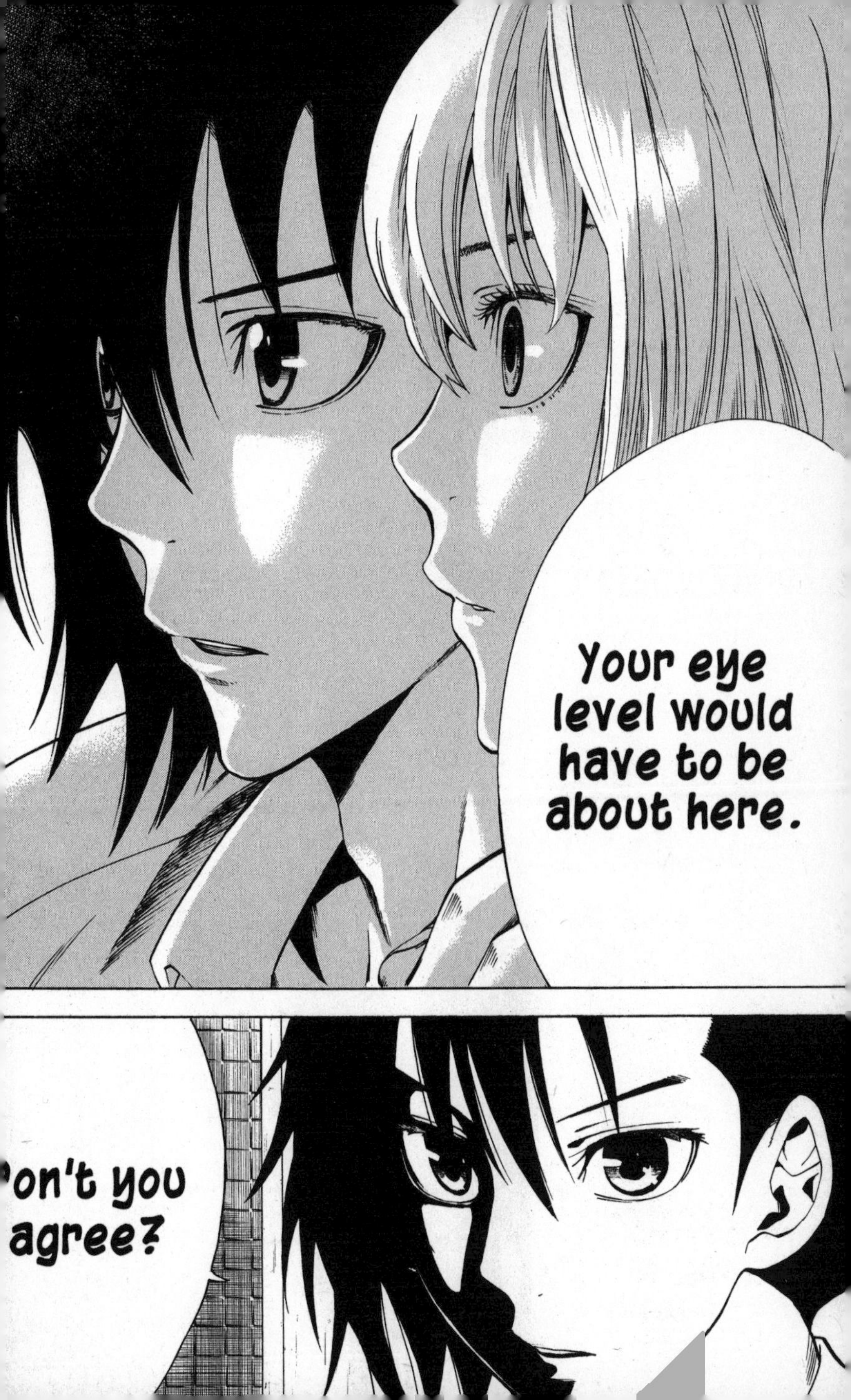
Your eye level would have to be about here.
on't you agree?

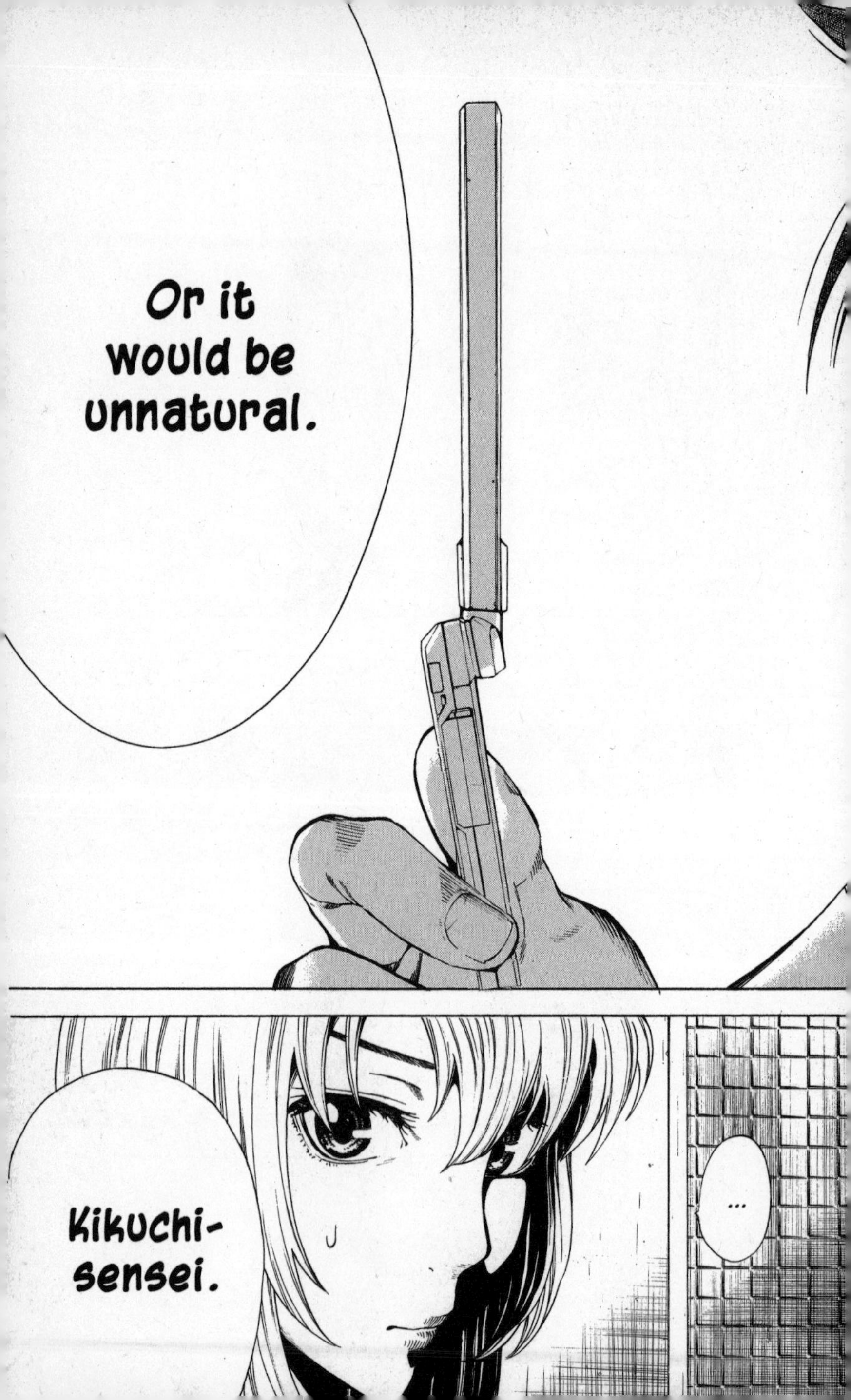
Or it would be unnatural.
...
Kikuchi-sensei.

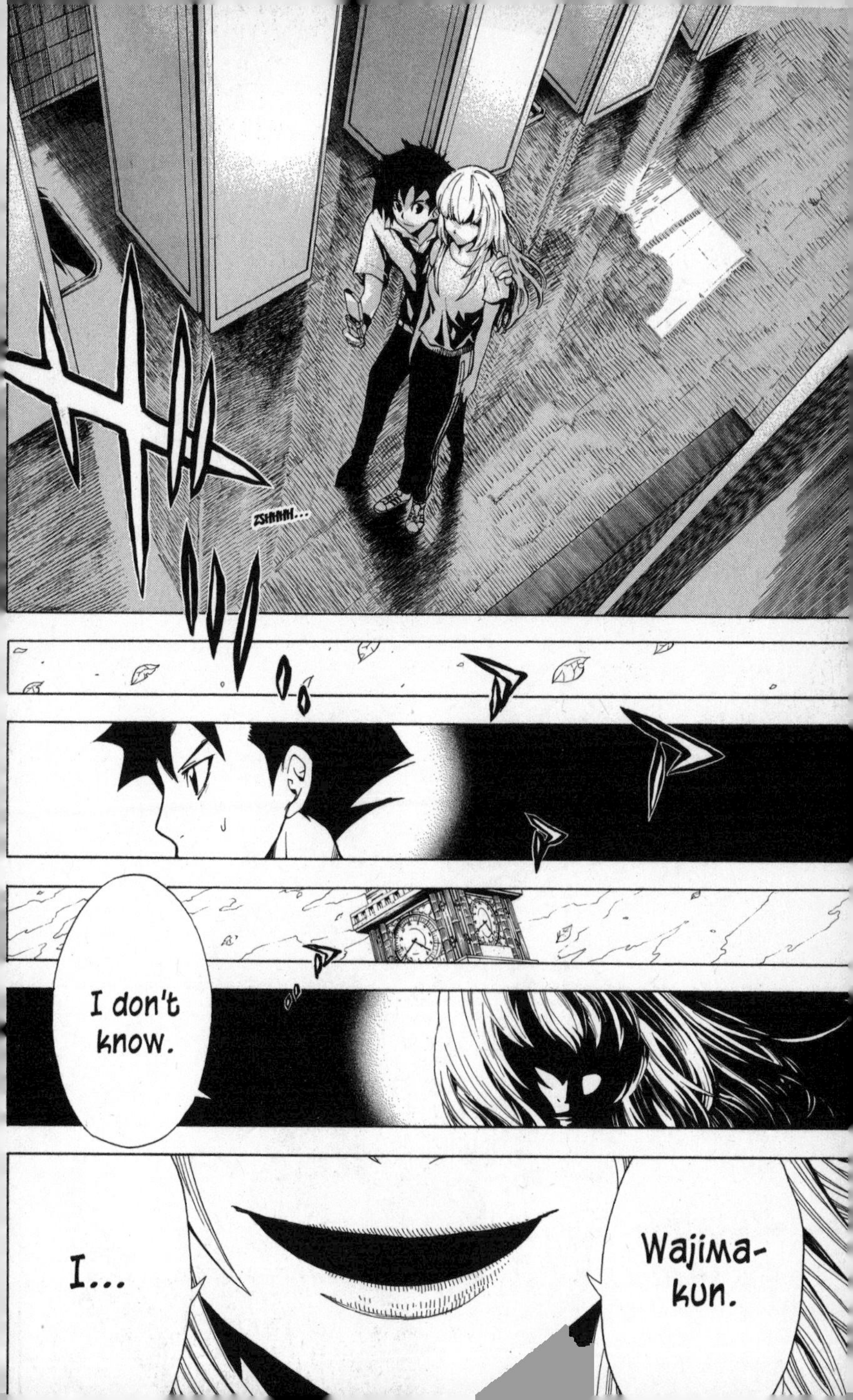

ZSHHHH...
I don't know.
Wajima-kun.
I...

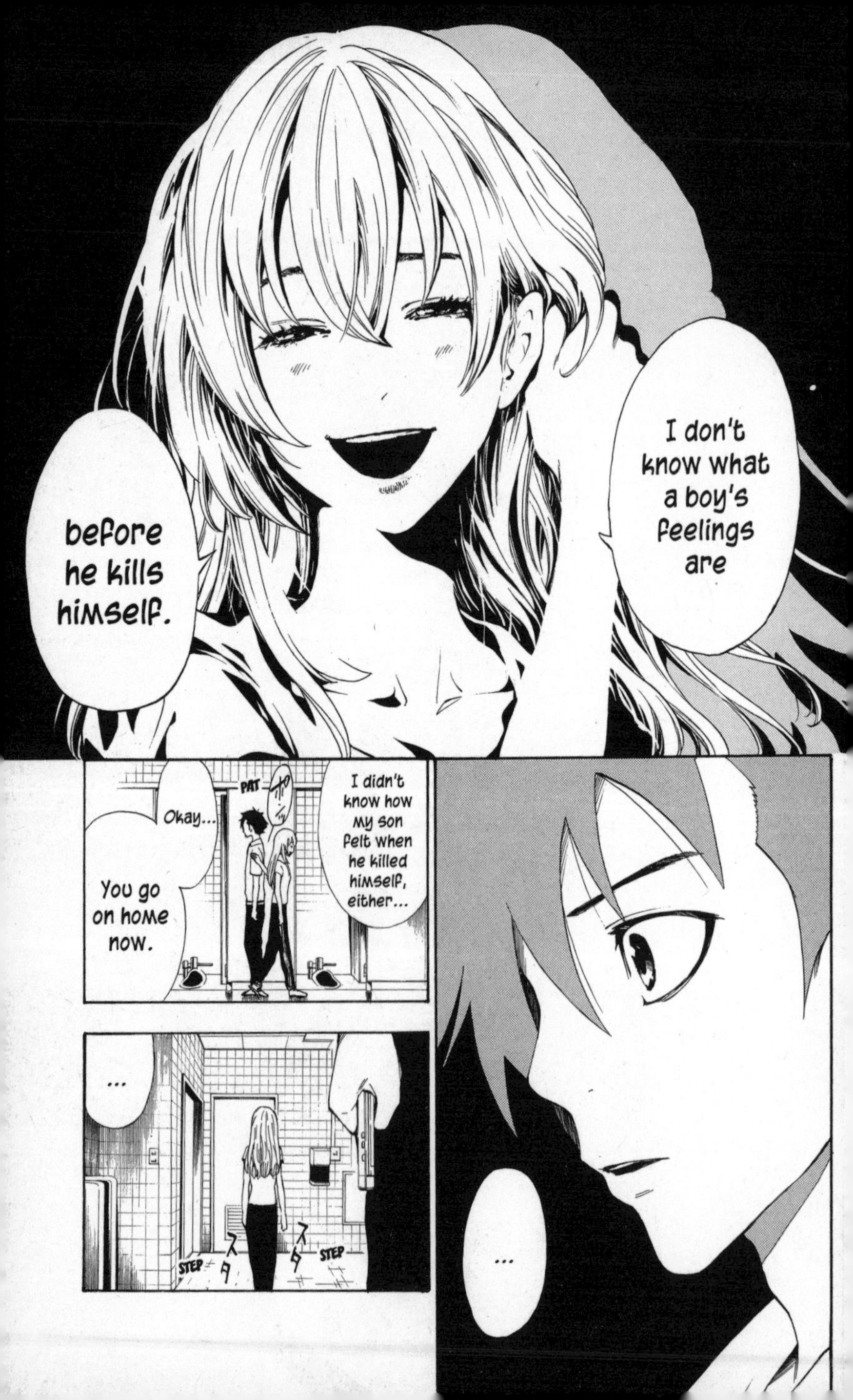

I don't know what a boy's feelings are
before he kills himself.
...
I didn't know how my son felt when he killed himself, either...
PAT
Okay...
You go on home now.
...
STEP
STEP

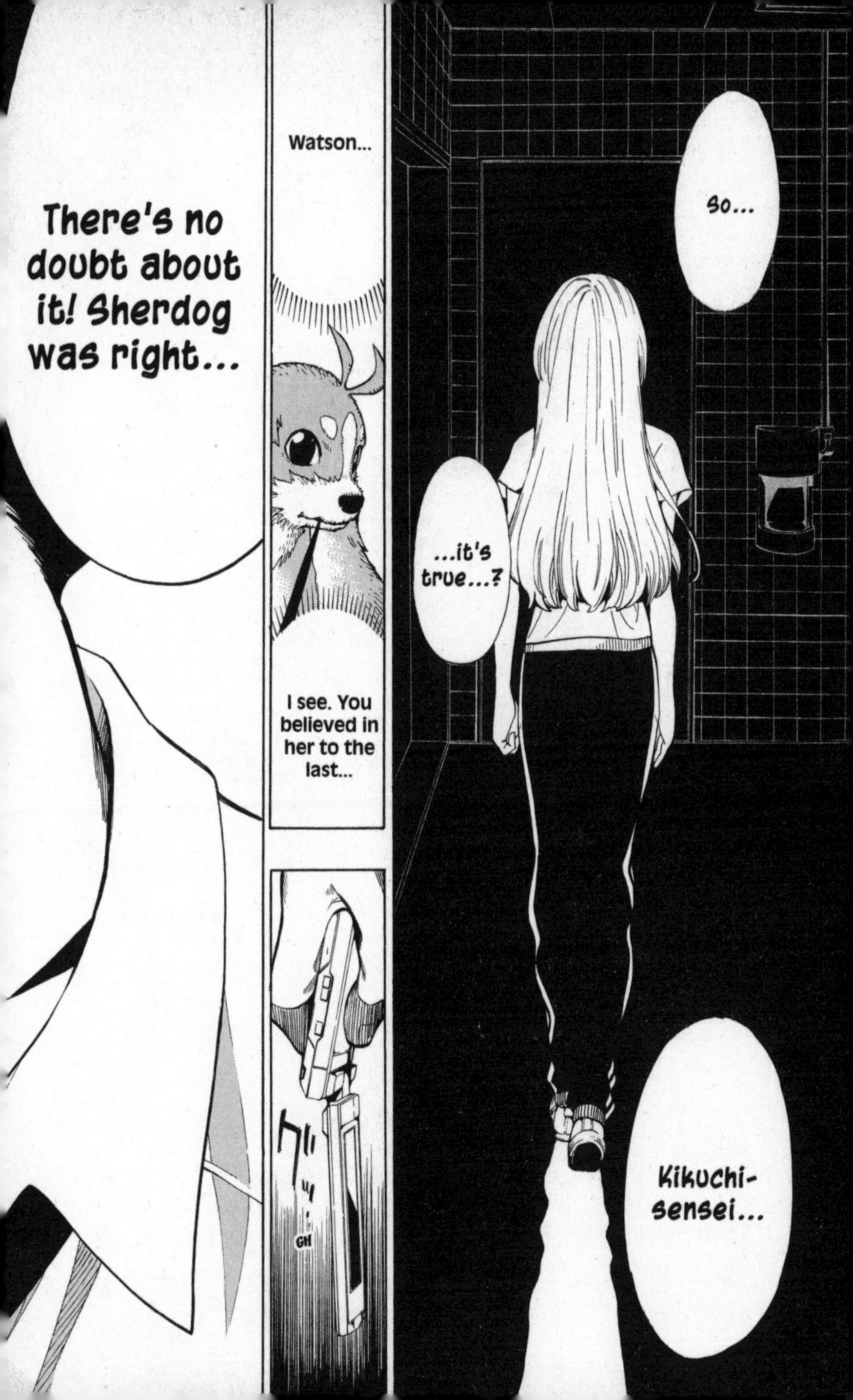
So...
...it's true...?
Kikuchi-sensei...
Watson...
I see. You believed in her to the last...
GH
There's no doubt about it! Sherdog was right...

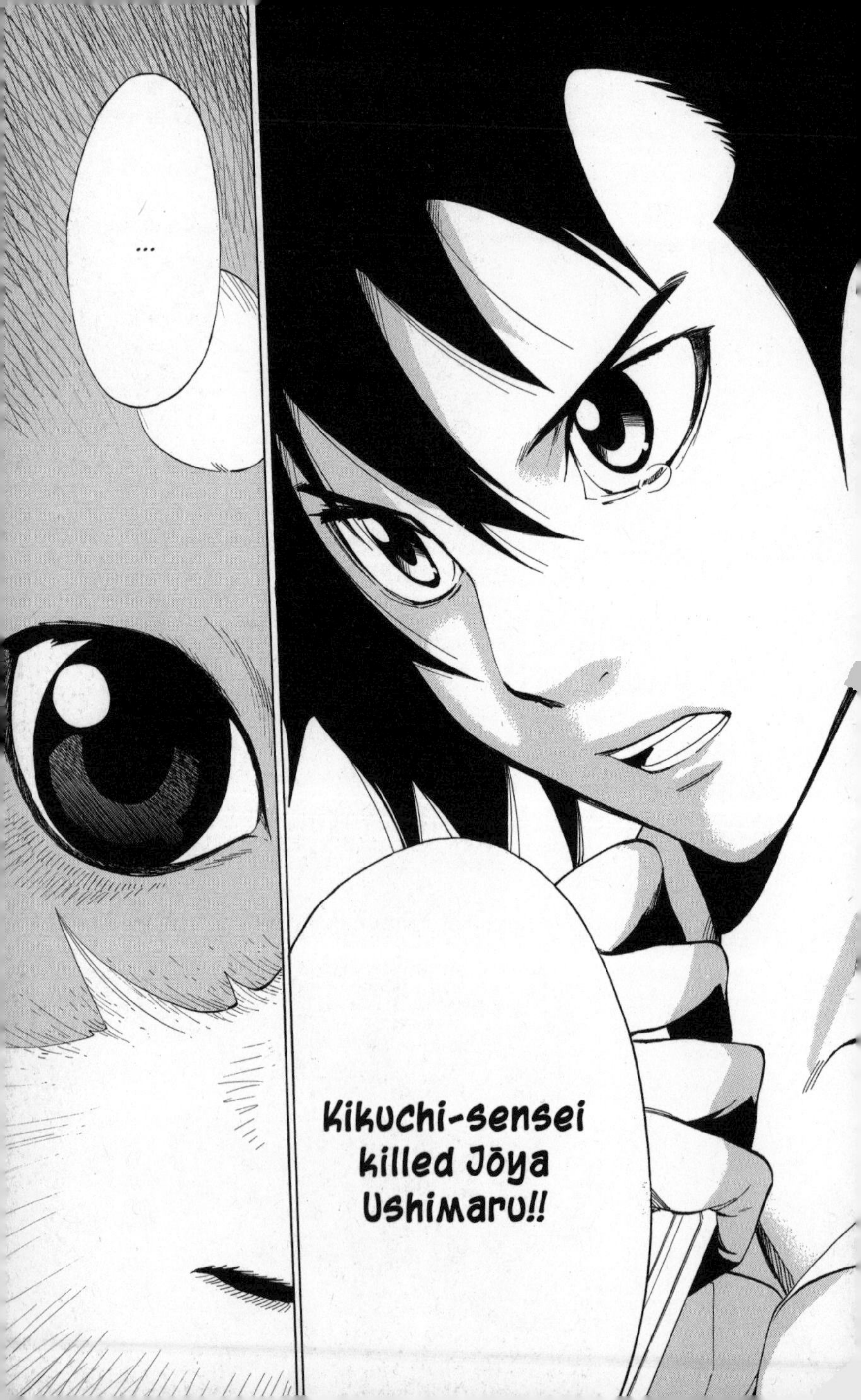
Kikuchi-sensei killed Jōya Ushimaru!!
...

SHERLOCK BONES

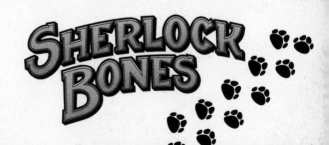

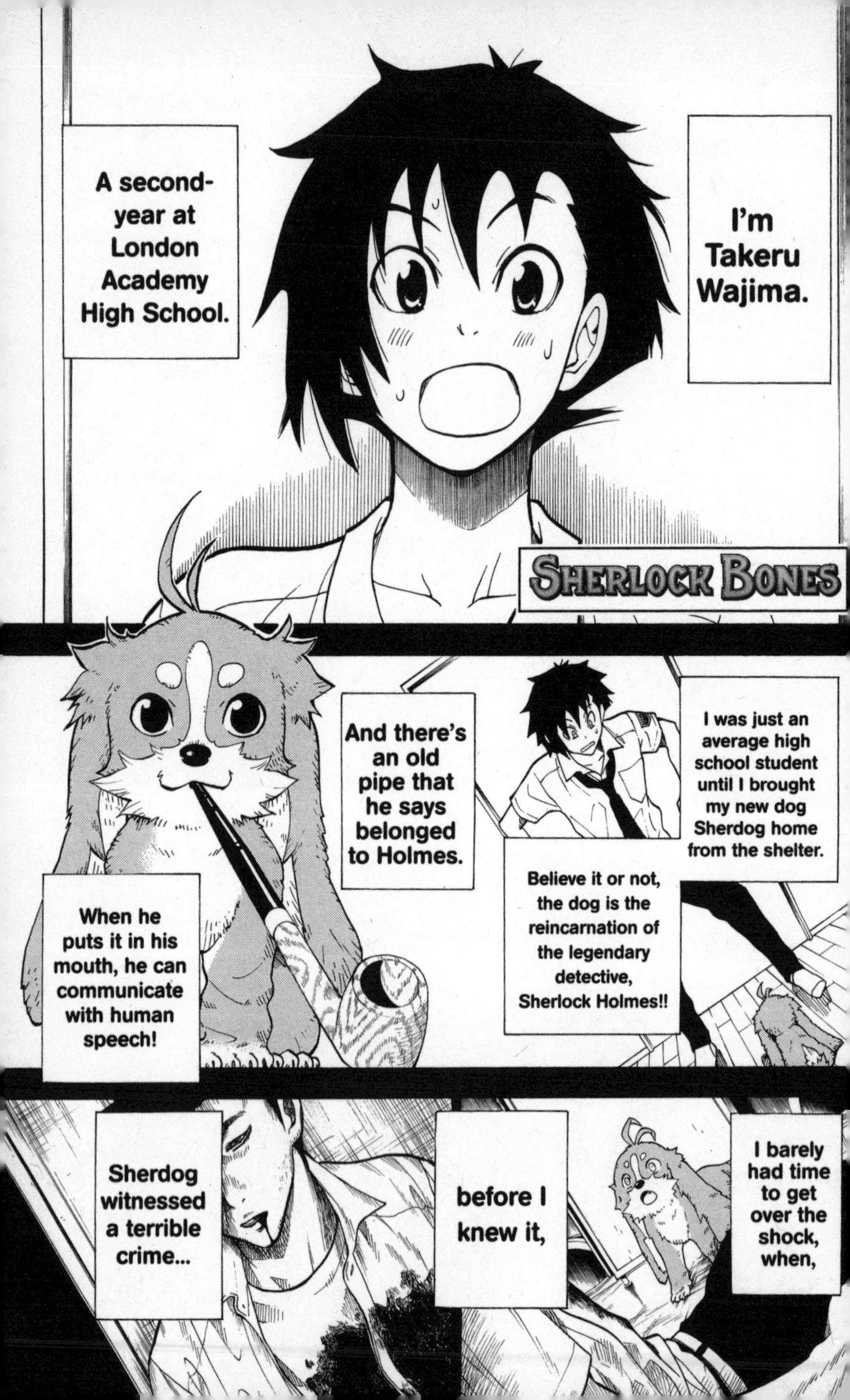
I'm Takeru Wajima.
A second-year at London Academy High School.
SHERLOCK BONES
I was just an average high school student until I brought my new dog Sherdog home from the shelter.
Believe it or not, the dog is the reincarnation of the legendary detective, Sherlock Holmes!!
And there's an old pipe that he says belonged to Holmes.
When he puts it in his mouth, he can communicate with human speech!
I barely had time to get over the shock, when,
before I knew it,
Sherdog witnessed a terrible crime...

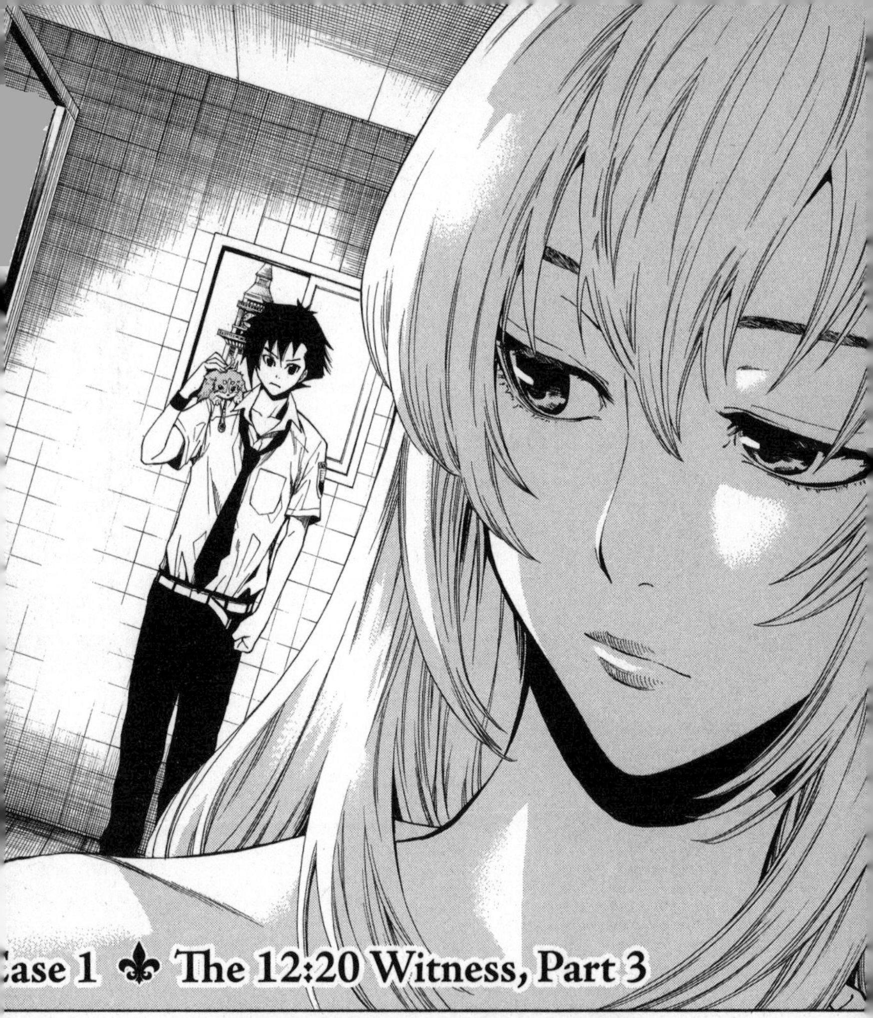

Case 1 ⚜ The 12:20 Witness, Part 3

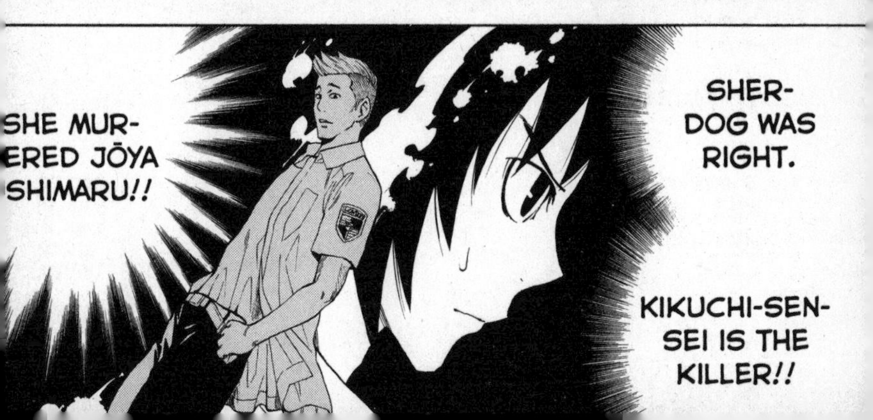
SHER-DOG WAS RIGHT.
KIKUCHI-SEN-SEI IS THE KILLER!!
SHE MUR-ERED JŌYA SHIMARU!!

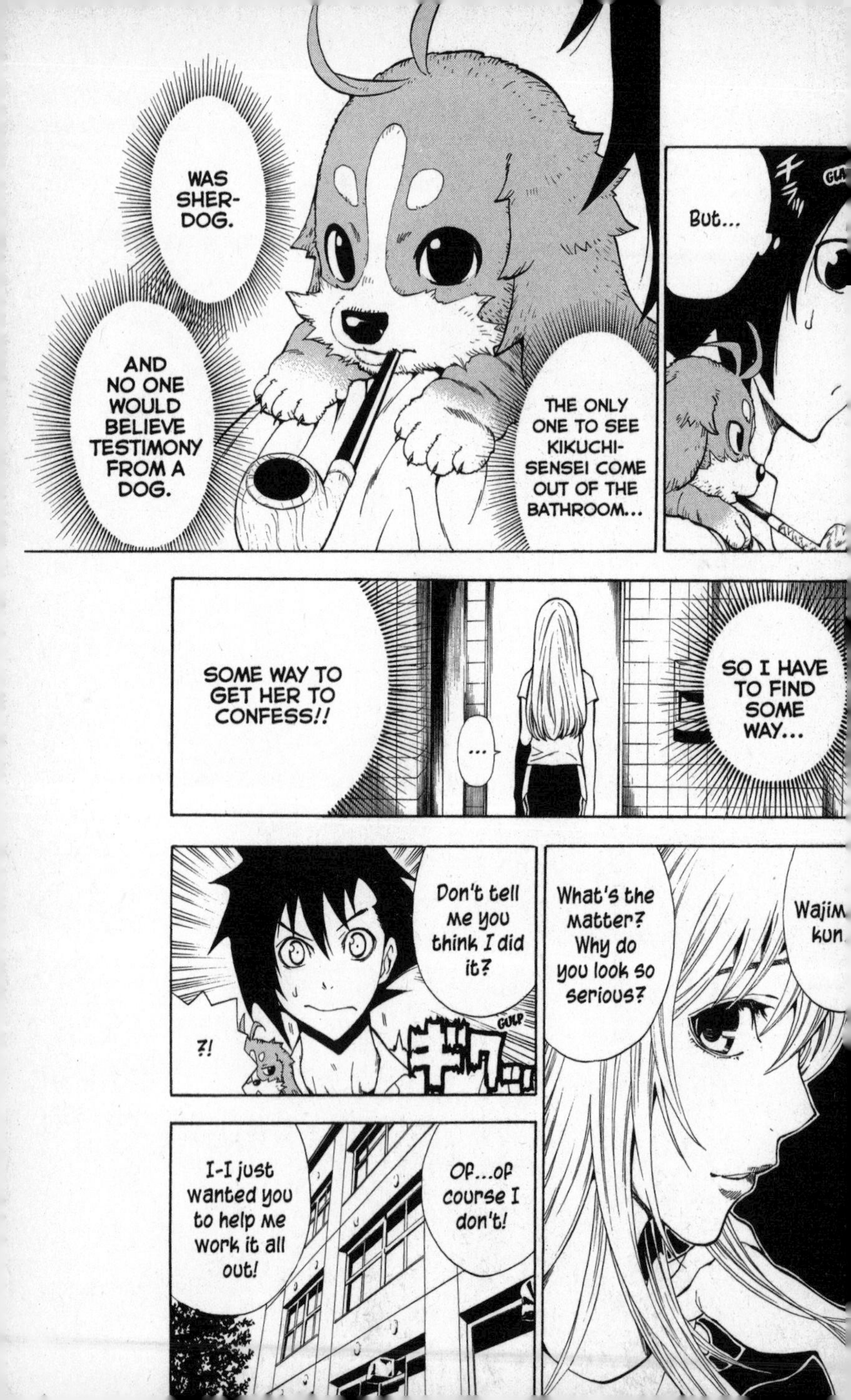
GLA
But...
THE ONLY ONE TO SEE KIKUCHI-SENSEI COME OUT OF THE BATHROOM...
WAS SHER-DOG.
AND NO ONE WOULD BELIEVE TESTIMONY FROM A DOG.
SO I HAVE TO FIND SOME WAY...
...
SOME WAY TO GET HER TO CONFESS!!
Wajim
kun
What's the matter? Why do you look so serious?
Don't tell me you think I did it?
GULP
?!
Of...of course I don't!
I-I just wanted you to help me work it all out!

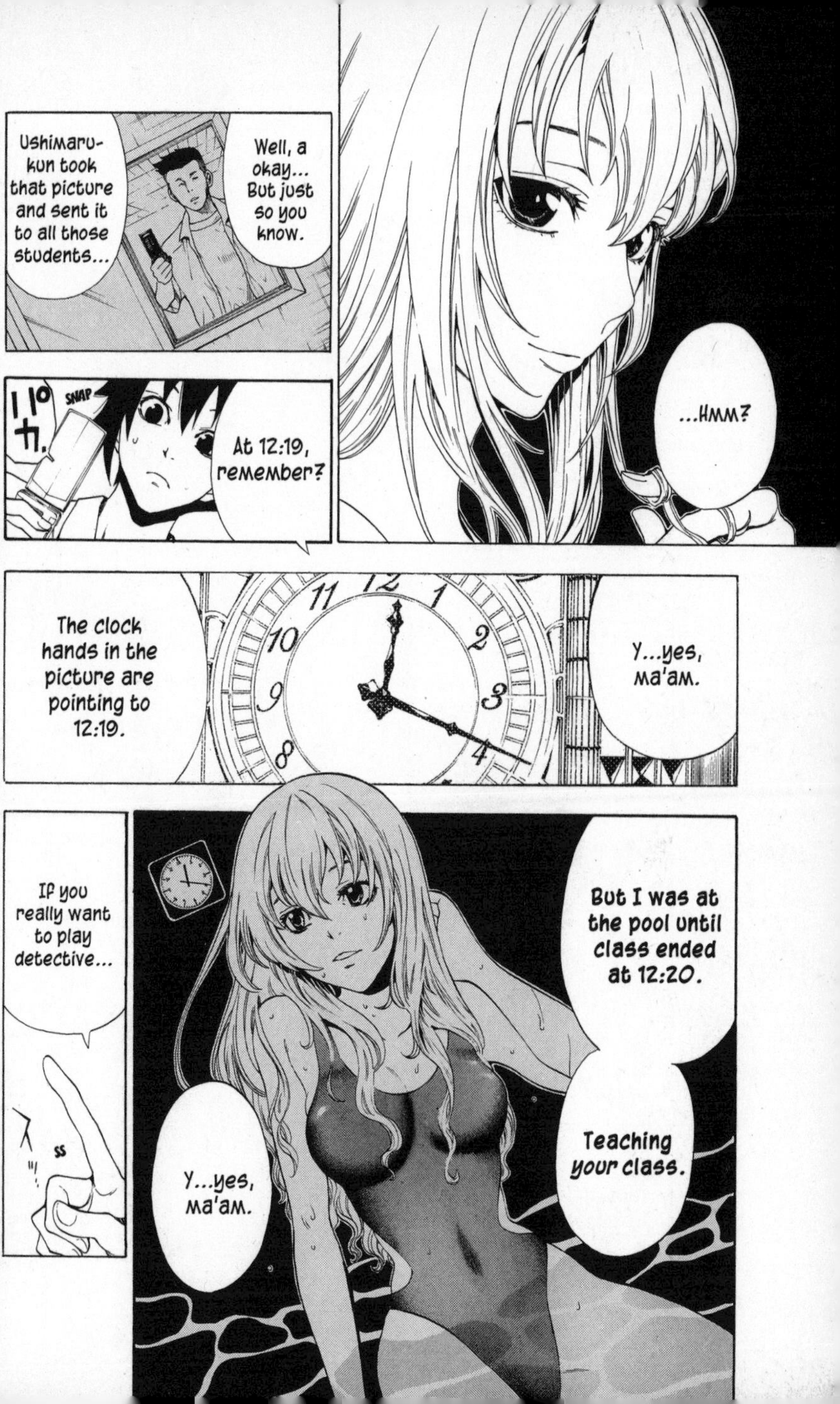
...HMM?
Well, a okay... But just so you know.
Ushimaru-kun took that picture and sent it to all those students...
SNAP
At 12:19, remember?
Y...yes, ma'am.
The clock hands in the picture are pointing to 12:19.
But I was at the pool until class ended at 12:20.
Teaching your class.
Y...yes, ma'am.
If you really want to play detective...
SS

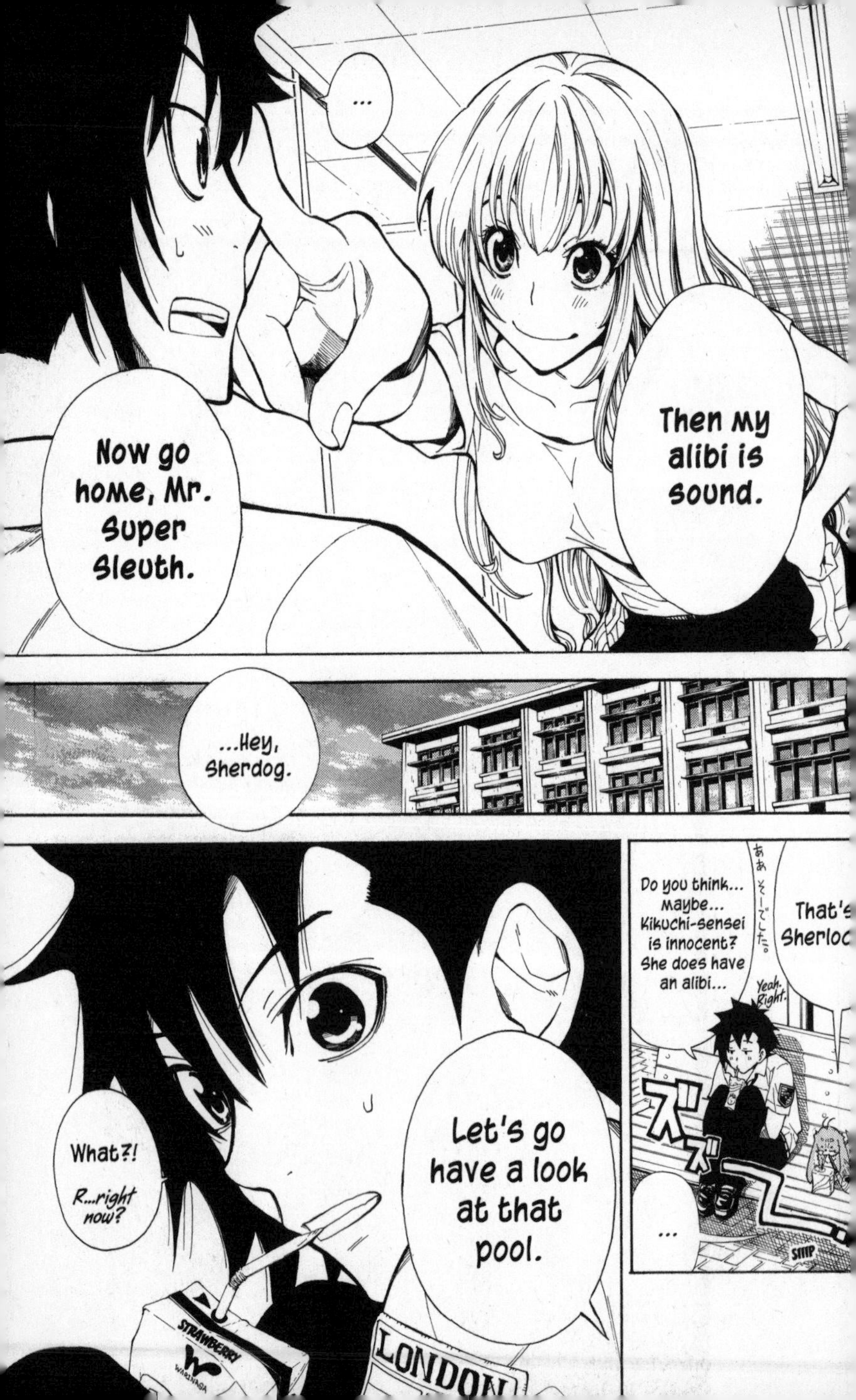
...
Then my alibi is sound.
Now go home, Mr. Super Sleuth.
...Hey, Sherdog.
That's Sherloc
ああそーでした。
Do you think... maybe... Kikuchi-sensei is innocent? She does have an alibi...
Yeah. Right.
ズズ
...
SIIP
Let's go have a look at that pool.
What?!
R...right now?
STRAWBERRY
LONDON

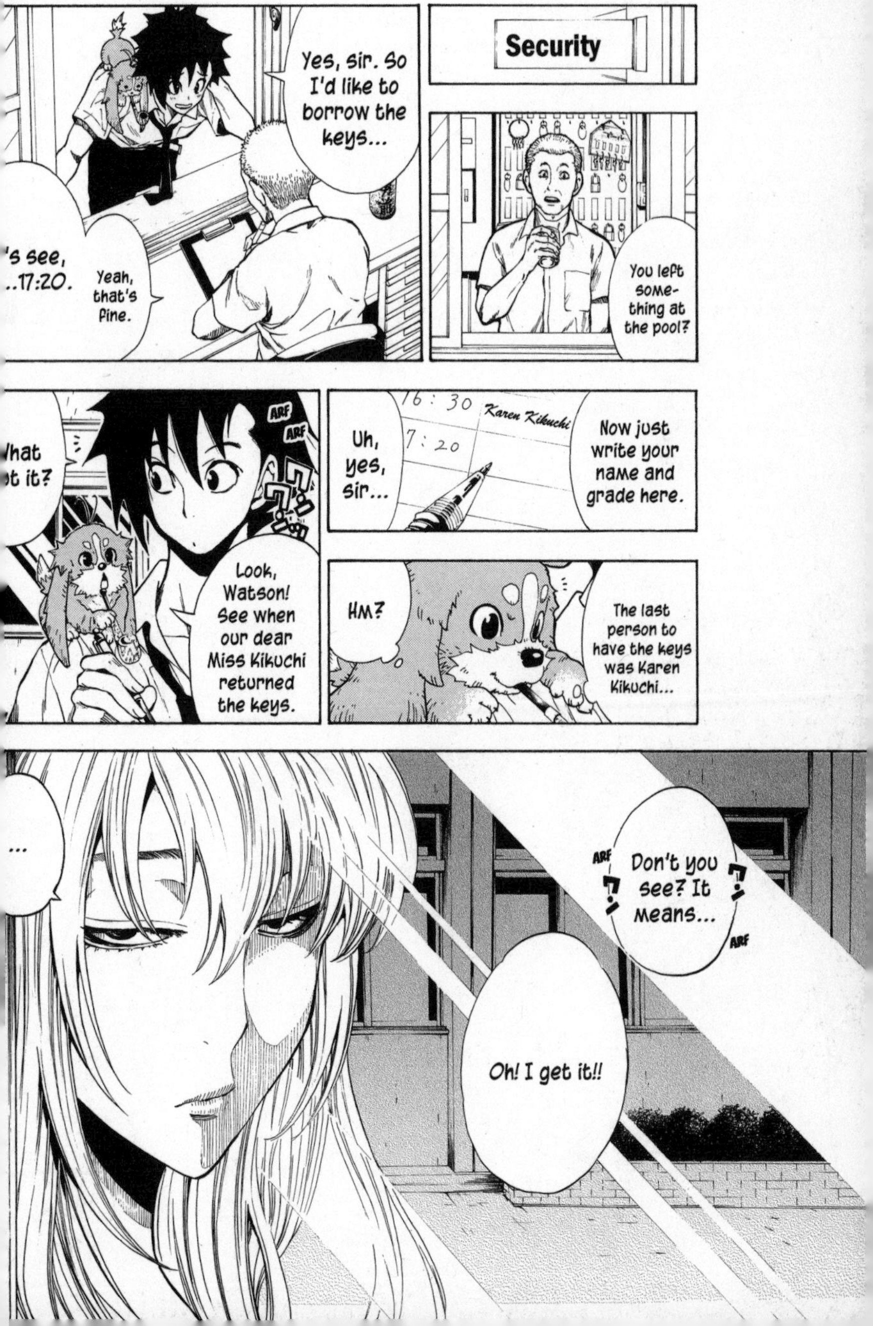
Security
You left something at the pool?
Yes, sir. So I'd like to borrow the keys...
Yeah, that's fine.
's see, ..17:20.
Now just write your name and grade here.
16:30 Karen Kikuchi
7:20
Uh, yes, sir...
The last person to have the keys was Karen Kikuchi...
HM?
ARF ARF
hat t it?
Look, Watson! See when our dear Miss Kikuchi returned the keys.
ARF
Don't you see? It means...
ARF
Oh! I get it!!
...

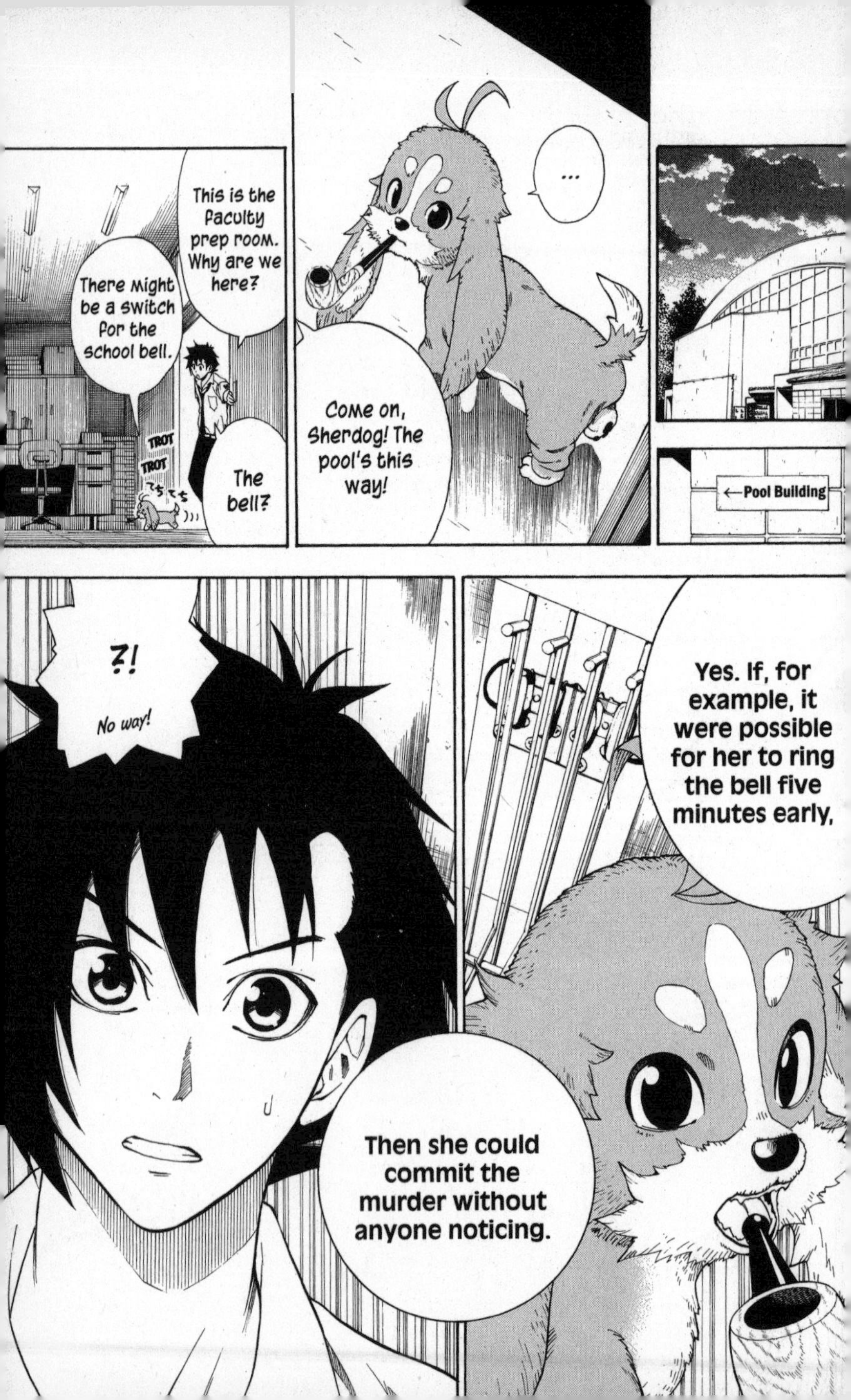
←Pool Building
...
Come on, Sherdog! The pool's this way!
This is the faculty prep room. Why are we here?
There might be a switch for the school bell.
TROT
TROT
The bell?
Yes. If, for example, it were possible for her to ring the bell five minutes early,
Then she could commit the murder without anyone noticing.
?!
No way!

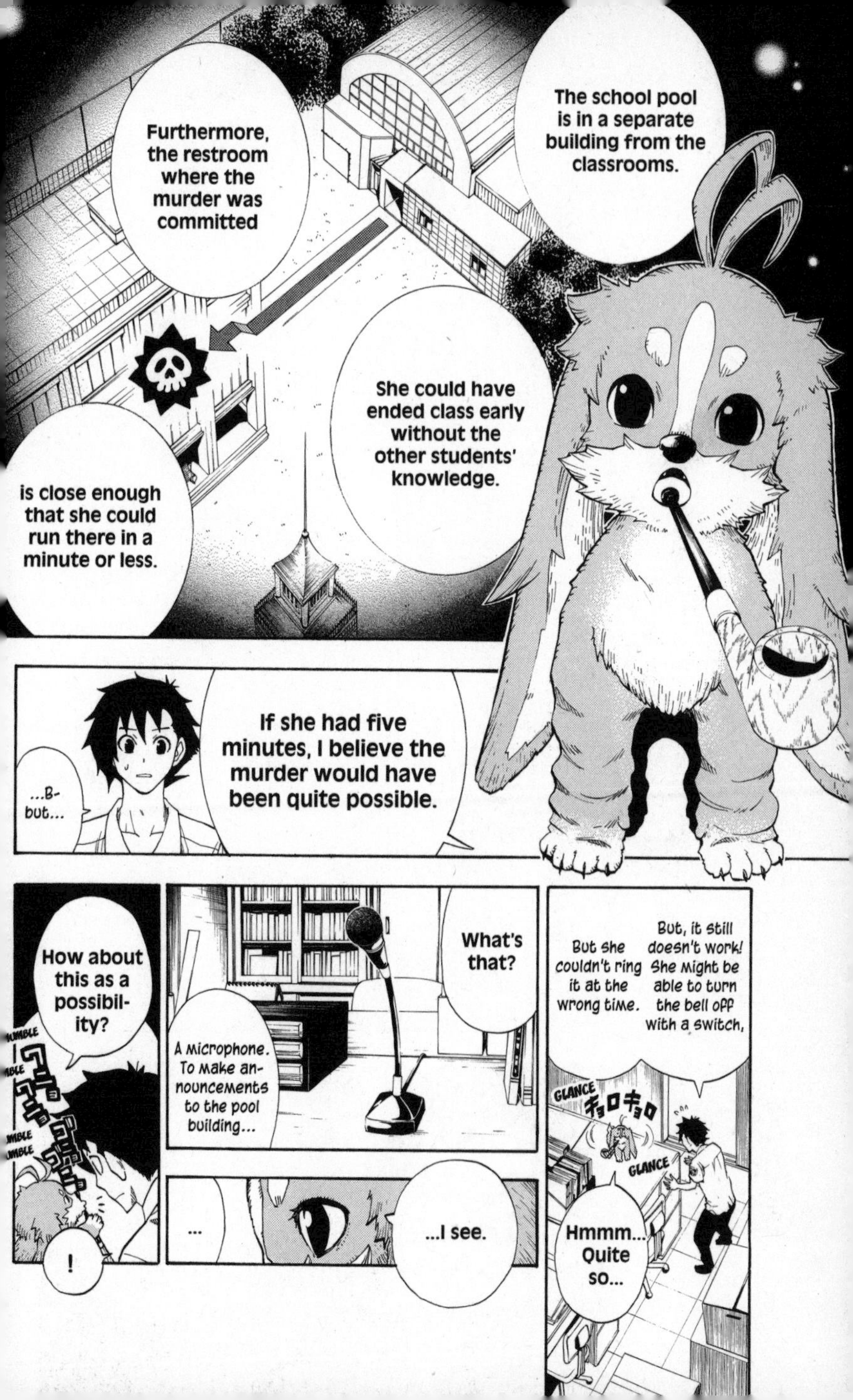
The school pool is in a separate building from the classrooms.
Furthermore, the restroom where the murder was committed
is close enough that she could run there in a minute or less.
She could have ended class early without the other students' knowledge.
If she had five minutes, I believe the murder would have been quite possible.
...B-but...
But, it still doesn't work! She might be able to turn the bell off with a switch,
But she couldn't ring it at the wrong time.
GLANCE
キョロキョロ
GLANCE
Hmmm... Quite so...
What's that?
A microphone. To make announcements to the pool building...
...I see.
...
How about this as a possibility?
!

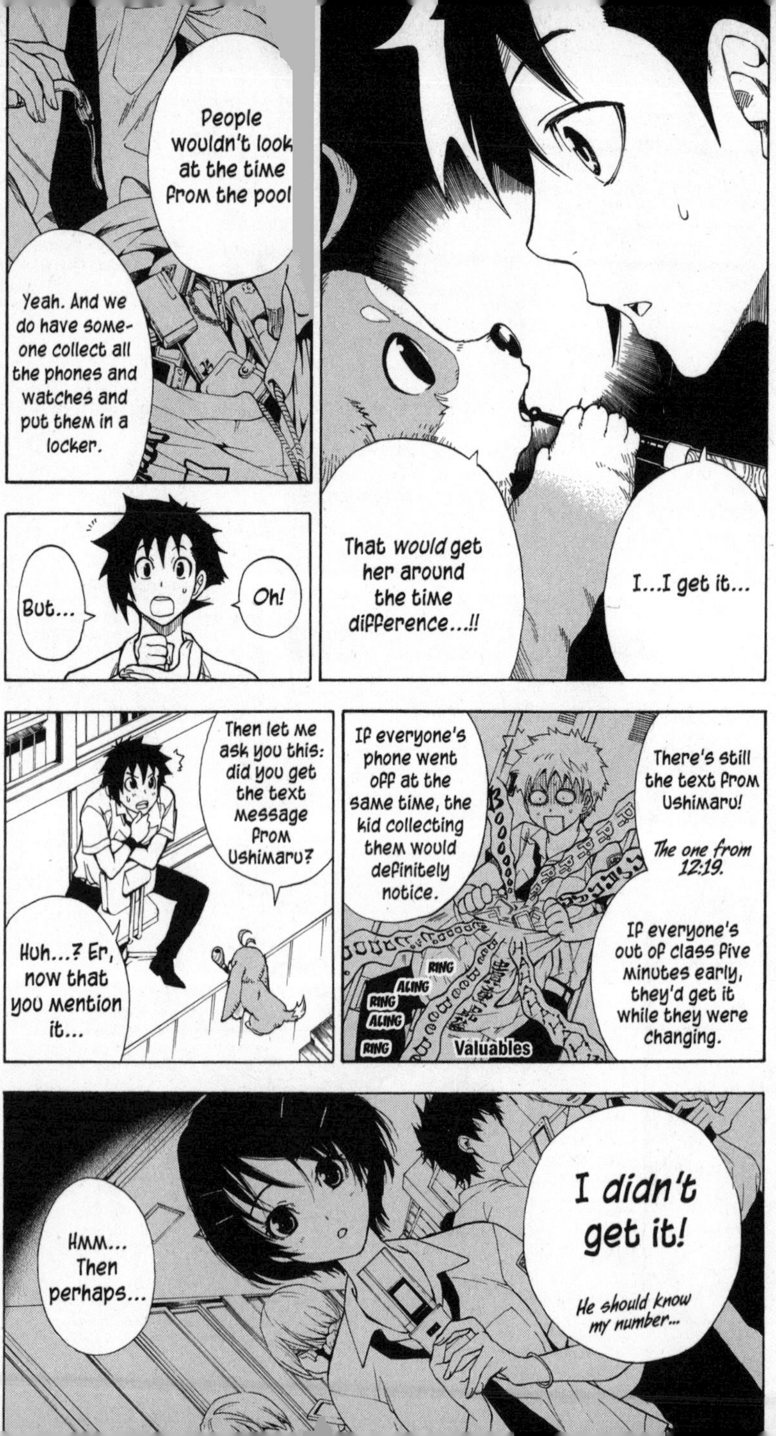
I...I get it...
That *would* get her around the time difference...!!
People wouldn't look at the time from the pool
Yeah. And we do have some-one collect all the phones and watches and put them in a locker.
Oh!
But...
There's still the text from Ushimaru!
The one from 12:19.
If everyone's phone went off at the same time, the kid collecting them would definitely notice.
If everyone's out of class five minutes early, they'd get it while they were changing.
RING
ALING
RING
ALING
RING
Valuables
Then let me ask you this: did you get the text message from Ushimaru?
Huh...? Er, now that you mention it...
I *didn't* get it!
He should know my number...
Hmm... Then perhaps...

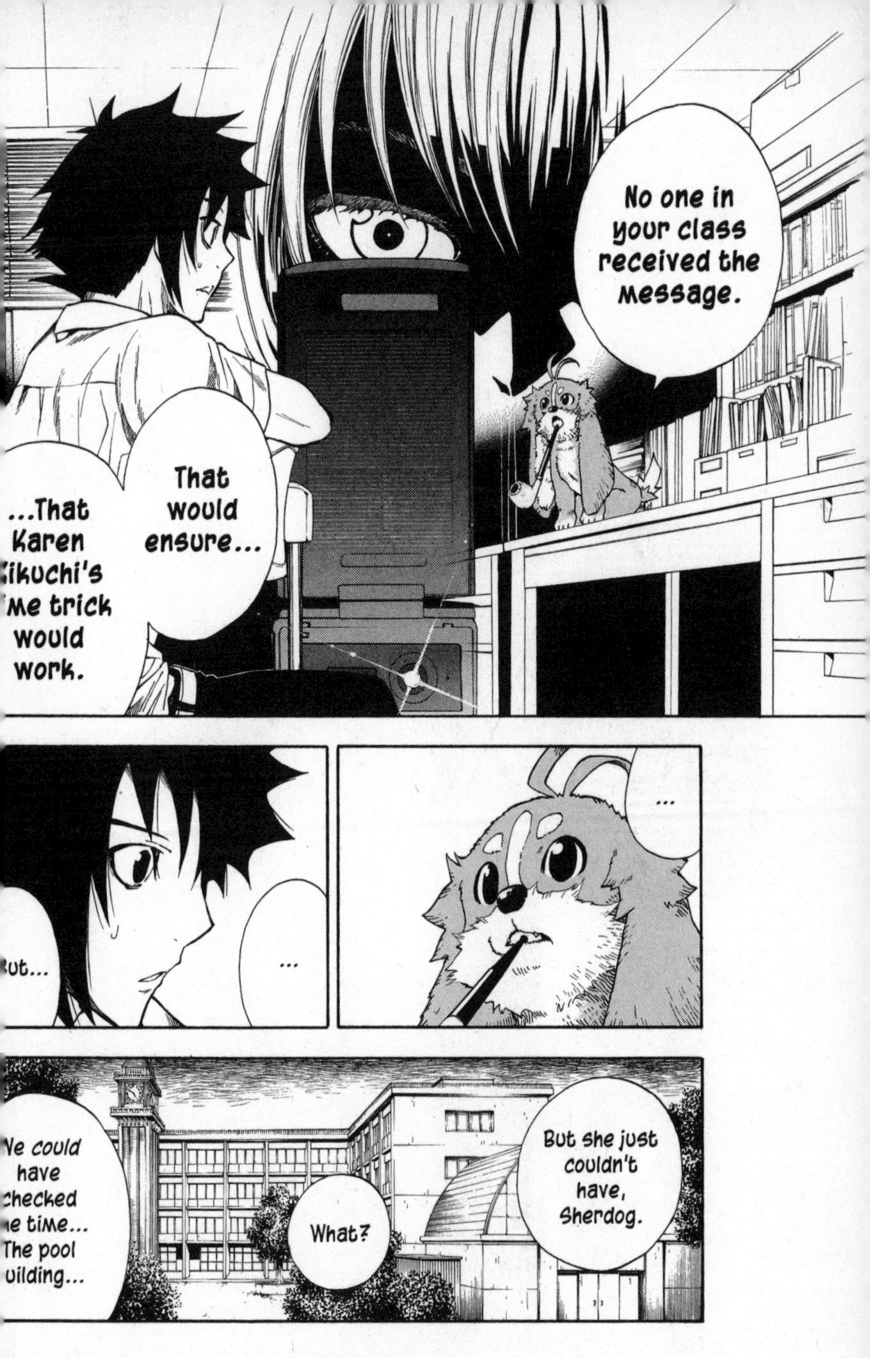
No one in your class received the message.
That would ensure...
...That Karen ikuchi's me trick would work.
...
...
ut...
But she just couldn't have, Sherdog.
What?
e could have hecked e time... The pool uilding...

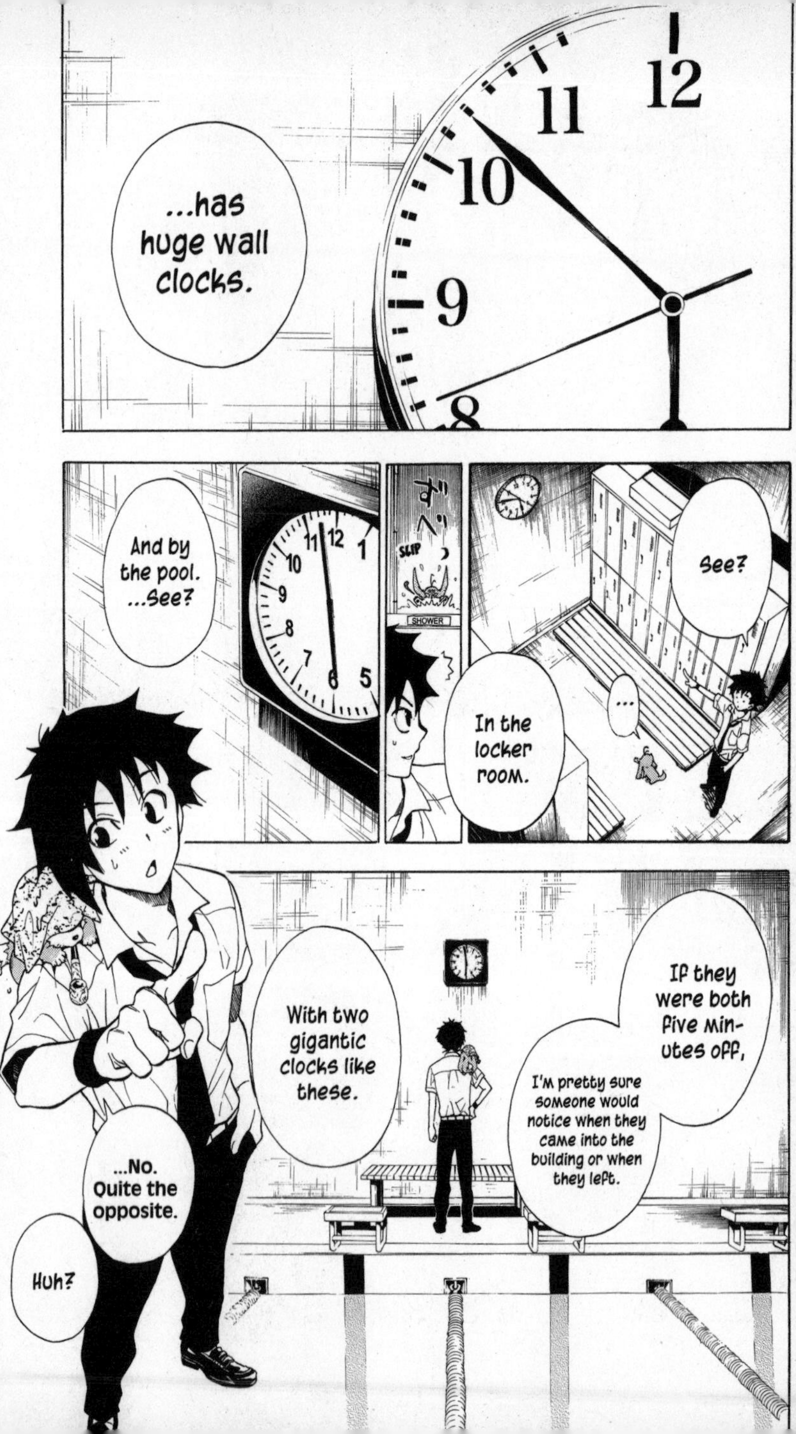
...has huge wall clocks.
See?
...
In the locker room.
ずべっ
SLIP
SHOWER
And by the pool. ...See?
If they were both five min-utes off,
I'm pretty sure someone would notice when they came into the building or when they left.
With two gigantic clocks like these.
...No. Quite the opposite.
Huh?

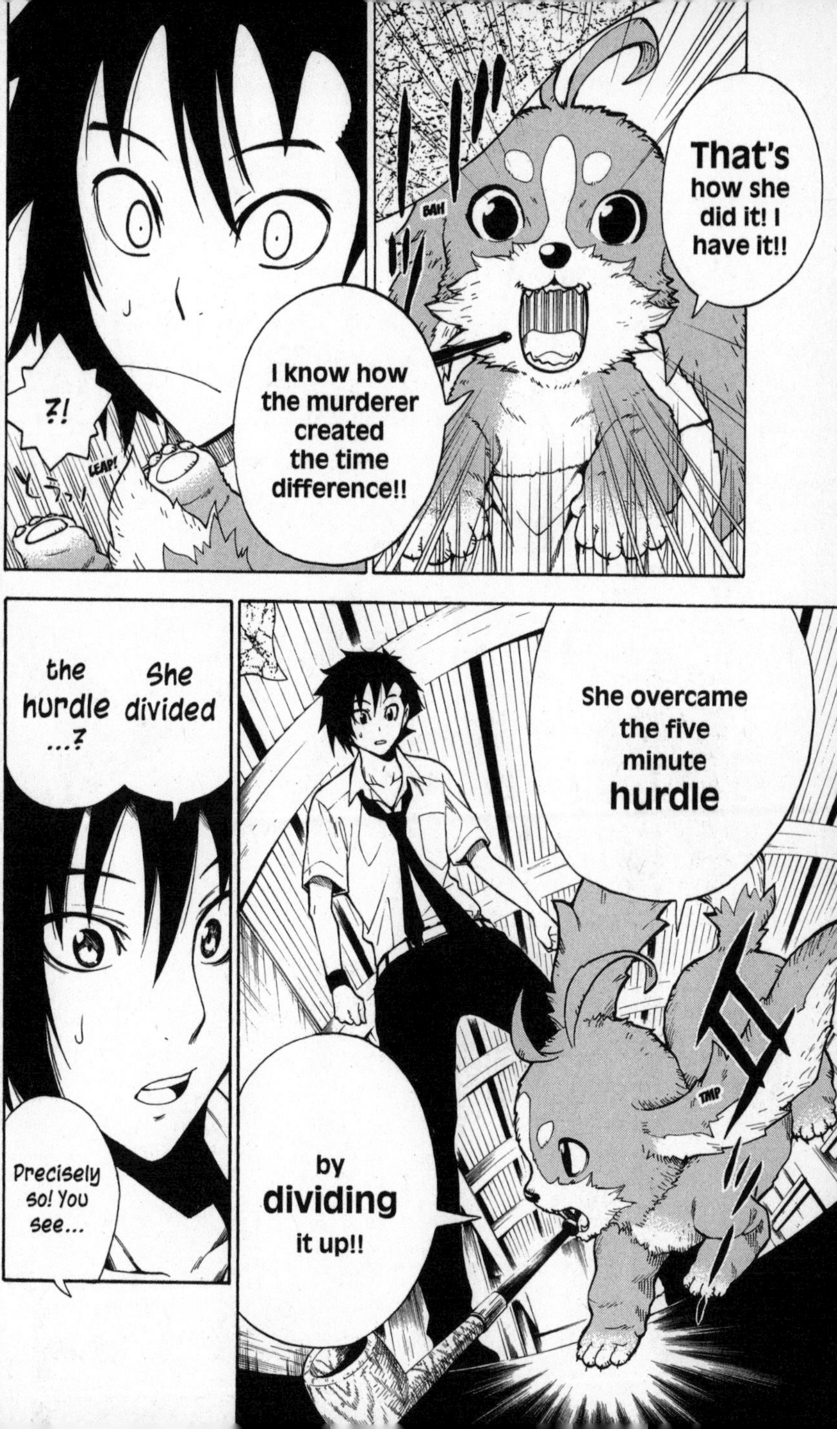
That's how she did it! I have it!!
BAH
I know how the murderer created the time difference!!
?!
LEAP!
She overcame the five minute hurdle
by dividing it up!!
TMP
She divided the hurdle ...?
Precisely so! You see...

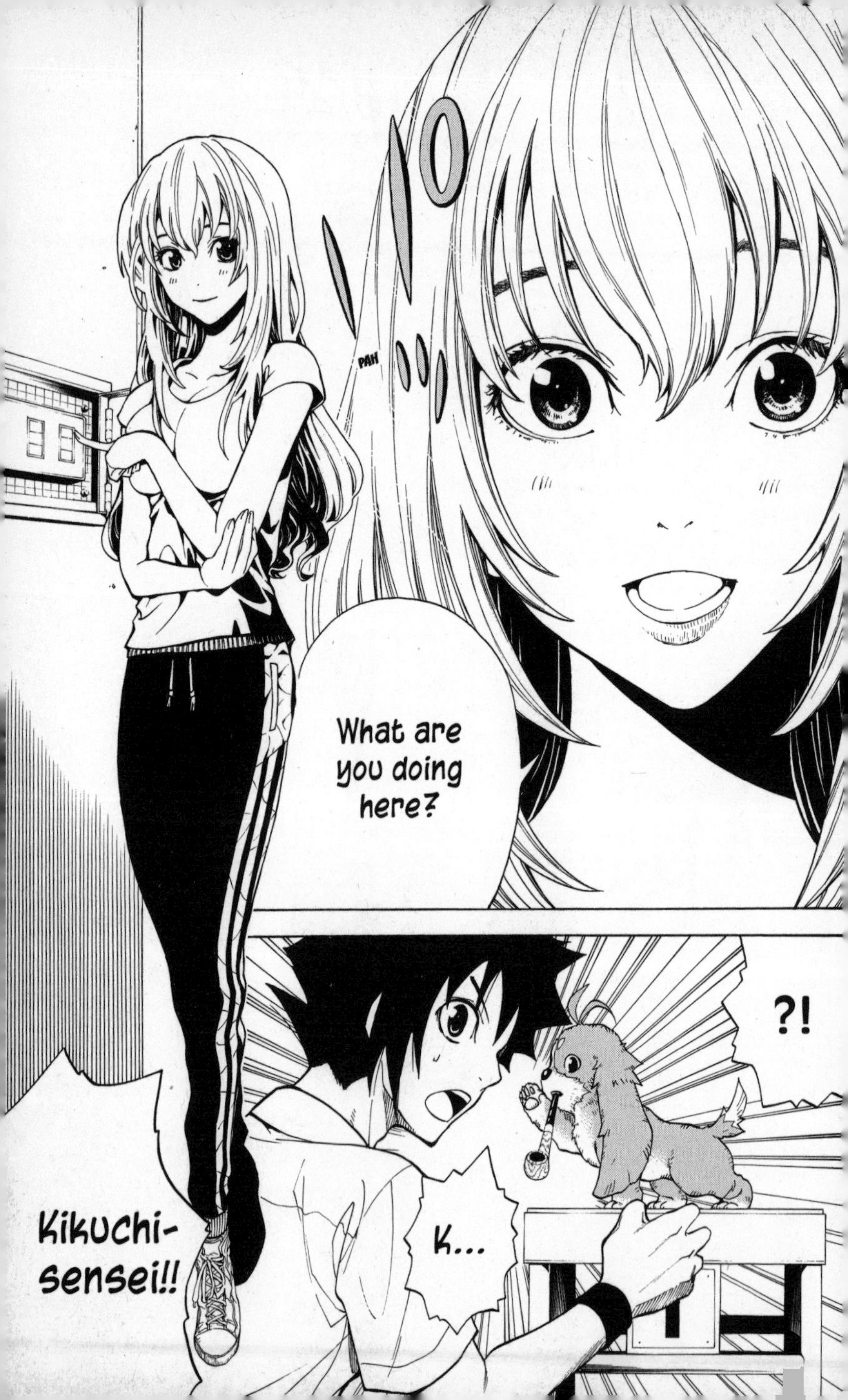
PAH
What are you doing here?
?!
K...
Kikuchi-sensei!!

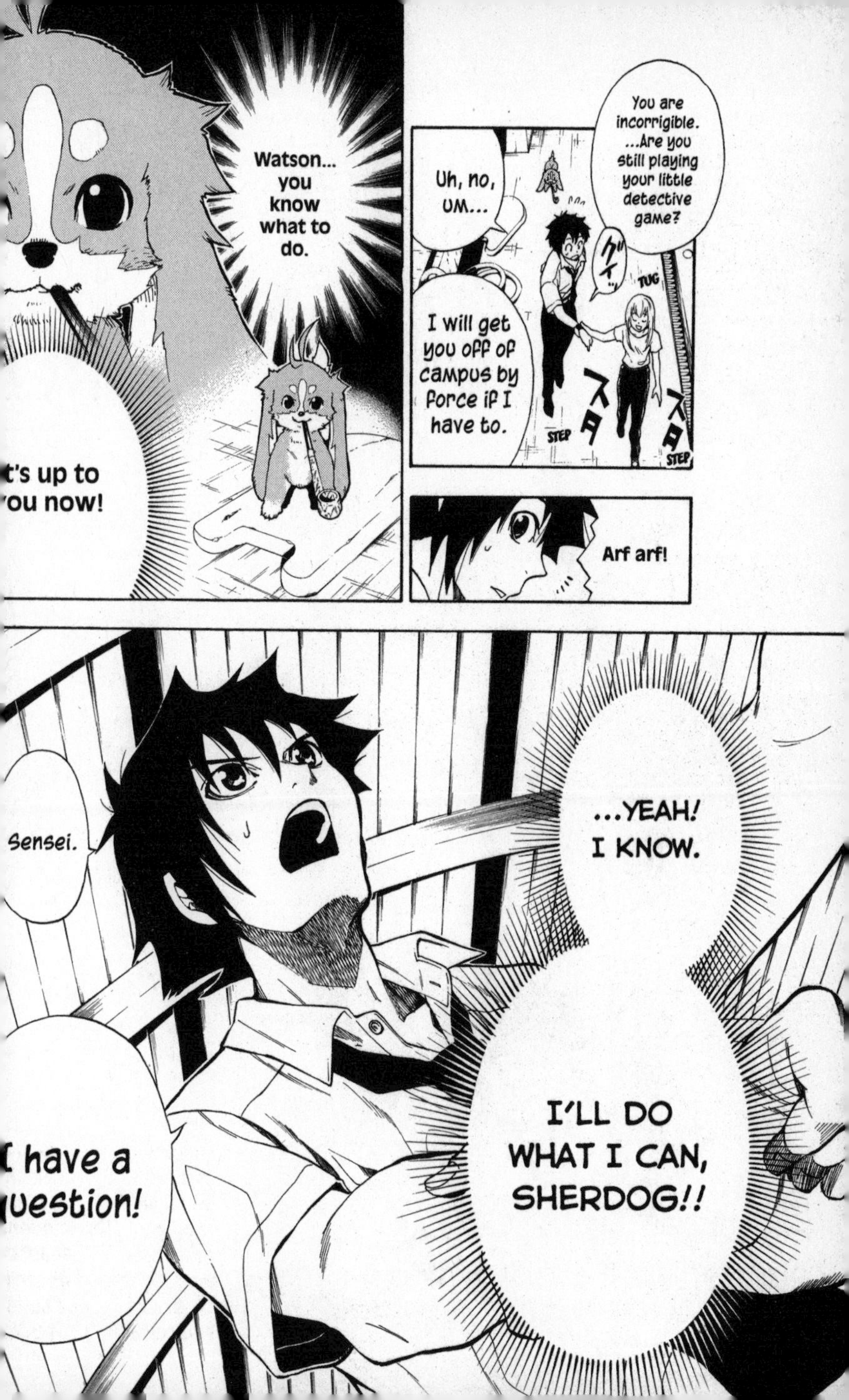
You are incorrigible. ...Are you still playing your little detective game?
グイ
TUG
Uh, no, UM...
I will get you off of campus by force if I have to.
スタ
STEP
スタ
STEP
Arf arf!
Watson... you know what to do.
t's up to ou now!
...YEAH! I KNOW.
I'LL DO WHAT I CAN, SHERDOG!!
Sensei.
have a uestion!

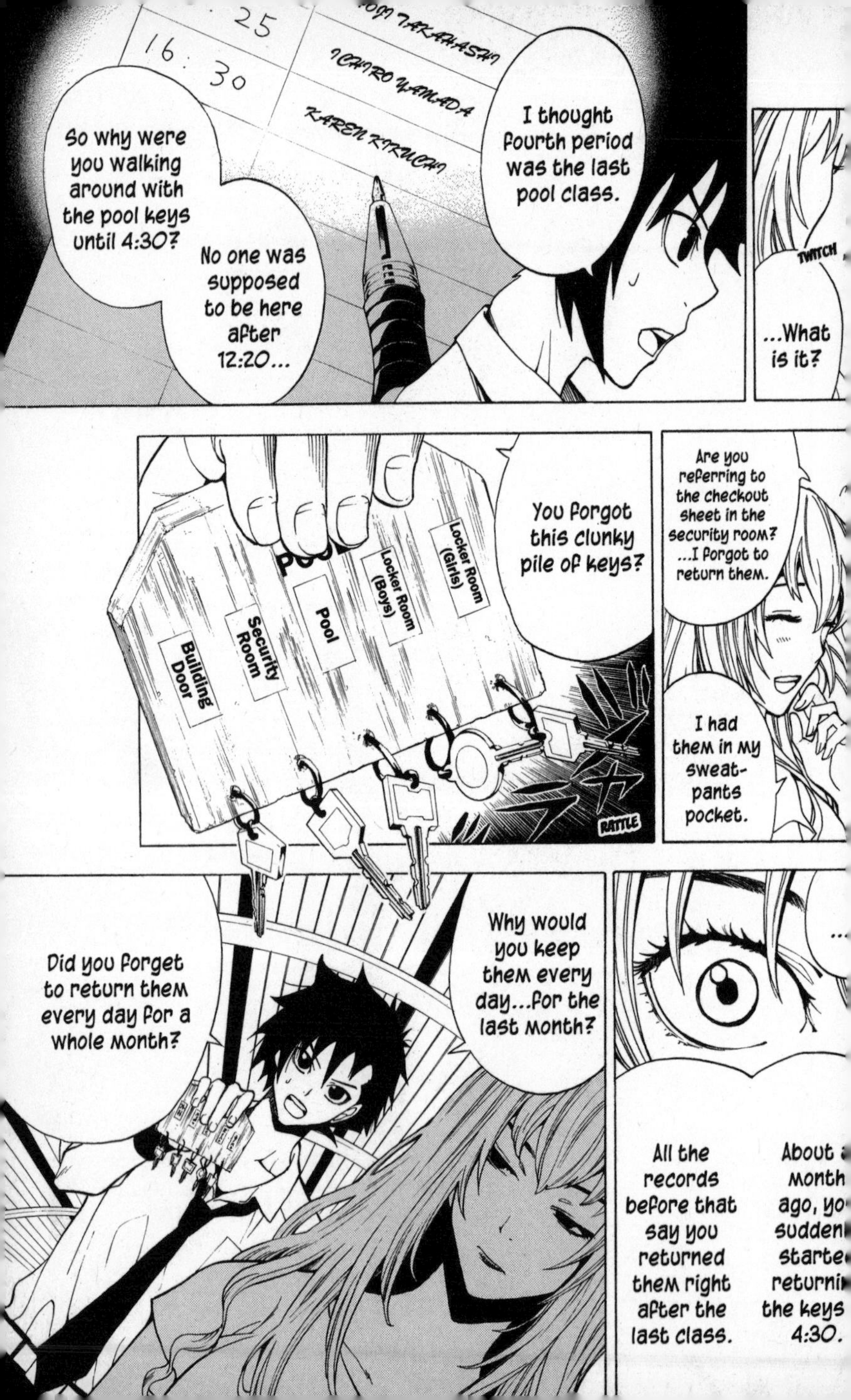

TWITCH
...What is it?
I thought fourth period was the last pool class.
25
16:30
ICHIRO YAMADA
KAREN KIKUCHI
So why were you walking around with the pool keys until 4:30?
No one was supposed to be here after 12:20...
Are you referring to the checkout sheet in the security room? ...I forgot to return them.
I had them in my sweat-pants pocket.
You forgot this clunky pile of keys?
POOL
Locker Room (Girls)
Locker Room (Boys)
Pool
Security Room
Building Door
RATTLE
...
About a month ago, yo sudden starte returni the keys 4:30.
All the records before that say you returned them right after the last class.
Why would you keep them every day...for the last month?
Did you forget to return them every day for a whole month?

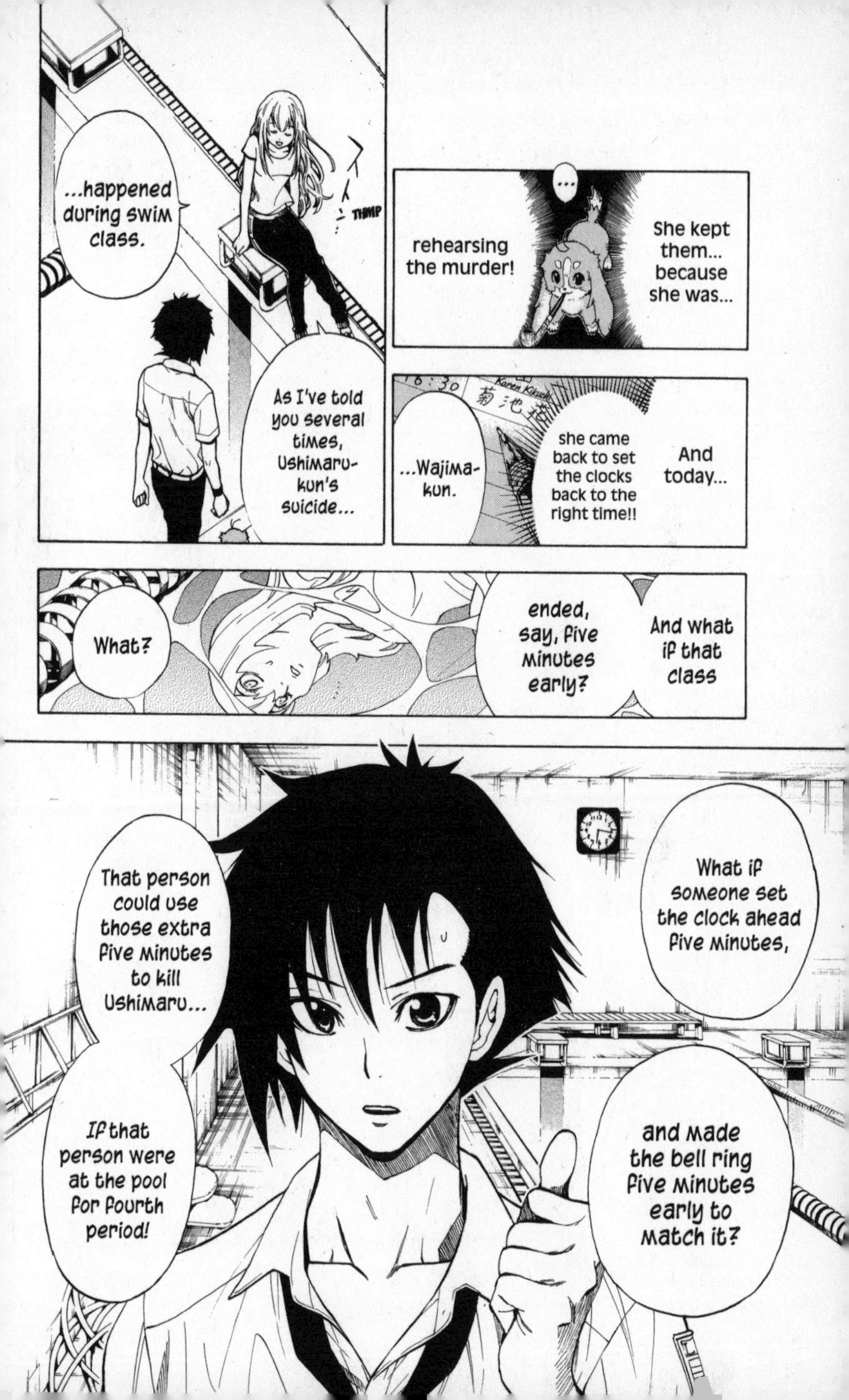

...
She kept them... because she was...
rehearsing the murder!
And today...
she came back to set the clocks back to the right time!!
Karen Kikuchi
...Wajima-kun.
THMP
As I've told you several times, Ushimaru-kun's suicide...
...happened during swim class.
And what if that class
ended, say, five minutes early?
What?
What if someone set the clock ahead five minutes,
and made the bell ring five minutes early to match it?
That person could use those extra five minutes to kill Ushimaru...
If that person were at the pool for fourth period!

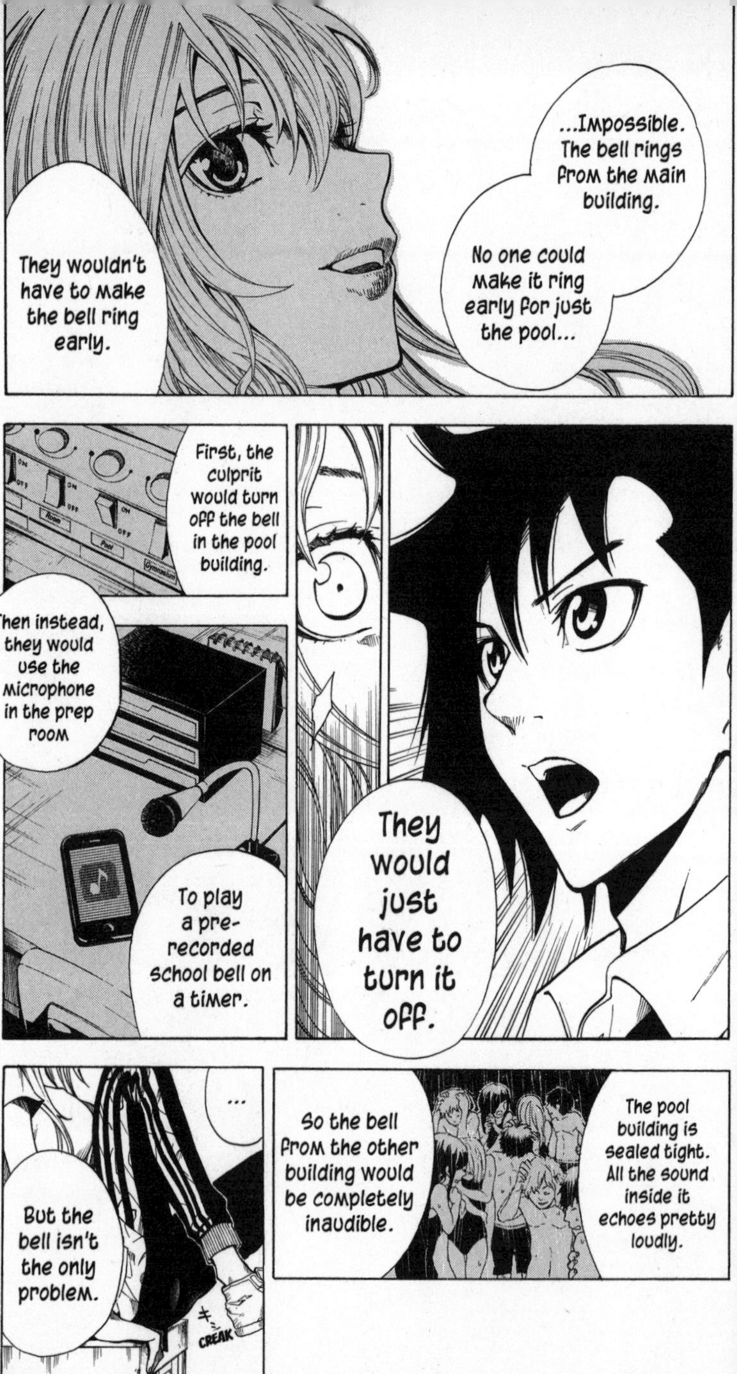
...Impossible. The bell rings from the main building.
No one could make it ring early for just the pool...
They wouldn't have to make the bell ring early.
They would just have to turn it off.
First, the culprit would turn off the bell in the pool building.
Then instead, they would use the microphone in the prep room
To play a pre-recorded school bell on a timer.
The pool building is sealed tight. All the sound inside it echoes pretty loudly.
So the bell from the other building would be completely inaudible.
...
But the bell isn't the only problem.
CREAK

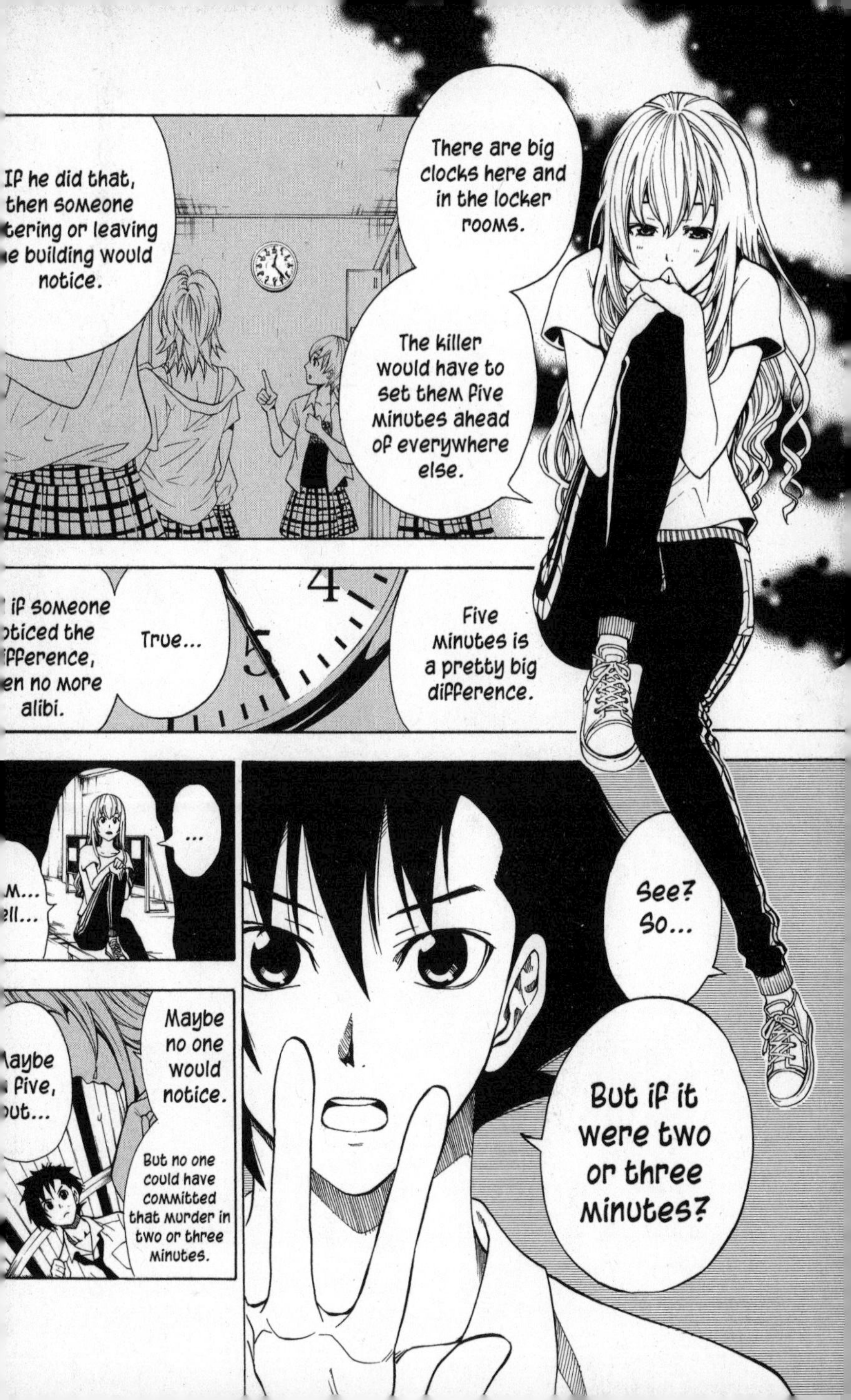

There are big clocks here and in the locker rooms.
The killer would have to set them five minutes ahead of everywhere else.
If he did that, then someone tering or leaving e building would notice.
Five minutes is a pretty big difference.
True...
if someone oticed the ifference, en no more alibi.
See? So...
But if it were two or three minutes?
...
M... ll...
Maybe no one would notice.
aybe five, ut...
But no one could have committed that murder in two or three minutes.

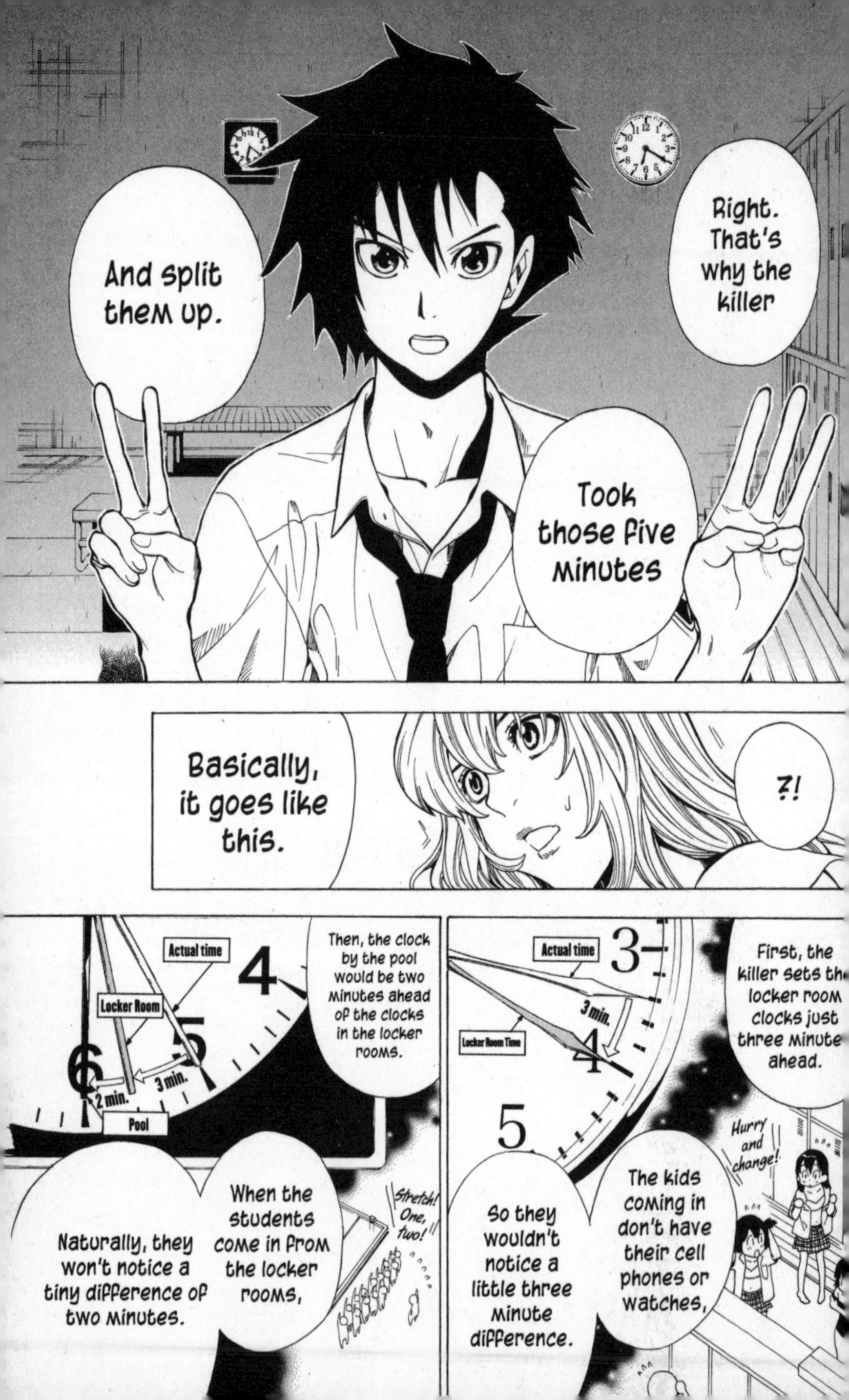
Right. That's why the killer
Took those five minutes
And split them up.
?!
Basically, it goes like this.
Actual time
3 min.
Locker Room Time
First, the killer sets the locker room clocks just three minute ahead.
Hurry and change!
The kids coming in don't have their cell phones or watches,
So they wouldn't notice a little three minute difference.
Actual time
Locker Room
3 min.
2 min.
Pool
Then, the clock by the pool would be two minutes ahead of the clocks in the locker rooms.
Stretch! One, two!
When the students come in from the locker rooms,
Naturally, they won't notice a tiny difference of two minutes.

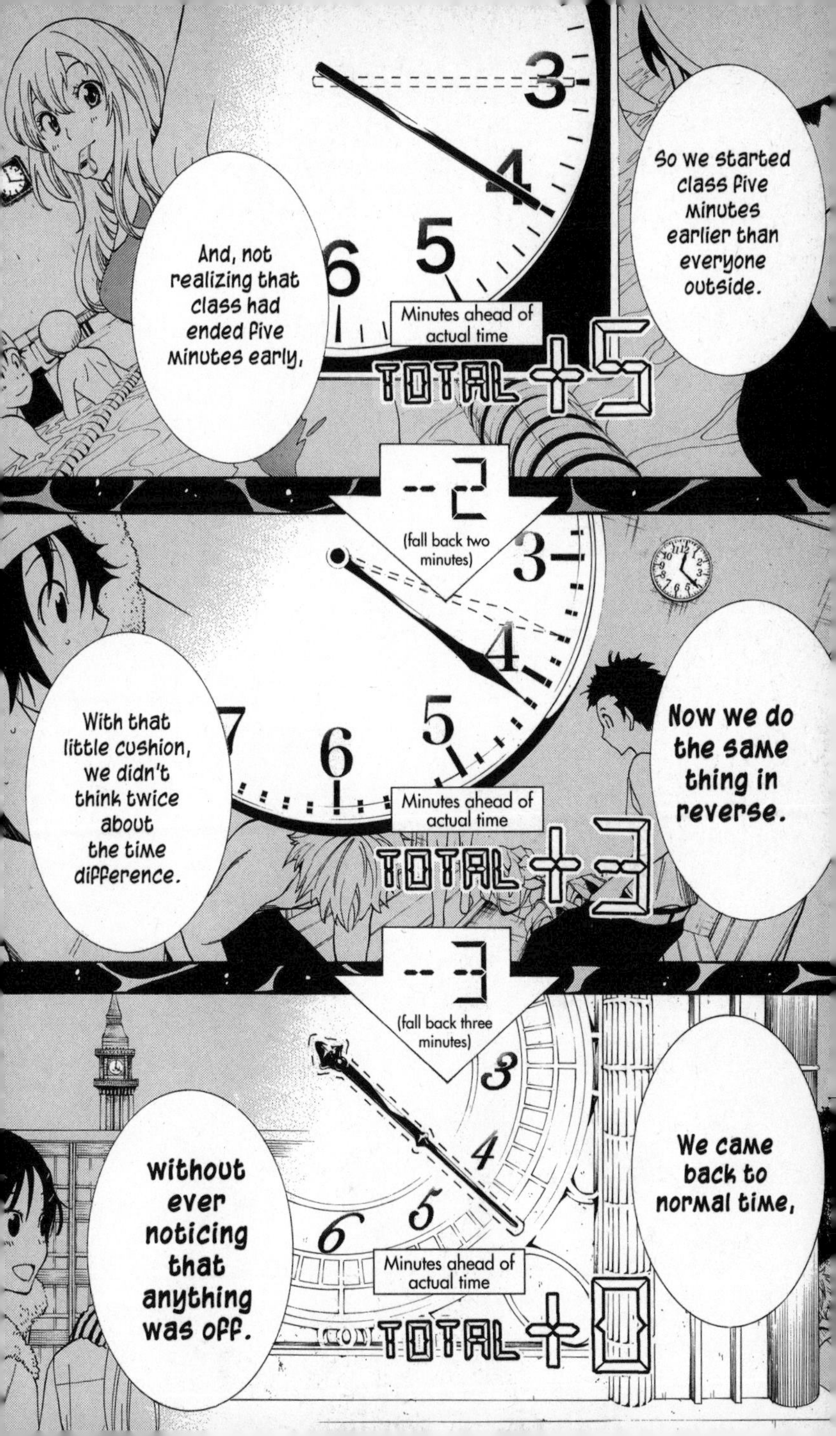
So we started class five minutes earlier than everyone outside.
And, not realizing that class had ended five minutes early,
Minutes ahead of actual time
TOTAL +5
-2
(fall back two minutes)
Now we do the same thing in reverse.
With that little cushion, we didn't think twice about the time difference.
Minutes ahead of actual time
TOTAL +3
-3
(fall back three minutes)
We came back to normal time,
without ever noticing that anything was off.
Minutes ahead of actual time
TOTAL +0

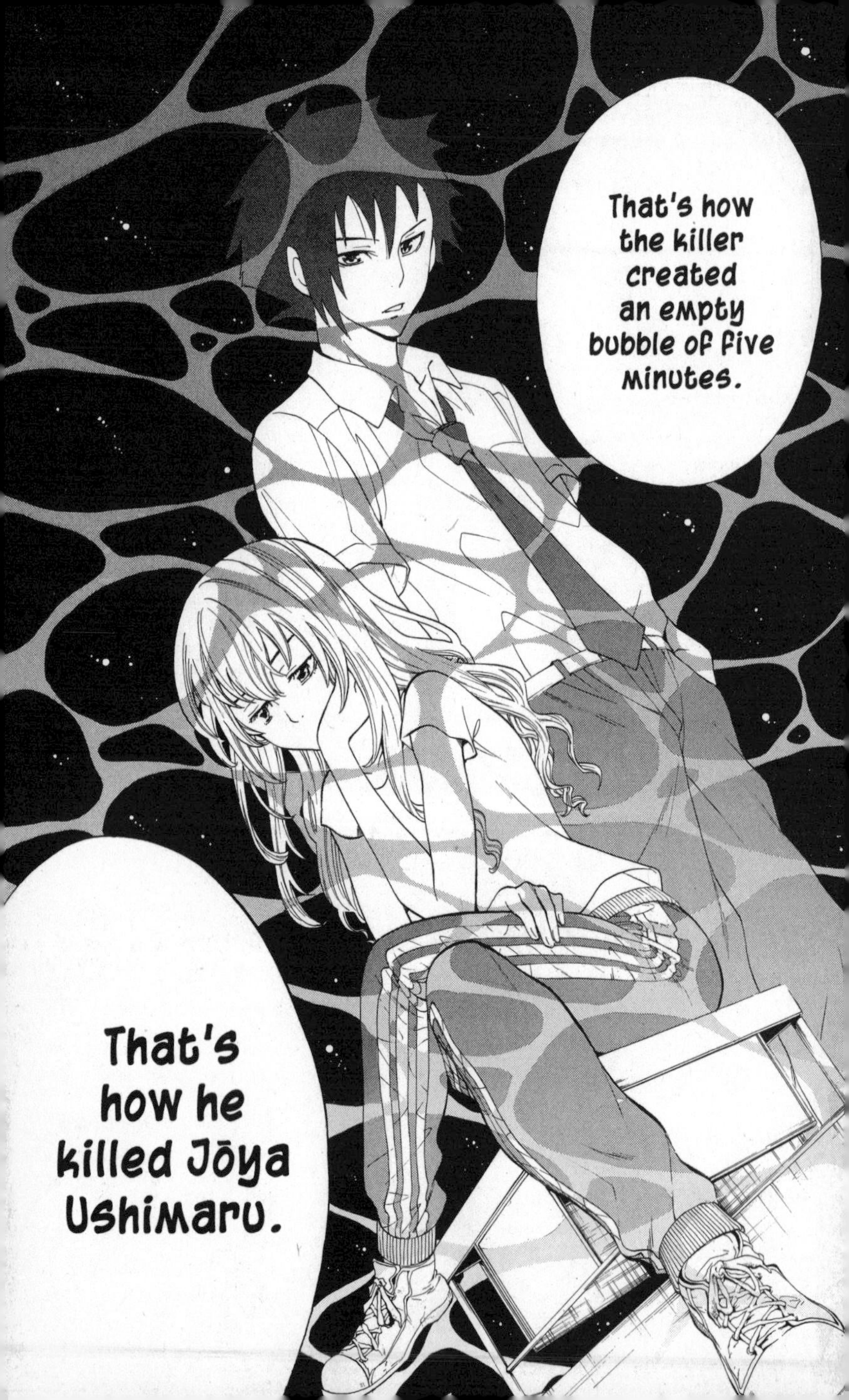
That's how the killer created an empty bubble of five minutes.
That's how he killed Jōya Ushimaru.

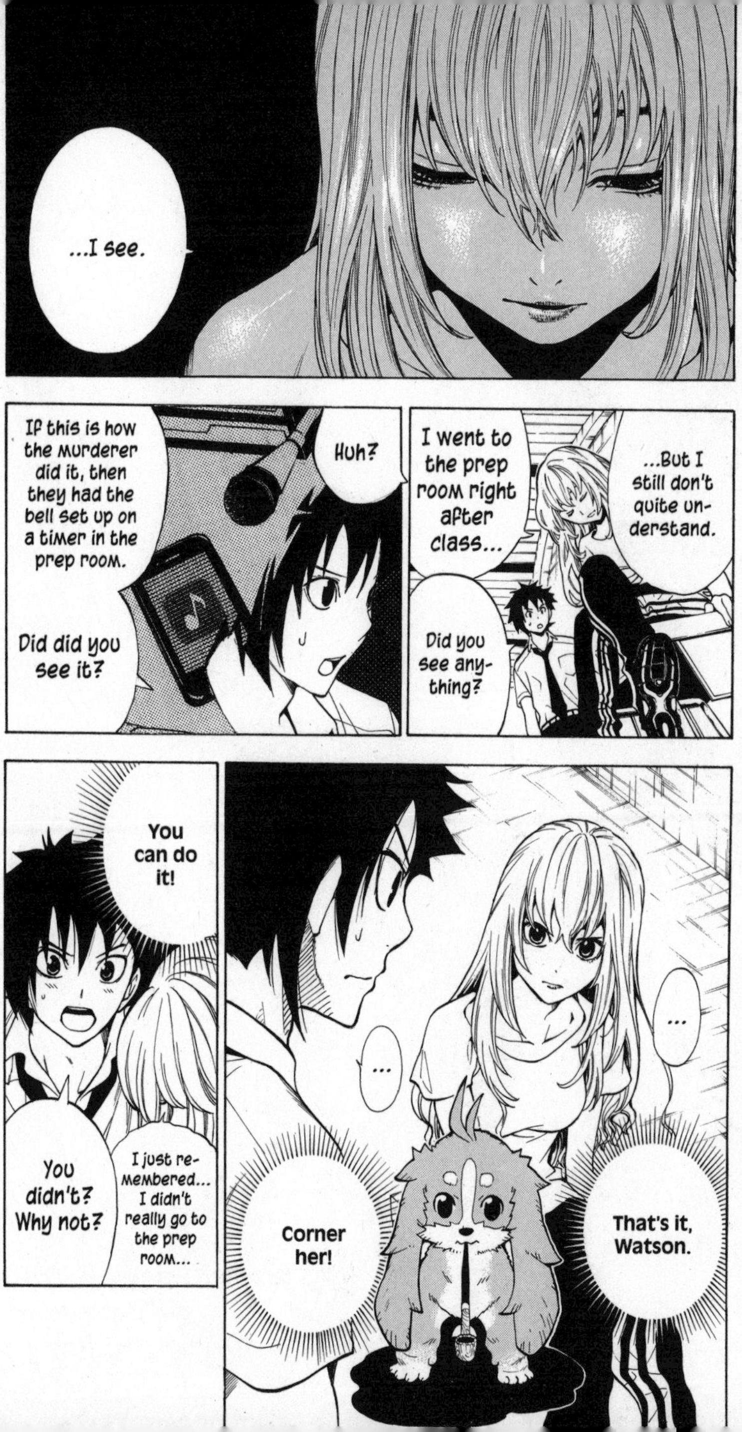
...I see.
...But I still don't quite un-derstand.
I went to the prep room right after class...
Did you see any-thing?
Huh?
If this is how the murderer did it, then they had the bell set up on a timer in the prep room.
Did did you see it?
...
...
That's it, Watson.
Corner her!
You can do it!
I just re-membered... I didn't really go to the prep room...
You didn't? Why not?

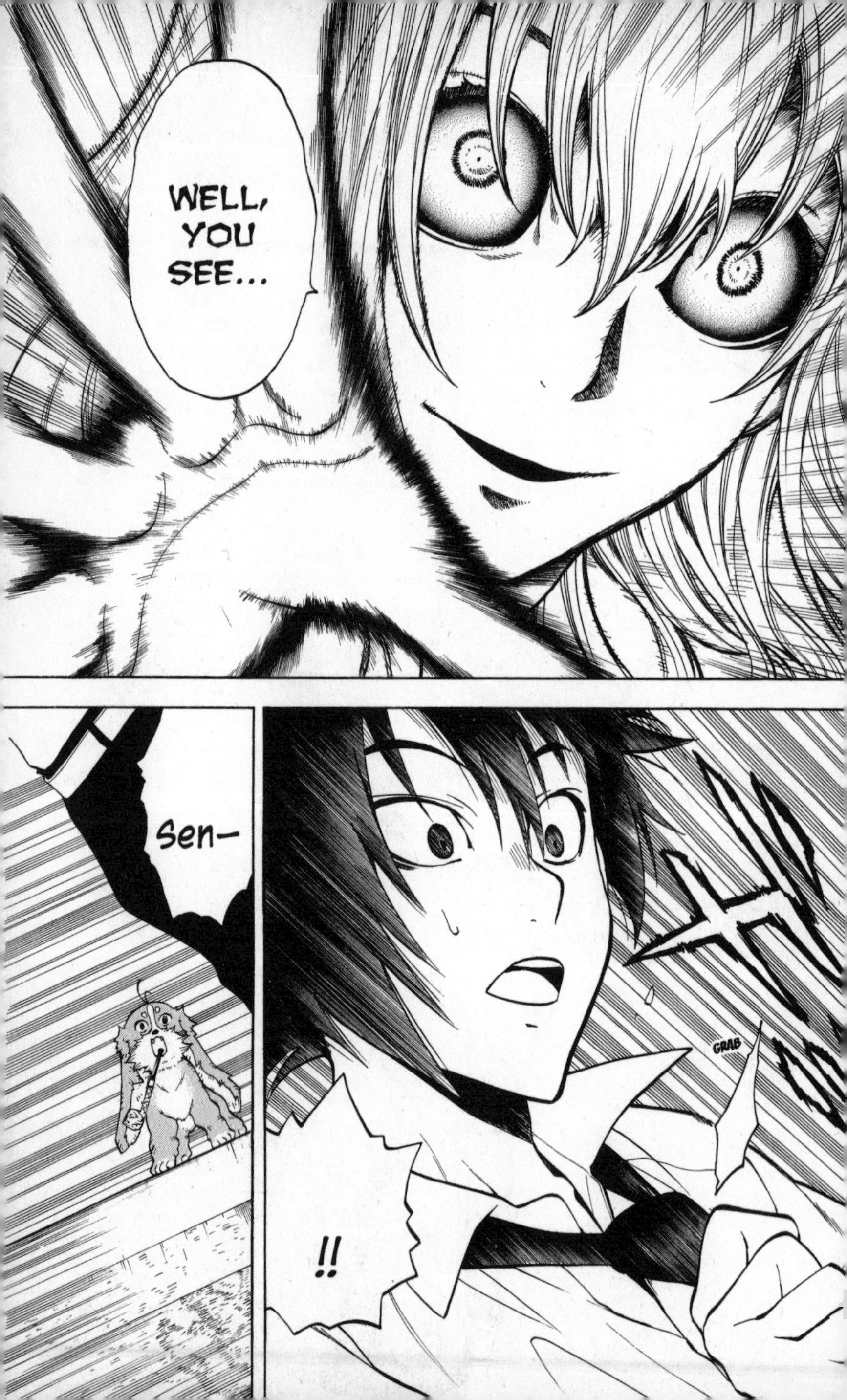
WELL, YOU SEE...
GRAB
!!
Sen-

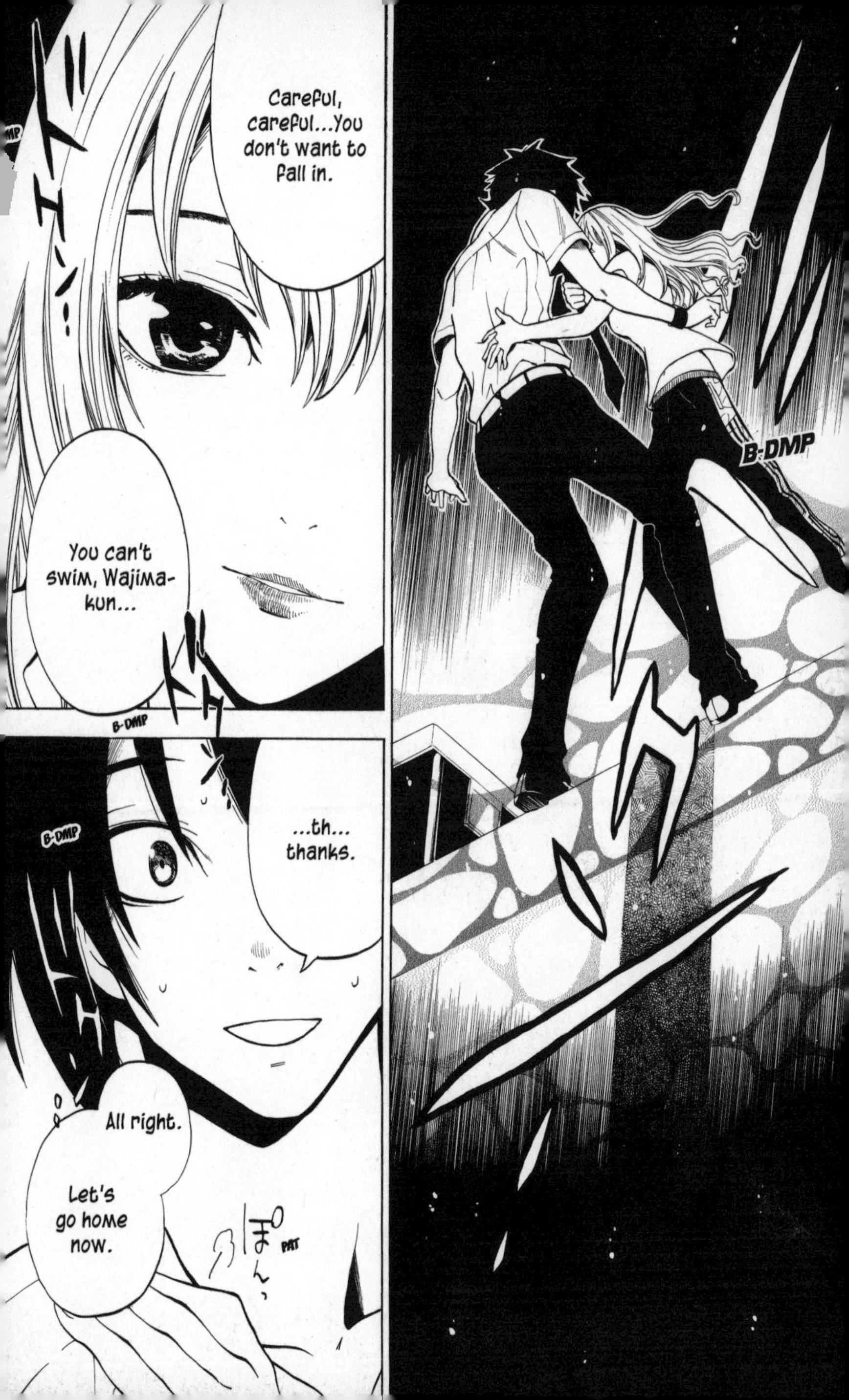
B-DMP
Careful, careful...You don't want to fall in.
You can't swim, Wajima-kun...
B-DMP
B-DMP
...th... thanks.
All right.
Let's go home now.
PAT

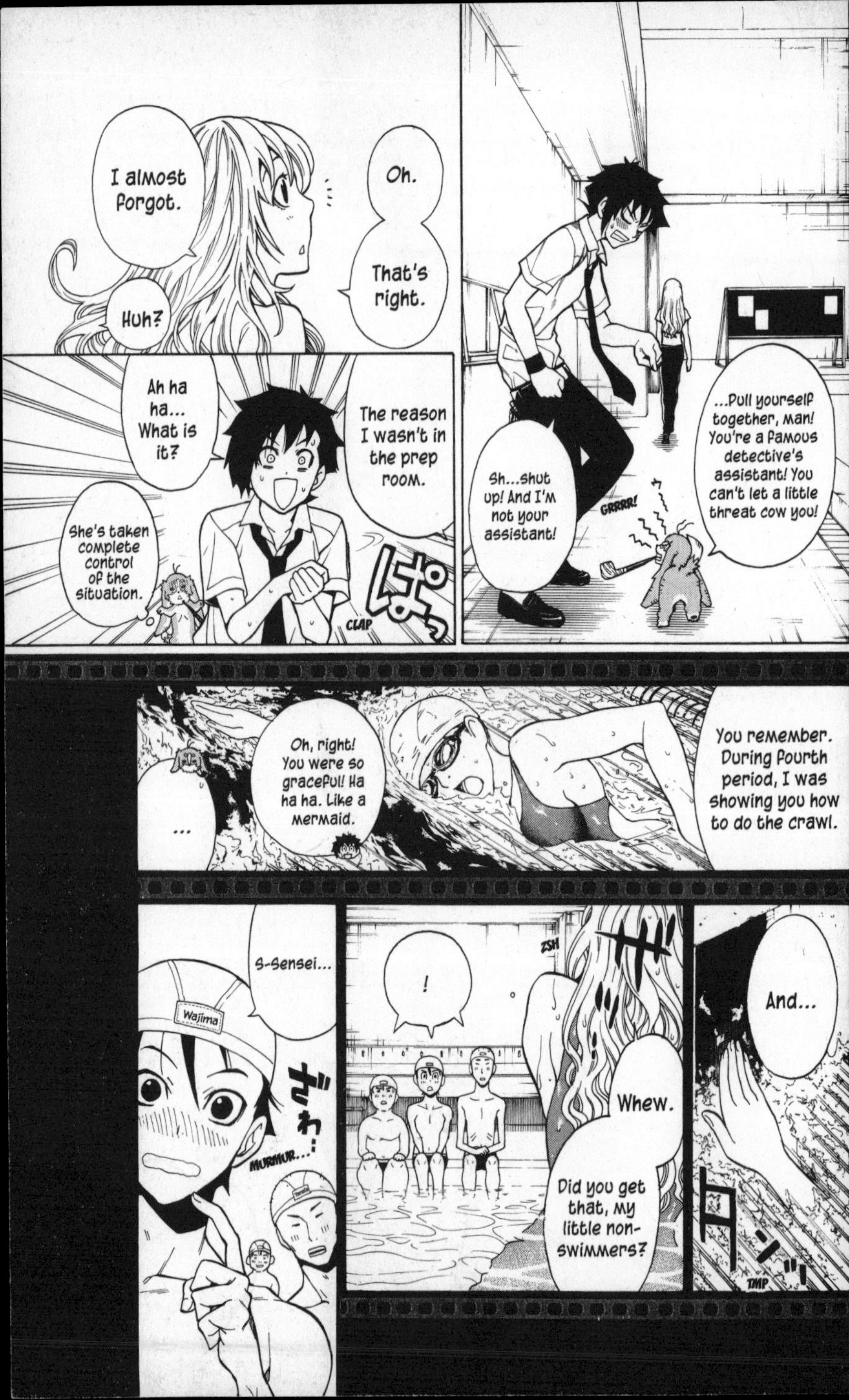
...Pull yourself together, man! You're a famous detective's assistant! You can't let a little threat cow you!
GRRRR!
Sh...shut up! And I'm not your assistant!
Oh.
That's right.
I almost forgot.
Huh?
The reason I wasn't in the prep room.
CLAP
Ah ha ha... What is it?
She's taken complete control of the situation.
You remember. During fourth period, I was showing you how to do the crawl.
Oh, right! You were so graceful! Ha ha ha. Like a mermaid.
...
And...
TMP
Whew.
Did you get that, my little non-swimmers?
ZSH
!
S-Sensei...
Wajima
MURMUR...

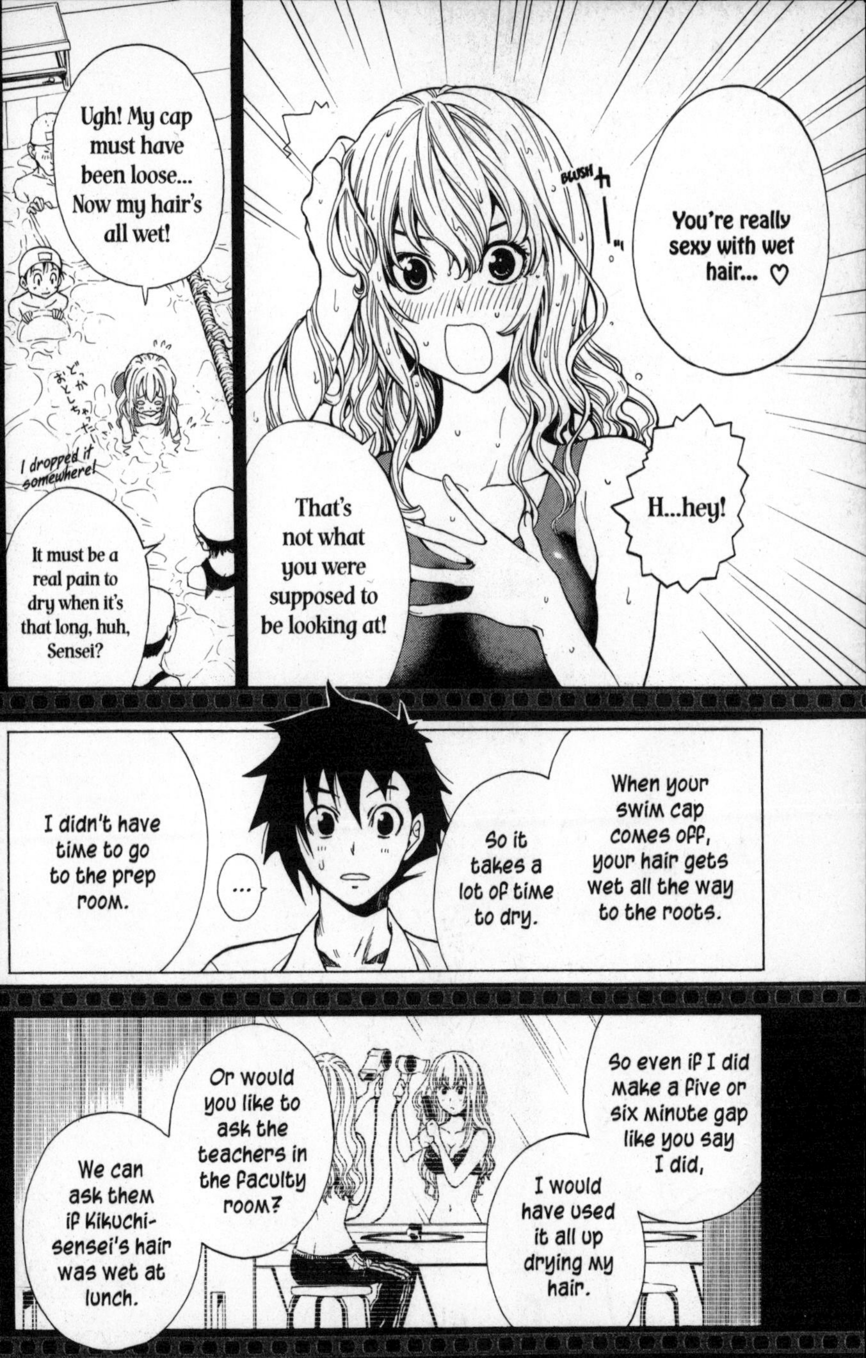
You're really sexy with wet hair... ♡
BLUSH
H...hey!
That's not what you were supposed to be looking at!
Ugh! My cap must have been loose... Now my hair's all wet!
I dropped it somewhere!
It must be a real pain to dry when it's that long, huh, Sensei?
When your swim cap comes off, your hair gets wet all the way to the roots.
So it takes a lot of time to dry.
...
I didn't have time to go to the prep room.
So even if I did make a five or six minute gap like you say I did,
I would have used it all up drying my hair.
Or would you like to ask the teachers in the faculty room?
We can ask them if Kikuchi-sensei's hair was wet at lunch.

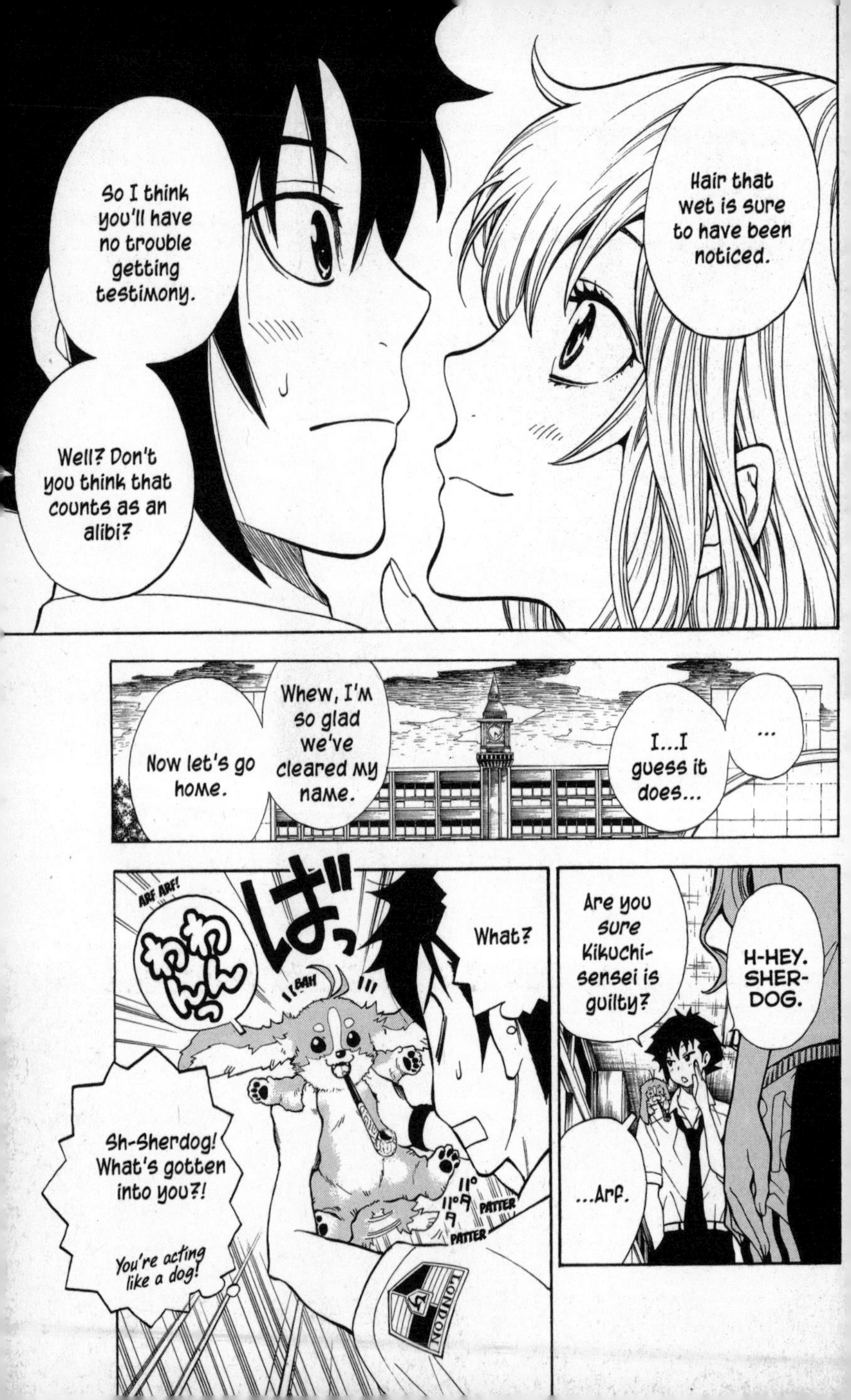
Hair that wet is sure to have been noticed.
So I think you'll have no trouble getting testimony.
Well? Don't you think that counts as an alibi?
...
I...I guess it does...
Whew, I'm so glad we've cleared my name.
Now let's go home.
H-HEY. SHER-DOG.
Are you sure Kikuchi-sensei is guilty?
...Arf.
What?
ばっ
BAH
わわんっ
ARF ARF!
PATTER
PATTER
Sh-Sherdog! What's gotten into you?!
You're acting like a dog!

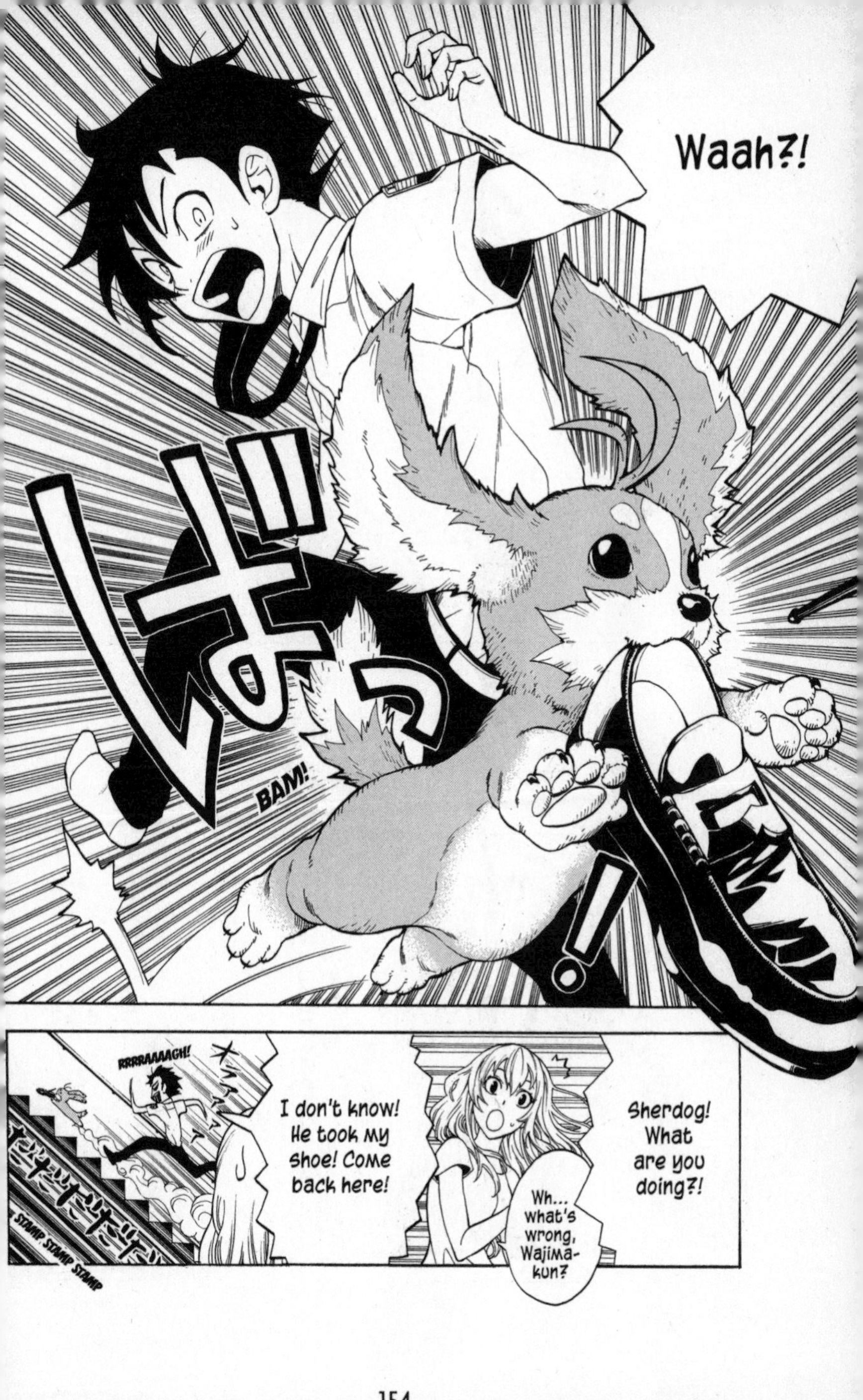
Waah?!
ばっ!
BAM!
Sherdog! What are you doing?!
Wh... what's wrong, Wajima-kun?
RRRRAAAAGH!
I don't know! He took my shoe! Come back here!
STAMP STAMP STAMP

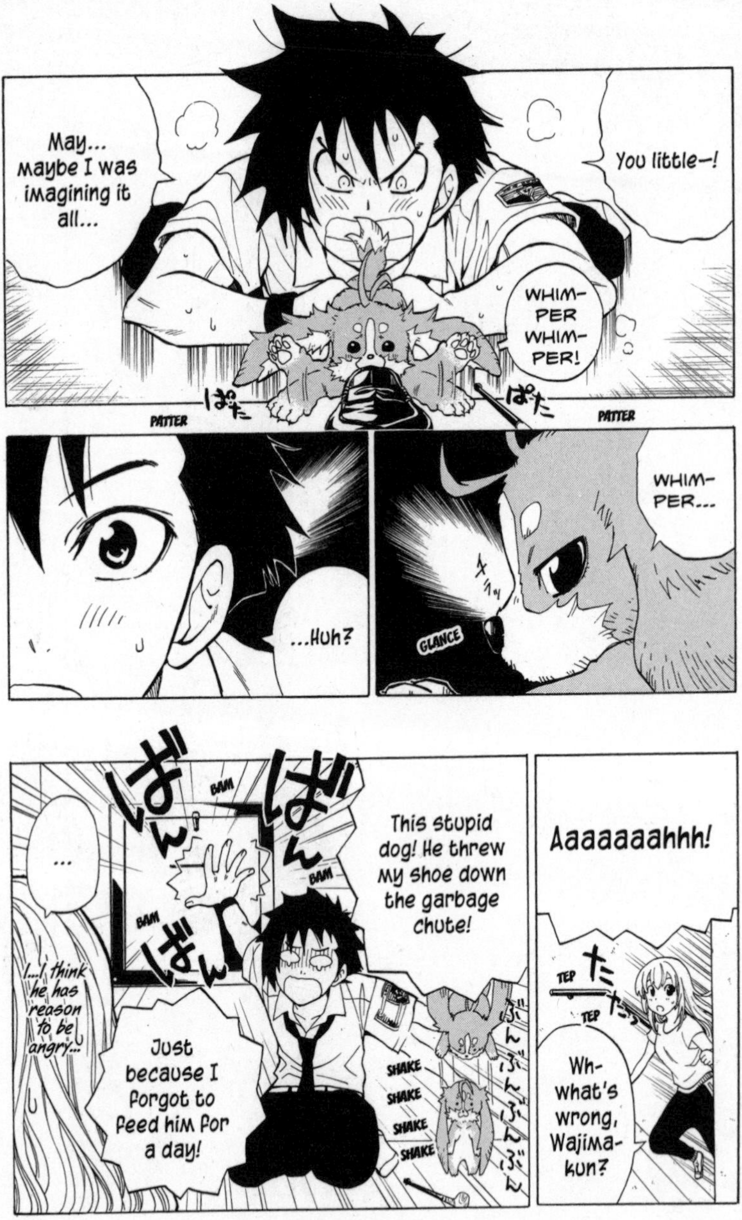
You little—!
May... maybe I was imagining it all...
WHIMPER-PER WHIMPER-PER!
ぱた
PATTER
ぱた
PATTER
WHIMPER...
GLANCE
...Huh?
Aaaaaaahhh!
TEP
TEP
Wh-what's wrong, Wajima-kun?
This stupid dog! He threw my shoe down the garbage chute!
BAM
BAM
BAM
SHAKE
SHAKE
SHAKE
SHAKE
...
Just because I forgot to feed him for a day!
I...I think he has reason to be angry...

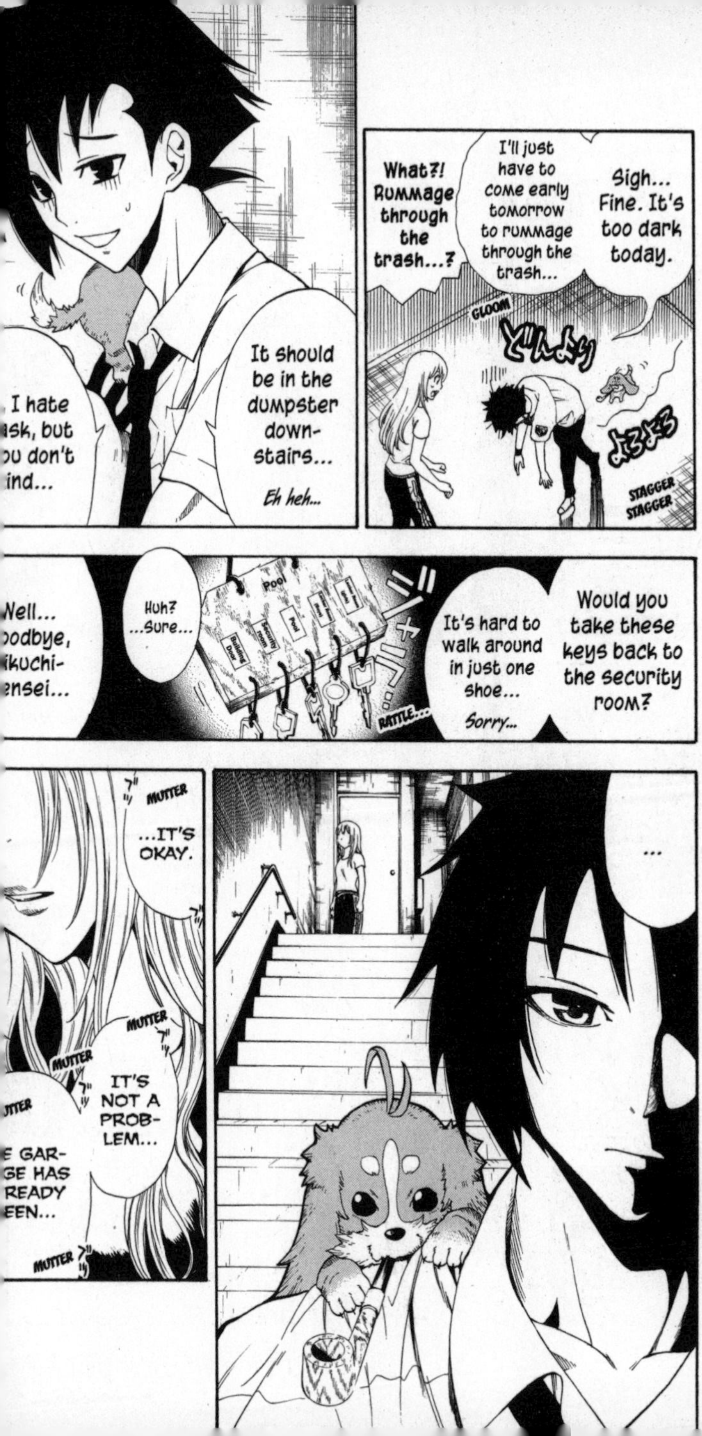
Sigh... Fine. It's too dark today.
I'll just have to come early tomorrow to rummage through the trash...
What?! Rummage through the trash...?
GLOOM
STAGGER STAGGER
It should be in the dumpster down-stairs...
Eh heh...
I hate
ask, but
ou don't
ind...
Would you take these keys back to the security room?
It's hard to walk around in just one shoe...
Sorry...
RATTLE...
Huh? ...Sure...
Well...
oodbye,
ikuchi-
ensei...
...
MUTTER
...IT'S OKAY.
MUTTER
MUTTER
IT'S NOT A PROB-LEM...
UTTER
E GAR-
GE HAS
READY
EEN...
MUTTER

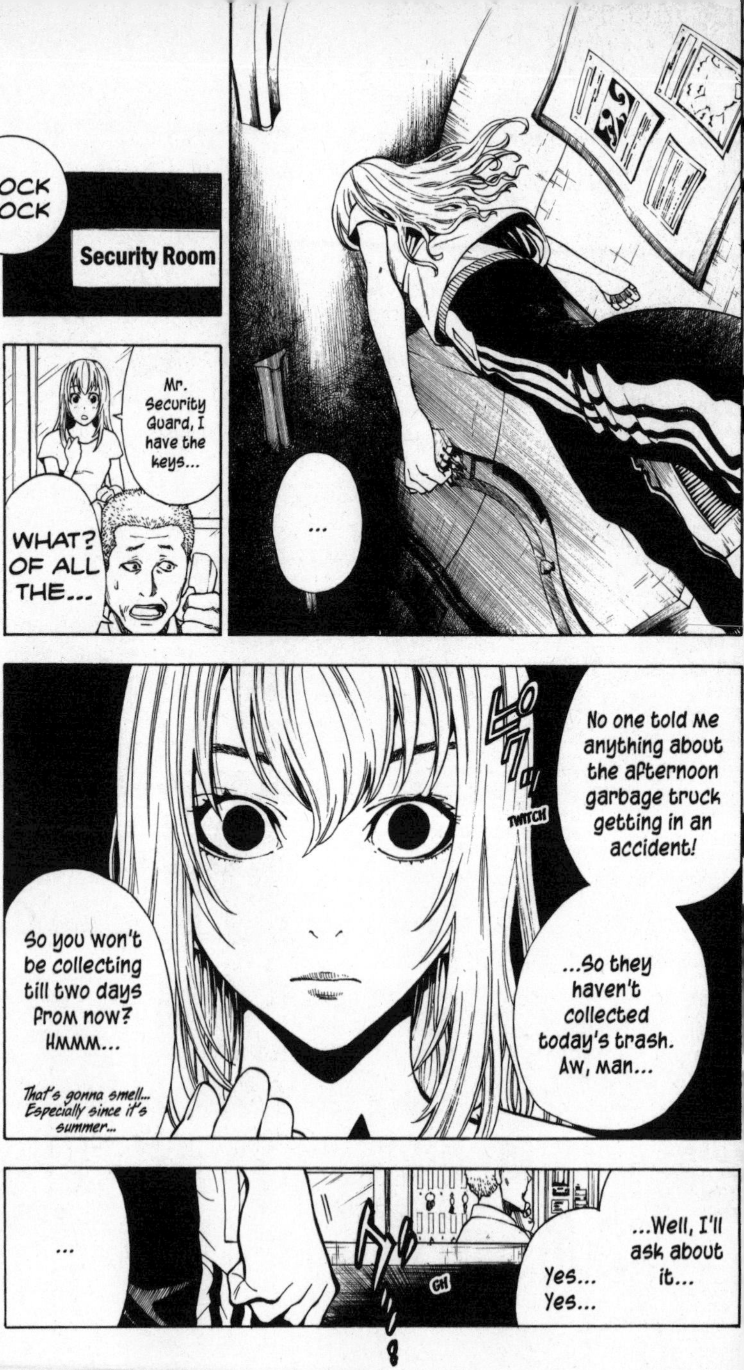
...
KNOCK KNOCK
Security Room
Mr. Security Guard, I have the keys...
WHAT? OF ALL THE...
No one told me anything about the afternoon garbage truck getting in an accident!
TWITCH
...So they haven't collected today's trash. Aw, man...
So you won't be collecting till two days from now? HMMM...
That's gonna smell... Especially since it's summer...
...Well, I'll ask about it...
Yes... Yes...
GH
...

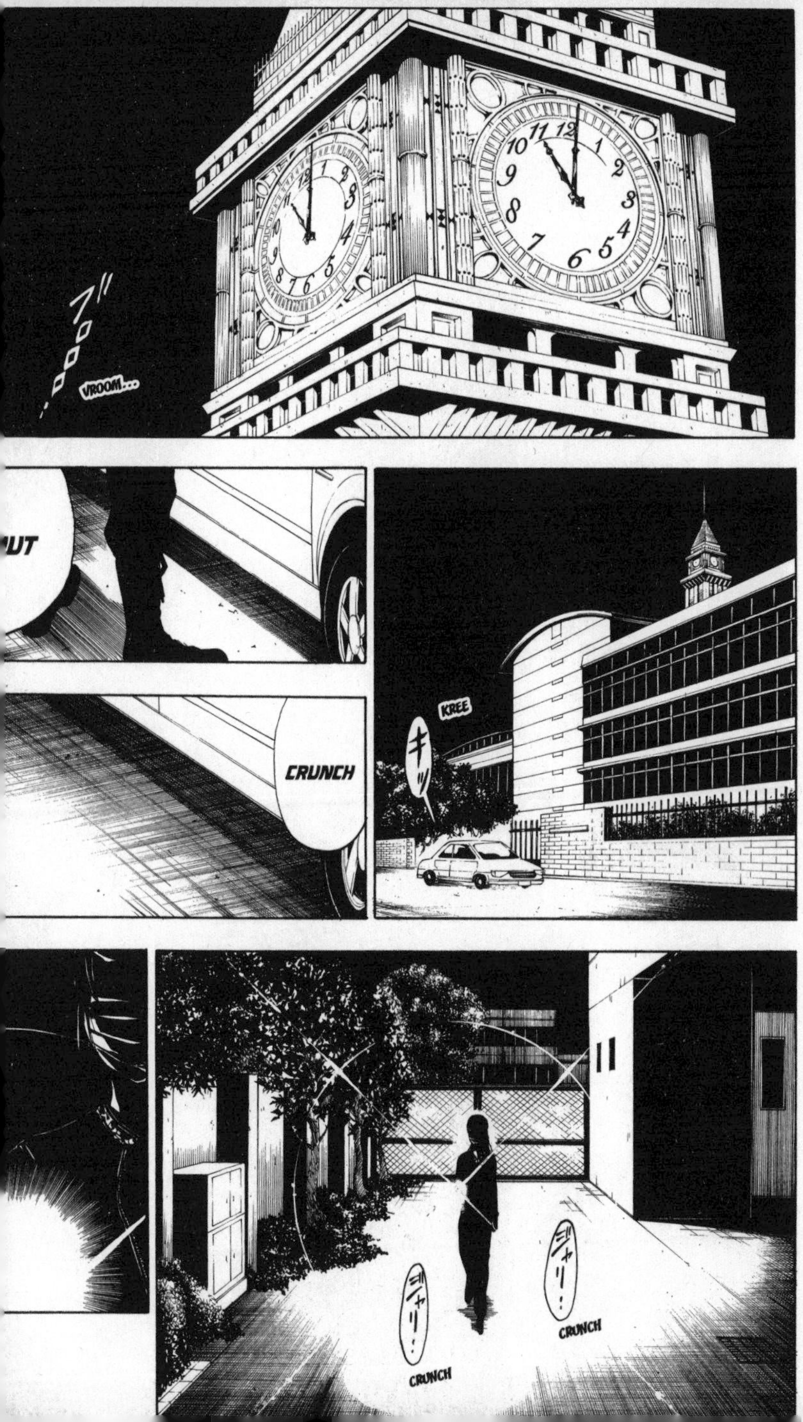

ブロロロ…
VROOM...
キッ
KREE
CRUNCH
ジャリ！
CRUNCH
ジャリ！
CRUNCH

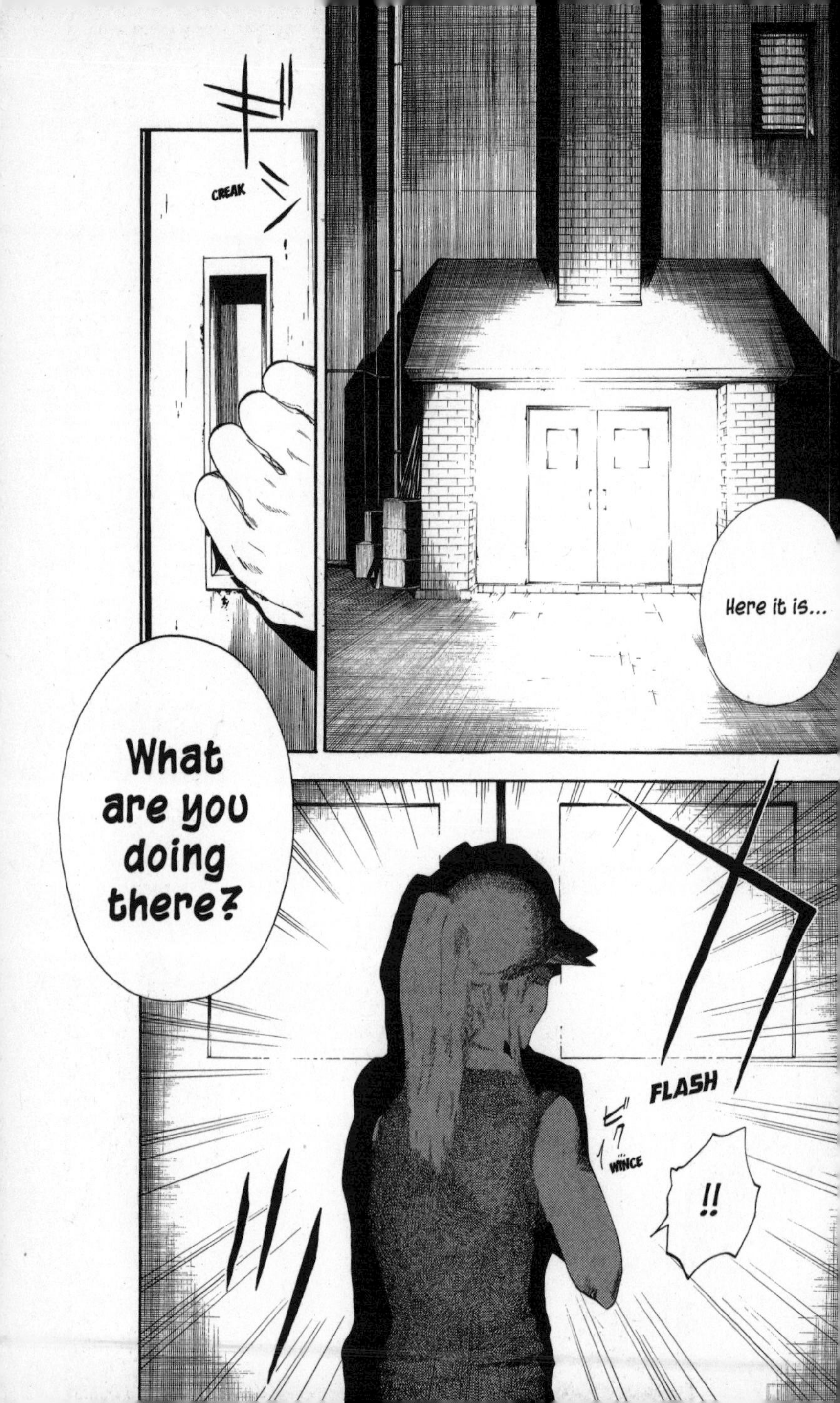
Here it is...
CREAK
What are you doing there?
FLASH
WINCE
!!

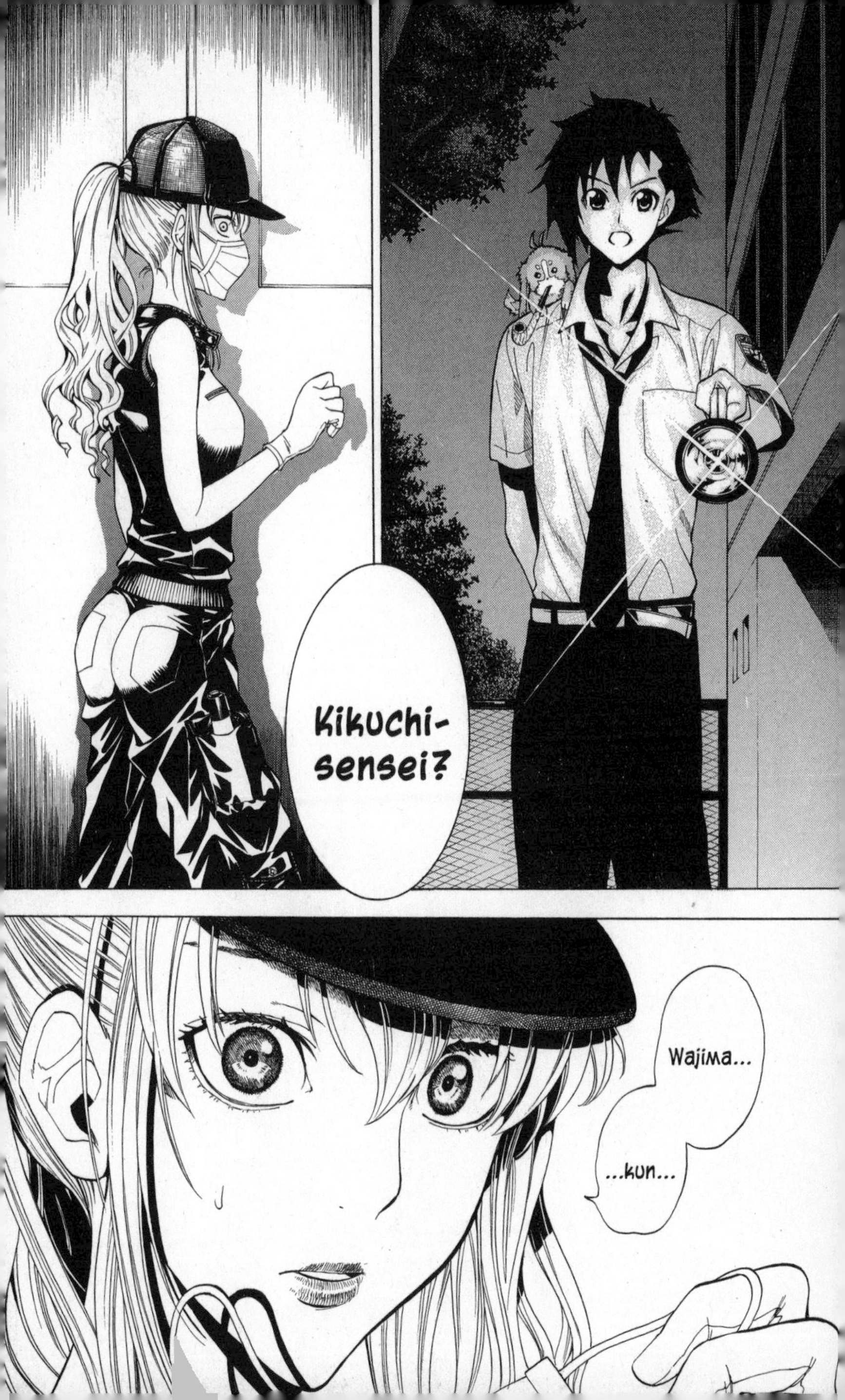
Kikuchi-sensei?
Wajima...
...kun...

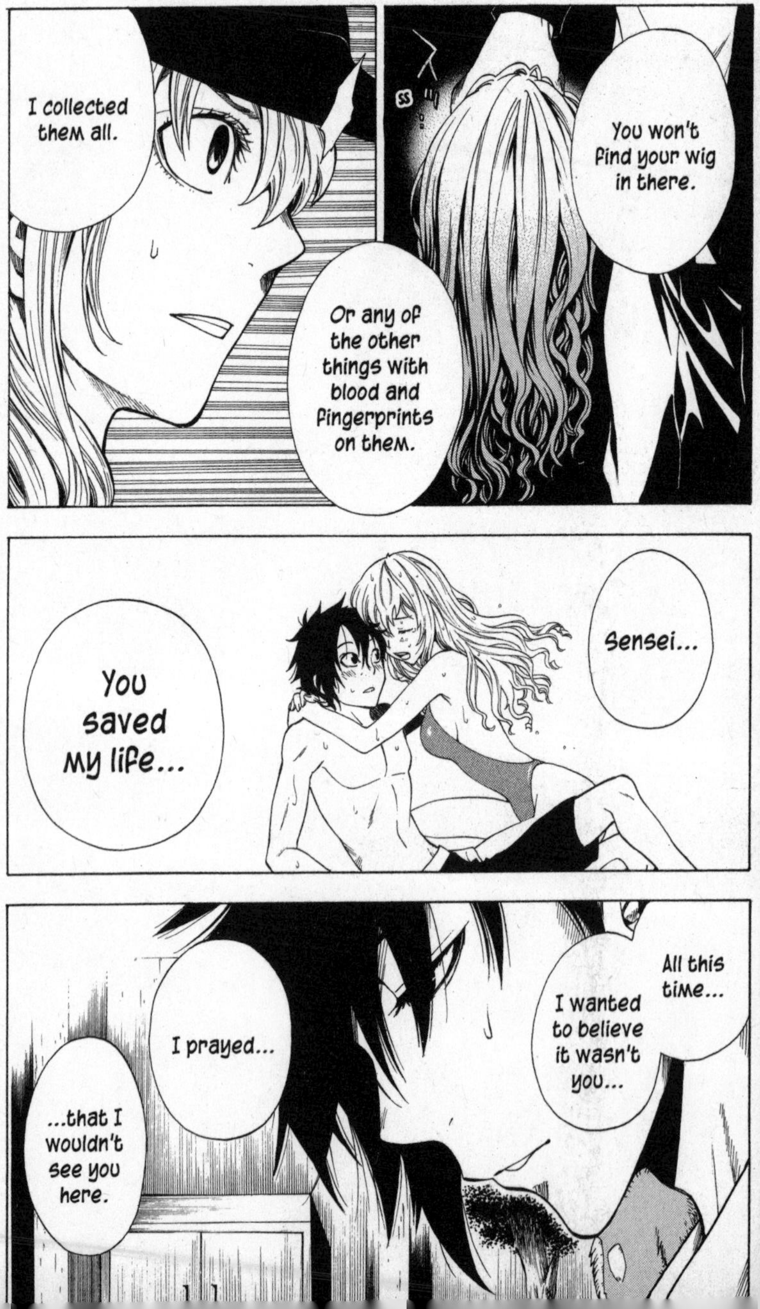

You won't find your wig in there.
SS
Or any of the other things with blood and fingerprints on them.
I collected them all.
Sensei...
You saved my life...
All this time...
I wanted to believe it wasn't you...
I prayed...
...that I wouldn't see you here.

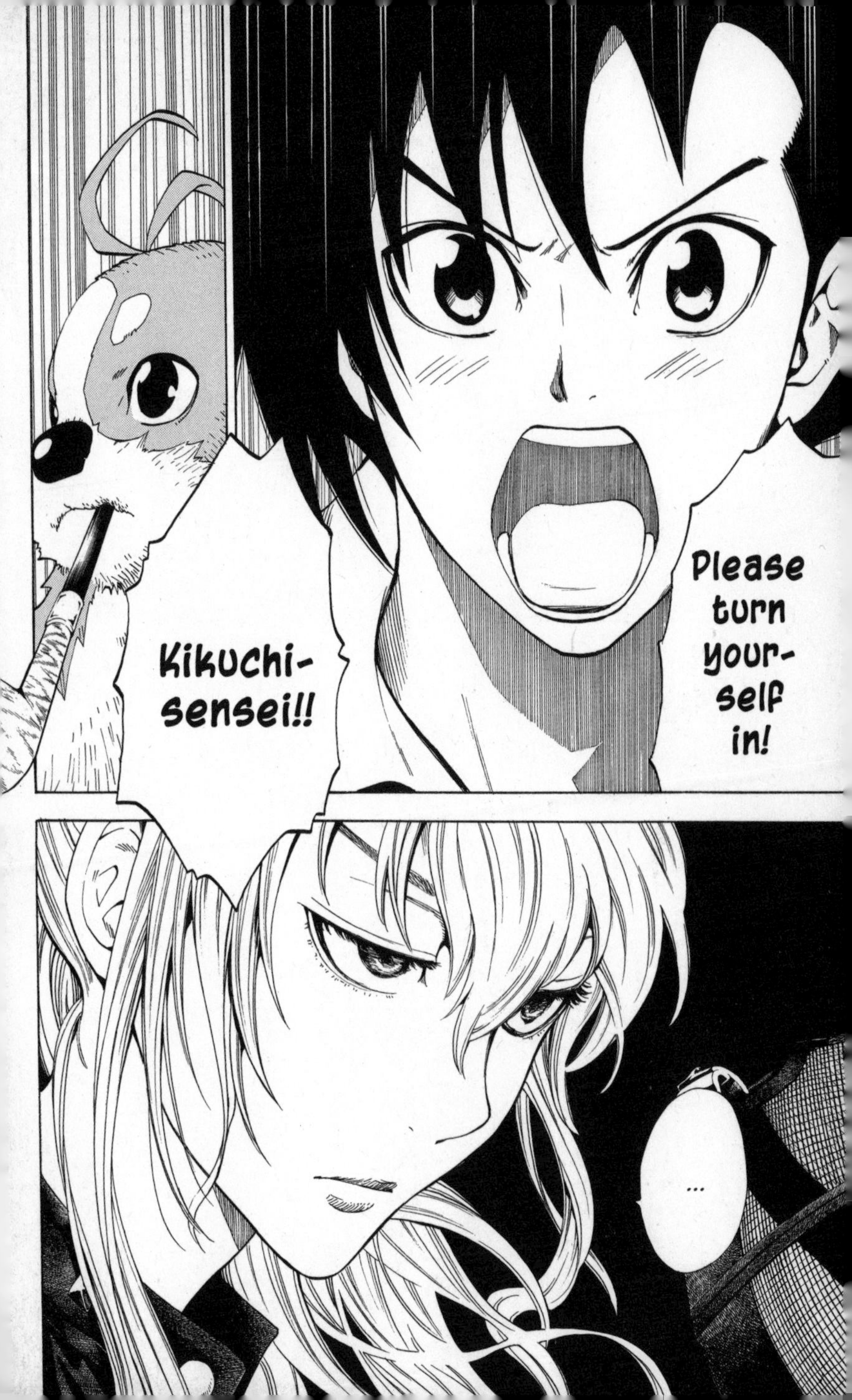
Please turn your-self in!
Kikuchi-sensei!!
...

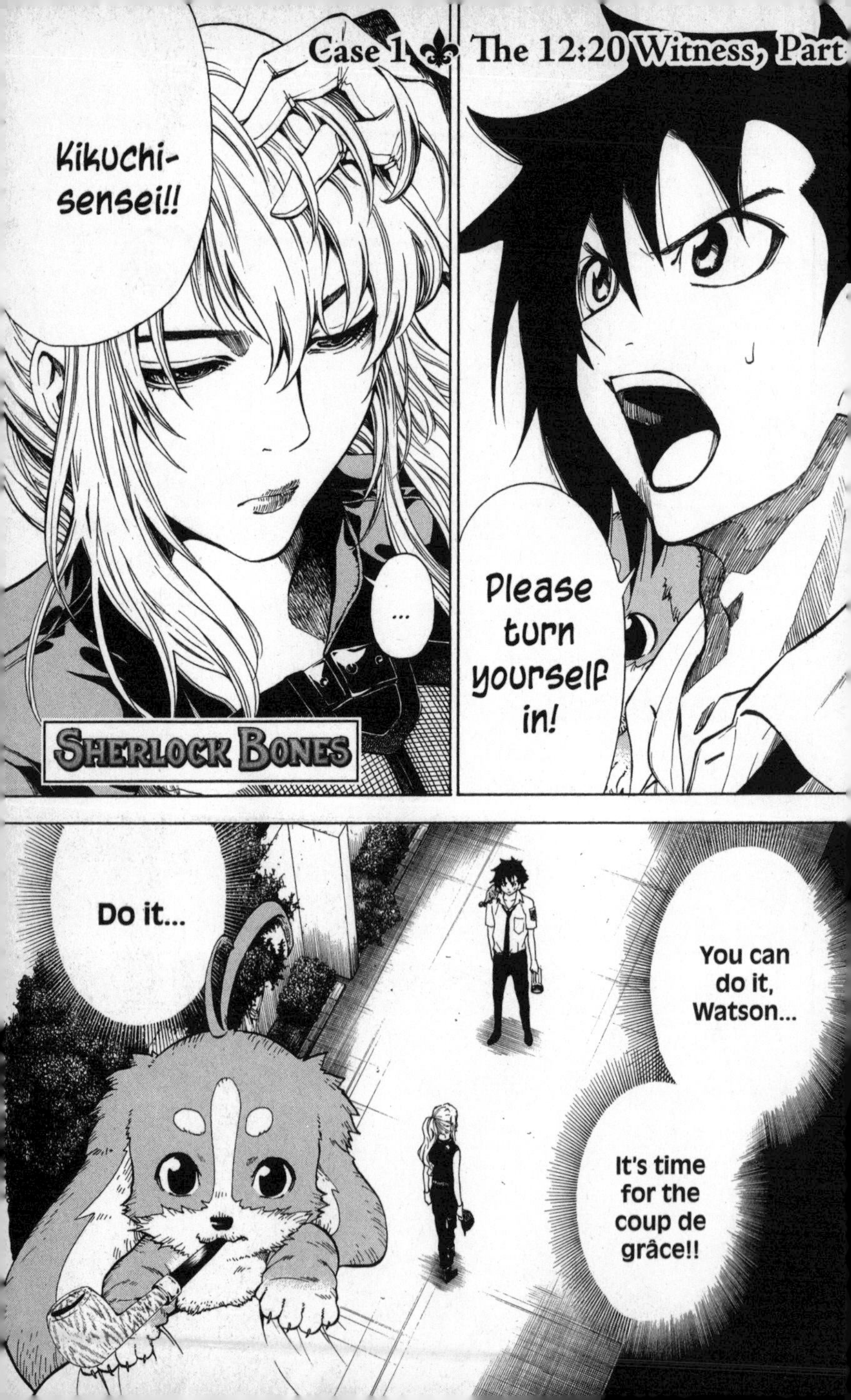
Case 1 The 12:20 Witness, Part
Please turn yourself in!
Kikuchi-sensei!!
...
Sherlock Bones
Do it...
You can do it, Watson...
It's time for the coup de grâce!!

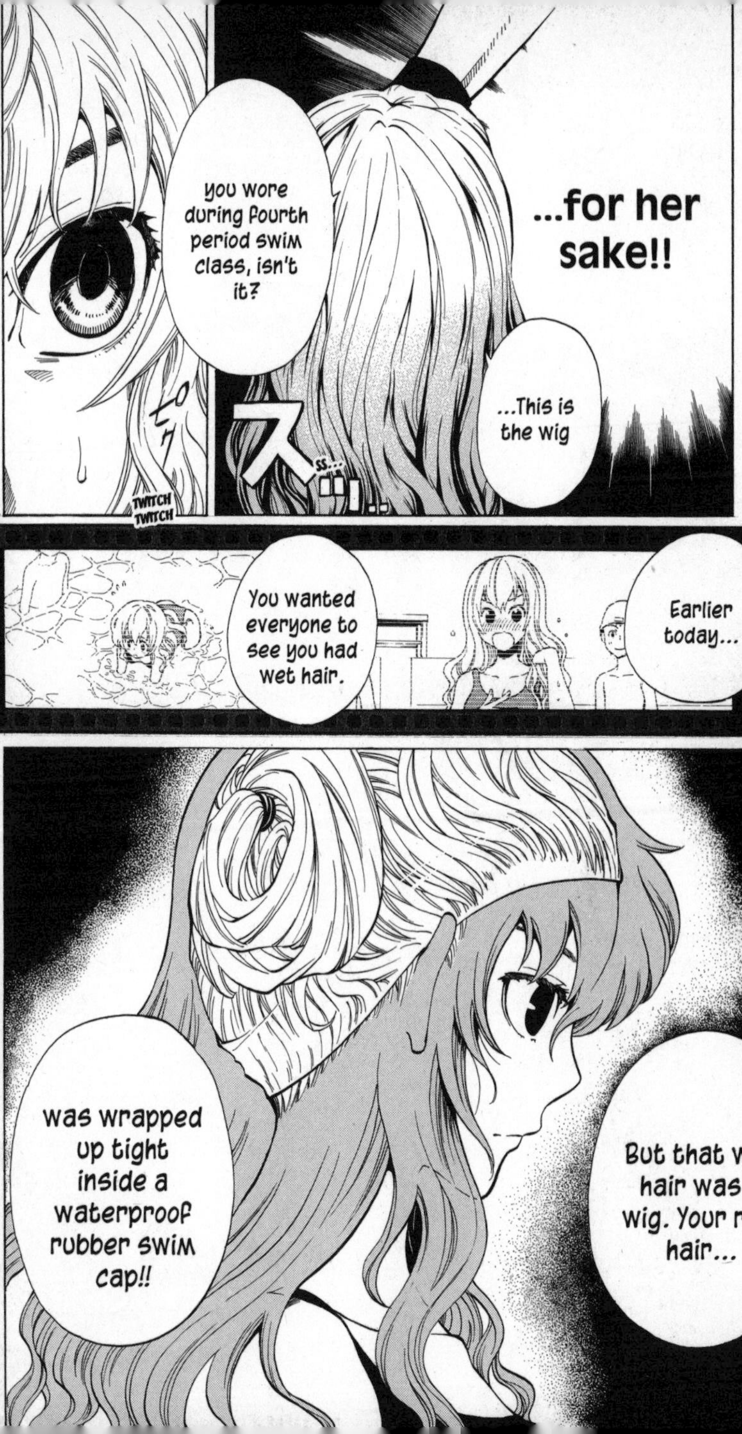

...for her sake!!
...This is the wig
you wore during fourth period swim class, isn't it?
SS...
TWITCH TWITCH
Earlier today...
You wanted everyone to see you had wet hair.
But that wet hair was a wig. Your real hair...
was wrapped up tight inside a waterproof rubber swim cap!!

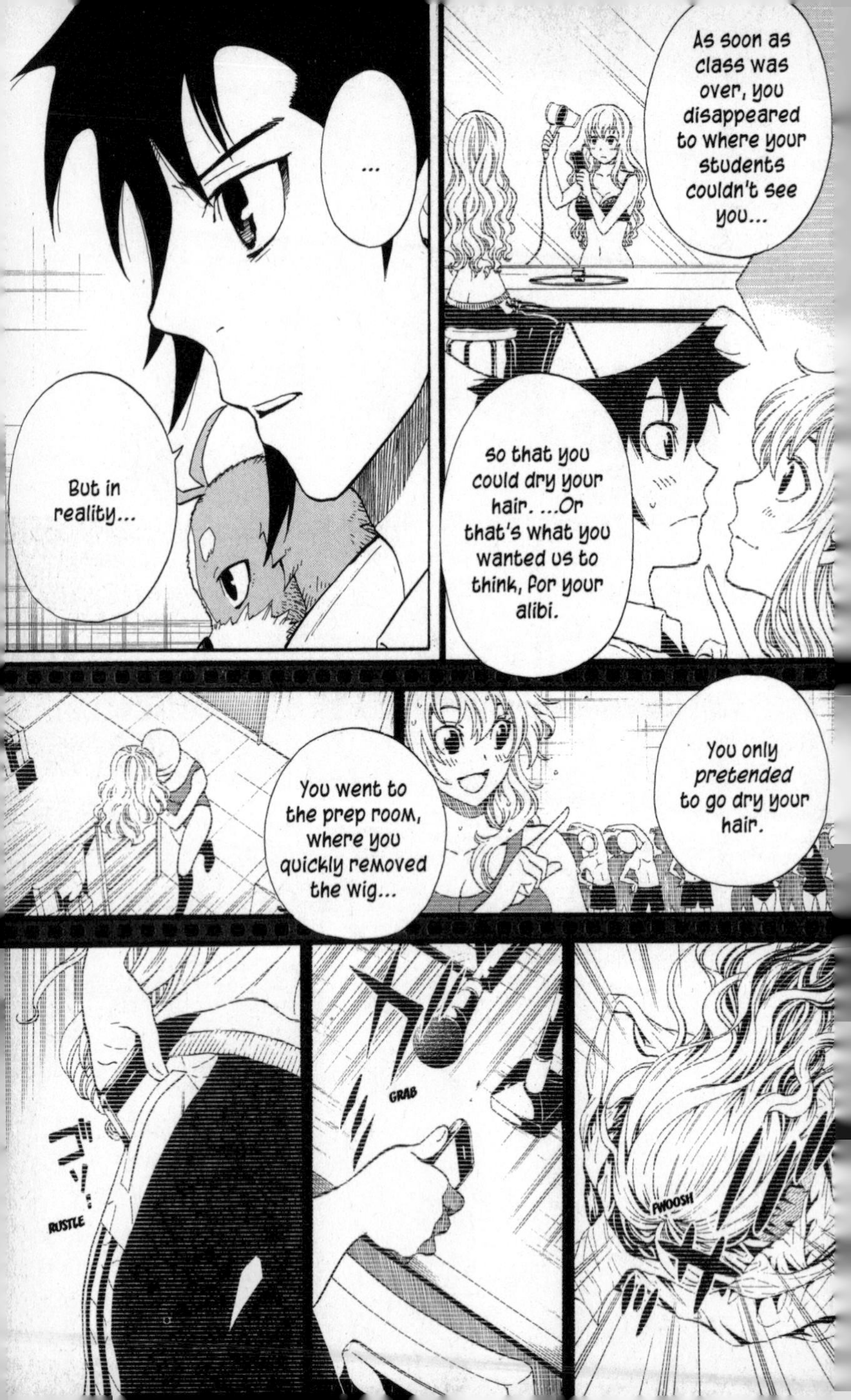
As soon as class was over, you disappeared to where your students couldn't see you...
so that you could dry your hair. ...Or that's what you wanted us to think, for your alibi.
...
But in reality...
You only *pretended* to go dry your hair.
You went to the prep room, where you quickly removed the wig...
FWOOSH
GRAB
RUSTLE

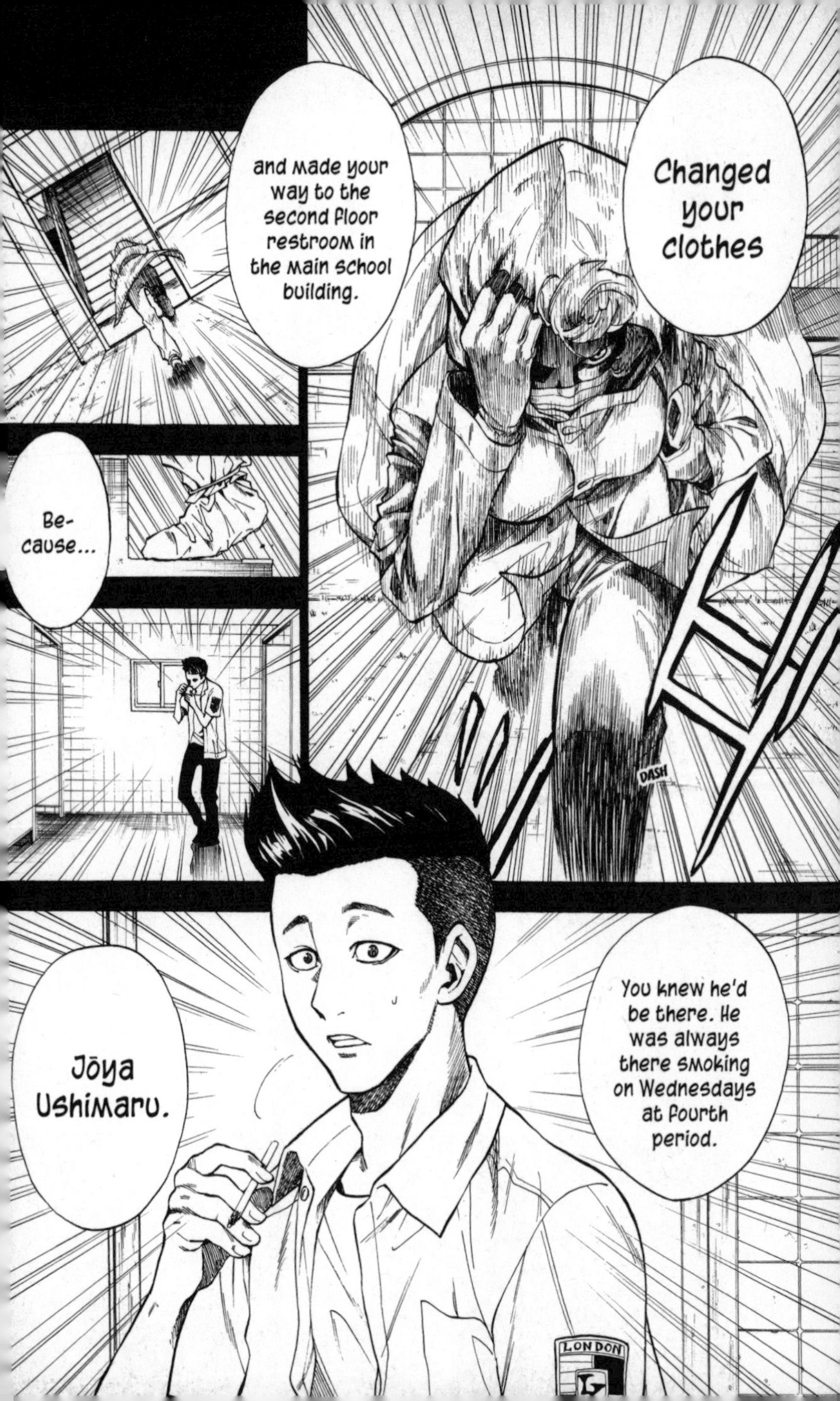
Changed your clothes
DASH
and made your way to the second floor restroom in the main school building.
Be-cause...
You knew he'd be there. He was always there smoking on Wednesdays at fourth period.
Jōya Ushimaru.
LONDON

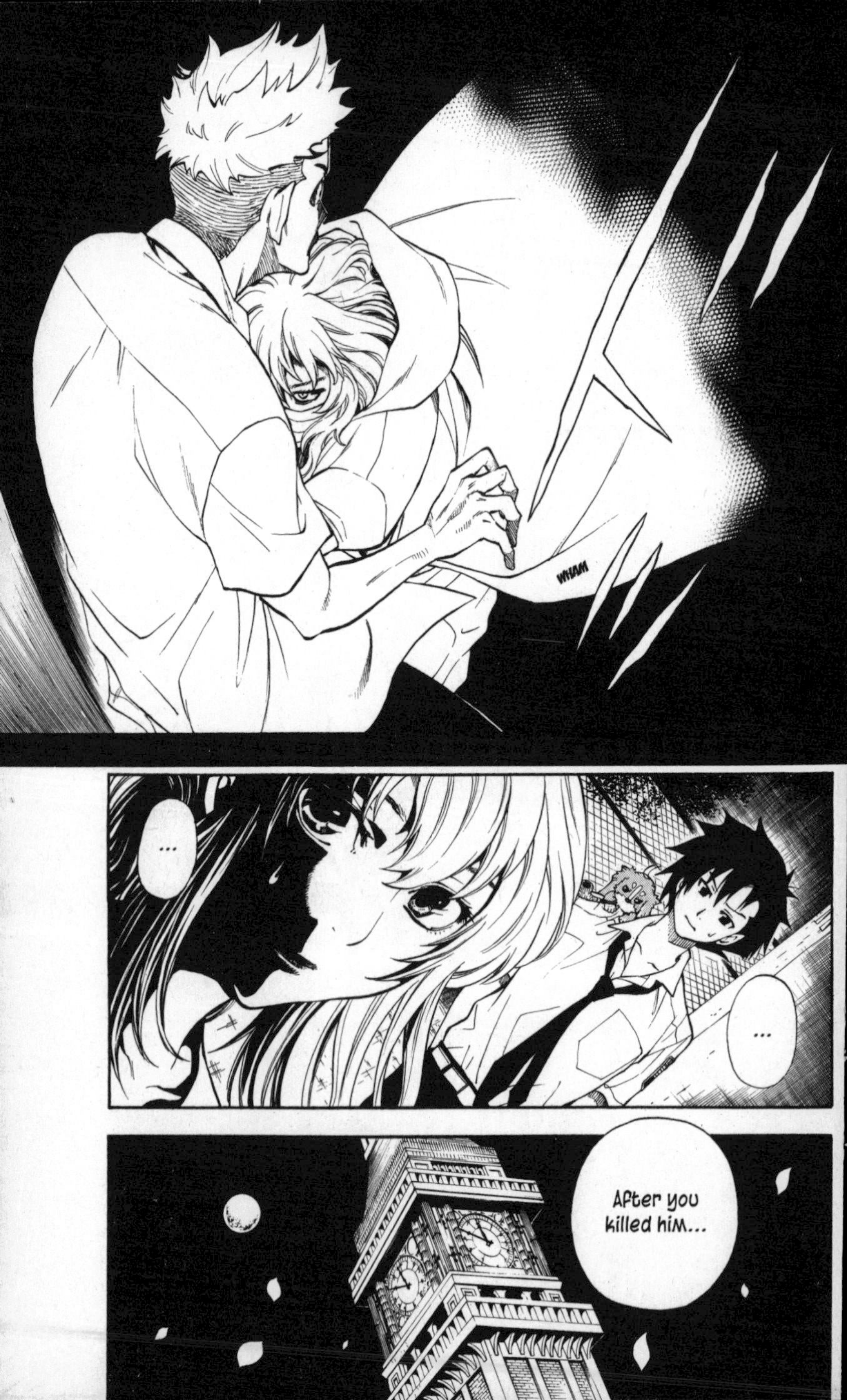
WHAM
...
...
After you killed him...

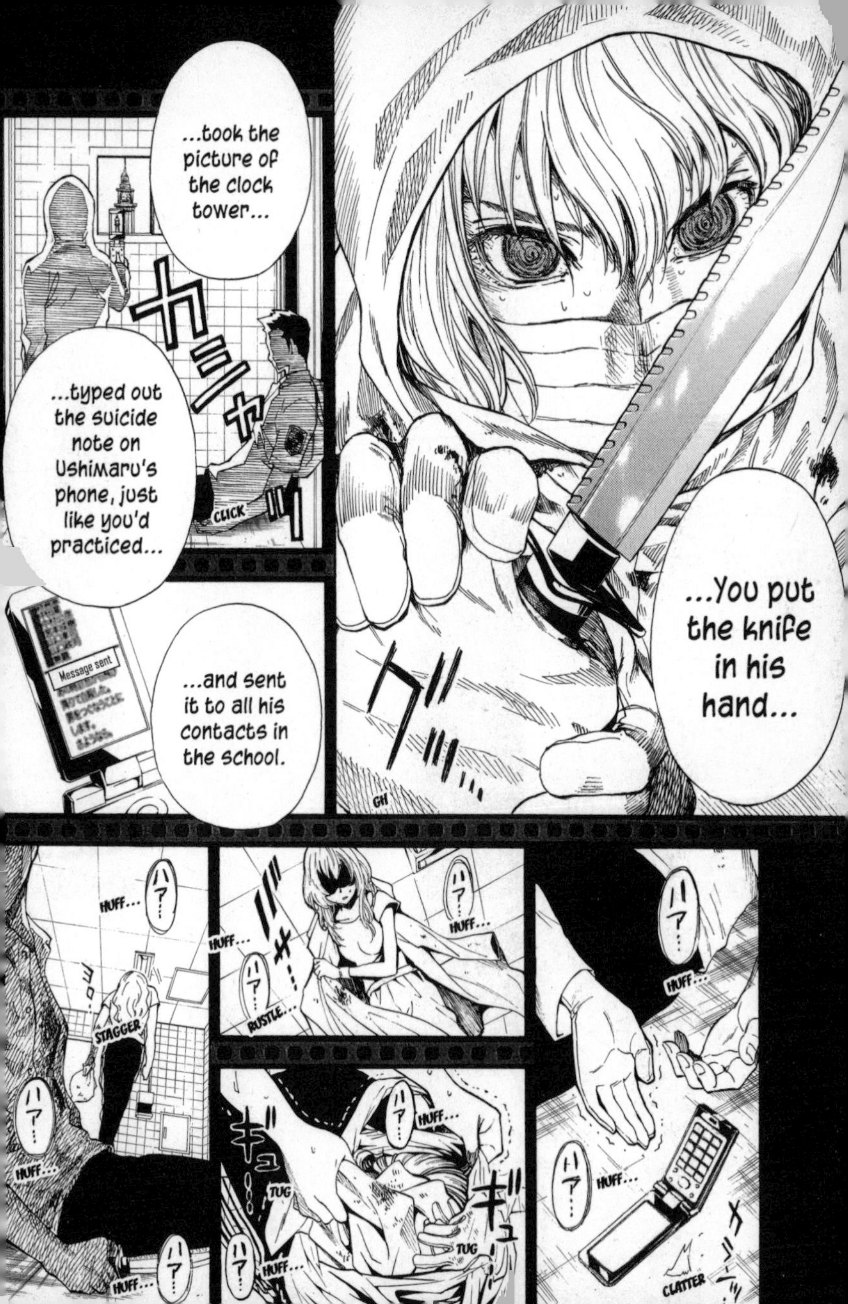
...You put the knife in his hand...
GH
...took the picture of the clock tower...
CLICK
...typed out the suicide note on Ushimaru's phone, just like you'd practiced...
Message sent
...and sent it to all his contacts in the school.
HUFF...
HUFF...
CLATTER
HUFF...
HUFF...
RUSTLE...
HUFF...
TUG
TUG
HUFF...
HUFF...
STAGGER
HUFF...
HUFF...

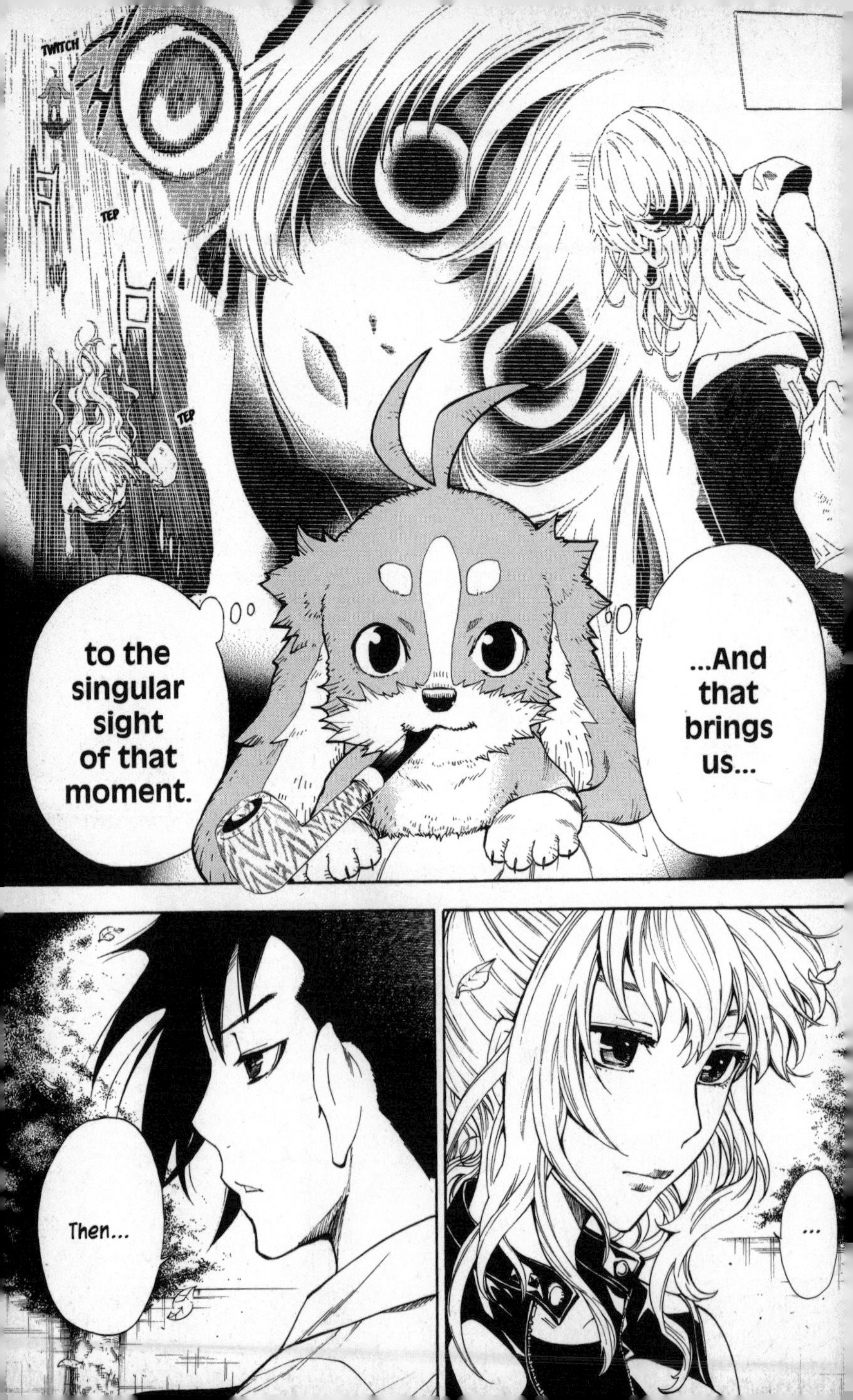
TWITCH
TEP
TEP
...And that brings us...
to the singular sight of that moment.
...
Then...

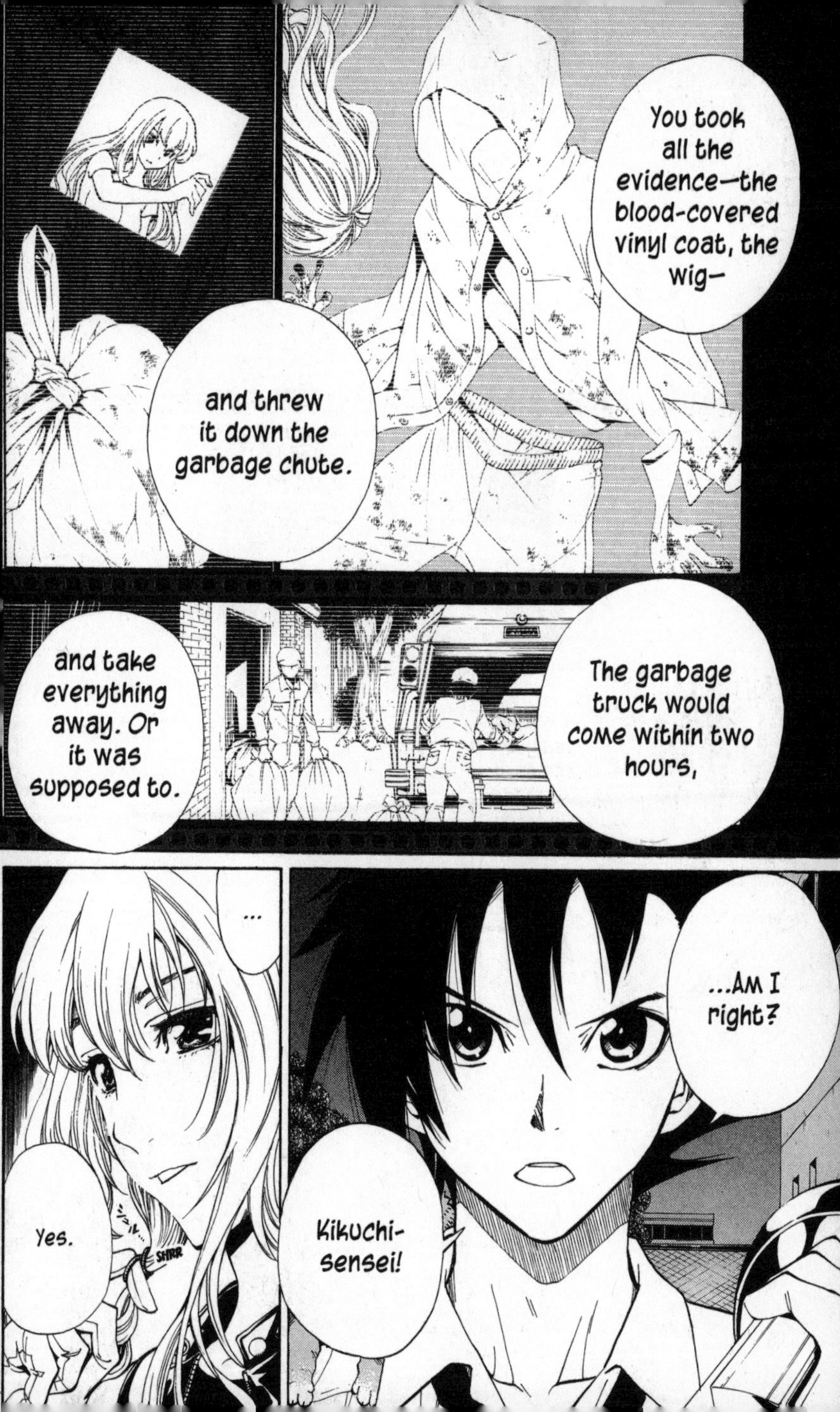
You took all the evidence—the blood-covered vinyl coat, the wig—
and threw it down the garbage chute.
The garbage truck would come within two hours,
and take everything away. Or it was supposed to.
...Am I right?
Kikuchi-sensei!
...
Yes.
SHRR

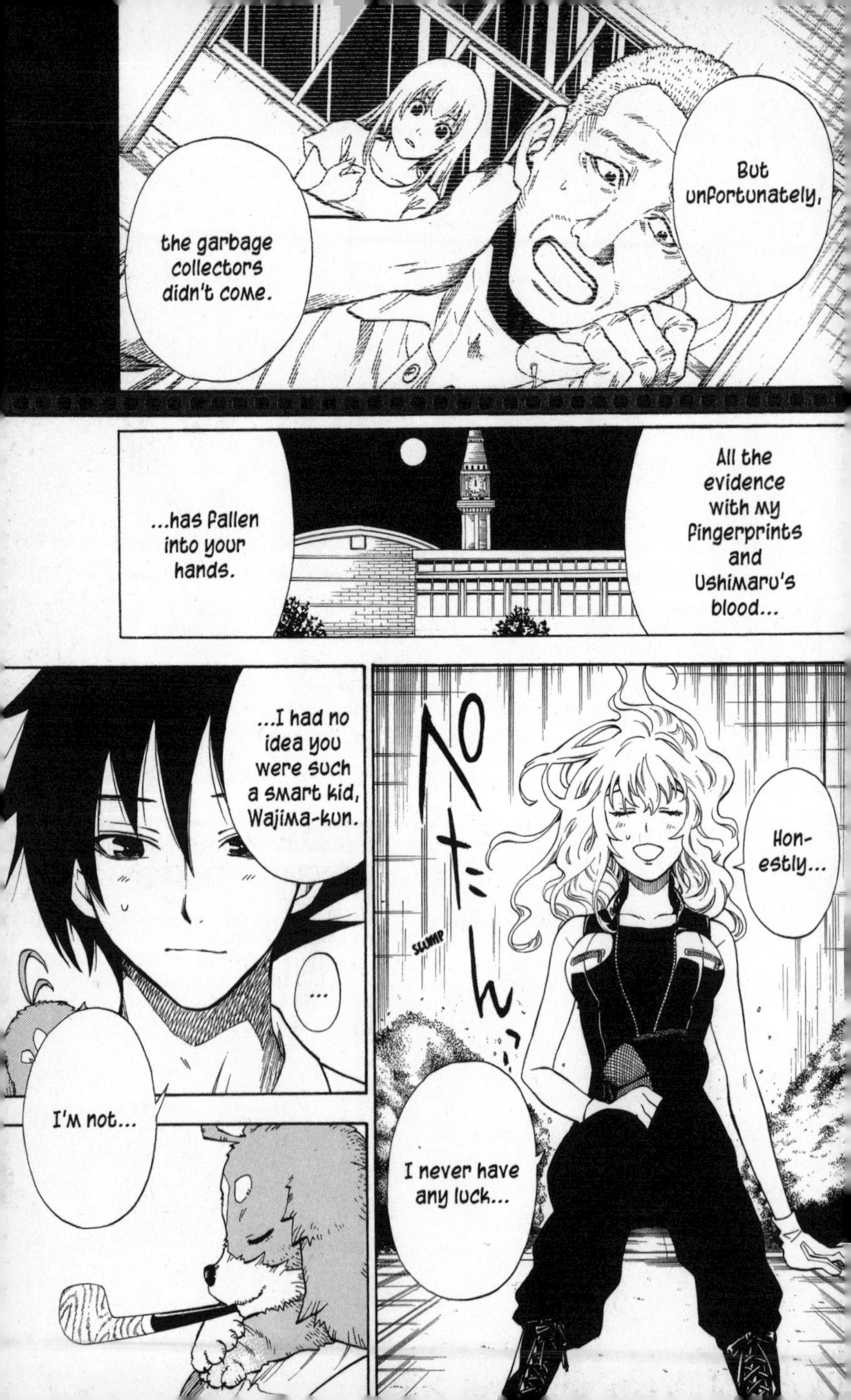
But unfortunately,
the garbage collectors didn't come.
All the evidence with my fingerprints and Ushimaru's blood...
...has fallen into your hands.
Hon-estly...
SLUMP
I never have any luck...
...I had no idea you were such a smart kid, Wajima-kun.
...
I'm not...

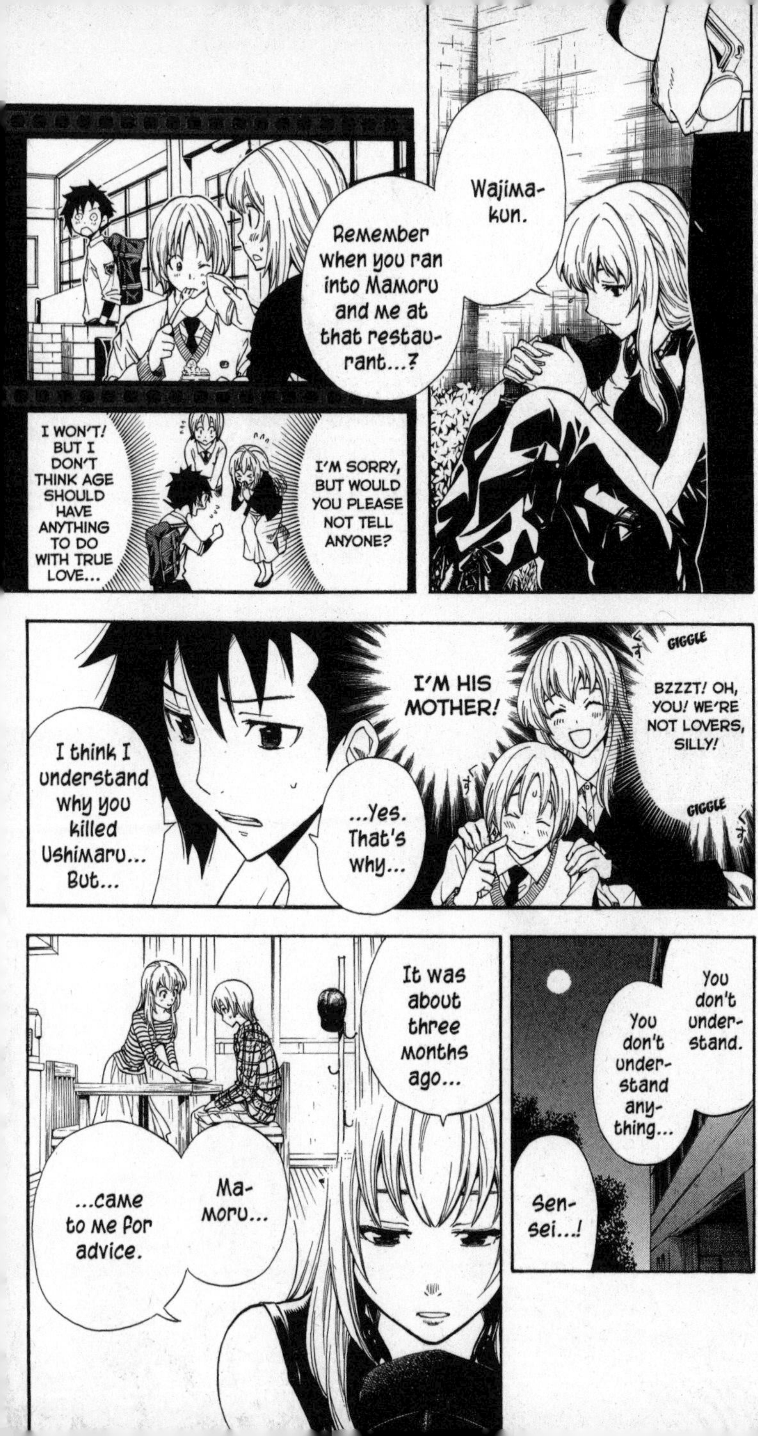
Wajima-kun.
Remember when you ran into Mamoru and me at that restaurant...?
I'M SORRY, BUT WOULD YOU PLEASE NOT TELL ANYONE?
I WON'T! BUT I DON'T THINK AGE SHOULD HAVE ANYTHING TO DO WITH TRUE LOVE...
GIGGLE
BZZZT! OH, YOU! WE'RE NOT LOVERS, SILLY!
GIGGLE
I'M HIS MOTHER!
...Yes. That's why...
I think I understand why you killed Ushimaru... But...
You don't understand.
You don't understand anything...
Sen-sei...!
It was about three months ago...
Ma-moru...
...came to me for advice.

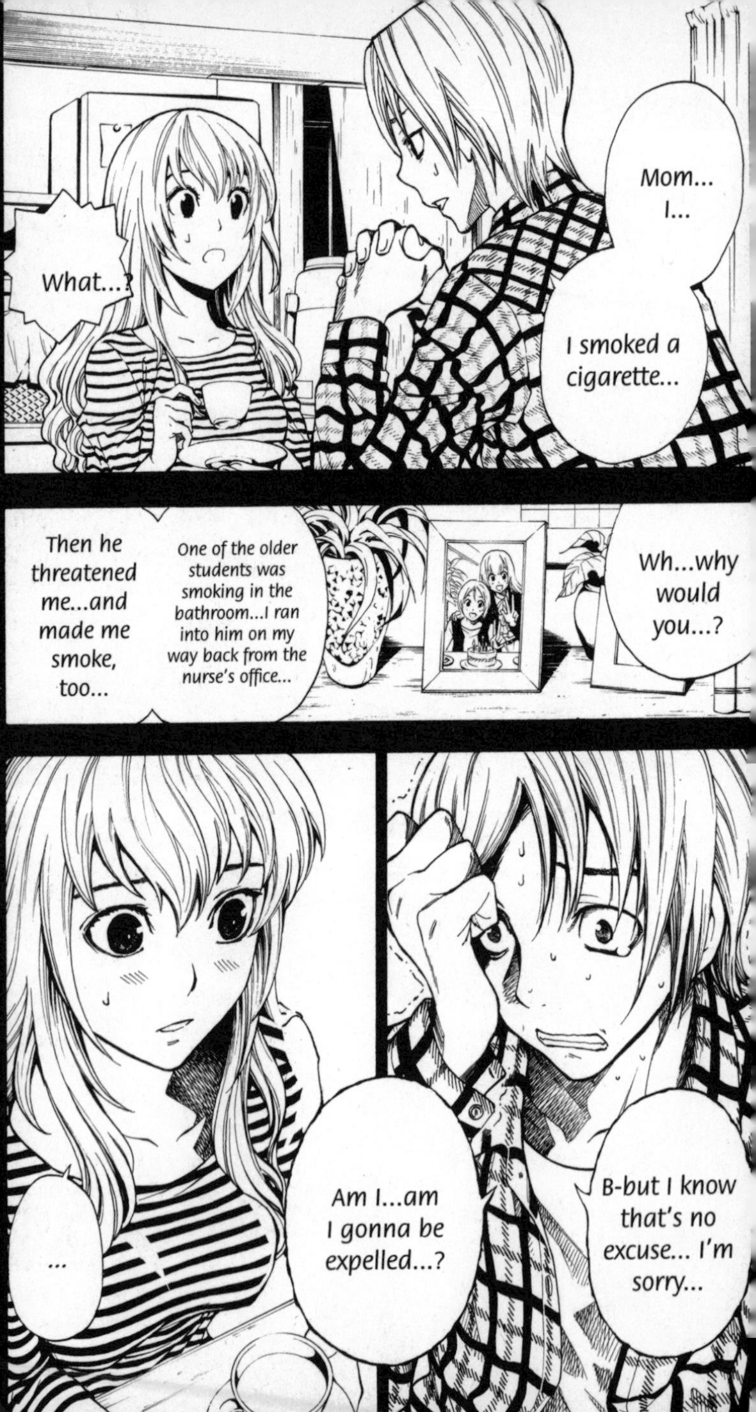
Mom... I...
I smoked a cigarette...
What...?
Wh...why would you...?
One of the older students was smoking in the bathroom...I ran into him on my way back from the nurse's office...
Then he threatened me...and made me smoke, too...
B-but I know that's no excuse... I'm sorry...
Am I...am I gonna be expelled...?
...

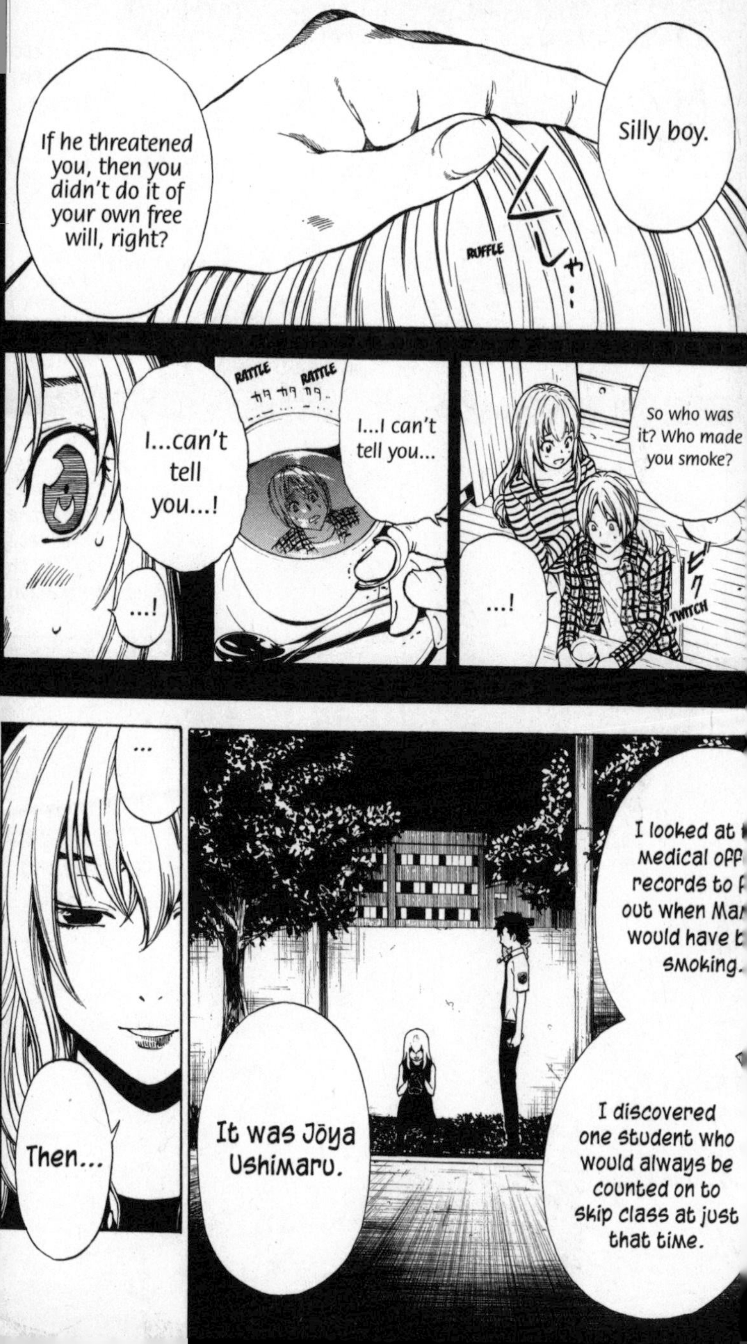
Silly boy.
RUFFLE
If he threatened you, then you didn't do it of your own free will, right?
So who was it? Who made you smoke?
TWITCH
...!
RATTLE RATTLE
I...I can't tell you...
I...can't tell you...!
...!
I looked at
medical off
records to
out when Ma
would have
smoking.
I discovered one student who would always be counted on to skip class at just that time.
It was Jōya Ushimaru.
...
Then...

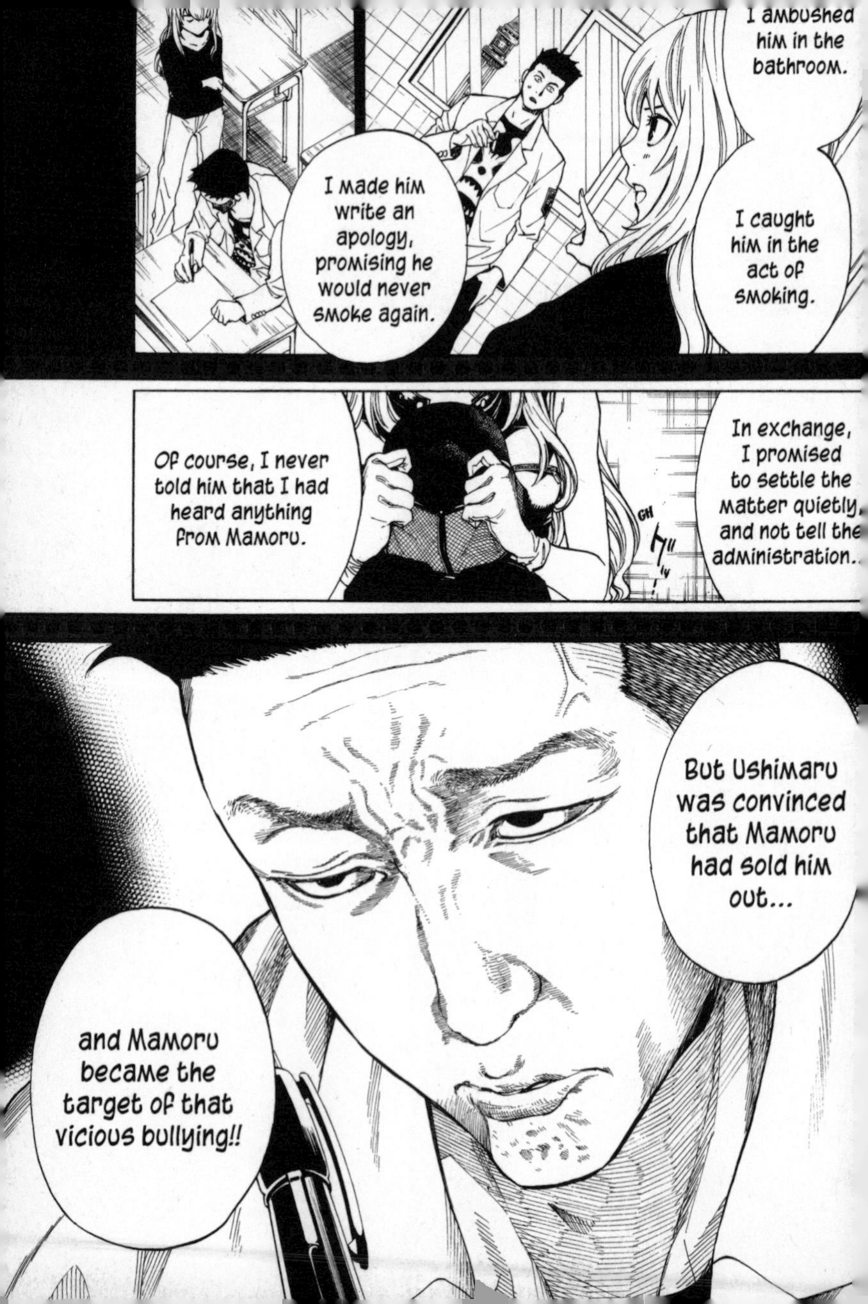
I ambushed him in the bathroom.
I caught him in the act of smoking.
I made him write an apology, promising he would never smoke again.
In exchange, I promised to settle the matter quietly, and not tell the administration...
GH
Of course, I never told him that I had heard anything from Mamoru.
But Ushimaru was convinced that Mamoru had sold him out...
and Mamoru became the target of that vicious bullying!!

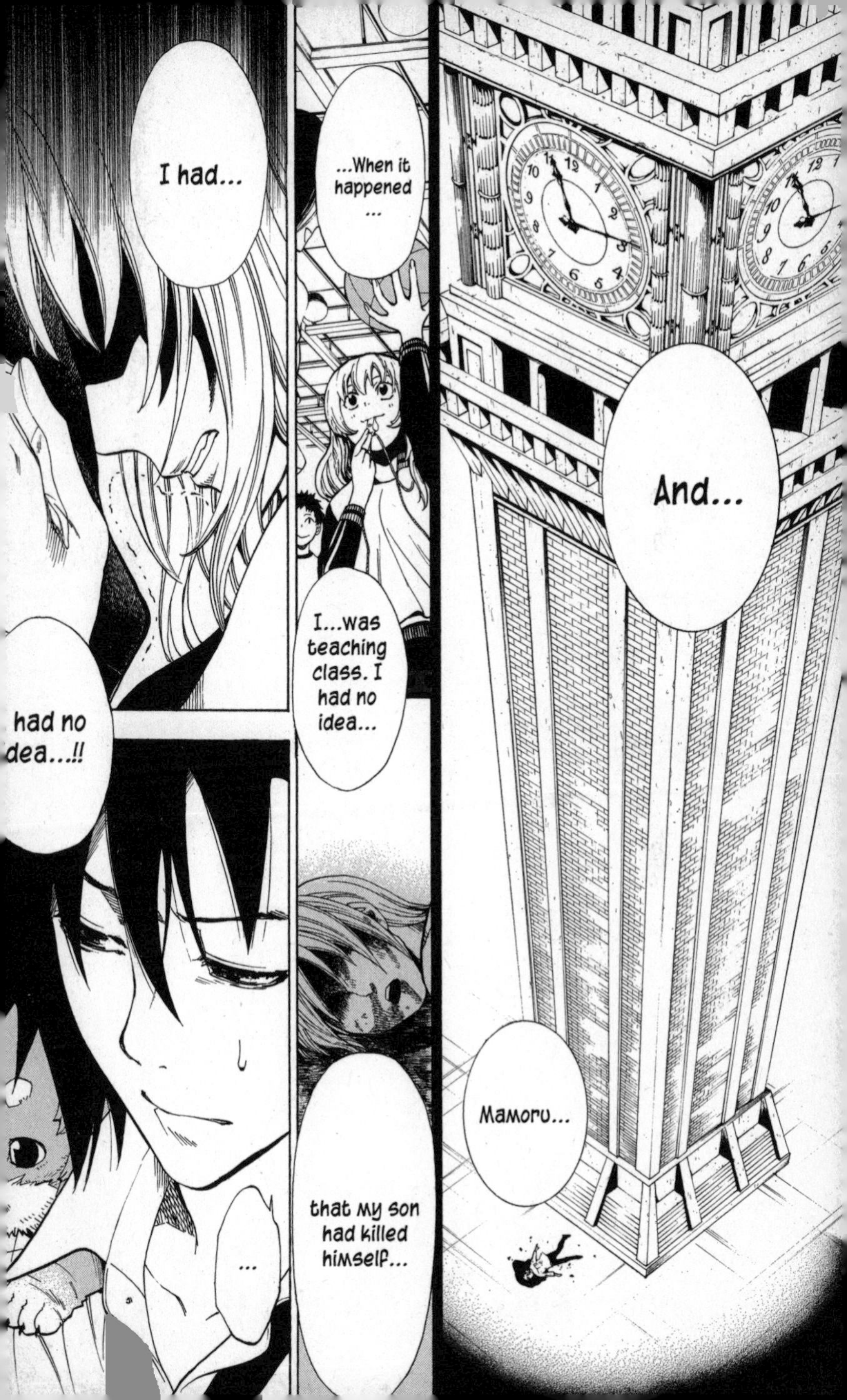
And...
Mamoru...
...When it happened ...
I...was teaching class. I had no idea...
that my son had killed himself...
I had...
had no dea...!!
...

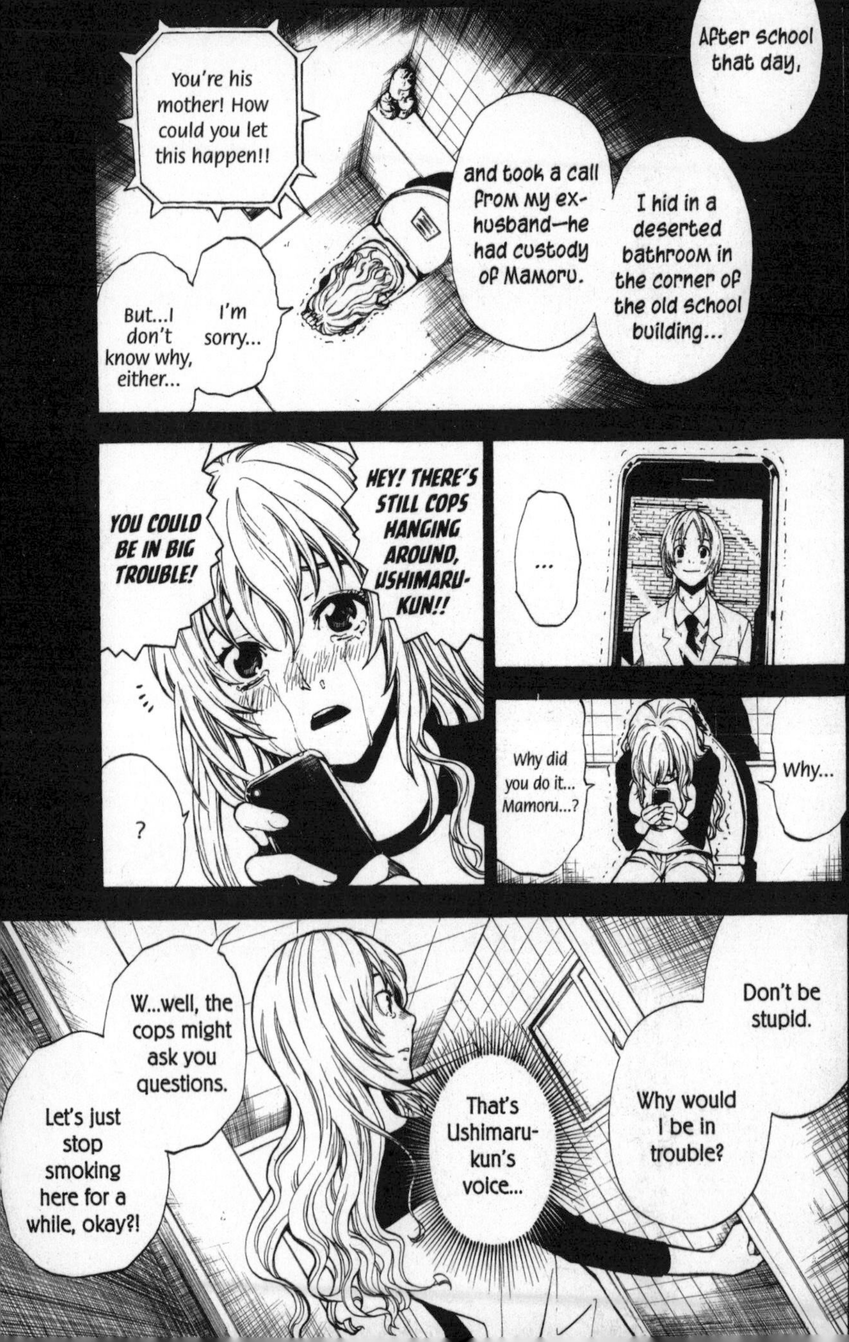
After school that day,
I hid in a deserted bathroom in the corner of the old school building...
and took a call from my ex-husband—he had custody of Mamoru.
You're his mother! How could you let this happen!!
I'm sorry...
But...I don't know why, either...
...
Why...
Why did you do it... Mamoru...?
HEY! THERE'S STILL COPS HANGING AROUND, USHIMARU-KUN!!
YOU COULD BE IN BIG TROUBLE!
?
Don't be stupid.
Why would I be in trouble?
That's Ushimaru-kun's voice...
W...well, the cops might ask you questions.
Let's just stop smoking here for a while, okay?!

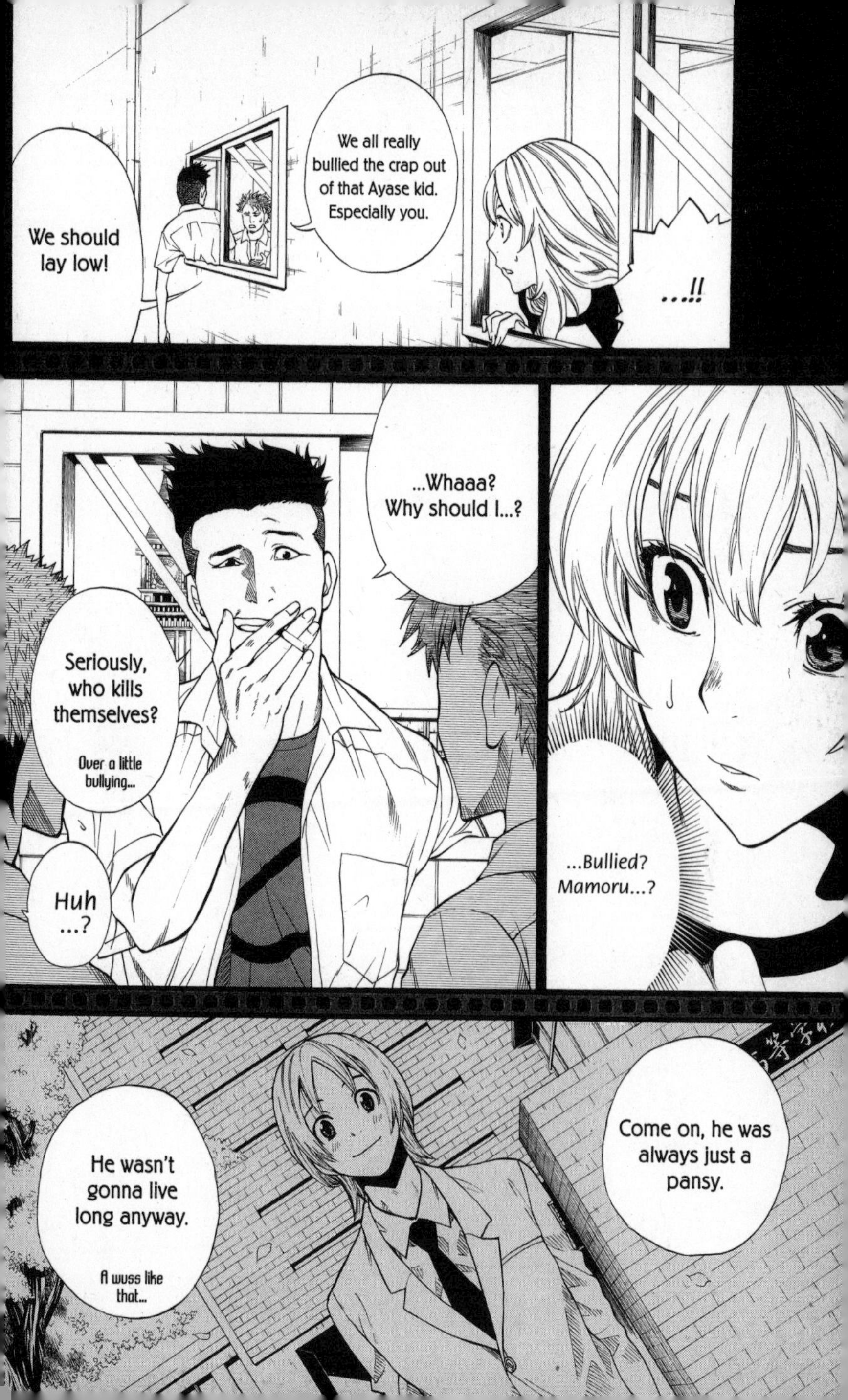

...!!
We all really bullied the crap out of that Ayase kid. Especially you.
We should lay low!
...Bullied? Mamoru...?
...Whaaa? Why should I...?
Seriously, who kills themselves?
Over a little bullying...
Huh ...?
Come on, he was always just a pansy.
He wasn't gonna live long anyway.
A wuss like that...

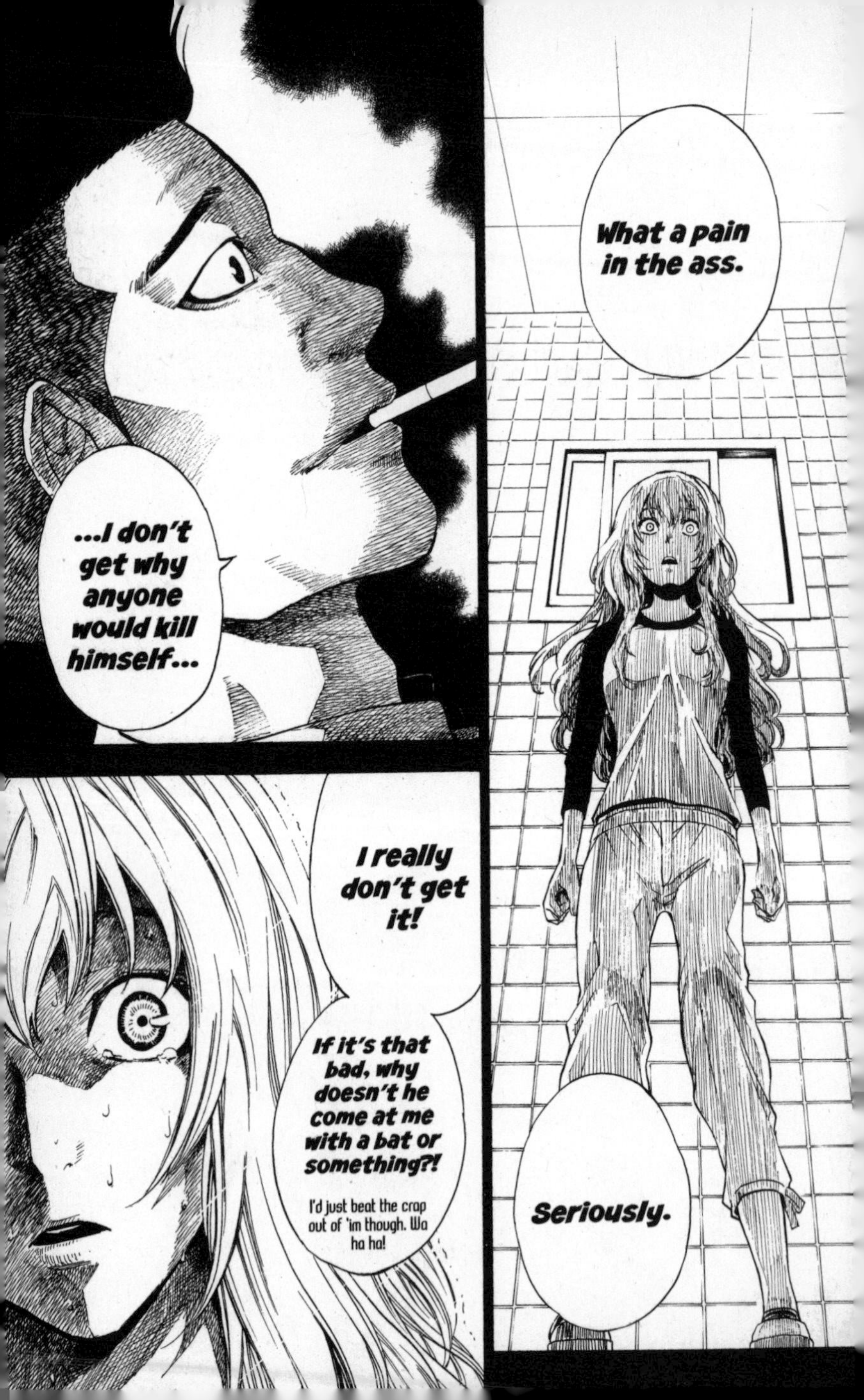
What a pain in the ass.
Seriously.
...I don't get why anyone would kill himself...
I really don't get it!
If it's that bad, why doesn't he come at me with a bat or something?!
I'd just beat the crap out of 'im though. Wa ha ha!

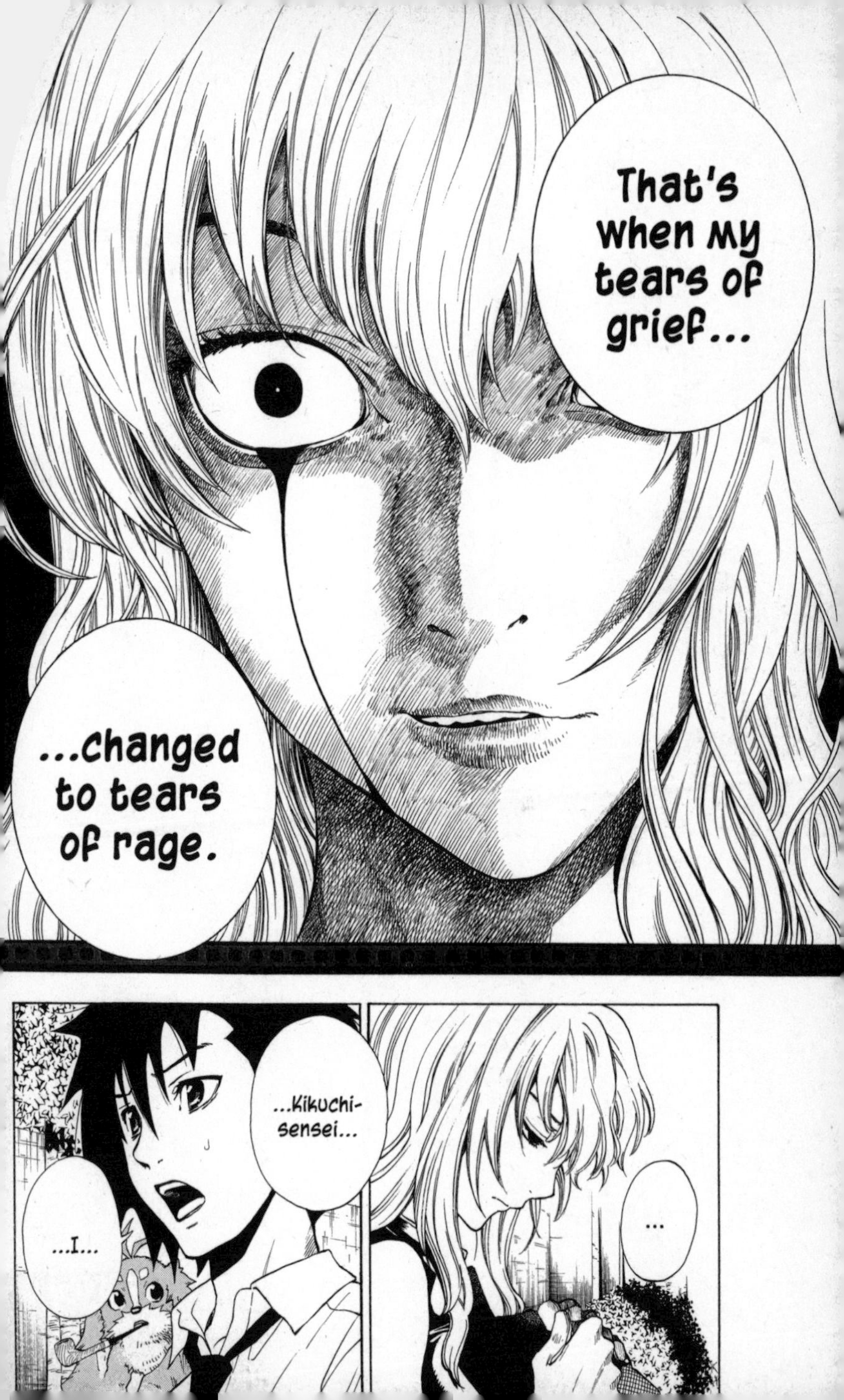
That's when my tears of grief...
...Changed to tears of rage.
...
...Kikuchi-sensei...
...I...

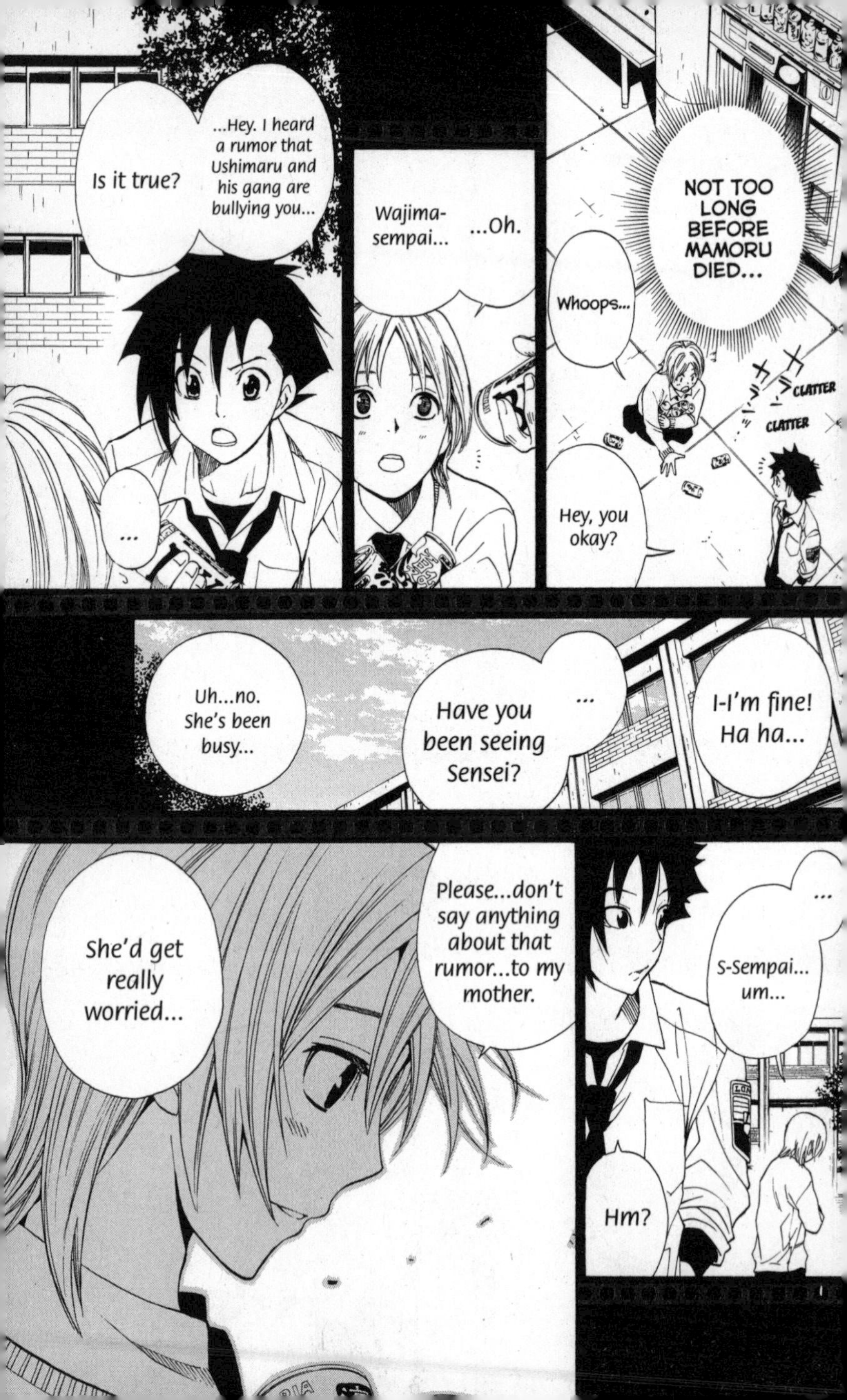
NOT TOO LONG BEFORE MAMORU DIED...
Whoops...
CLATTER
CLATTER
Hey, you okay?
Wajima-sempai...
...Oh.
...Hey. I heard a rumor that Ushimaru and his gang are bullying you...
Is it true?
...
I-I'm fine! Ha ha...
...
Have you been seeing Sensei?
Uh...no. She's been busy...
...
S-Sempai... um...
Hm?
Please...don't say anything about that rumor...to my mother.
She'd get really worried...

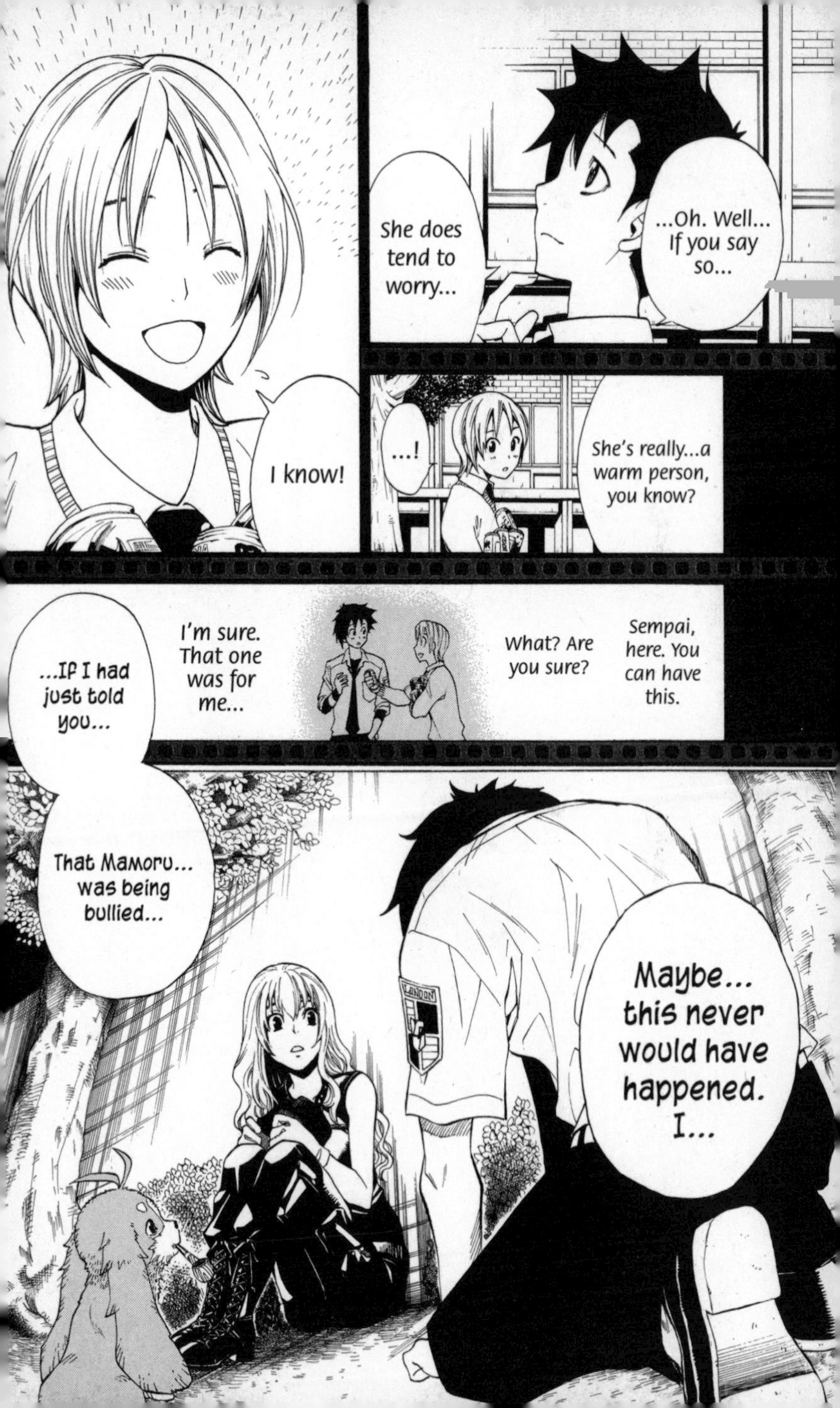
...Oh. Well... If you say so...
She does tend to worry...
She's really...a warm person, you know?
...!
I know!
Sempai, here. You can have this.
What? Are you sure?
I'm sure. That one was for me...
...If I had just told you...
That Mamoru... was being bullied...
Maybe... this never would have happened. I...
LONDON

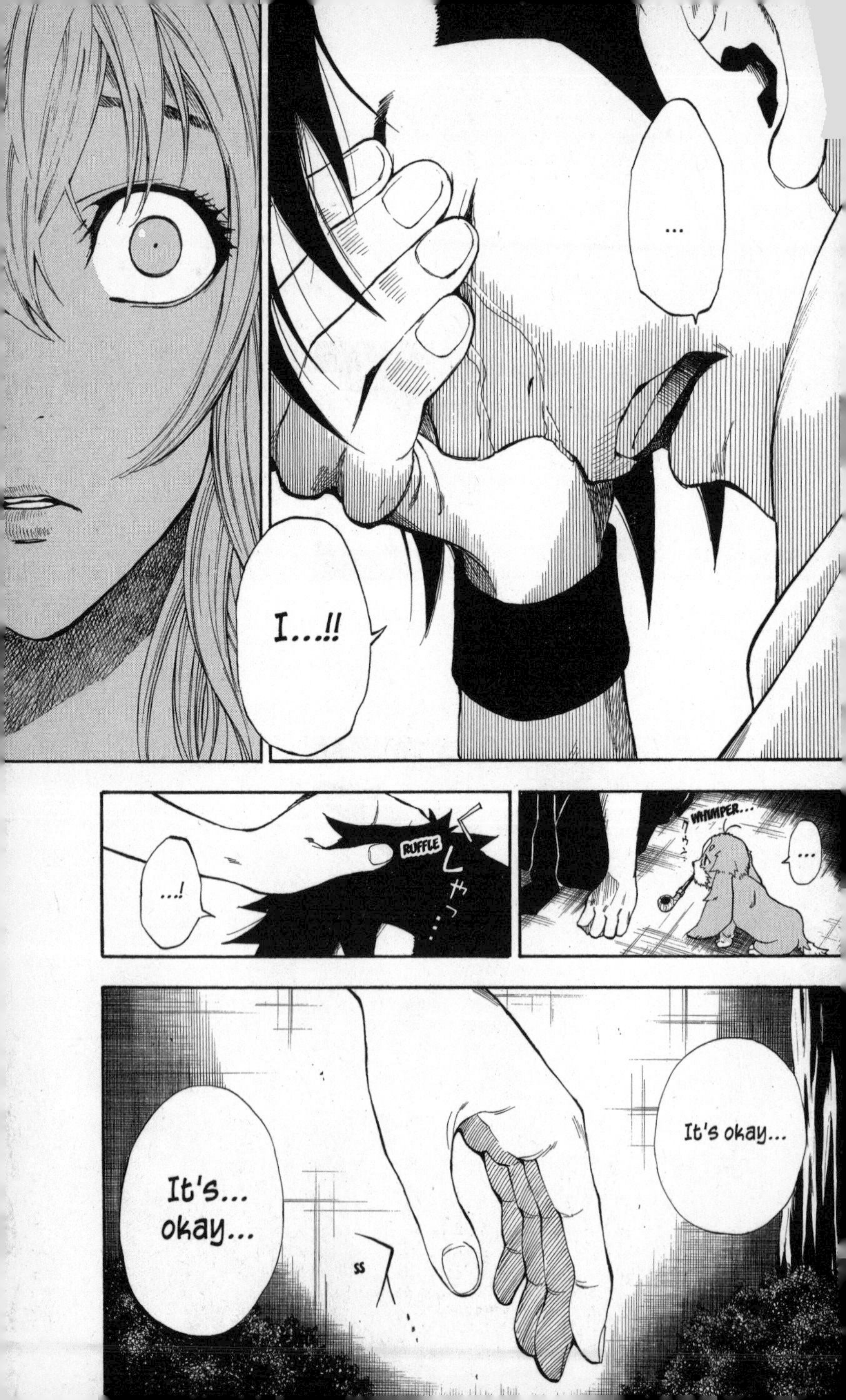

...
I...!!
WHIMPER...
...
RUFFLE
...!
It's okay...
It's... okay...
SS

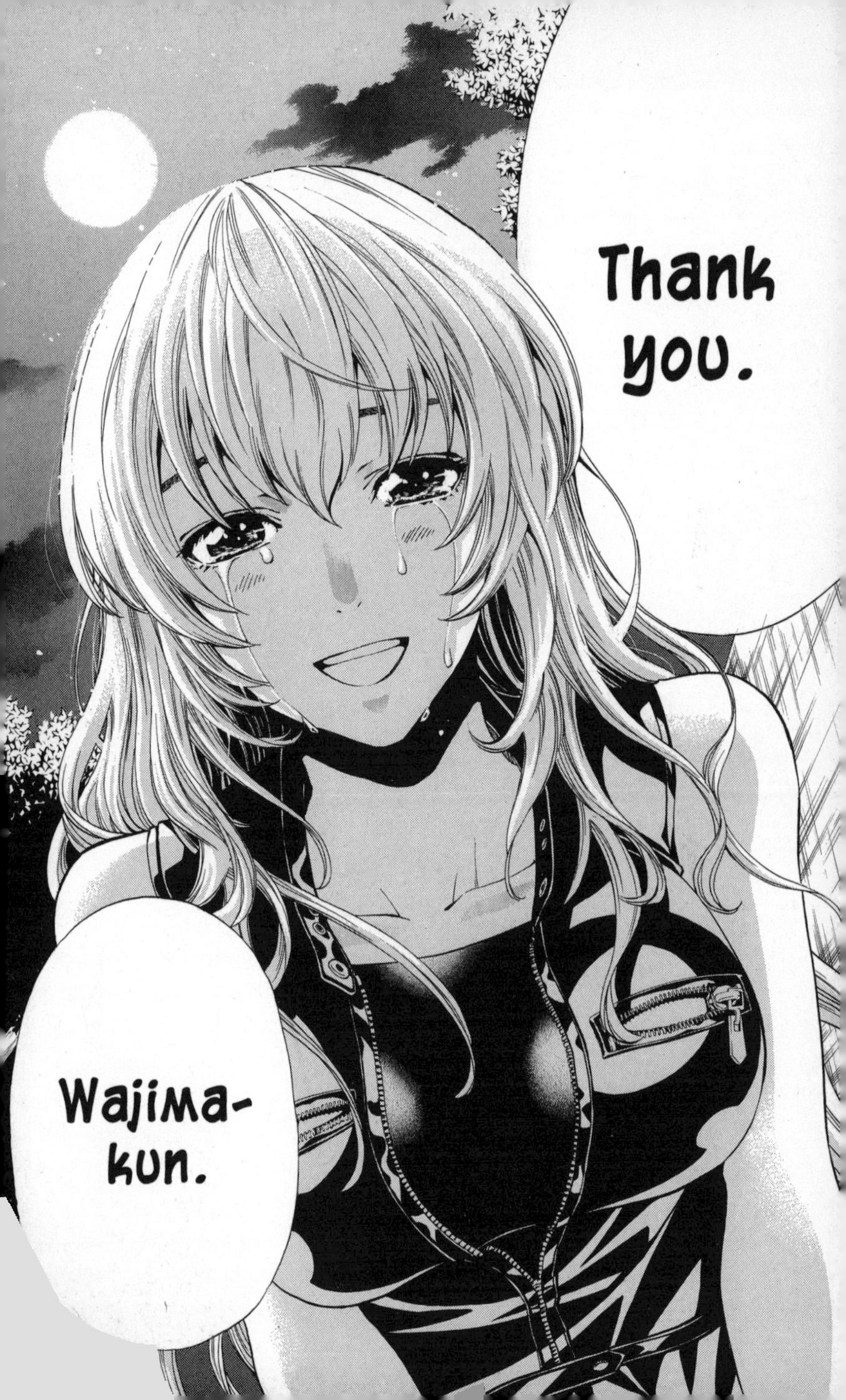
Thank you.
Wajima-kun.

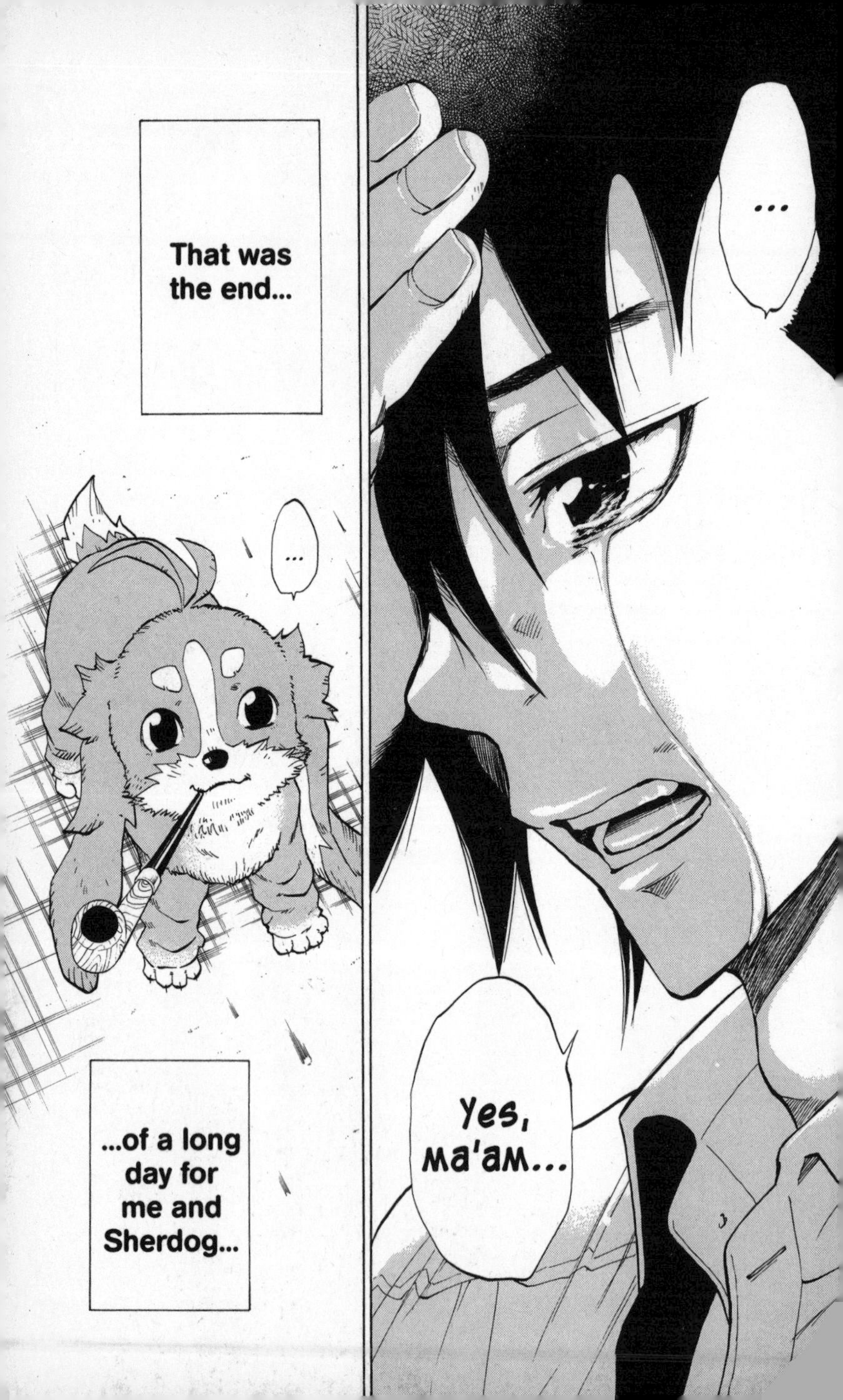
...
Yes, ma'am...
That was the end...
...
...of a long day for me and Sherdog...

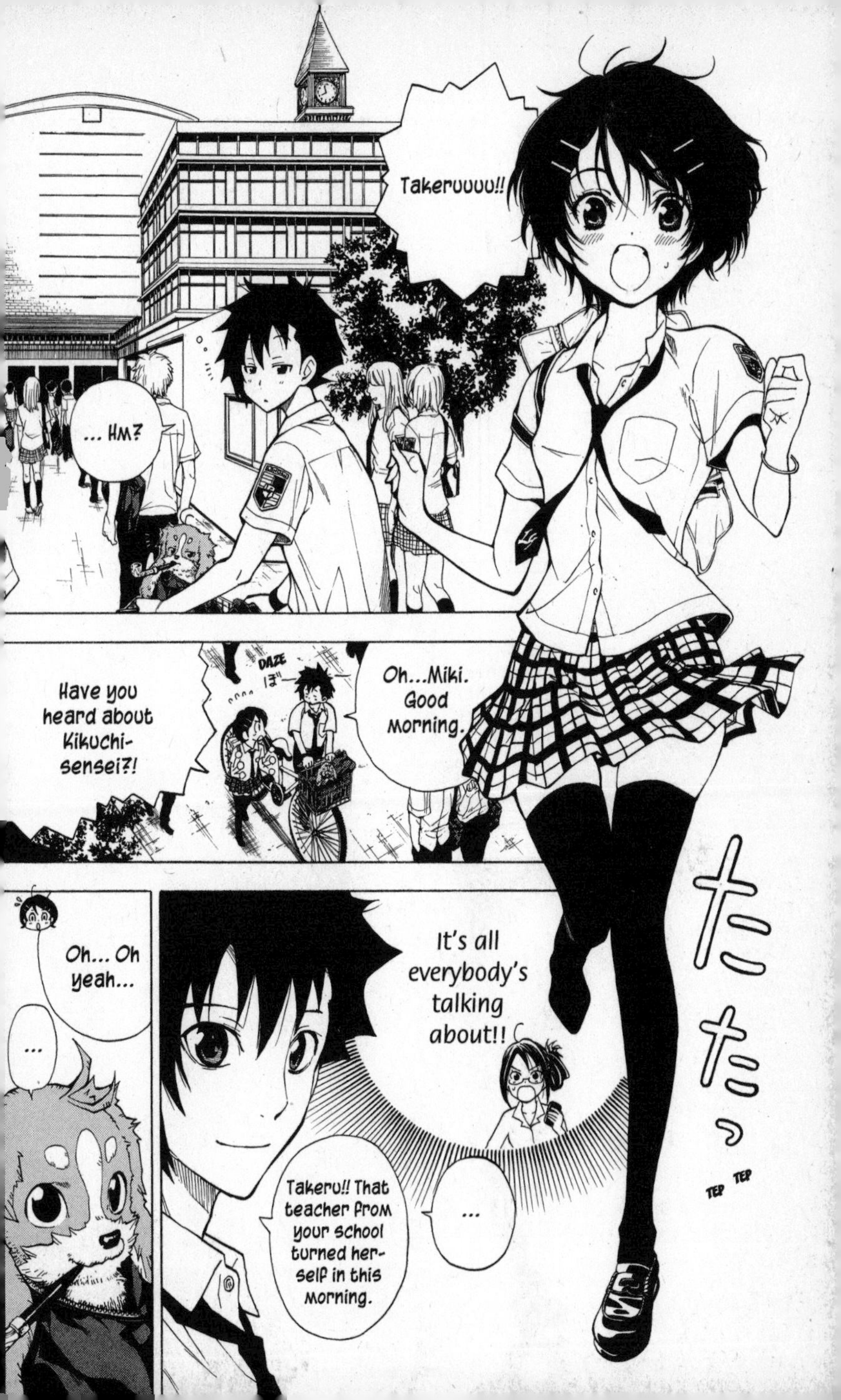
Takeruuuu!!
たたっ
TEP TEP
... Hm?
Oh...Miki. Good morning.
DAZE ぼ
Have you heard about Kikuchi-sensei?!
It's all everybody's talking about!!
Takeru!! That teacher from your school turned her-self in this morning.
...
Oh... Oh yeah...
...

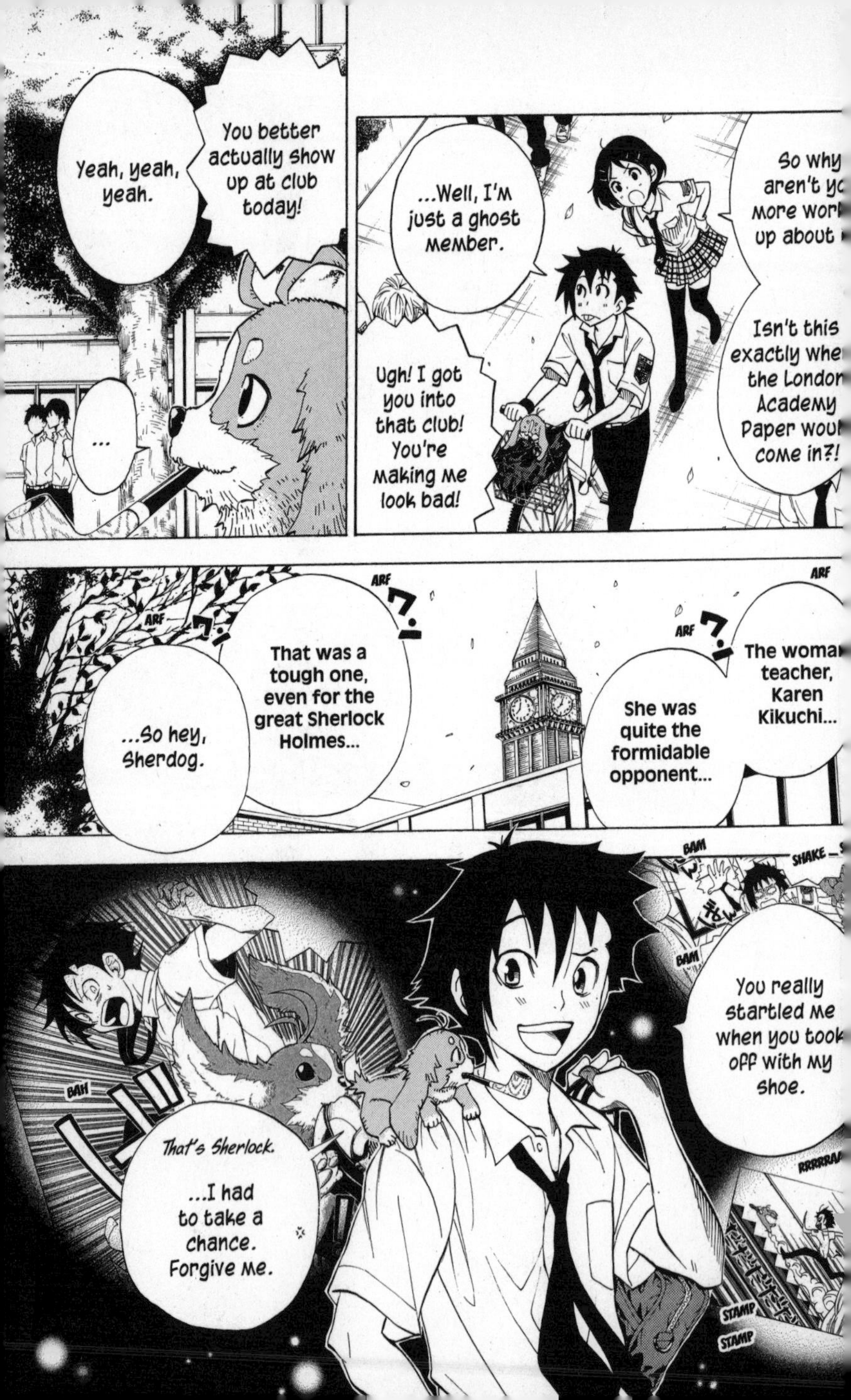
So why aren't yo more wor up about
Isn't this exactly whe the London Academy Paper wou come in?!
...Well, I'm just a ghost member.
Ugh! I got you into that club! You're making me look bad!
You better actually show up at club today!
Yeah, yeah, yeah.
...
ARF
The woma teacher, Karen Kikuchi...
ARF
She was quite the formidable opponent...
ARF
That was a tough one, even for the great Sherlock Holmes...
ARF
...So hey, Sherdog.
SHAKE
BAM
BAM
You really startled me when you took off with my shoe.
RRRRRA
STAMP
STAMP
That's Sherlock.
...I had to take a chance. Forgive me.
BAH

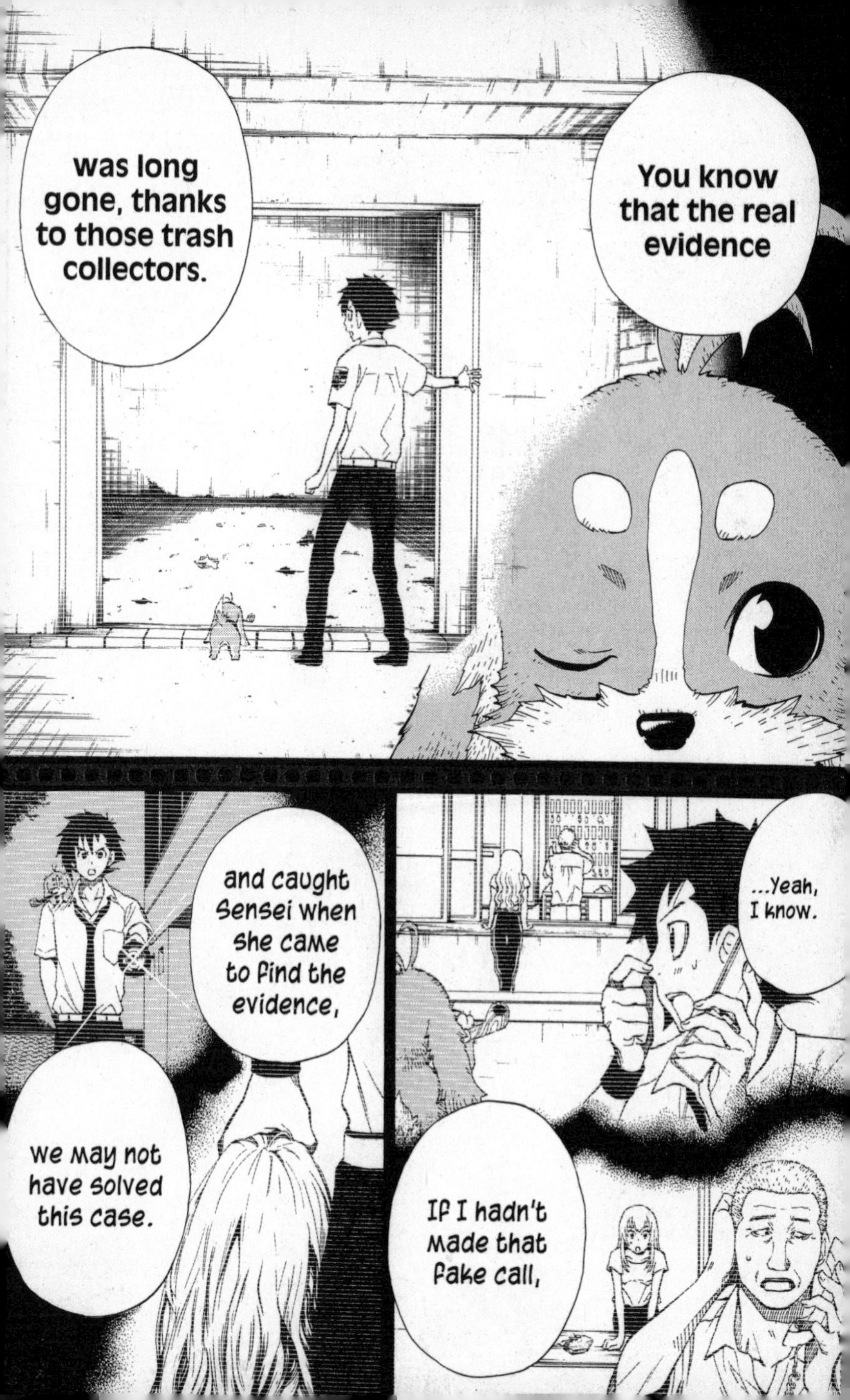
You know that the real evidence
was long gone, thanks to those trash collectors.
...Yeah, I know.
If I hadn't made that fake call,
and caught Sensei when she came to find the evidence,
we may not have solved this case.

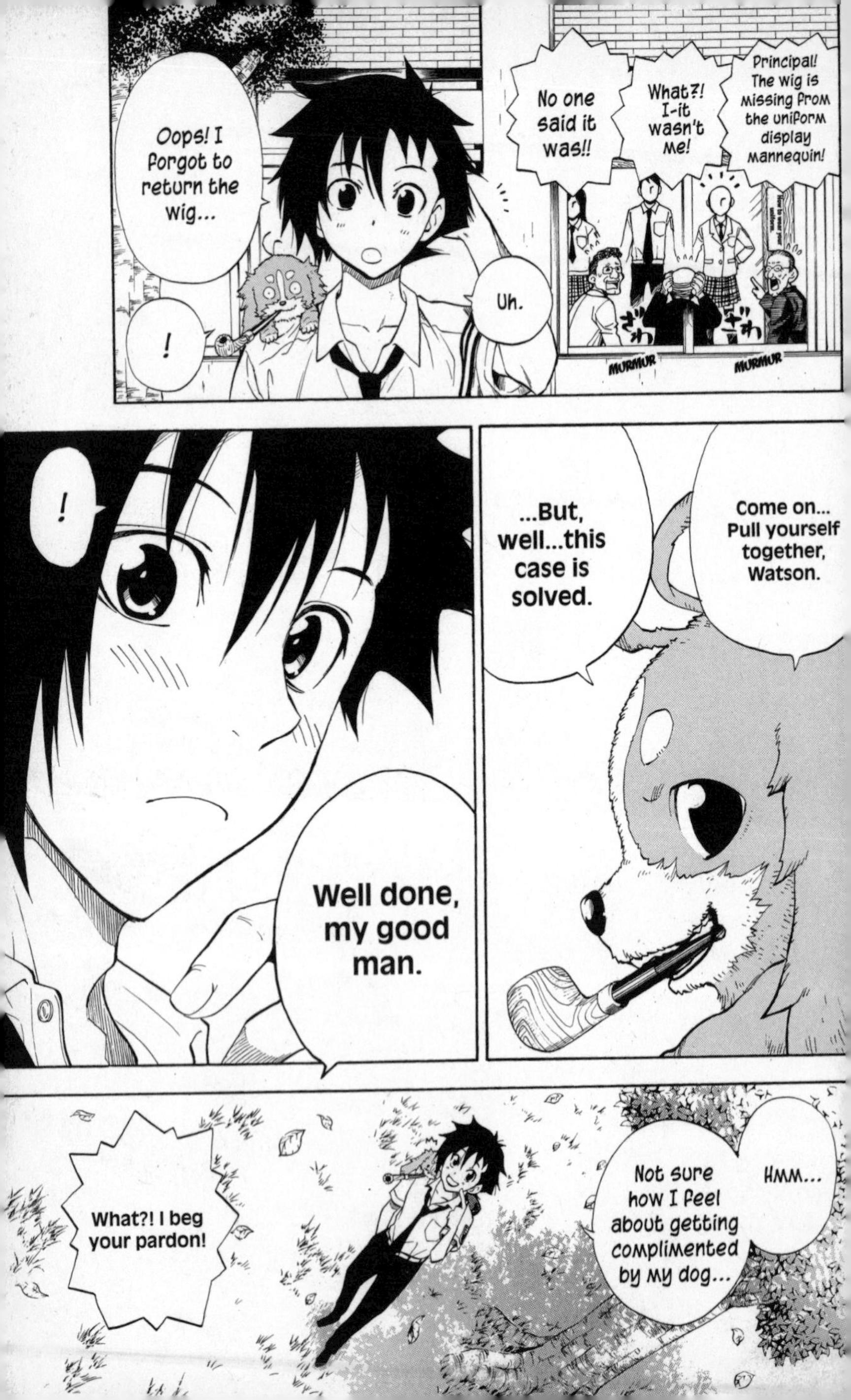
Principal! The wig is missing from the uniform display mannequin!
What?! I-it wasn't me!
No one said it was!!
ざわ
ざわ
MURMUR
MURMUR
Uh.
Oops! I forgot to return the wig...
!
Come on... Pull yourself together, Watson.
...But, well...this case is solved.
!
Well done, my good man.
HMM...
Not sure how I feel about getting complimented by my dog...
What?! I beg your pardon!

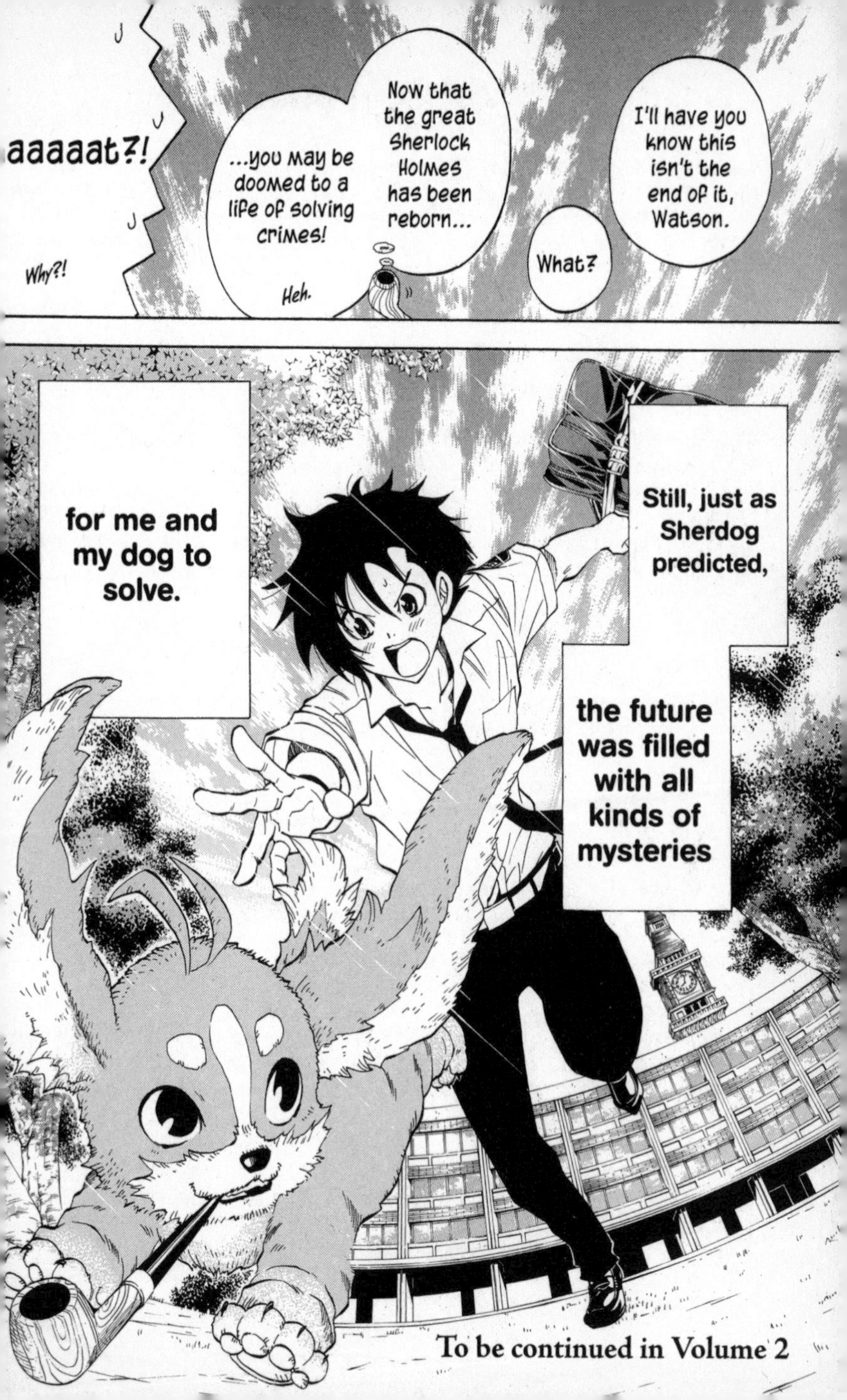
I'll have you know this isn't the end of it, Watson.
What?
Now that the great Sherlock Holmes has been reborn...
...you may be doomed to a life of solving crimes!
Heh.
aaaaat?!
Why?!
Still, just as Sherdog predicted,
the future was filled with all kinds of mysteries
for me and my dog to solve.
To be continued in Volume 2

Translation Notes

Japanese is a tricky language for most Westerners, and translation is often more art than science. For your edification and reading pleasure, here are notes on some of the places where we could have gone in a different direction with our translation of the work, or where a Japanese cultural reference is used.

Taro and Jiro (page 16)

As Takeru's father suggests, there is a movie Nankyoku Monogatari (released in the United States as Antarctica) about a Japanese expedition to the South Pole, and the fate of the dogs that were left behind when the expedition failed. The two lead dogs are Taro and Jiro. The other dog names suggested by Takeru's father are Pochi, the Japanese equivalent of Spot; Hachikō, after the faithful dog who waited for his master every day at the Shibuya train station; Patrasche, the title dog in the book A Dog of Flanders; and Shiro, meaning White.

In my office (page 20)

Officer Wajima's office will be found at the nearby kōban, loosely translated as "police box." Kōban are like miniature police stations, spread throughout the community, bringing the police close to the community so they can respond more readily to the citizens' needs.

Wa To Son (page 35)

While they usually represent ideas (words), Chinese characters can be used to represent syllables or sounds to spell foreign words phonetically. The name written on Takeru's bike is, of course, his name, Wajima Takeru (with his family name first, as is the custom in Asian languages). The three characters in his name can be pronounced Wa Jima Takeru, or Wa To Son. The O after the T is swallowed (almost silent), and so when said quickly, it forms the name Watson.

Plum Group, (page 38)

The closest thing Takeru has to the sort of hat Sherlock Holmes is known for wearing is his old preschool hat. You can tell it's from his earlier education based on the fact that his class, instead of having a number or letter, is named after a fruit.

Non-swimmers (page 151)

Just a bit of trivia: what Karen Kikuchi actually called this bunch was "hammer boys," because in Japan, someone who can't swim is called a "hammer."

W9-BHN-936

Sherlock Bones volume 1 is a work of fiction. Names, characters, places, and incidents are the products of the author's imagination or are used fictitiously. Any resemblance to actual events, locales, or persons, living or dead, is entirely coincidental.

A Kodansha Comics Trade Paperback Original.

Sherlock Bones volume 1 copyright © 2012 Yuma Ando & Yuki Sato
English translation copyright © 2013 Yuma Ando & Yuki Sato

Published in the United States by Kodansha Comics,
an imprint of Kodansha USA Publishing, LLC, New York.

Publication rights for this English edition arranged through Kodansha Ltd., Tokyo.

First published in Japan in 2012 by Kodansha Ltd., Tokyo, as *Tanteiken Sherdock* volume 1.

ISBN 978-1-61262-444-0

Printed in the United States of America.

www.kodanshacomics.com

9 8 7 6 5 4 3 2 1

Translator: Alethea Nibley and Athena Nibley
Lettering: Kiyoko Shiromasa